Contents

THIRTY YEARS IN REVIEW

Over the years we've seen changes in what *you cook,* how *you cook it, and even* who *cooks it. Walk down memory lane from the early '70s through the '90s as we reminisce about the changing world of food.*

FOOD IN THE 1970s

Stuffed vegetable "boats" were big. We scooped out and stuffed zucchini, eggplant, potatoes, peppers, and mushrooms.

Those decorative little pimiento peppers popped up in sandwich spreads, salads, casseroles, and as the universal garnish.

Shrimp Creole recipes abounded as we explored the secrets of Creole cooking.

Kitchen colors were avocado, harvest gold, paprika, and coppertone.

Country ham and redeye gravy and biscuits were on the breakfast table.

We made cookies with potato chips and corn flakes cereal.

Steak was in style—Swiss Steak to Steak Kabobs to Steak Parmigiana.

Pork was prominent as thick chops baked in the oven or browned in a skillet.

A keen interest in home canning helped preserve fresh produce and save on food costs.

We were nuts for nog. Eggnog appeared eight ways for the holidays in '72 alone. By decade's end, eggnog flavored pies, buttercream frosting, and Nutty Eggnog Christmas Bread.

Curry dishes were cutting edge.

Canned mushrooms were a luxury ingredient—they dressed up simple dishes, topped veal, stuffed tomatoes, and filled quiche.

These were the salad days for sure! Molded fruit salad for lunch, frozen salads for Christmas, broccoli or carrot salad for summer suppers.

Crêpes anyone? We had 'em for breakfast, dinner, and dessert, filled with sausage, zucchini, crabmeat, and even cherries.

Charlotte Russe, Frozen Bombes, Cherries Jubilee, and Steamed Pudding were posh.

Southern Living

DECEMBER 1972 · 50¢

The toast-R-oven, country kettle, chafing dish, fondue pot, wok, and percolator were common in kitchens across the country.

Men were cooking and claiming "more flair and less fuss." Who besides men really liked the recipe called He-Man Supper in '71 that simmered steak strips in French dressing?

We made meat loaf a dozen ways, so then we turned to ham loaf and tuna-cheese loaf.

We weren't intimidated by soufflés in the '70s.

Budget entrées to boast about— Corned Beef and Cabbage, Beef Stroganoff, Old-Fashioned Chicken and Dumplings, Biscuit-Topped Tuna Casserole, Creamy Chipped Beef and Toast, and Chicken à la King.

"New" idea for leftover chicken: crescent dinner rolls for chicken in a biscuit.

Fresh herbs on the rise? Parsley and mint were mainstream greenery.

Veal and quiche were vogue. And so were poached eggs and Chicken Liver Pâté.

Chablis and Burgundy were the table wines to pour.

Veggie Tales: cabbage, cauliflower, and broccoli filled grocery bags. Recipes helped us scallop, stuff, soufflé, and fry them.

We were fearless for oysters every which way—fried, scalloped, on the half shell, and even skewered.

Ubiquitous seasonings: Onion and garlic powder, pie spice, and poultry seasoning.

"In" ingredients were Minute Rice, cottage cheese, canned shrimp, canned crabmeat, deviled ham, smoked oysters, envelopes of onion soup mix, canned mushrooms, rock Cornish game hens, and cured boneless ham.

We've always been thankful for the bronzed holiday bird. And we garnished it with lots of parsley back then.

Frankly speaking, franks were in. We even served Oriental Franks, Batter-Fried Franks, Creole Franks, and Sweet-and-Sour, too.

Unchartered territory: In '75 "Beef Cuts You May Not Know" featured Oven-Barbecued Brisket and Stuffed Flank Steak. In '78 "Getting to Know the Scallop" showcased the milky white mollusk bacon-wrapped, marinated, scalloped, and fried.

Layer cakes like Old Time Fudge Cake said Southern tradition.

We clamored for congealed salads—shapely ones in varying colors and flavors—carrot, avocado, and strawberry. And casseroles, most containing rice, were all the rage.

Soup was elegant appetizer fare. We ladled Curried Tomato Bisque, Creamy Asparagus Soup, Summer Borscht, Iced Avocado Soup, and Crème Vichyssoise.

We labeled the classic Chicken Kiev as "ultimate elegant entrée."

We put on lotsa pot roast . . . from Bavarian to barbecued. And round steak "rounded out the budget."

We stored our recipes in little boxes.

Flounder and mullet were the catch of the day.

Trés elegante: Sherried Baked Duck and Rice Ring with Beets.

FOOD IN THE 1980s

We savored a profusion of stuffed green peppers. They were stuffed with ham, macaroni and cheese, rice, and a Mexican ground beef mixture.

Low Country cooking captured the spotlight with Seafood Boil, Savannah Red Rice, Crab-Stuffed Flounder, Benne Seed Bites, Old-South Carrot Cake, and Chatham Artillery Punch.

Tuna stretched the budget with Tuna Mousse, Tuna Ring, and Tuna-Egg Croquettes.

The holiday table had Roast Turkey with oyster stuffing, Holiday Duckling, Country Ham in Apple Cider, Standing Rib Roast with Yorkshire Pudding.

Strawberry Shortcake graced magazine covers across the South in '81.

Southerners served a lot of iced tea in the early '80s—after steeping it in the kitchen, and even outside in the sun!

Casseroles came from the microwave and so did everything else: Microwave meat loaf in a ring, potatoes, manicotti, and lasagna. Even a layer cake.

Company chicken meant Chicken Cacciatore, Chicken Crêpes, and Sherried Chicken Divan.

We had a flair for the Orient. Egg Foo Yong, Chicken in a Garden, Stir-Fry Beef and Pea Pods, and Egg Fried Rice.

Curry came on strong—in Chicken Divan, Shrimp Curry, Lamb Curry with Rice, and Curry Dip.

We enjoyed Caesar Salad with the coddled (partially cooked) egg!

Kabobs were frequently on the scene—and on the grill.

We celebrated spring outdoors with shrimp salad and wine spritzers.

Simple vegetables were served in a skillet. And so was stroganoff.

We found time to make our own mayonnaise and pizza from scratch.

Home-style baking was hot.

If it grew in the garden, we pickled it–cucumbers, corn, okra, squash, and watermelon.

Where's the beef? We had it in Beef Noodle Bake, Simple Sloppy Joes, Skillet Beef and Macaroni, and Mexicali Hot Dogs.

Round steak made the rounds. Again.

Cabbage was queen.

Home gardening was a hot hobby. Vegetable dinners included stuffed squash, potato salad, okra and tomatoes, and corn on the cob.

Chicken casseroles cut the food bill.

Pork chop dinners were popular.

1982 saw the birth of our monthly "Cooking Light" column touting low calorie and low-sodium recipes. Light desserts were among the first to debut.

"From Our Kitchen To Yours" column was introduced, answering reader questions about cooking.

Cooking en papillote gave paper new purpose.

Groovy garnishes: tomato roses, frosted grapes, butter curls, and radish roses.

Stuffing was in, but not just bread. Cantaloupe halves were scalloped and stuffed with melon balls. We fixed Sweet Potato-Stuffed Orange Cups. We ate chicken salad in scooped out avocados. And, of course, we stuffed celery sticks.

We had ham however—Cheesy Ham Towers, Ham Tetrazzini, and Cranberry-Ham Loaf.

Fried food, fancy that! Fried cheese, fried pickles, french-fried mushrooms, fish fry, even crispy frog legs.

Eggs all around. We ate Rolled Mushroom Omelet, Texas Brunch, Baked Eggs in Spinach Nests, Eggs in Brandied Cream Sauce, and Saucy Deviled Eggs.

Fresh mushrooms made the scene. We stuffed 'em, marinated 'em, and sherried 'em.

Everything was coming up okra ... fried, pilaf, and in vegetable medleys.

We plugged in food processors, pressure cookers, and microwaves to help us cook quickly.

The chafing dish was a centerpiece and serving piece.

Can you say olé?! Tex-Mex tacos, flautas, tostadas, vegetable burritos, and cheese enchiladas were mainstream.

Chef Paul Prudhomme's fame flared with blackened redfish. Other Cajun recipes were also the rage— Red Beans and Rice, Seafood Gumbo, and Crawfish Étouffée.

We had time to bake in the '80s. Recipes for glazed doughnuts and chocolate doughnuts and yeast bread rings were favorites.

Stuffed potatoes spread excitement for side dishes taking center stage. Potatoes were chili-topped, Mexican-topped, broccoli-topped, and sweet-and-sour.

We purposely left the peel on for our mashed potatoes.

Cheesecakes were chic. We even introduced our first appetizer cheesecake.

Shapely dishes took form as aspics, chicken liver pâté, gelatin salads, and molded desserts.

The Southern adage "waste not, want not" brought creative ways with leftover bread: day-old bread slices in meat loaf, cornbread in dressing, and biscuits in Apple Brown Betty.

Swirled soups were as pleasing to see as to savor.

Cornish hens set the style for elegant entertaining.

The sizzling fajita surfaced.

Fruit kabobs began the decade. Venison kabobs ended it.

We piped fancy potatoes as nests, croquettes, and duchesse.

"In" ingredients were cream cheese, pork sausage, fresh spinach, Cheddar cheese, refrigerated crescent dinner rolls, fresh button mushrooms, egg noodles, macaroni, diced pimiento, grated Parmesan cheese, Italian dressing, and sherry.

Ads of the day: Jello pudding, boil-in-bag rice, and unflavored gelatin.

Men were in the kitchen loud and clear. That is when they weren't out on the patio firing up the grill.

Sassy seasonings were Worcestershire sauce, teriyaki sauce, and lemon pepper.

FOOD IN THE 1990s

Salsa snuck past ketchup in popularity.

We snubbed salt and fat in favor of fresh herbs and other seasonings.

We rapped about food and then wrapped it up in pitas and tortillas.

Olive oil was everywhere, thanks to the Mediterranean diet buzz.

Tall food
was tops. We ate towering appetizers and desserts.

We saw a movement toward fresh ingredients and refreshing flavors. Herbs and spices even infused desserts including Jalapeño-Mint Sherbet, Fennel Ice Cream, Roasted Garlic Crème Brûlée.

With fragrant green thumbs, we got bold and grew herbs—cilantro, basil, rosemary, mint, and many more.

Scones, biscuit's shapely cousins, proudly baked all across the country.

There was confusion over *fusion.* Fusion cooking crossed all borders.

What was brewing? Coffee became a luxurious dessert, as in Java Cream Puffs, Coffee Crème Brûlée, and Coffee Tart.

Perfect *al dente* was the heart's desire as pasta moved to main dish.

Southwestern roundup gave us Fiery Steak with Pimiento Cheese Salsa.

Vegetables became more than meat's sidekick, especially when roasted or grilled.

Chili was still being spooned out . . . but into bowls made of biscuits.

We seasoned our food with fresh garlic and ginger, flavored oils and vinegars, freshly ground pepper, and bottled herb blends.

A farmhouse breakfast was not grits but baked polenta with cheese. And for a fancy supper we served Spoonbread Grits with Savory Mushroom Sauce.

We went crazy caramelizing onions–and a lot of other foods, too.

Move over Chicken Salad. Make room for Tuscan Feta Salad Sandwiches.

The bang and tang of balsamic vinegar took over in dressings, marinades, and sometimes dessert (we served strawberries with black pepper and balsamic vinegar).

We mixed and matched china and flatware for fresh new settings.

We still enjoyed picking berries, and we put them in unexpected places, like on Smoked Turkey, Mozzarella, and Blackberry Sandwiches.

We kicked up flavors a notch with Jamaican Jerk seasoning.

We ate rustic cobblers and chocolate chip cookies and called them comfort food.

Holiday Fare: Acorn Squash-Thyme Soup, Apple-Rosemary Roasted Turkey, Caramelized Onion and Pecan Brussels Sprouts.

"In" ingredients were olive oil, balsamic vinegar, fresh garlic, roasted red pepper, goat cheese, and couscous.

We kept bread machines, coffee grinders, and mini choppers busy on our kitchen counters.

Goat cheese got the vote for best appetizer.

Haute Hors d'oeuvres: Blue Cheese Olive Ball, Black Truffle Bruschetta, Smoked Salmon Canapés, and Goat Cheese Wrapped in Phyllo.

It was peak season for mashed potatoes.

Still giving the gift of chocolate? At the end of the decade we ran a recipe for a Chocolate Mousse Present.

Vegetarian cooking caught on.

Gulp. Gulp. Bottled water was our favorite drink.

Couscous was cool—and quick.

Fine wine with good food reigned. And there were no rules anymore as we sipped Pinot Noir with swordfish and salmon, and slurped oaky Chardonnay with steak.

Risotto stirred up a new creamy rice sensation.

Trés elegante in the '90s: Sweet Corn Soup with Shiitakes and Shrimp, Mashed Potatoes with Crab Marinière.

The USDA convinced us to cook all our eggs.

The holiday table would not have been complete without a to-die-for coconut cake for Christmas.

Our Top-Rated Recipes of 1995

Southern Living

DECEMBER 1995 • $3.50

Sharing Family Food Traditions

Easy & Natural Decorations

Getaways for The Holidays

Two Looks From One Centerpiece

Holiday desserts got transformed. There was Pecan Pie Cake (pictured) and Cracked Caramel Pumpkin Pie.

Appetizers and Beverages

Whet your appetite and excite the
palate with some bite-size finger
food that sports big flavor.

Toasted Pecans (page 14), Wine Welcomer (page 28)

TOASTED PECANS

make ahead

½ cup butter or margarine, melted
3 cups pecan halves
½ teaspoon salt

• **Combine** butter and pecans in a bowl, stirring to coat. Using a slotted spoon, spread pecans on a 15- x 10-inch jellyroll pan; sprinkle with salt. Bake at 275° for 1 hour, stirring occasionally. Yield: 3 cups.

SWEDISH NUTS

make ahead

This trio of sweet snacking nuts bakes with a sugary coating.

1 cup whole blanched almonds
½ cup butter or margarine
2 egg whites
¾ cup sugar
Dash of salt
1 cup walnut halves
1 cup pecan halves

• **Spread** almonds evenly on an ungreased baking sheet. Roast at 325° for 15 minutes or until lightly browned, stirring occasionally; remove from oven, and cool. Place butter in a 13- x 9-inch pan; place in oven to melt butter.
• **Beat** egg whites in a large mixing bowl at high speed with an electric mixer until stiff peaks form. Gradually add sugar and salt, beating until mixture is stiff (2 to 4 minutes). Gently fold in almonds, walnuts, and pecans; spread nut mixture evenly over melted butter in pan.
• **Bake** at 325° for 35 minutes or until mixture is browned and butter is absorbed, stirring every 10 minutes. Cool completely. Store in an airtight container. Yield: 5 cups.

GARLIC COCKTAIL OLIVES

make ahead

The longer these olives marinate, the more pronounced the flavors become.

1 (8-ounce) jar kalamata olives, drained
1 (7-ounce) jar whole green olives, drained
3 large cloves garlic, slivered
⅓ cup olive oil
1 tablespoon chopped fresh rosemary
½ teaspoon freshly ground pepper

• **Combine** all ingredients; cover and let stand at room temperature 1 hour before serving. To make olives ahead, refrigerate up to 5 days; then let stand at room temperature 1 hour before serving. Yield: 2½ cups.

PARTY MIX

make ahead

½ cup butter or margarine, melted
2 teaspoons Worcestershire sauce
1 teaspoon hot sauce
1½ teaspoons garlic salt
6 cups corn-and-rice cereal
2 cups toasted oat O-shaped cereal
1 cup mixed nuts
1 cup pretzel sticks

• **Stir** together first 4 ingredients in a roasting pan. Add cereals, nuts, and pretzels, stirring to coat.
• **Bake** mixture at 200° for 1 hour or until toasted, stirring every 15 minutes. Cool. Yield: 10 cups.

SALLY'S CHEESE STRAWS

family favorite, make ahead

1 pound sharp Cheddar cheese, cut into pieces
1½ cups all-purpose flour
¼ cup butter, softened
1 teaspoon salt
¼ teaspoon ground red pepper

• **Shred** cheese in a food processor; cover and let stand at room temperature 1 hour.
• **Process** cheese, flour, and remaining ingredients in food processor about 30 seconds or until mixture forms a ball.
• **Use** a cookie press fitted with a star-shaped disc to shape mixture into straws, following manufacturer's instructions. Press onto an ungreased baking sheet.
• **Bake** at 375° for 8 to 10 minutes or until lightly browned. Transfer to wire racks to cool. Yield: about 8 dozen.

DATE-FILLED CHEESE PASTRIES

make ahead

1½ cups (6 ounces) shredded Cheddar cheese
1 cup all-purpose flour
1 teaspoon salt
¼ teaspoon ground red pepper
⅓ cup butter or margarine, melted
24 pitted dates
24 pecan halves, toasted

• **Combine** first 4 ingredients in a bowl, stirring well. Add butter, stirring just until dry ingredients are moistened. (Dough will be crumbly.) Shape dough into a ball.

• **Make** a lengthwise slit in each date, and stuff each date with a pecan half. Press 1 generous tablespoon cheese mixture around each date, covering completely. Cover and chill 45 minutes. (You can cover and freeze dates up to 1 month. Thaw in refrigerator before baking.)
• **Place** dates on a greased baking sheet. Bake at 350° for 25 minutes. Remove dates to a wire rack to cool. Serve warm or at room temperature. Yield: 2 dozen.

WARM NACHO DIP

family favorite

2 (16-ounce) cans refried beans
1 (4.5-ounce) can chopped green chiles, drained
1 (1.25-ounce) package taco seasoning
2 cups (8 ounces) shredded Monterey Jack cheese with jalapeño peppers
1 (6-ounce) can frozen avocado dip, thawed
1 (8-ounce) carton sour cream
1 cup chopped tomato
6 green onions, thinly sliced
1 (4.5-ounce) can sliced ripe olives, drained

• **Combine** first 3 ingredients; spread mixture in a lightly greased 11- x 7-inch baking dish. Bake, uncovered, at 350° for 20 minutes or until thoroughly heated. Sprinkle with cheese; bake 5 more minutes or until cheese melts.
• **Spread** avocado dip over warm bean mixture; spread sour cream over avocado dip. Top with tomato, green onions, and olives. Serve warm with tortilla chips or corn chips. Yield: 12 appetizer servings.

HOT CRAB DIP

quick

3 tablespoons butter or margarine, divided
2 shallots, minced
1 1/2 tablespoons all-purpose flour
3/4 cup milk
1/2 cup whipping cream
2 teaspoons lemon juice
1/2 teaspoon salt
1/2 teaspoon ground white pepper
Dash of Worcestershire sauce
1 pound fresh lump crabmeat, drained
1 tablespoon dry sherry

• **Melt** 2 tablespoons butter in a heavy saucepan over medium-high heat; add shallots. Sauté shallots until tender; remove from saucepan, and set aside.
• **Melt** remaining 1 tablespoon butter in saucepan over low heat, and whisk in flour until smooth. Cook 1 minute, whisking constantly. Gradually add milk, whisking until mixture is thickened and bubbly.
• **Whisk** in shallots, cream, and next 4 ingredients; cook mixture over low heat until thoroughly heated. Stir in crabmeat and sherry. Serve dip warm with assorted crackers or Melba toast. Yield: 2 1/2 cups.

BLACK-EYED PEA DIP

make ahead, quick

You can chill this dip overnight. Then just microwave briefly until thoroughly heated.

1/4 cup butter or margarine
2 (15.8-ounce) cans black-eyed peas, undrained
1 cup (4 ounces) shredded Cheddar cheese
1/2 cup (2 ounces) shredded mozzarella cheese
2 tablespoons blackened seasoning (we tested with Paul Prudhomme's)
3 green onions, chopped
1/4 cup chopped green pepper
3/4 cup chopped cooked ham

• **Microwave** butter in a 2-quart microwave-safe bowl at HIGH 30 seconds or until melted. Stir in peas and next 5 ingredients; microwave at HIGH 7 to 8 minutes or until cheese melts, stirring every 2 minutes.
• **Add** ham; spoon dip into a chafing dish. Serve warm with tortilla chips. Yield: 4 cups.

The No-Brainer Appetizer

What's the easiest appetizer to make in a hurry?

70s Onion-sour cream dip. Blend dried onion soup mix with a carton of sour cream. Serve with potato chips.

80s Nachos. Sprinkle shredded Monterey Jack cheese and pickled jalapeño slices over a bed of tortilla chips. Broil or heat in the microwave oven until cheese bubbles.

90s Crostini. Brush little toasts with olive oil, and add a savory topping such as chopped tomato, cheese, or shrimp.

SIMPLE BLUE CHEESE SPREAD

The serious blue cheese fan will enjoy this three-ingredient spread.

1 (4-ounce) package blue cheese
1 (3-ounce) package cream cheese, softened
3 tablespoons brandy

• **Crumble** and mash blue cheese in a bowl. Add cream cheese; beat at medium speed with an electric mixer until smooth. Add brandy, beating until mixture is blended. Cover and chill. Serve with assorted crackers, pumpernickel or rye party rounds, or apple and pear slices. Yield: 1 cup.

FRESH BASIL-CHEESE SPREAD

$^3/_4$ cup chopped walnuts
$^1/_4$ cup coarsely chopped fresh basil leaves
1 green onion, chopped
1 garlic clove, halved
2 (8-ounce) packages cream cheese, softened
1 cup freshly grated Parmesan cheese
$^1/_2$ cup olive oil

• **Bake** walnuts in a shallow pan at 350° for 5 to 10 minutes or until toasted, stirring occasionally. Cool.
• **Pulse** basil, green onion, and garlic in a food processor until minced. Add walnuts, cream cheese, Parmesan cheese, and oil; process until smooth. Cover and chill. Serve spread with crackers or toasted pita wedges. Yield: 3 cups.

HEARTS OF PALM SPREAD

1 (14.4-ounce) can hearts of palm, drained and chopped
1 cup (4 ounces) shredded mozzarella cheese
$^3/_4$ cup mayonnaise
$^1/_2$ cup grated Parmesan cheese
$^1/_4$ cup sour cream
1 green onion, minced

• **Combine** all ingredients; spoon mixture into a lightly greased 9-inch quiche dish or pieplate. Bake, uncovered, at 350° for 20 minutes or until hot and bubbly. Serve with crackers or Melba rounds. Yield: 2 cups.

MEXICAN CHEESE SPREAD

2 cups (8 ounces) shredded sharp Cheddar cheese
$^1/_2$ cup sour cream
$^1/_4$ cup butter or margarine, softened
2 green onions, chopped
1 (2-ounce) jar diced pimiento, drained
2 tablespoons chopped green chiles

• **Combine** first 3 ingredients in a mixing bowl; beat at medium speed with an electric mixer until blended.
• **Stir** in green onions, pimiento, and chiles. Cover and chill, if desired. Serve with crackers. Yield: 2 cups.

Layered Cheese Torta

Four-Cheese Pâté

LAYERED CHEESE TORTA

⌁ make ahead ⌁

This rich cheese blend goes a long way at a party. Be sure to layer the cheese mixtures according to directions so you'll have three even ribbons of color. Then give the mold plenty of time to chill.

1 (8-ounce) package cream cheese, softened
$^1/_4$ cup crumbled blue cheese
1 (8-ounce) can crushed pineapple, drained
$^1/_8$ teaspoon ground ginger
$^1/_2$ cup chopped pecans
1 (3-ounce) package cream cheese, softened
$^1/_3$ cup milk
2 cups (8 ounces) shredded Cheddar cheese
6 slices bacon, cooked and crumbled
1 teaspoon grated onion
$^1/_4$ teaspoon hot sauce
Garnishes: chopped pecans, fresh parsley sprigs

• **Combine** first 4 ingredients in a bowl. Beat at medium speed with an electric mixer until blended; stir in pecans.
• **Line** a lightly greased 4-cup fluted mold or a $7^3/_8$- x $3^5/_8$-inch loafpan with plastic wrap, allowing edges to extend over sides of pan. Spread one-third of blue cheese mixture into mold; chill 1 hour.
• **Combine** remaining 3-ounce package cream cheese and milk, beating well. Add Cheddar cheese and next 3 ingredients, mixing well. Spread over chilled blue cheese mixture in mold. Top with remaining two-thirds blue cheese mixture, spreading evenly. Cover with plastic wrap; chill at least 8 hours or up to 3 days. Unmold onto a serving platter. Remove plastic wrap. Garnish, if desired. Serve with gingersnaps or assorted crackers. Yield: 3 cups.

FOUR-CHEESE PÂTÉ

⌁ make ahead ⌁

This snowy white pâté makes an impressive appetizer. Toasty pecans enhance the mild blend of cheeses.

1 (8-ounce) package cream cheese, softened
2 tablespoons milk
1 cup chopped pecans, toasted
2 (8-ounce) packages cream cheese, softened
1 ($4^1/_2$-ounce) package Camembert cheese, softened
1 (4-ounce) package blue cheese
1 cup (4 ounces) shredded Swiss cheese
Garnishes: red and green grapes

• **Line** a lightly greased 8-inch round cakepan with plastic wrap; set aside. Combine 1 package cream cheese and milk in a medium mixing bowl; beat at medium speed with an electric mixer until smooth. Spread mixture into prepared pan; sprinkle evenly with chopped pecans. Cover and chill.
• **Combine** remaining 2 packages cream cheese, Camembert cheese (including rind), blue cheese, and Swiss cheese in bowl; beat until blended. Spoon mixture over pecan layer, spreading to edge of pan. Cover and chill at least 4 hours or up to 1 week.
• **To serve,** invert pâté onto a serving plate; carefully remove plastic wrap. Garnish pâté, if desired. Serve with apple wedges, gingersnaps, or assorted crackers. Yield: $4^1/_2$ cups.

NOTE: Be sure to sprinkle the pecans to the edge of the pan so when the pâté is inverted for serving, a ring of pecans shows around the edge.

MINIATURE CHEESE QUICHES

These little pastries can serve almost any occasion—a breakfast or brunch, bridal shower, baby shower, or perhaps a picnic.

2 large eggs, lightly beaten
$^1/_2$ cup milk
$1^1/_2$ tablespoons butter or margarine, melted
1 cup (4 ounces) shredded Cheddar cheese or
   Monterey Jack cheese with peppers
Pastry shells
Ground red pepper or paprika (optional)

• **Combine** first 4 ingredients, stirring well. Spoon filling into pastry shells. Sprinkle with red pepper, if desired. Bake at 350° for 25 minutes or until set and golden. Yield: 2 dozen.

Pastry Shells

$1^1/_4$ cups all-purpose flour
1 teaspoon salt
3 tablespoons butter or margarine, melted
1 egg yolk
3 to 4 tablespoons ice water

• **Combine** flour and salt, stirring well; add butter, mixing well. Add egg yolk and ice water; stir with a fork just until dry ingredients are moistened.
• **Shape** dough into 24 (1-inch) balls. Place in lightly greased $1^3/_4$-inch miniature muffin pans, shaping each into a shell. Chill until ready to bake. Yield: 2 dozen.

SWISS CHEESE CROSTINI

1 French baguette
4 cups (16 ounces) shredded Swiss cheese
$^1/_4$ cup beer
2 tablespoons tomato paste
1 tablespoon spicy brown mustard
$^1/_4$ teaspoon garlic powder
$^1/_8$ teaspoon hot sauce

• **Cut** baguette into $^1/_4$-inch-thick slices, and place on an aluminum foil-lined baking sheet.
• **Bake** at 400° for 5 minutes or until lightly browned.
• **Combine** cheese and next 5 ingredients; spread on bread slices.
• **Bake** at 400° for 5 minutes or until cheese melts. Serve immediately. Yield: 3 dozen.

Chippety-Doo-Dah

90s If you said "Please pass the chips" in the late '90s, you might have gotten blue corn or lime tortilla chips, specialty thick-cut, kettle-fried potato chips, or terra chips sliced from sweet potatoes, yuca, and colored with natural beet juice. Even with all these chips available, in 1997 more Americans chose plain ol' potato chips than any other savory/salty snack. Tortilla chips edged in as a close second.

Stuffed Brie en Croûte

make ahead

1 small red pepper
1 (8-ounce) round Brie, chilled
¹/₄ cup coarsely chopped ripe olives
¹/₂ (17¹/₄-ounce) package frozen puff pastry
      sheets, thawed
2 egg yolks, lightly beaten
2 tablespoons water

• **Place** pepper on an aluminum foil-lined baking sheet.
• **Broil** pepper 5¹/₂ inches from heat 5 minutes or until pepper looks blistered, turning twice.
• **Place** pepper in a heavy-duty, zip-top plastic bag; seal and let stand 10 minutes. Peel pepper; remove core and seeds. Coarsely chop pepper.
• **Cut** Brie in half horizontally with a serrated knife. Place pepper and olives on bottom half of Brie; replace top half, and set aside.
• **Unfold** puff pastry sheet onto a lightly floured surface. Fold corners 2 inches toward center; roll pastry into a 14-inch circle.
• **Place** Brie in center of pastry circle; bring pastry together, pinching seams, to resemble a bundle. Tie with kitchen string. Cover and chill up to 8 hours, if desired.
• **Place** pastry-wrapped Brie on a lightly greased baking sheet. Combine egg yolks and water; brush over pastry.
• **Bake** at 400° for 30 to 35 minutes or until golden. Cool 10 minutes; remove string. Transfer to a small cutting board; cut into wedges. Serve warm. Yield: 4 servings.

Hot Mushroom Turnovers

Tender cream cheese pastry surrounds a rich, flavorful filling.

1 (8-ounce) package cream cheese, softened
¹/₂ cup butter or margarine, softened
1³/₄ cups all-purpose flour
3 tablespoons butter or margarine
1 (8-ounce) package fresh mushrooms, minced
1 large onion, minced
¹/₂ cup sour cream
2 tablespoons all-purpose flour
1 teaspoon salt
¹/₄ teaspoon dried thyme
1 large egg, lightly beaten

• **Beat** cream cheese and ¹/₂ cup butter at medium speed with an electric mixer until creamy; gradually add 1³/₄ cups flour, beating well.
• **Divide** dough in half; shape each portion into a ball. Cover and chill 1 hour.
• **Melt** 3 tablespoons butter in a large skillet. Add mushrooms and onion; sauté until tender. Stir in sour cream and next 3 ingredients; set aside.
• **Roll** 1 portion of dough to ¹/₈-inch thickness on a lightly floured surface; cut with a 2¹/₂-inch round cutter. Place rounds on greased baking sheets. Repeat procedure with remaining dough.
• **Spoon** 1 teaspoon mushroom mixture onto half of each dough circle. Moisten edges with egg, and fold dough over filling. Press edges with a fork to seal; prick tops. Brush turnovers with egg.
• **Bake** at 450° for 8 to 10 minutes or until golden. Serve hot. Yield: 3¹/₂ dozen.

Shrimp Tarts

SHRIMP TARTS

Asiago cheese updates the pastry in these rich appetizer tarts meant for a party.

2 pounds unpeeled large fresh shrimp
²/₃ cup finely chopped green onions
¹/₂ cup finely chopped fresh parsley
²/₃ cup mayonnaise
2 tablespoons capers
1 teaspoon lemon juice
¹/₂ teaspoon salt
¹/₄ teaspoon ground red pepper
1 clove garlic, minced
Tart shells
Garnish: thin diagonal slices of green onion

• **Bring** 6 cups water to a boil; add shrimp, and cook 3 to 5 minutes or until shrimp turn pink. Drain well; rinse with cold water. Cover and chill. Peel, devein, and coarsely chop shrimp.
• **Combine** chopped shrimp, green onions, and next 7 ingredients in a large bowl. Spoon mixture evenly into baked tart shells. Garnish, if desired. Yield: 3 dozen.

Tart Shells
¹/₂ cup butter, softened
¹/₂ (8-ounce) package cream cheese, softened
1¹/₄ cups all-purpose flour
¹/₄ cup grated Asiago cheese
¹/₄ teaspoon salt

• **Combine** butter and cream cheese; stir until blended. Add flour, cheese, and salt, blending well. Cover and chill dough 1 hour. Divide dough into 3 portions. Shape each portion into 12 balls.
• **Press** dough onto bottom and up sides of lightly greased 1³/₄-inch miniature muffin pans. Bake at 350° for 15 to 17 minutes or until golden. Cool. Remove from pans. Yield: 3 dozen.

COQUILLES ST. JACQUES

Though coquilles is French for scallop, we've added fresh crabmeat for another layer of flavor in this recipe. This classic dish is often served as an entrée; here it doubles as sumptuous pickup food.

¹/₄ cup plus 2 tablespoons butter or margarine, divided
3 tablespoons all-purpose flour
2 cups half-and-half
1 teaspoon salt
¹/₈ teaspoon ground white pepper
1 pound bay scallops
¹/₄ cup finely chopped green onions
¹/₂ cup chopped fresh mushrooms
¹/₂ pound fresh crabmeat, drained and flaked
3 tablespoons dry white wine or dry vermouth
4 (2.1-ounce) packages frozen mini fillo dough shells, thawed (we tested with Athens)*

• **Melt** 3 tablespoons butter in a heavy saucepan over low heat; add flour, stirring until smooth. Cook 1 minute, stirring constantly. Gradually add half-and-half; cook over medium heat, stirring constantly, until mixture is thickened and bubbly. Stir in salt and white pepper; set aside.
• **Melt** remaining 3 tablespoons butter in a large skillet over medium heat. Add scallops and green onions; cook 3 minutes, stirring constantly. Add mushrooms, and cook 3 more minutes.
• **Stir** cream sauce, crabmeat, and wine into scallop mixture; cook just until thoroughly heated. To serve, spoon about 1 tablespoon seafood mixture into each fillo shell. Yield: 5 dozen appetizers.

*You can substitute frozen 1-inch patty or pastry shells for fillo shells; just thaw and bake according to package directions.

CRAB-STUFFED MUSHROOMS

1½ pounds very large fresh mushrooms (about 18)
3 tablespoons butter or margarine
½ cup chopped onion
1 clove garlic, minced
½ cup soft breadcrumbs
¼ cup chopped fresh parsley
¼ cup mayonnaise
3 tablespoons grated Parmesan cheese
2 tablespoons dry sherry
½ teaspoon Worcestershire sauce
½ teaspoon salt
¼ teaspoon ground red pepper
8 ounces fresh lump crabmeat, drained
2 tablespoons butter or margarine, melted

• **Remove** and chop mushroom stems; set mushroom caps aside.
• **Melt** 3 tablespoons butter in a large skillet. Add chopped mushroom stems, onion, and garlic; sauté 3 to 5 minutes or until tender. Stir in breadcrumbs and next 7 ingredients until mixture is well blended; gently stir in crabmeat.
• **Spoon** crabmeat mixture evenly into mushroom caps; place on a rack in a broiler pan. Drizzle with melted butter.
• **Bake** at 350° for 20 minutes. Serve hot. Yield: about 1½ dozen.

SPICED ICED TEA

make ahead, quick

2 quarts water
2 (3-inch) cinnamon sticks
½ teaspoon whole cloves
¼ teaspoon ground nutmeg
3 family-size tea bags
½ cup sugar
1 (6-ounce) can frozen orange juice concentrate, undiluted
1 (6-ounce) can frozen lemonade concentrate, undiluted
Garnishes: orange and lemon slices

• **Bring** first 4 ingredients to a boil in a Dutch oven.
• **Remove** mixture from heat, and add tea bags; cover and steep 5 minutes. Using a slotted spoon, remove and discard tea bags, cinnamon, and cloves.
• **Stir** in sugar until dissolved; stir in concentrates. Chill; serve over ice. Garnish, if desired. Yield: 8 cups.

LIME-MINT TEA

make ahead, quick

8½ cups water, divided
6 regular-size tea bags
2 cups loosely packed fresh mint leaves, chopped
1½ cups sugar
1¼ cups lemon juice
⅓ cup fresh lime juice
Garnish: fresh mint

• **Bring** 4 cups water to a boil in a large saucepan; pour over tea bags. Cover and steep 5 minutes; discard tea bags.
• **Stir** in mint; let stand 15 minutes. Pour tea through a wire-mesh strainer into a bowl, discarding mint.
• **Bring** remaining 4½ cups water and sugar to a boil in saucepan; cool. Stir in tea and juices. Chill; serve over ice. Garnish, if desired. Yield: 10 cups.

Spiced Iced Tea

Lime-Mint Tea

FRONT PORCH LEMONADE

♥ family favorite, make ahead ♥

You'll need about 10 to 12 lemons and your juicer to make this old-fashioned sip of summertime.

1¼ cups sugar
½ cup boiling water
1 teaspoon grated lemon rind
1½ cups fresh lemon juice
4½ cups cold water
Garnish: lemon slices

• **Combine** sugar and boiling water, stirring until sugar dissolves. Add lemon rind, juice, and cold water; stir well. Chill and serve over ice. Garnish, if desired. Yield: 7 cups.

Front Porch Limeade: Substitute fresh lime rind and juice for the lemon, if desired.

CHAMPAGNE-STRAWBERRY PUNCH

♥ make ahead ♥

Pale pink and effervescent best describe this punch that's perfect for a wedding or anniversary celebration.

3 (6-ounce) cans frozen lemonade concentrate, thawed and undiluted
5 cups water
1 pint fresh strawberries, sliced
1 (1-liter) bottle ginger ale, chilled
2 (750-milliliter) bottles dry champagne, chilled

• **Combine** first 3 ingredients; cover and chill thoroughly. Gently stir in ginger ale and champagne just before serving. Yield: 20 cups.

Sparkling Strawberry Punch: Substitute 6 cups lemon-lime soft drink for champagne, if desired.

NOTE: You can make strawberry ice cubes for the punch by placing a strawberry half in each compartment of an ice cube tray. Fill tray with water or ginger ale, and freeze until firm. Add ice cubes to punch just before serving.

OPEN-HOUSE PUNCH

♥ quick ♥

Bourbon carries the flavor in this party drink.

1 (12-ounce) can frozen lemonade concentrate, thawed and undiluted
1 (6-ounce) can frozen orange juice concentrate, thawed and undiluted
2½ cups bourbon
⅔ cup lemon juice
1 (2-liter) bottle lemon-lime carbonated beverage, chilled
Garnishes: lemon slices, fresh mint

• **Combine** first 4 ingredients; stir well. Add carbonated beverage just before serving. Garnish, if desired. Yield: 14 cups.

The Daily Grind

90s Nineties coffee drinkers discovered common ground at the coffeehouse. Between 1991 and 1997 the number of coffeehouses across the United States soared—from fewer than 500 to more than 5600. At home, java lovers elbowed Mr. Coffee aside for espresso machines, French press pots, and coffee grinders.

Plantation Coffee Punch

Brew your favorite specialty coffee for a subtle play of flavors in this rich, creamy punch.

2 quarts freshly brewed coffee
½ cup sugar
2 quarts coffee ice cream, softened
1 quart chocolate milk
1 tablespoon vanilla extract
Whipped cream
Shaved semisweet chocolate (optional)

• **Combine** hot coffee and sugar, stirring until sugar dissolves. Cover and chill thoroughly. Combine chilled coffee mixture, ice cream, milk, and vanilla in a punch bowl; stir gently until ice cream melts. Top with dollops of whipped cream; sprinkle with shaved chocolate, if desired. Yield: 20 cups.

Maple Coffee

◦ quick ◦

Maple syrup sweetens this rich dessert coffee that resembles café au lait.

1 cup half-and-half
¼ cup maple syrup
1 cup freshly brewed coffee
Sweetened whipped cream

• **Combine** half-and-half and syrup in a saucepan over medium heat, stirring constantly, until thoroughly heated (do not boil).
• **Stir** in coffee; serve with sweetened whipped cream. Yield: 2¼ cups.

Coconut Coffee

◦ quick ◦

2 cups half-and-half
1 (15-ounce) can cream of coconut
4 cups freshly brewed coffee
Sweetened whipped cream

• **Bring** half-and-half and cream of coconut to a boil in a large saucepan over medium heat, stirring constantly.
• **Stir** in coffee; serve with sweetened whipped cream. Yield: 8 cups.

Hot Spiced Cider

◦ quick ◦

Simmering cider on the cooktop creates a spicy aroma that will fill your home. You can simmer the cider continuously, replenishing the apple cider as needed.

4 (4-inch) cinnamon sticks
20 whole cloves
1 gallon apple cider
½ cup firmly packed brown sugar
½ teaspoon ground nutmeg
1 (6-ounce) can frozen orange juice concentrate, undiluted
½ cup lemon juice
Garnish: additional cinnamon sticks

• **Tie** cinnamon sticks and cloves in a cheesecloth bag. Combine spice bag, cider, brown sugar, and nutmeg in a Dutch oven. Bring to a boil; reduce heat, and simmer, uncovered, 10 minutes. Remove and discard spice bag.
• **Add** orange juice concentrate and lemon juice; stir until thoroughly heated. Garnish, if desired. Yield: 1 gallon.

SLUSHY WHISKEY SOURS

~ make ahead ~

Bourbon lovers will relish this bracing cocktail. In particular, it's great for tailgating or a beach party.

1 (6-ounce) can frozen lemonade concentrate, thawed and undiluted
½ (6-ounce) can frozen orange juice concentrate, thawed and undiluted
1¾ cups lemon-lime carbonated beverage
1¼ cups bourbon
¾ to 1 cup water
Garnish: maraschino cherries with stems

• **Combine** first 5 ingredients; freeze overnight or up to 1 month. To serve, stir well until mixture is slushy. Garnish, if desired. Yield: 4½ cups.

WINE WELCOMER

~ quick ~

Try this invigorating beverage; it's like a wine spritzer spiked with a little orange liqueur.

1 (750-milliliter) bottle dry white wine such as Chardonnay
1 (6-ounce) can frozen lemonade concentrate, thawed and undiluted
2 cups orange juice
1 cup Cointreau or other orange-flavored liqueur
1 (1-liter) bottle club soda
Orange slices (optional)

• **Combine** first 4 ingredients in a punch bowl; add club soda, stirring gently. Serve over ice with orange slices, if desired. Yield: 12 cups.

Smooth Operator

80ˢ We Southerners fell for smoothies in 1981 when we published our first recipe, Tropical Smoothie. Dozens of variations followed; hundreds when you count shakes, flips, frostees, coolers, crushes, and slushes. They were usually fruit flavored and healthy, but occasionally we got sidetracked, as exemplified by Kahlúa Smoothie, published in 1987. Smoothies went mainstream in the 1990s as popularity spread nationwide.

FRUITED HONEY-YOGURT SMOOTHIE

~ quick ~

Serve this thick, fruity treat as a beverage, healthy light breakfast, or even dessert.

1 (8-ounce) carton vanilla or fruit-flavored low-fat yogurt
1 (6-ounce) can frozen orange juice concentrate, thawed and undiluted
½ cup water
⅓ cup honey
1½ teaspoons vanilla extract
Ice cubes

• **Process** first 5 ingredients in container of an electric blender until combined; add enough ice cubes to bring mixture to 4½-cup level. Process until smooth. Serve immediately. Yield: 4½ cups.

EASY EGGNOG

quick

½ gallon vanilla ice cream, softened
2 quarts commercial refrigerated eggnog
1½ cups bourbon
Freshly grated nutmeg or ground nutmeg
    (optional)

• **Spoon** softened ice cream into a large punch bowl. Add eggnog and bourbon, stirring gently to blend. Sprinkle with nutmeg, if desired. Serve immediately. Yield: about 18 cups.

ORANGE MILK SHAKE

quick

2 cups milk
1 cup vanilla ice cream
½ cup frozen orange juice concentrate, undiluted
Garnish: orange slices

• **Process** first 3 ingredients in container of an electric blender until smooth. Pour into chilled glasses; garnish, if desired. Serve immediately. Yield: 4 cups.

WHISPERS

quick

This luxurious blend of liqueurs and ice cream makes a potent after-dinner drink.

1 quart coffee ice cream, slightly softened
¼ cup cognac
¼ cup crème de cacao
¼ cup Kahlúa or other coffee-flavored liqueur

• **Process** all ingredients in container of an electric blender until smooth. Pour mixture into chilled stemmed glasses; serve immediately. Yield: 3 cups.

CHOCOLATE MALTED

quick

If you like really thick shakes, increase the ice cream to 4 cups.

3 cups vanilla ice cream
½ cup milk
⅓ cup chocolate syrup
2 tablespoons malt-flavored drink mix
    (we tested with Ovaltine)

• **Combine** first 3 ingredients in container of an electric blender; process just until smooth, stopping once to scrape down sides. Stir in drink mix. Serve immediately. Yield: 3 cups.

PEACH-GINGER FROST

quick

3 ripe peaches, peeled and quartered
    (1 pound)
⅓ cup light corn syrup
¼ teaspoon ground ginger
1 cup pineapple or lemon sherbet
1 cup vanilla ice cream
½ cup ginger ale
Garnish: peach slices

• **Process** first 3 ingredients in container of an electric blender until smooth. Add sherbet and ice cream; process just until smooth. Add ginger ale; process 30 seconds. Garnish, if desired. Serve immediately. Yield: 4 cups.

Breads

Baked in the oven to produce one of life's most marvelous aromas, bread is a welcome staple on any table. Its many names, shapes, and textures match easily with an endless array of foods for any meal.

Flaky Buttermilk Biscuits (next page) and
Molasses-Oat Bread (page 47)

FLAKY BUTTERMILK BISCUITS

family favorite, quick

½ cup cold butter or margarine, cut up
2 cups self-rising flour
¾ cup buttermilk
Butter or margarine, melted

• **Cut** ½ cup butter into flour with a pastry blender until mixture is crumbly. Add buttermilk, stirring with a fork just until flour is moistened. Turn dough out onto a lightly floured surface, and knead 4 or 5 times.
• **Roll** dough to ¾-inch thickness; cut with a 2-inch biscuit cutter. Place biscuits on a greased baking sheet.
• **Bake** at 450° for 8 to 10 minutes or until golden. Remove biscuits from oven, and brush with melted butter. Yield: 16 biscuits.

SOUR CREAM BISCUITS

3 cups all-purpose flour
2 tablespoons baking powder
1 teaspoon salt
½ cup cold butter or margarine, cut up
½ cup milk
½ cup buttermilk
⅓ cup sour cream
⅛ teaspoon sugar
⅛ teaspoon vanilla extract

• **Combine** first 3 ingredients; cut in butter with a pastry blender until mixture is crumbly.
• **Combine** milk and next 4 ingredients; add to dry ingredients, stirring with a fork just until dry ingredients are moistened.
• **Turn** dough out onto a floured surface; knead 3 or 4 times. Roll to ½-inch thickness; cut with a 1½-inch biscuit cutter, and place on lightly greased baking sheets.
• **Bake** at 450° for 7 to 9 minutes. Yield: about 3 dozen.

SWEET POTATO BISCUITS

1 large sweet potato
2 cups self-rising flour
¼ cup sugar
3 tablespoons shortening
2 tablespoons cold butter or margarine, cut up
⅓ cup milk

• **Pierce** sweet potato several times with a fork. Microwave at HIGH 6 minutes or until tender; cool slightly. Peel and mash; cool.
• **Combine** flour and sugar in a medium bowl. Cut shortening and butter into flour mixture with a pastry blender until crumbly; add mashed sweet potato and milk, stirring just until dry ingredients are moistened.
• **Turn** dough out onto a floured surface; knead 3 or 4 times. Roll dough to ½-inch thickness; cut with a 2-inch biscuit cutter. Place on a greased baking sheet.
• **Bake** at 400° for 15 minutes or until golden. Yield: 10 biscuits.

CREAM SCONES

quick

In Britain, plain scones (offered with jam and clotted cream) are served with afternoon tea. As a nod to this tradition, we serve Cream Scones with preserves and whipped cream.

2 cups all-purpose flour
¼ cup sugar
1 tablespoon baking powder
¼ teaspoon salt
⅓ cup cold butter, cut up
1 cup whipping cream

• **Combine** first 4 ingredients; cut in butter with a pastry blender until crumbly.
• **Add** whipping cream to flour mixture, stirring just until moistened.

• **Turn** dough out onto a lightly floured surface; knead 5 or 6 times. Roll to ½-inch thickness; cut with a 2-inch biscuit cutter, and place in lightly greased muffin pans or 2 inches apart on greased baking sheets.
• **Bake** at 375° for 15 minutes or until golden. Serve with preserves and whipped cream. Yield: 1 dozen.

ORANGE-CURRANT SCONES

quick

This Scottish quick bread is spiked with currants and orange essence. The key to tender, flaky scones is to work quickly when cutting cold butter into the dough and to handle the dough as little as possible.

⅓ cup currants
¾ cup buttermilk
2 cups all-purpose flour
2 tablespoons sugar
2 teaspoons baking powder
¼ teaspoon baking soda
¼ teaspoon salt
1 tablespoon grated orange rind
⅓ cup cold butter or margarine, cut up
Milk
Sugar

• **Combine** currants and buttermilk in a small bowl.
• **Combine** flour and next 5 ingredients, stirring well. Cut in butter with a pastry blender until mixture is crumbly. Gradually add currants and buttermilk, stirring just until dry ingredients are moistened.
• **Turn** dough out onto a lightly floured surface, and knead 4 or 5 times. Pat dough to ¾-inch thickness; cut with a 3-inch biscuit cutter. Place scones on a lightly greased baking sheet. Brush scones with milk, and sprinkle with sugar.
• **Bake** at 400° for 18 minutes or until golden. Yield: 6 scones.

COFFEE CAKE MUFFINS

Cinnamon streusel runs throughout and crowns the top of these sweet muffins that are perfect for breakfast or brunch.

¼ cup firmly packed brown sugar
¼ cup chopped pecans
1 teaspoon ground cinnamon
1½ cups all-purpose flour
½ cup sugar
2 teaspoons baking powder
¼ teaspoon baking soda
¼ teaspoon salt
1 large egg
¾ cup milk
⅓ cup vegetable oil
Vegetable cooking spray

• **Combine** first 3 ingredients; set aside.
• **Stir** together flour and next 4 ingredients in a large bowl; make a well in center of mixture.
• **Stir** together egg, milk, and oil; add to flour mixture, stirring just until dry ingredients are moistened.
• **Place** paper baking cups in muffin pans, and lightly coat with cooking spray.
• **Spoon** about 1 tablespoon batter into each of 12 cups; sprinkle evenly with half of brown sugar mixture. Top evenly with remaining batter, and sprinkle with remaining brown sugar mixture.
• **Bake** at 400° for 22 to 24 minutes or until lightly browned. Remove from pan immediately; cool on a wire rack. Yield: 1 dozen.

LEMON MUFFINS

~ quick ~

These tender muffins are best served warm from the oven. If you have leftovers, split and toast them, and add a drizzle of honey.

1 cup shortening
1 cup sugar
4 large eggs, separated
2 cups all-purpose flour
2 teaspoons baking powder
1 teaspoon salt
½ cup fresh lemon juice
2 teaspoons grated lemon rind

• **Beat** shortening at medium speed with an electric mixer until fluffy; gradually add sugar, beating well. Add egg yolks, 1 at a time, beating after each addition.
• **Combine** flour, baking powder, and salt; add to shortening mixture alternately with lemon juice, beginning and ending with flour mixture. Beat at low speed after each addition until blended. Stir in lemon rind.
• **Beat** egg whites at high speed until stiff peaks form. Gently fold beaten egg whites into batter. Spoon into lightly greased muffin pans, filling three-fourths full.
• **Bake** at 375° for 18 to 19 minutes. Remove from pans immediately. Serve warm. Yield: 1½ dozen.

BLUEBERRY STREUSEL MUFFINS

~ family favorite ~

¼ cup pecan halves
¼ cup firmly packed brown sugar
1 tablespoon all-purpose flour
2 tablespoons butter or margarine
½ cup uncooked regular oats
2 cups all-purpose flour
½ cup sugar
2 teaspoons baking powder
¼ teaspoon baking soda
¼ teaspoon salt
2 teaspoons grated lemon rind
1¼ cups fresh or frozen blueberries
1 large egg, lightly beaten
¾ cup buttermilk
¼ cup vegetable oil

• **Process** pecans in a food processor 2 or 3 times or until chopped. Add brown sugar and 1 tablespoon flour; process 5 seconds. Add butter; pulse 5 times or until mixture is crumbly. Stir in oats; set aside.
• **Combine** 2 cups flour and next 5 ingredients in a large bowl; add blueberries, tossing gently. Make a well in center of mixture.
• **Combine** egg, buttermilk, and oil; add to flour mixture, stirring just until moistened. Spoon batter into greased muffin pans, filling two-thirds full; sprinkle with oat mixture.
• **Bake** at 400° for 15 to 20 minutes or until golden. Remove from pans immediately; cool on wire racks. Yield: 1 dozen.

Buzz Words

70ˢ Veggies, Munchies, Nouvelle cuisine

80ˢ Lite/Low-Fat/Natural, California Spa cuisine, Cocooning

90ˢ Fusion cooking, Med-Rim cuisine, Grazing, HMR (Home meal replacement), MRE (Meals ready to eat)

Blueberry Streusel Muffins

SAUSAGE-CHEDDAR MUFFINS

Serve these savory muffins for breakfast or with soup and salad.

¹/₂ pound ground pork sausage
2 cups all-purpose flour
2 tablespoons sugar
1 tablespoon baking powder
¹/₄ teaspoon salt
1 cup milk
1 large egg, lightly beaten
¹/₄ cup butter or margarine, melted
¹/₂ cup (2 ounces) shredded sharp Cheddar cheese
Vegetable cooking spray

• **Brown** sausage in a large skillet, stirring until it crumbles; drain. Set sausage aside.
• **Combine** flour and next 3 ingredients; make a well in center of mixture.
• **Combine** milk, egg, and butter; add to dry mixture, stirring just until moistened. Stir in sausage and cheese.
• **Place** paper baking cups in muffin pans, and coat lightly with cooking spray. Spoon batter into cups, filling two-thirds full.
• **Bake** at 375° for 20 minutes or until golden. Remove from pans immediately. Yield: 1 dozen.

Hot Biscuits or Bust

Southerners love their biscuits, hot, steaming, and dripping with butter and honey or homemade jam. Self-rising flour made biscuits easy; packaged mixes made them even easier. Canned biscuits eliminated measuring and mixing altogether. The '90s hot biscuit trail often lead directly to Hardee's drive-through—but, there's still nothing like a hot biscuit from scratch.

ORANGE-GLAZED TEA ROLLS

family favorite

Turn out these petite tea rolls for your next luncheon or baby shower.

1 (8-ounce) package refrigerated crescent dinner rolls
1 tablespoon butter or margarine, melted
¹/₃ cup sugar
¹/₄ teaspoon ground cinnamon
Orange Glaze

• **Unroll** crescent roll dough onto lightly floured wax paper; press perforations to seal. Brush dough with melted butter. Combine sugar and cinnamon; sprinkle over dough.
• **Roll** up, jellyroll fashion, starting at long side, and cut into 1-inch-thick slices. Place slices, cut sides down, in lightly greased miniature (1³/₄-inch) muffin pans.
• **Bake** at 375° for 11 to 13 minutes or until golden. Remove from pans immediately, and drizzle with Orange Glaze. Yield: 1 dozen.

Orange Glaze
²/₃ cup sifted powdered sugar
2 tablespoons frozen orange juice concentrate, thawed and undiluted
2 teaspoons water

• **Combine** all ingredients in a small bowl, stirring until smooth. Yield: ¹/₄ cup.

ZUCCHINI BREAD

family favorite

Zucchini bread is great for breakfast, lunch, or snacking any time of day. This recipe makes two loaves, so you can enjoy one right away and freeze the other one or share it with a friend.

3 cups all-purpose flour
1 tablespoon baking powder
½ teaspoon baking soda
¾ teaspoon salt
1 teaspoon ground cinnamon
1 teaspoon ground nutmeg
2 cups sugar
¾ cup vegetable oil
3 large eggs, lightly beaten
2 teaspoons vanilla extract
3 cups shredded zucchini (about 2 large)
1 cup chopped pecans or walnuts

• **Combine** first 6 ingredients in a large bowl; make a well in center of mixture.
• **Combine** sugar, oil, eggs, and vanilla; stir well. Add to dry ingredients, stirring just until moistened. Stir in zucchini and pecans.
• **Spoon** batter into two lightly greased 8½- x 4½-inch loafpans.
• **Bake** at 350° for 50 minutes or until a wooden pick inserted in center comes out clean. Cool in pans on wire racks 10 minutes; remove from pans, and cool completely on wire racks. Yield: 2 loaves.

HONEY-BANANA BREAD

family favorite

Honey instead of sugar sweetens this homespun banana bread. When bananas become fragrant and the peels turn black, it's time to bake this timeless loaf.

½ cup butter or margarine, softened
¾ cup honey
2 large eggs
1 cup mashed ripe banana
2 cups all-purpose flour
1 teaspoon baking soda
¼ teaspoon salt
1 cup chopped pecans, toasted

• **Beat** butter at medium speed with an electric mixer in a large mixing bowl; add honey, beating well. Add eggs, 1 at a time, beating after each addition. Add banana, and mix well.
• **Combine** flour, baking soda, and salt; stir in pecans. Add to butter mixture, stirring just until dry ingredients are moistened.
• **Spoon** batter into a lightly greased and floured 9- x 5-inch loafpan.
• **Bake** at 350° for 50 to 55 minutes or until a wooden pick inserted in center comes out clean. Shield with aluminum foil, if necessary. Cool in pan on a wire rack 10 minutes; remove from pan, and cool completely on wire rack. Yield: 1 loaf.

SOUR CREAM CORN STICKS

family favorite

3 large eggs, lightly beaten
1 cup self-rising cornmeal
1 (8¾-ounce) can cream-style corn
1 (8-ounce) carton sour cream
¼ cup vegetable oil

• **Heat** lightly greased cast-iron corn stick pans in a 400° oven for 5 minutes.
• **Combine** all ingredients, stirring just until cornmeal is moistened.
• **Remove** cast-iron pans from oven, and spoon batter into hot pans.
• **Bake** at 400° for 16 to 18 minutes or until golden. Yield: 16 corn sticks.

SOUTHERN CORNCAKES

quick

Enjoy these sizzling Southern pancakes for breakfast alongside crisp bacon and fluffy scrambled eggs.

1½ cups self-rising cornmeal
1¼ cups buttermilk
1 tablespoon sugar
1 tablespoon vegetable oil
1 large egg, lightly beaten
Vegetable oil

• **Combine** first 5 ingredients in a large bowl, stirring just until dry ingredients are moistened.
• **Pour** oil to depth of ¼ inch into a large heavy skillet. For each corncake, pour ¼ cup batter into skillet. Fry corncakes in hot oil over medium-high heat 3 minutes on each side or until golden. Serve immediately. Yield: 8 corncakes.

MEXICAN CORNBREAD

Green chiles give this crusty cornbread its Mexican slant. Corn and Cheddar cheese are a pleasant surprise in the batter as well. This cornbread is the ideal complement to a bowl of chili.

1 tablespoon shortening
1 cup yellow cornmeal
1 teaspoon baking powder
½ teaspoon baking soda
½ teaspoon salt
1 (8-ounce) carton sour cream
1 (8½-ounce) can cream-style corn
2 large eggs, lightly beaten
1 cup (4 ounces) shredded Cheddar cheese
1 (4.5-ounce) can chopped green chiles, drained

• **Place** shortening in a 9-inch cast-iron skillet, and heat in a 450° oven for 3 to 5 minutes or until fat smokes.
• **Combine** cornmeal, baking powder, soda, and salt; blend well. Combine sour cream, corn, and eggs, mixing well. Add to dry ingredients, stirring just until moistened.
• **Spoon** half of batter into hot skillet. Sprinkle with cheese and chiles; top with remaining batter.
• **Bake** at 450° for 23 to 25 minutes or until brown. Let stand 5 minutes before serving. Yield: 8 servings.

CORN SPOONBREAD

Muffin mix and two cans of corn make this cross between cornbread and spoonbread quick and easy.

2 large eggs, lightly beaten
1 (8½-ounce) package corn muffin mix
1 (8-ounce) can cream-style corn
1 (8-ounce) can whole kernel corn, drained
1 (8-ounce) container sour cream
½ cup butter or margarine, melted

• **Combine** all ingredients, stirring just until muffin mix is moistened; pour batter into a lightly greased 11- x 7-inch baking dish.
• **Bake** at 350° for 35 to 40 minutes or until golden. Yield: 12 servings.

CORNBREAD DRESSING

⁓ make ahead ⁓

Don't wait until Thanksgiving to try this moist dressing. With hints of sage and onion, it pairs nicely with a pork roast.

Cornbread
10 to 12 slices day-old white or wheat bread
½ (2-ounce) package onion soup mix
1 teaspoon rubbed sage
1 teaspoon poultry seasoning
¼ teaspoon pepper
2 large eggs, lightly beaten
2 (10¾-ounce) cans cream of celery soup
2 (10¾-ounce) cans cream of chicken soup
1½ to 2 cups chicken or turkey broth

• **Crumble** cornbread and bread slices into a large bowl; add onion soup mix and next 3 ingredients to bowl. Stir in beaten eggs, soups, and enough broth to make a moist dressing.
• **Spoon** dressing into a lightly greased 13- x 9-inch baking dish. Bake, uncovered, at 400° for 30 to 35 minutes or until browned. Yield: 12 servings.

Cornbread
1 cup cornmeal
1 cup all-purpose flour
1 tablespoon baking powder
1 large egg, lightly beaten
1 cup milk
¼ cup shortening

• **Combine** first 3 ingredients in a bowl; add egg and milk, stirring just until dry ingredients are moistened.
• **Place** shortening in a 10-inch cast-iron skillet. Place skillet in a 425° oven for 5 minutes or until shortening melts. Remove from oven, and pour melted shortening into batter; stir well. Pour batter into hot skillet.
• **Bake** at 425° for 25 minutes or until golden. Yield: 1 (10-inch) wheel.

NOTE: This dressing freezes well. Divide dressing between two (8-inch) square pans. Bake one; cover and freeze the other. Let dressing thaw in refrigerator overnight before baking.

Redefining Dixie Dining

New South cuisine honors tradition and takes the region's bounty to a new level. What a heritage! Western European cooking styles meet African foods and techniques plus a mix of American Indian food culture. We partake of absolutely fresh, absolutely delicious pork, ham, chicken, sweet potatoes, biscuits, black-eyed peas, and pound cake. And, never forget the banana cream pie.

Sopaipillas

SOPAIPILLAS

Your family will enjoy this Southwestern bread that looks like puffy little pillows. To guarantee their "puff," it's important to maintain the oil's heat at 375°. Clip a candy thermometer to the side of the pan to help regulate the heat.

1¾ cups all-purpose flour
1 tablespoon sugar
2 teaspoons baking powder
1 teaspoon salt
2 tablespoons shortening
⅔ cup milk
Vegetable oil
Honey
Cinnamon sugar

• **Combine** first 4 ingredients; cut in shortening with a pastry blender until mixture is crumbly. Add milk, stirring with a fork just until dry ingredients are moistened; shape into a ball.
• **Turn** dough out onto a lightly floured surface, and knead gently until smooth (about 1 minute). Cover dough, and let rest 1 hour.
• **Roll** dough to ¹⁄₁₆-inch thickness with a floured rolling pin. Using a pizza cutter, cut dough into 3-inch squares. Cover dough with a damp towel or cloth.
• **Pour** oil to depth of 2 inches in a Dutch oven; heat to 375°. Drop dough, a few squares at a time, into hot oil, turning immediately to allow even puffing; turn back over, and cook until both sides are lightly browned. Drain on paper towels. Repeat with remaining dough squares. Serve immediately with honey and cinnamon sugar. Yield: 22 sopaipillas.

NOTE: Make your own cinnamon sugar, if desired, by combining ½ cup sugar and 1 tablespoon ground cinnamon.

BELGIAN WAFFLES

family favorite

These waffles are baked in a Belgian waffle iron which has larger, deeper grids than the traditional appliance. You can use a regular waffle iron if you prefer. Either way, heap fresh strawberries and whipped cream on waffles to maintain the Belgian influence.

4 large eggs, separated
3 tablespoons butter or margarine, melted
½ teaspoon vanilla extract
1 cup all-purpose flour
½ teaspoon salt
1 cup milk
Sweetened whipped cream
Sliced fresh strawberries

• **Beat** egg yolks at medium speed with an electric mixer until thick and pale. Add butter and vanilla, beating until blended. Set aside.
• **Combine** flour and salt. Add flour mixture and milk to egg mixture, beating until smooth. Set aside.
• **Beat** egg whites until stiff peaks form, and gently fold into batter.
• **Bake** waffles in batches in a preheated, oiled Belgian waffle iron until golden. Serve with sweetened whipped cream and strawberries. Yield: 8 (4-inch) waffles.

Buttermilk Pancakes

BUTTERMILK PANCAKES

family favorite, quick

1¼ cups all-purpose flour
2 tablespoons sugar
2 teaspoons baking powder
½ teaspoon baking soda
¾ teaspoon salt
1 large egg, lightly beaten
1¼ cups buttermilk
3 tablespoons vegetable oil
1 cup chopped pecans, toasted (optional)

• **Stir** together first 5 ingredients in a large bowl; make a well in center of mixture.
• **Stir** together egg, buttermilk, and oil; add to dry ingredients, stirring just until moistened. Add pecans, if desired.
• **For** each pancake, pour about ¼ cup batter onto a hot, lightly greased griddle.
• **Cook** pancakes until tops are covered with bubbles and edges look cooked; turn and cook other side. Serve with butter, warm maple syrup, and fresh berries. Yield: 9 (4-inch) pancakes.

AMARETTO FRENCH TOAST

make ahead

6 (1-inch-thick) French bread slices
4 large eggs
½ cup milk
1 tablespoon dark brown sugar
1 teaspoon almond extract
½ teaspoon ground nutmeg
2 tablespoons amaretto (optional)
3 tablespoons butter or margarine
¼ cup sliced almonds, toasted
Powdered sugar
Maple syrup, warmed

• **Arrange** bread slices in a lightly greased 13- x 9-inch baking dish. Whisk together eggs, next 4 ingredients, and, if desired, liqueur; pour over bread. Let stand 3 minutes; then gently turn bread over in pan to evenly absorb egg mixture. Chill 8 hours, if desired.
• **Melt** butter at 400° in a 15- x 10-inch jellyroll pan; add soaked bread. Bake at 400° for 15 minutes; turn. Bake 8 more minutes or until golden. Sprinkle French toast with almonds and powdered sugar. Serve with syrup. Yield: 3 servings.

An Exploding Market

70s College students plugged in the popcorn popper for heating canned soup or warming a late-night snack.

80s The popper's popularity plopped. Even Jiffy Pop popcorn seemed slow when popcorn appeared on the market in ready-to-microwave bags.

90s Jiffy Pop still had a modest following. But microwaveable popcorn stood out in the popcorn field. Across the U.S., consumers spent twice as much on it as they did for supermarket bags of popped corn and the traditional kernels combined. Plus, microwave-ready popcorn catered to every taste: low salt, low fat, extra butter, even Cheddar cheese and caramel, and, of course regular!

HOMEMADE RAISIN BREAD

~family favorite~

The aroma of homemade bread baking is one of life's simple pleasures. Try the main recipe below or the Cinnamon-Raisin version, which is a bit sweeter.

1 cup raisins
2 packages active dry yeast
½ cup warm water (105° to 115°)
3 tablespoons sugar
⅔ cup shortening
1⅓ cups milk
½ cup sugar
1½ teaspoons salt
6 to 6½ cups bread flour, divided
2 large eggs, lightly beaten
1 large egg, lightly beaten
2 tablespoons butter or margarine, melted

• **Place** raisins in a small saucepan; add water to cover. Bring to a boil; remove from heat. Drain and cool.
• **Combine** yeast and warm water in a 2-cup liquid measuring cup; stir in 3 tablespoons sugar, and let stand 5 minutes. Combine shortening and next 3 ingredients in a saucepan over medium heat until shortening melts; remove from heat. Let mixture cool to lukewarm (105° to 115°).
• **Combine** yeast mixture, shortening mixture, 2 cups flour, and 2 eggs in a large mixing bowl. Beat at medium speed with an electric mixer until blended. Gradually stir in enough remaining flour to make a soft dough.
• **Turn** dough out onto a floured surface; add raisins, and knead until smooth and elastic (8 to 10 minutes). Place in a well-greased bowl, turning to grease top. Cover and let rise in a warm place (85°), free from drafts, 1 hour or until doubled in bulk.
• **Punch** dough down, and divide in half. Roll each half of dough into a 15- x 7-inch rectangle on a lightly floured surface; roll up, jellyroll fashion, starting at narrow end. Pinch seams and ends to seal. Place loaves, seam side down, in two well-greased 9- x 5-inch loafpans. Cover and let rise 30 to 45 minutes or until doubled in bulk.
• **Brush** tops of loaves with remaining beaten egg. Bake at 350° for 30 minutes or until loaves sound hollow when tapped. Brush tops of loaves with melted butter. Yield: 2 loaves.

Cinnamon-Raisin Bread: Prepare dough as directed at left. Combine 3 tablespoons sugar and 1 tablespoon ground cinnamon; sift across dough before rolling up, jellyroll fashion. Combine 1 cup sifted powdered sugar and 1½ tablespoons milk, stirring until smooth. Drizzle glaze over barely warm baked loaves.

VIENNA BRIOCHE LOAVES

~make ahead~

4½ cups all-purpose flour, divided
¼ cup sugar
1 teaspoon salt
1 teaspoon grated lemon rind
1 package active dry yeast
1 cup butter
½ cup water
6 large eggs
3 tablespoons butter, softened
⅔ cup firmly packed brown sugar
2 tablespoons milk
¼ teaspoon vanilla extract
2 egg yolks, lightly beaten
2 cups finely chopped pecans
Melted butter
Powdered sugar (optional)

• **Combine** 1¾ cups flour, ¼ cup sugar, and next 3 ingredients in a large mixing bowl; stir well. Combine

1 cup butter and water in a saucepan; heat until butter melts, stirring occasionally. Cool to 120° to 130°.

• **Gradually** add liquid mixture to flour mixture, beating well at low speed with an electric mixer. Beat an additional 2 minutes at medium speed. Add 6 eggs; beat well. Gradually stir in remaining flour. Cover and let rise in a warm place (85°), free from drafts, 1 hour or until doubled in bulk. Cover and chill at least 8 hours.

• **Combine** 3 tablespoons butter and next 4 ingredients in a medium bowl; stir well. Stir in pecans, and set aside.

• **Punch** dough down; turn out onto a lightly floured surface, and knead 4 or 5 times. Divide dough in half. Work with 1 portion of dough at a time, refrigerating other portion. Roll dough into a 14- x 9-inch rectangle; brush with melted butter. Spread half of pecan mixture over dough to within ½ inch of edge. Roll up 1 side of dough, starting at short side and ending at middle of dough. Roll up remaining side of dough until rolls meet in the middle.

• **Place** dough in a well-greased 9- x 5-inch loafpan, rolled side up. Gently brush loaf with melted butter. Repeat procedure with remaining portion of dough and pecan mixture. Cover and let rise in a warm place, free from drafts, 45 minutes or until doubled in bulk.

• **Bake** at 350° for 20 minutes; cover with aluminum foil, and bake 15 more minutes or until golden. Remove bread from pans immediately; cool on wire racks. Sprinkle with powdered sugar, if desired. Yield: 2 loaves.

NOTE: You can prepare loaves ahead and freeze. Bake loaves as directed; let cool. Wrap tightly in aluminum foil, and freeze up to 1 month. Let thaw, covered, at room temperature. Reheat in foil at 350° for 10 to 15 minutes, if desired.

MOLASSES-OAT BREAD

family favorite

A sprinkling of oats speckles the top of this attractive loaf.

1 cup uncooked regular oats
2 cups boiling water
2 packages active dry yeast
⅓ cup warm water (105° to 115°)
½ cup molasses
¼ cup honey
2 tablespoons butter or margarine, softened
2½ teaspoons salt
6 to 6½ cups all-purpose flour, divided
1 large egg, lightly beaten
2 tablespoons uncooked regular oats

• **Combine** 1 cup oats and boiling water, stirring well. Let stand 20 minutes or until mixture reaches 115°.

• **Combine** yeast and ⅓ cup warm water in a 1-cup liquid measuring cup; let stand 5 minutes.

• **Combine** yeast, oats mixture, molasses, and next 3 ingredients in a large mixing bowl, mixing well. Add 2 cups flour, and stir until smooth. Gradually add enough remaining flour to make a soft dough.

• **Turn** dough out onto a well-floured surface, and knead until smooth and elastic (about 8 minutes). Place in a well-greased bowl, turning to grease top. Cover and let rise in a warm place (85°), free from drafts, 45 minutes or until doubled in bulk.

• **Punch** dough down, and divide in half; roll 1 portion into a 14- x 7-inch rectangle. Roll up dough, starting at narrow end, pressing firmly to eliminate air pockets; pinch ends to seal. Place dough, seam side down, in a well-greased 9- x 5-inch loafpan. Repeat procedure with remaining portion of dough. Brush loaves with beaten egg, and sprinkle with 2 tablespoons oats. Cover and let rise in a warm place, free from drafts, 45 minutes or until doubled in bulk.

• **Bake** at 350° for 30 to 35 minutes or until loaves sound hollow when tapped. Remove from pans immediately; cool on wire racks. Yield: 2 loaves.

DILLY CASSEROLE BREAD

Here's an old-fashioned batter bread that ranks as high in popularity today as it did in the seventies. Serve it warm with grilled chicken or as an accompaniment with vegetable soup.

1 cup small-curd cottage cheese
1 large egg, lightly beaten
1½ tablespoons butter or margarine
1 tablespoon sugar
1 tablespoon dried minced onion
2 teaspoons dill seeds
1 teaspoon salt
¼ teaspoon baking soda
1 package active dry yeast
1 tablespoon sugar
¼ cup warm water (105° to 115°)
2½ cups all-purpose flour
Melted butter
Coarse salt

• **Combine** first 8 ingredients in a small saucepan. Cook over medium heat until butter melts, stirring occasionally. Let cool to 105° to 115°.
• **Combine** yeast, 1 tablespoon sugar, and warm water in a 1-cup liquid measuring cup; let stand 5 minutes.
• **Combine** cottage cheese mixture, yeast mixture, and flour; stir well. (Dough will be sticky.) Cover and let rise in a warm place (85°), free from drafts, 45 minutes or until doubled in bulk.
• **Stir** dough down, and spoon into a well-greased 2-quart casserole or any other round baking dish. Cover and let rise in a warm place, free from drafts, 30 minutes or until doubled in bulk.
• **Bake** at 350° for 25 to 30 minutes or until brown. Brush with melted butter, and sprinkle lightly with coarse salt. Remove from dish; cool on a wire rack. Yield: 1 loaf.

BLACK BREAD

Serve wedges of this dark bread with cheese and white wine or your favorite brew.

1 package active dry yeast
2 cups warm water (105° to 115°)
3 to 4 cups all-purpose flour, divided
2 tablespoons shortening, melted and cooled
2 tablespoons sugar
2 teaspoons salt
3 cups rye flour
1 tablespoon caraway seeds
1 tablespoon dill seeds
3 tablespoons dark molasses
Butter or margarine, melted

• **Combine** yeast and warm water in a 2-cup liquid measuring cup; let stand 5 minutes. Combine yeast mixture, 3 cups all-purpose flour, shortening, sugar, and salt in a large mixing bowl; beat at medium speed with an electric mixer until well blended. Add rye flour and next 3 ingredients; mix well. Gradually stir in enough remaining all-purpose flour to form a soft dough.
• **Turn** dough out onto a well-floured surface, and knead until smooth and elastic (about 8 to 10 minutes). Place in a well-greased bowl, turning to grease top. Cover and let rise in a warm place (85°), free from drafts, 1 hour or until doubled in bulk.
• **Punch** dough down, and divide in half; shape each portion into a smooth ball. Place on a large greased baking sheet, and lightly press to flatten bottom. Slash tops of loaves with a razor blade or sharp knife. Cover and let rise in a warm place, free from drafts, 1 hour or until doubled in bulk.
• **Bake** at 400° for 30 minutes or until loaves sound hollow when tapped. Brush bread with melted butter. Remove to wire racks to cool. Yield: 2 loaves.

CHRISTMAS COFFEE CAKE RING

~ family favorite ~

This buttery-rich yeast bread tastes like German stollen, but the ring shape makes it different. It's just what you'll want to serve family and friends during the holiday season.

1 cup milk
1 cup butter or margarine
½ cup water
5¼ cups all-purpose flour
¼ cup sugar
1 teaspoon salt
2 packages active dry yeast
2 large eggs, lightly beaten
½ teaspoon grated lemon rind
½ teaspoon grated orange rind
½ cup raisins
¼ cup chopped candied red cherries
¼ cup chopped candied green cherries
½ cup chopped pecans
3 tablespoons butter or margarine, softened
½ cup sugar
1 tablespoon ground cinnamon
1 cup sifted powdered sugar
2 to 3 tablespoons milk
¼ teaspoon vanilla extract
Candied cherry halves

• **Combine** 1 cup milk, 1 cup butter, and ½ cup water in a small saucepan; place over low heat until butter melts and a thermometer registers 120° to 130°.
• **Combine** flour, ¼ cup sugar, salt, and yeast in a large mixing bowl; stir in warm milk mixture and eggs, beating at medium speed with an electric mixer. Add grated lemon and orange rinds, raisins, chopped candied cherries, and pecans; mix well. Cover and chill dough 8 hours or overnight.
• **Place** chilled dough on a floured surface; roll into an 18- x 12-inch rectangle; spread with 3 tablespoons

softened butter. Combine ½ cup sugar and cinnamon; sprinkle cinnamon-sugar over butter.
• **Beginning** with long side, roll up dough, jellyroll fashion, pinching edges to seal. Place roll on a large greased large baking sheet, and shape into a ring (it should resemble a large doughnut). Brush ends of roll with water, and pinch to seal.
• **Using** kitchen shears, make cuts in dough every inch around ring, cutting two-thirds of the way through roll at each cut. Gently turn each piece of dough on its side, slightly overlapping the previous piece.
• **Let** rise, uncovered, in a warm place (85°), free from drafts 30 minutes or until doubled in bulk. Bake at 350° for 25 to 28 minutes or until golden.
• **Combine** powdered sugar, 2 to 3 tablespoons milk, and vanilla; drizzle over warm coffee cake ring. Decorate with candied cherry halves. Yield: 1 coffee cake ring.

Cheers

What's the all-time most popular spirited beverage? Punch. Seventy recipes were published in Southern Living *alone from 1979 to 1999. Here's a toast and tribute to some of our other favorite drinks.*

70s Bloody Marys, Irish coffee, Martinis

80s Frozen Daiquiris, Margaritas, Sangría

90s Bellinis, Martinis again

ALMOND DANISH

make ahead

1 cup butter, slightly softened
2 packages active dry yeast
½ cup warm water (105° to 115°)
⅓ cup sugar
¾ cup milk
2 large eggs

4¼ to 4¾ cups all-purpose flour
1 teaspoon salt
Almond Filling, divided
1 large egg, lightly beaten
Sugar
¼ cup sliced almonds

• **Place** 2 sticks butter 1 inch apart between two sheets of wax paper; roll into a 12-inch square, using a rolling pin. Place on a baking sheet, and chill.

• **Combine** yeast, warm water, and ½ teaspoon sugar in a 1-cup liquid measuring cup; let stand 5 minutes. Combine yeast mixture, remaining sugar, milk, 2 eggs, 3 cups flour, and salt in a large mixing bowl; beat at medium speed with an electric mixer 3 minutes. Gradually stir in enough remaining flour to make a soft dough. Cover and chill dough 30 minutes.

• **Place** dough on a lightly floured surface; roll into an 18- x 13-inch rectangle. Peel top sheet of wax paper from chilled butter; invert butter on 1 end of dough, covering two-thirds of dough. Peel off remaining wax paper from butter. Fold uncovered third of dough over middle third; gently fold remaining third over middle third. Turn dough so that long side is toward you. Roll dough into a 24- x 12-inch rectangle. Fold ends to center; then fold dough in half. Turn dough so that the long side is toward you again. Repeat rolling and folding procedure twice; cover and chill dough 1 hour.

• **Divide** dough in half. Place half of dough on a lightly floured surface; refrigerate unused portion. Roll dough into a 30- x 9-inch rectangle. Cut lengthwise into 3 strips. Gently spread ¼ cup Almond Filling evenly down center of each strip. Fold edges of strips over filling, and seal. Place 3 ropes, side by side, on a large ungreased baking sheet; braid. Join ends of dough to make a 9-inch ring. Repeat procedure with remaining dough and filling.

• **Let** dough rise in a warm place (85°), free from drafts, 30 minutes or until doubled in bulk. Brush with beaten egg; sprinkle with sugar and almonds. Bake at 350° for 25 to 30 minutes or until golden. Transfer coffee cakes to wire racks to cool. Yield: 2 coffee cakes.

Almond Filling

1 (8-ounce) can almond paste, crumbled

½ cup butter or margarine, softened
½ cup sugar

• **Combine** all ingredients in a bowl; beat at medium speed with an electric mixer until mixture is blended. Yield: 1½ cups.

NOTE: To freeze, bake as directed; let cool. Wrap tightly in aluminum foil; freeze. To serve, let thaw, covered, in refrigerator; reheat in foil at 350° for 15 to 20 minutes.

Almond Danish

Dried Fruit Galette

DRIED FRUIT GALETTE

A French galette *is a round, flat cake or tart filled with fruit, jam, nuts, or cheese.*

1 package active dry yeast
¼ cup warm water (105° to 115°)
2 cups all-purpose flour
¼ cup sugar
1 teaspoon salt
¾ cup butter or margarine, cut into pieces
1 large egg, lightly beaten
1 teaspoon vanilla extract
Fruit Filling
2 tablespoons turbinado sugar or sugar

• **Combine** yeast and warm water in a 1-cup liquid measuring cup; let stand 5 minutes.
• **Combine** flour, ¼ cup sugar, and salt in a large mixing bowl; cut in butter with a pastry blender until mixture is crumbly. Combine yeast mixture, egg, and vanilla; stir into flour mixture, blending well. Shape dough into a flat disc; cover and chill.
• **Roll** dough into a 14-inch circle on a large greased baking sheet. Spread Fruit Filling over dough to within 3 inches of edge. Fold edges of dough over fruit, leaving center of fruit uncovered. Sprinkle dough with turbinado sugar. Bake at 400° for 25 minutes or until golden. Serve warm. Yield: 6 servings.

Fruit Filling

⅔ cup dried prunes
⅔ cup dried apricot halves
1 (8¼-ounce) can crushed pineapple in heavy
    syrup, undrained
½ cup sugar
1½ tablespoons quick-cooking tapioca

• **Cook** prunes and apricots in boiling water to cover 10 minutes; drain and chop fruit. Combine fruit, pineapple, sugar, and tapioca, stirring well. Yield: 2¼ cups.

COUNTY FAIR EGG BREAD

The recipe title tells you that this showy braided bread has won some blue ribbons over the years—for flavor and appearance.

1 package active dry yeast
¼ cup warm water (105° to 115°)
1 cup milk
¼ cup water
¼ cup sugar
¼ cup shortening
2 teaspoons salt
2 large eggs, beaten
4½ to 5½ cups all-purpose flour, divided
Butter or margarine, melted

• **Combine** yeast and warm water in a 1-cup liquid measuring cup; let stand 5 minutes. Combine milk and next 4 ingredients in a saucepan; place over low heat, stirring constantly, until mixture reaches 105° to 115°. Remove from heat.
• **Combine** yeast mixture, milk mixture, eggs, and 2 cups flour; beat at low speed with an electric mixer until smooth. Stir in enough remaining flour to make a soft dough.
• **Place** dough in a well-greased bowl, turning to grease top. Cover and let rise in a warm place (85°), free from drafts, 1½ hours or until doubled in bulk. Punch dough down; cover dough, and let rest 10 minutes.
• **Divide** dough into thirds; shape each portion of dough into a 12- to 14-inch rope. Place ropes on a lightly greased baking sheet, pinching at 1 end to seal. Braid ropes; pinch ends to seal, and tuck ends under. Cover and let rise in a warm place, free from drafts, 45 minutes or until doubled in bulk.
• **Bake** at 375° for 20 minutes or until evenly browned. Brush bread with melted butter. Remove to wire rack to cool. Yield: 1 loaf.

Cakes

Simple or stately, a beautiful cake
always takes center stage on the
Southern sideboard. Great cakes
come in many sizes. And they're
the quintessential symbol of
fine hospitality.

Coconut-Cream Cheese Pound Cake (page 56)

MILK CHOCOLATE POUND CAKE

~ family favorite ~

Melted candy bars make this pound cake supermoist.

1 cup butter or margarine, softened
1½ cups sugar
4 large eggs
6 (1.55-ounce) milk chocolate candy bars, melted (we tested with Hershey's)
2½ cups all-purpose flour
¼ teaspoon baking soda
⅛ teaspoon salt
1 cup buttermilk
1 cup chopped pecans
½ cup chocolate syrup (we tested with Hershey's)
2 teaspoons vanilla extract
Powdered sugar (optional)

• **Beat** butter at medium speed with an electric mixer 2 minutes or until creamy. Gradually add sugar, beating 5 to 7 minutes. Add eggs, 1 at a time, beating after each addition just until yellow disappears. Add melted candy bars, stirring well.
• **Combine** flour, baking soda, and salt; add to butter mixture alternately with buttermilk, beginning and ending with flour mixture. Mix at low speed after each addition just until blended. Stir in pecans, chocolate syrup, and vanilla.
• **Pour** batter into a greased and floured 10-inch tube pan or 12-cup Bundt pan. Bake at 325° for 1 hour and 5 minutes or until a wooden pick inserted in center comes out clean. Cool in pan on a wire rack 10 to 15 minutes; remove from pan, and cool completely on wire rack. Sprinkle with powdered sugar, if desired. Yield: 1 (10-inch) cake.

COCONUT-CREAM CHEESE POUND CAKE

~ family favorite ~

Cream cheese and coconut put this pound cake in a rich and tender category all its own.

½ cup butter or margarine, softened
½ cup shortening
1 (8-ounce) package cream cheese, softened
3 cups sugar
6 large eggs
3 cups all-purpose flour
¼ teaspoon baking soda
¼ teaspoon salt
1 (6-ounce) package frozen flake grated coconut, thawed (1¾ cups) (we tested with Tropic Isle)
1 teaspoon vanilla extract
1 teaspoon coconut flavoring

• **Beat** butter, shortening, and cream cheese at medium speed with an electric mixer 2 minutes or until creamy. Gradually add sugar, beating 5 to 7 minutes. Add eggs, 1 at a time, beating after each addition just until yellow disappears.
• **Combine** flour, baking soda, and salt; add to butter mixture, beating at low speed just until blended. Stir in coconut, vanilla, and coconut flavoring.
• **Pour** batter into a greased and floured 10-inch tube pan. Bake at 325° for 1 hour and 30 to 40 minutes or until a wooden pick inserted in center comes out clean. Cool in pan on a wire rack 10 to 15 minutes; remove from pan, and cool completely on wire rack. Yield: 1 (10-inch) cake.

PEACH BRANDY POUND CAKE

1 cup butter or margarine, softened
3 cups sugar
6 large eggs
3 cups all-purpose flour
¼ teaspoon baking soda
⅛ teaspoon salt
1 (8-ounce) carton sour cream
½ cup peach brandy
2 teaspoons dark rum
1 teaspoon orange extract
1 teaspoon vanilla extract
½ teaspoon lemon extract
¼ teaspoon almond extract

• **Beat** butter at medium speed with an electric mixer 2 minutes. Gradually add sugar, beating at medium speed 5 minutes. Add eggs, 1 at a time, beating after each addition just until yellow disappears.
• **Combine** flour, baking soda, and salt; add to butter mixture alternately with sour cream, beginning and ending with flour mixture. Mix at low speed just until blended after each addition. Stir in brandy and remaining ingredients.
• **Pour** batter into a greased and floured 10-inch tube pan. Bake at 325° for 1½ hours or until a wooden pick inserted in center comes out clean. Cool in pan on a wire rack 10 to 15 minutes; remove from pan, and cool completely on wire rack. Yield: 1 (10-inch) cake.

Cake Mix Mania

Southern cooks took to cake mixes like bees to honey. We made them even better by adding pudding mix, sour cream, nuts, fruit, and other goodies. We bake 'em in fluted Bundt pans and drizzle frosting over the top. We pat cake mixes into pans as the base for bar cookies and sprinkle mixes as streusel topping for muffins and coffee cake. And that's just until we come up with the next great idea!

CHOCOLATE-PECAN SNACK CAKE

Chocolate morsels and pecans create a pebbled top for this cake that kids will devour.

1 cup chopped dates
1 cup boiling water
1 teaspoon baking soda
½ cup shortening
1 cup sugar
2 large eggs
1 tablespoon cocoa
1 teaspoon vanilla extract
1¾ cups all-purpose flour
½ teaspoon cream of tartar
½ teaspoon salt
1 cup (6 ounces) semisweet chocolate morsels
¾ cup chopped pecans

• **Combine** first 3 ingredients in a small bowl; stir well. Cool to room temperature. (Do not drain.)
• **Beat** shortening at medium speed with an electric mixer 2 minutes or until creamy. Gradually add sugar, beating well. Add eggs, 1 at a time, beating just until yellow disappears. Add cocoa and vanilla; beat well.
• **Combine** flour, cream of tartar, and salt; add to shortening mixture alternately with date mixture, beginning and ending with flour mixture. Mix at low speed after each addition just until blended.
• **Pour** batter into a lightly greased 13- x 9-inch pan. Sprinkle chocolate morsels and pecans evenly over batter. Bake at 350° for 26 to 28 minutes. Cool in pan on a wire rack. Cut into squares to serve. Cover and store in pan. Yield: 20 servings.

Mississippi Mud Cake

MISSISSIPPI MUD CAKE

family favorite

In the culinary world, Mississippi mud refers to a rich and gooey chocolaty dessert. This cake certainly lives up to the description.

1 cup butter or margarine
½ cup cocoa
2 cups sugar
4 large eggs, lightly beaten
1½ cups all-purpose flour
Dash of salt
1 teaspoon vanilla extract
1½ cups chopped pecans
4 cups miniature marshmallows
Chocolate Frosting

• **Combine** butter and cocoa in a medium saucepan. Cook over medium heat until butter melts. Remove from heat; transfer to a large mixing bowl. Add sugar and eggs; beat at medium speed with an electric mixer until blended. Add flour, salt, and vanilla; beat until blended. Stir in pecans. Spoon batter into a lightly greased 13- x 9-inch pan.
• **Bake** at 350° for 35 minutes. Remove from oven, and sprinkle marshmallows over hot cake. Immediately spread frosting over marshmallows on cake. Cool in pan on a wire rack. Cut into squares to serve. (Chill before slicing for neater squares.) Yield: 15 servings.

Chocolate Frosting

1 (16-ounce) package powdered sugar, sifted
½ cup milk
⅓ cup cocoa
¼ cup butter or margarine, softened

• **Combine** all ingredients in a large bowl; beat at medium speed until smooth, adding an additional tablespoon of milk if frosting is too stiff. Yield: 2 cups.

DOUBLE GINGER GINGERBREAD

family favorite

Fresh ginger enlivens this homey cake.

½ cup butter, softened
½ cup sugar
1 large egg
1 cup molasses
½ cup finely grated fresh ginger
2½ cups all-purpose flour
1½ teaspoons baking soda
½ teaspoon baking powder
1 teaspoon ground cinnamon
1 teaspoon ground ginger
½ teaspoon ground cloves
1 cup hot water

• **Beat** butter at medium speed with an electric mixer until creamy; gradually add sugar, beating well. Add egg and molasses, beating until blended. Add fresh ginger, beating until blended.
• **Combine** flour and next 5 ingredients; add to butter mixture alternately with hot water, beginning and ending with flour mixture. Beat at low speed until blended after each addition; beat 1 more minute or until very smooth. Pour batter into a greased 13- x 9-inch pan.
• **Bake** at 350° for 40 minutes or until a wooden pick inserted in center comes out clean. Cool in pan on a wire rack.
• **Cut** into squares; serve with vanilla ice cream. Yield: 12 servings.

GINGERBREAD CAKE ROLL

⸺ make ahead ⸺

The old-fashioned goodness of gingerbread is rolled up and frosted with cinnamon whipped cream. Offer this dessert during the holiday season.

3 large eggs, separated
1 tablespoon butter or margarine, melted
½ cup molasses
¼ cup sugar
1 cup all-purpose flour
¾ teaspoon baking powder
¾ teaspoon baking soda

⅛ teaspoon salt
½ teaspoon ground cinnamon
½ teaspoon ground cloves
½ teaspoon ground ginger
2 tablespoons powdered sugar
Spiced Cream
Garnishes: pecan halves or edible pansies

• **Line** a greased 15- x 10-inch jellyroll pan with wax paper; grease and flour wax paper. Set pan aside.

• **Beat** egg yolks at high speed with an electric mixer until thick and pale. Gradually add butter and molasses, beating until blended.

• **Beat** egg whites at high speed until foamy. Gradually add sugar, 1 tablespoon at a time, beating until stiff peaks form and sugar dissolves (2 to 4 minutes). Fold egg whites into yolk mixture.

• **Combine** flour and next 6 ingredients; gradually fold flour mixture into egg mixture. Spread batter evenly into prepared pan. Bake at 350° for 8 to 10 minutes or just until cake springs back when lightly touched.

• **Sift** powdered sugar in a 15- x 10-inch rectangle on a cloth towel. When cake is done, immediately loosen from sides of pan, and turn out onto sugared towel. Peel off wax paper. Starting at narrow end, roll up cake and towel together; cool completely on a wire rack, seam side down.

• **Unroll** cake; spread with half of Spiced Cream; carefully reroll. Place on a serving plate, seam side down. Spread remaining Spiced Cream on all sides. Pull a fork or an icing comb down length of frosting, if desired. Cover loosely, and chill until ready to serve. Garnish, if desired. Yield: 10 servings.

Spiced Cream

1½ cups whipping cream
⅓ cup sifted powdered sugar
1 teaspoon ground cinnamon

¼ teaspoon ground cloves
1 teaspoon vanilla extract

• **Combine** all ingredients; beat at medium speed until soft peaks form. Yield: 3½ cups.

NOTE: Pansies are edible as long as they haven't been sprayed with insecticide. Use pansies from your garden or those labeled edible in supermarkets.

Gingerbread Cake Roll

OLD-FASHIONED JELLYROLL

A jellyroll is a thin sponge cake spread with jelly, rolled tightly, and sprinkled with sugar. When sliced, it displays a pretty pinwheel design.

¾ cup all-purpose flour
1 teaspoon baking powder
¼ teaspoon salt
¾ cup sugar
4 large eggs
1 teaspoon vanilla extract
2 tablespoons powdered sugar
1 cup jelly, jam, or preserves
Additional powdered sugar

• **Grease** a 15- x 10-inch jellyroll pan; line with wax paper, and grease wax paper. Set pan aside.
• **Combine** flour, baking powder, and salt; sift together 3 times.
• **Beat** sugar and eggs at medium speed with an electric mixer 10 minutes or until thick and pale and tripled in volume. Sift flour mixture over batter, and gently fold in flour mixture and vanilla.
• **Spread** batter evenly into prepared pan. Bake at 400° for 7 to 9 minutes or just until cake springs back when lightly touched. Do not overbake.
• **Sift** powdered sugar in a 15- x 10-inch rectangle on a cloth towel. Run knife around edge of pan to release cake. Turn cake out onto sugared towel. Carefully peel off wax paper.
• **Starting** at narrow end, roll up cake and towel together. Cool completely on a wire rack, seam side down. Unroll cake, and remove towel. Spread cake with jelly; carefully reroll. Place on a serving plate, seam side down. Sprinkle with additional powdered sugar, if desired. Chill 1 to 2 hours before serving. Yield: 8 servings.

ROULAGE
✑ family favorite, make ahead ✑

Roulage is a popular cake roll. Ours is chocolate enhanced with lightly sweetened whipped cream. Try serving it partially frozen; it's like an ice cream sandwich.

5 large eggs, separated
1 cup sugar
¼ cup cocoa
¼ teaspoon salt
2 tablespoons cocoa, divided
1 teaspoon unflavored gelatin
2 tablespoons cold water
1¼ cups whipping cream
3 tablespoons powdered sugar
1 teaspoon vanilla extract
Garnish: fresh strawberries

• **Grease** bottom and sides of a 15- x 10- inch jellyroll pan; line with wax paper, and grease and flour wax paper. Set pan aside.
• **Beat** egg yolks at high speed with an electric mixer until thick and pale. Gradually add 1 cup sugar, beating until blended. Stir in ¼ cup cocoa and salt; set batter aside.
• **Beat** egg whites in a large mixing bowl at high speed until stiff peaks form. Fold one-third of egg white mixture into chocolate batter. Gently fold remaining egg white mixture into batter. Spread batter evenly into prepared pan. Bake at 325° for 15 to 17 minutes or just until cake springs back when lightly touched.
• **Sift** 1 tablespoon cocoa in a 15- x 10-inch rectangle on a cloth towel. When cake is done, immediately loosen from sides of pan, and turn out onto towel; carefully peel off wax paper. Dust top of cake with remaining 1 tablespoon cocoa. Starting at narrow end, roll up cake and towel together; cool 30 minutes on a wire rack, seam side down.
• **Sprinkle** gelatin over cold water in a small saucepan; let stand 1 minute. Cook over low heat, stirring until gelatin dissolves. Set aside. Beat whipping cream at low

speed, gradually adding gelatin mixture. Increase to medium speed, and beat until mixture begins to thicken. Add powdered sugar and vanilla, and beat until soft peaks form.

• **Unroll** cake, and remove towel. Spread cake with whipped cream, leaving 1-inch margins, and carefully reroll. Place cake on a serving plate, seam side down. Cover and chill or partially freeze Roulage, if desired. Before serving, let stand 1 hour at room temperature to partially thaw. Garnish, if desired. Yield: 8 servings.

APRICOT SPICE CAKE

You won't need a mixer to whip up this favorite dump-and-stir cake.

2 cups self-rising flour
1¾ cups sugar
1 cup chopped pecans
1 cup vegetable oil
1 (6-ounce) jar apricot baby food
1 teaspoon ground cinnamon
1 teaspoon ground allspice
3 large eggs, lightly beaten
Cream Cheese Glaze

• **Combine** first 8 ingredients in a large bowl; stir until blended. Pour batter into a heavily greased and floured 12-cup Bundt pan. (Batter will be shallow in pan.) Bake at 350° for 50 minutes or until a wooden pick inserted in center comes out clean. Cool in pan on a wire rack 10 minutes. Remove from pan, and cool completely on wire rack. Drizzle Cream Cheese Glaze over cake. Yield: 1 (10-inch) cake.

Cream Cheese Glaze
1 (3-ounce) package cream cheese, softened
3 tablespoons milk
1 teaspoon vanilla extract
Dash of salt
1½ cups sifted powdered sugar

• **Combine** first 4 ingredients; beat at medium speed with an electric mixer until smooth. Gradually add powdered sugar, beating at low speed until glaze is smooth. Yield: 1 cup.

NOTE: Don't substitute a tube pan in this recipe—the cake will be too shallow.

APPLE CAKE WITH BROWN SUGAR GLAZE

2 cups sugar
1 cup vegetable oil
3 large eggs
3 cups all-purpose flour
1 teaspoon baking soda
½ teaspoon salt
1 teaspoon ground cinnamon
3 cups peeled, finely chopped cooking apple
½ cup chopped pecans
Brown Sugar Glaze

• **Beat** first 3 ingredients at medium speed with an electric mixer until creamy.
• **Combine** flour and next 3 ingredients; add to sugar mixture, beating well. Stir in apple and pecans.
• **Pour** batter into a greased and floured 12-cup Bundt pan. Bake at 350° for 1 hour and 20 minutes or until a wooden pick inserted in center comes out clean. Cool in pan on a wire rack 10 to 15 minutes; remove from pan, and cool completely on wire rack. Drizzle Brown Sugar Glaze over cake. Yield: 1 (10-inch) cake.

Brown Sugar Glaze
½ cup firmly packed brown sugar
¼ cup butter or margarine
2 tablespoons evaporated milk

• **Combine** all ingredients in a small saucepan; cook over high heat, stirring constantly, 2 minutes or until butter melts. Cool to lukewarm. Yield: ½ cup.

PEANUT BUTTER CAKE

Peanut butter and caramel are a luscious combination in this cake. This particular Caramel Frosting is a staff favorite—it's easy to make and tastes divine.

½ cup shortening
1 cup creamy peanut butter
1 cup sugar
2 large eggs
1½ cups all-purpose flour
1 tablespoon baking powder
½ teaspoon salt
1 cup milk
½ teaspoon vanilla extract
Caramel Frosting

• **Beat** shortening and peanut butter at medium speed with an electric mixer until creamy; gradually add sugar, beating well. Add eggs, 1 at a time, beating after each addition.
• **Combine** flour, baking powder, and salt; add to shortening mixture alternately with milk, beginning and ending with flour mixture. Mix at low speed after each addition until blended. Stir in vanilla. Pour batter into two lightly greased and floured 9-inch round cakepans.
• **Bake** at 350° for 25 to 27 minutes or until a wooden pick inserted in center comes out clean. Cool in pans on wire racks 10 minutes; remove from pans, and cool completely on wire racks.
• **Spread** Caramel Frosting between layers and on top and sides of cake. Yield: 1 (2-layer) cake.

Caramel Frosting
2 cups sugar
1 cup butter
1 cup evaporated milk
1 teaspoon vanilla extract

• **Combine** sugar, butter, and milk in a large heavy saucepan; bring to a boil over medium heat. Cover and cook 2 to 3 minutes to wash down sugar crystals from sides of pan. Uncover and cook, stirring constantly, until mixture reaches soft ball stage or candy thermometer registers 234°. Remove from heat, and add vanilla (do not stir). Cool 10 minutes. Beat at medium speed with an electric mixer 8 to 10 minutes or until frosting is spreading consistency. Yield: 2½ cups.

SUPERFUDGE CAKE

family favorite

In the mood for chocolaty cake layers smothered with a fudgy frosting? This layer cake is like candy and cake all in one.

⅔ cup milk chocolate morsels
½ cup boiling water
1 cup butter or margarine, softened
2 cups sugar
4 large eggs, separated
1 teaspoon vanilla extract
2½ cups all-purpose flour
1 teaspoon baking soda
½ teaspoon salt
1 cup buttermilk
Chocolate Fudge Frosting

• **Grease** three 9-inch round cakepans; line with wax paper. Grease wax paper. Set pans aside.
• **Combine** milk chocolate morsels and water in a small bowl, stirring until morsels melt; cool.
• **Beat** butter at medium speed with an electric mixer until creamy; gradually add sugar, beating well. Add egg yolks, 1 at a time, beating after each addition. Add chocolate mixture and vanilla; mix well.
• **Combine** flour, baking soda, and salt; add to butter mixture alternately with buttermilk, beginning and ending with flour mixture. Mix at low speed after each addition until blended.
• **Beat** egg whites at high speed until soft peaks form. Fold one-fourth of beaten egg whites into batter; fold in remaining beaten egg whites. Pour batter into prepared pans.

• **Bake** at 350° for 25 to 28 minutes or until a wooden pick inserted in center comes out clean. Cool layers in pans 10 minutes; remove from pans, and cool completely on wire racks.
• **Spread** Chocolate Fudge Frosting between layers and on top and sides of cake. Yield: 1 (3-layer) cake.

Chocolate Fudge Frosting
1 cup butter
2¾ cups sugar
⅔ cocoa
⅔ cup milk
1½ teaspoons vanilla extract

• **Melt** butter over low heat in a 3-quart heavy saucepan; add sugar, cocoa, and milk. Cook until sugar dissolves, stirring constantly. Bring to a boil over medium-high heat; boil until a candy thermometer registers 230° (about 4 minutes).
• **Remove** from heat; transfer to a large mixing bowl, and add vanilla. Let stand until completely cool (do not stir). Beat at high speed with a heavy-duty stand mixer until spreading consistency (5 to 10 minutes). Yield: 3¼ cups.

NOTE: It's important to allow this fudgelike frosting to cool before beating it. Shorten the beating time by placing the bowl of warm frosting in ice water and stirring briefly to cool mixture quickly before beating. This may be particularly necessary if using a glass mixing bowl.

Just say "Chocolate."

70ˢ Chocolate anything.

80ˢ Chocolate anything.

90ˢ Chocolate anything.

COCONUT CAKE

1 cup butter or margarine, softened
2 cups sugar
4 large eggs
3¼ cups all-purpose flour
1 tablespoon baking powder
1¼ cups milk
1 teaspoon vanilla extract
Sour Cream-Coconut Filling

• **Beat** butter at medium speed with an electric mixer until fluffy. Gradually add sugar, beating well. Add eggs, 1 at a time, beating mixture after each addition.
• **Combine** flour and baking powder; add to butter mixture alternately with milk, beginning and ending with flour mixture. Mix just until blended after each addition. Stir in vanilla. Pour batter into three greased and floured 9-inch round cakepans.
• **Bake** at 350° for 18 minutes or until a wooden pick inserted in center comes out clean. Cool in pans on wire racks 10 minutes; remove from pans, and cool completely on wire racks.
• **Split** each layer in half horizontally. Spread Sour Cream-Coconut Filling between layers and on top of cake. Cover and chill at least 3 hours before serving. Yield: 1 (3-layer) cake.

Sour Cream-Coconut Filling
2 cups sifted powdered sugar
1 (16-ounce) carton sour cream
1 (8-ounce) container frozen whipped topping, thawed
2 (6-ounce) packages frozen coconut, thawed

• **Combine** first 3 ingredients; stir in coconut. Yield: about 5½ cups.

CHOCOLATE ALMOND CAKE

½ cup cocoa
½ cup boiling water
⅔ cup shortening
1¾ cups sugar
2 large eggs
2¼ cups all-purpose flour
1½ teaspoons baking soda

¼ teaspoon salt
1½ cups buttermilk
1 teaspoon vanilla extract
Almond Cream Filling
Chocolate Frosting
Garnishes: toasted sliced almonds,
    candied violets

• **Grease** three 8-inch round cakepans. Line bottoms of pans with wax paper; grease wax paper. Flour wax paper and sides of pans. Set aside.
• **Combine** cocoa and boiling water in a small bowl; stir until smooth. Set aside.
• **Beat** shortening at medium speed with an electric mixer until fluffy; gradually add sugar, beating well. Add eggs, 1 at a time, beating after each addition.
• **Combine** flour, soda, and salt; add to shortening mixture alternately with buttermilk, beginning and ending with flour mixture. Mix after each addition. Stir in cocoa mixture and vanilla.
• **Pour** batter into prepared pans. Bake at 350° for 25 minutes or until a wooden pick inserted in center comes out clean. Cool in pans on wire racks 10 minutes; remove from pans, and cool completely on wire racks.
• **Spread** Almond Cream Filling between layers to within ½ inch of edge. Reserve 1 cup Chocolate Frosting; spread remaining frosting on top and sides of cake. Using a star tip, pipe reserved frosting on top of cake. Garnish, if desired. Yield: 1 (3-layer) cake.

Almond Cream Filling

2 tablespoons all-purpose flour
¼ cup plus 1 tablespoon milk
¼ cup shortening
2 tablespoons butter, softened

½ teaspoon almond extract
⅛ teaspoon salt
2 cups sifted powdered sugar

• **Combine** flour and milk in a saucepan; cook over low heat, stirring constantly with a wire whisk, until mixture is thick enough to hold its shape and resembles a soft frosting. (Do not boil.) Remove from heat; cool completely. Beat shortening and butter at medium speed with an electric mixer until creamy; add flour mixture, almond extract, and salt, beating well. Gradually add sugar, beating at high speed 4 minutes or until fluffy. Yield: 1½ cups.

Chocolate Frosting

½ cup butter or margarine, softened
3 (1-ounce) squares unsweetened
    chocolate, melted

½ cup milk
1 teaspoon vanilla extract
1 (16-ounce) package powdered sugar

• **Beat** butter at medium speed with an electric mixer until creamy. Add melted chocolate, milk, and vanilla; beat well. Gradually add powdered sugar, beating at high speed about 5 minutes or until mixture is spreading consistency. Yield: enough for 1 (3-layer) cake.

AMBROSIA CAKE

1 cup butter, softened
1¾ cups sugar
4 large eggs
3 cups sifted cake flour
2½ teaspoons baking powder
½ teaspoon salt

1 cup milk
1 teaspoon butter flavoring
1 teaspoon vanilla extract
Orange Filling
Divinity Frosting
½ cup flaked coconut

• **Beat** butter at medium speed with an electric mixer until creamy; gradually add sugar, beating well. Add eggs, 1 at a time, beating after each addition.
• **Combine** flour, baking powder, and salt; add to butter mixture alternately with milk, beginning and ending with flour mixture. Mix at low speed after each addition until blended. Stir in flavorings.
• **Pour** batter into three greased and floured 9-inch round cakepans. Bake at 350° for 20 minutes or until a wooden pick inserted in center comes out clean. Cool in pans on wire racks 10 minutes; remove from pans, and cool completely on wire racks.
• **Spread** Orange Filling between layers; spread Divinity Frosting on top and sides of cake. Sprinkle cake with coconut. Yield: 1 (3-layer) cake.

Orange Filling

1 cup sugar
3 tablespoons cornstarch
¼ teaspoon salt
¾ cup fresh orange juice

¼ cup lemon juice
½ cup water
3 egg yolks, beaten
1 tablespoon grated orange rind

• **Combine** sugar, cornstarch, and salt in a small saucepan; gradually stir in fruit juices and water. Cook over medium heat, stirring constantly, until mixture thickens and boils.
• **Gradually** stir about one-fourth of hot mixture into yolks; add to remaining hot mixture, stirring constantly. Cook 3 more minutes, stirring constantly. Remove from heat, and stir in orange rind. Cool completely; cover and chill. Yield:1¾ cups.

Divinity Frosting

1½ cups sugar
½ teaspoon cream of tartar
½ cup water

3 egg whites
½ teaspoon vanilla extract

• **Combine** sugar, cream of tartar, and water in a heavy saucepan. Cook over medium heat, stirring constantly, until clear. Cook, without stirring, to soft ball stage (240°).
• **While** syrup cooks, beat egg whites until soft peaks form; continue to beat, adding hot syrup in a heavy stream. Add vanilla; continue beating just until stiff peaks form and frosting is thick enough to spread. Immediately spread frosting on cake. Yield: 4¾ cups.

Tart Lemon-Cheese Cake

TART LEMON-CHEESE CAKE

~ make ahead ~

There's no cheese in this stately cake; however, it was justly named for its luscious cheeselike lemon curd filling.

1 cup butter, softened
2 cups sugar
¾ cup water
¼ cup milk
3¼ cups sifted cake flour
2¾ teaspoons baking powder
½ teaspoon salt
½ teaspoon rum flavoring or 1 teaspoon vanilla extract
6 egg whites
Lemon-Cheese Filling
Lemony White Frosting
Lemon slices (optional)

• **Beat** butter at medium speed with an electric mixer until creamy; gradually add sugar, beating well.
• **Combine** water and milk in a small bowl; set aside.
• **Combine** flour, baking powder, and salt; add to butter mixture alternately with milk mixture, beginning and ending with flour mixture. Mix at low speed after each addition until blended. Stir in rum flavoring.
• **Beat** egg whites at high speed until stiff peaks form; gently fold into batter. Pour batter into three greased and floured 9-inch round cakepans.
• **Bake** at 350° for 20 to 25 minutes or until a wooden pick inserted in center comes out clean. Cool in pans on wire racks 10 minutes; remove from pans, and cool completely.
• **Spread** Lemon-Cheese Filling between layers and on top of cake. Spread Lemony White Frosting on sides. Garnish, if desired. Yield: 1 (3-layer) cake.

Lemon-Cheese Filling

1 cup sugar
3 tablespoons cornstarch
⅛ teaspoon salt
2 tablespoons grated lemon rind
1 cup fresh lemon juice (about 4 large lemons)
6 egg yolks, beaten
⅓ cup butter or margarine

• **Combine** sugar, cornstarch, and salt in a heavy saucepan; stir well.
• **Add** lemon rind and juice; cook over medium heat, stirring constantly, until mixture thickens and comes to a boil. Boil 1 minute, stirring constantly.
• **Gradually** stir half of hot mixture into egg yolks; add to remaining hot mixture, stirring constantly. Cook, stirring constantly, 1 minute or until thoroughly heated. Remove from heat. Add butter, stirring until butter melts; cool completely. Yield: 2 cups.

Lemony White Frosting

1 cup sugar
⅓ cup water
2 tablespoons light corn syrup
2 egg whites
¼ cup sifted powdered sugar
½ teaspoon lemon extract

• **Combine** 1 cup sugar, water, and corn syrup in a large heavy saucepan. Cook over medium heat, stirring constantly, until clear. Cook, without stirring, until candy thermometer registers 240°.
• **Beat** egg whites at high speed with an electric mixer until soft peaks form; continue to beat, adding hot syrup mixture in a heavy stream. Add powdered sugar and lemon extract to mixture; continue beating until stiff peaks form and frosting is thick enough to spread (see note). Yield: about 3 cups.

NOTE: If you're using a metal bowl and a heavy-duty stand mixer to beat the frosting, it will take 3 to 4 minutes to reach a spreadable consistency. Frosting may take twice as long to thicken if using another type of mixer and a glass bowl.

BLACK WALNUT CAKE

½ cup butter or margarine, softened
½ cup shortening
2 cups sugar
5 large eggs, separated
1 cup buttermilk
1 teaspoon baking soda
2 cups all-purpose flour
1 teaspoon vanilla extract
1 cup chopped black walnuts
1 (3-ounce) can flaked coconut
½ teaspoon cream of tartar
Cream Cheese Frosting
Chopped black walnuts

• **Beat** butter and shortening at medium speed with an electric mixer until creamy. Gradually add sugar, beating well. Add egg yolks, 1 at a time, beating well after each addition.
• **Combine** buttermilk and soda; stir until soda dissolves.
• **Add** flour to butter mixture alternately with buttermilk mixture, beginning and ending with flour. Mix after each addition. Stir in vanilla. Add 1 cup walnuts and coconut, stirring well.
• **Beat** egg whites and cream of tartar until stiff peaks form; fold into batter.
• **Pour** batter into three greased and floured 9-inch round cakepans. Bake at 350° for 22 to 25 minutes or until a wooden pick inserted in center comes out clean. Cool in pans 10 minutes; remove from pans, and cool completely on wire racks.
• **Spread** Cream Cheese Frosting between layers and on top and sides of cake; press additional chopped walnuts onto sides of cake. Yield: 1 (3-layer) cake.

Cream Cheese Frosting
¾ cup butter, softened
1 (8-ounce) package cream cheese, softened
1 (3-ounce) package cream cheese, softened
6¾ cups sifted powdered sugar
1½ teaspoons vanilla extract

• **Beat** butter and cream cheese at medium speed until creamy. Gradually add powdered sugar, beating until mixture is light and fluffy. Stir in vanilla. Yield: enough for 1 (3-layer) cake.

OLD-FASHIONED CARROT CAKE
family favorite

3 cups shredded carrot
2 cups all-purpose flour
2 cups sugar
1 teaspoon baking powder
1 teaspoon baking soda
1 teaspoon ground cinnamon
½ teaspoon salt
4 large eggs, lightly beaten
¾ cup vegetable oil
1 teaspoon vanilla extract
Cream Cheese Frosting

• **Grease** three 9-inch round cakepans and line with wax paper; grease and flour wax paper.
• **Combine** first 7 ingredients in a large bowl; add eggs, oil, and vanilla, stirring until blended. Pour into prepared pans.
• **Bake** at 350° for 25 minutes or until a wooden pick inserted in center comes out clean. Cool in pans on wire racks 10 minutes; remove from pans, and cool completely on wire racks.
• **Spread** Cream Cheese Frosting between layers and on top and sides of cake. Chill. Freeze cake up to 3 months, if desired. Yield: 1 (3-layer) cake.

Cream Cheese Frosting
1 (8-ounce) package cream cheese, softened
½ cup butter or margarine, softened
1 (16-ounce) package powdered sugar, sifted
1 teaspoon vanilla extract

• **Beat** cream cheese and butter at medium speed with an electric mixer until fluffy; gradually add sugar, beating well. Stir in vanilla. Yield: about 3 cups.

Old-Fashioned Carrot Sheet Cake: Line a 13- x 9-inch pan with wax paper; grease and flour wax paper. Spoon batter into pan; bake at 350° for 35 minutes. Cool in pan on a wire rack. Spread with frosting. Yield: 15 servings.

APPLE STACK CAKE

make ahead

Let this multilayered apple cake, traditional of the Appalachian area, set up overnight. Its layers will absorb moisture from the buttery cinnamon-apple filling.

½ cup butter or margarine, softened
1 cup sugar
1 large egg
3½ cups all-purpose flour
1½ teaspoons baking powder
½ teaspoon baking soda
½ teaspoon salt
½ cup buttermilk
1 teaspoon vanilla extract
¼ cup butter or margarine, melted
Dried Apple Filling
Sifted powdered sugar (optional)

• **Beat** ½ cup butter at medium speed with an electric mixer until creamy; gradually add sugar, beating well. Add egg; beat just until blended.
• **Combine** flour, baking powder, soda, and salt; add to butter mixture alternately with buttermilk, beginning and ending with flour mixture. Beat at low speed after each addition until blended. Stir in vanilla.
• **Divide** dough into 6 equal portions; pat 3 portions into three lightly greased 9-inch round cakepans. Prick dough several times with a fork. (Cover remaining

dough, and set aside while first layers bake.) Bake at 400° for 10 minutes or until lightly browned. Carefully remove layers to a wire rack; cool completely. Repeat procedure with remaining 3 portions of dough.
• **Stack** cake, spreading ¼ cup melted butter and Dried Apple Filling between each layer. Cover and chill 8 hours before serving. Sprinkle cake with powdered sugar before serving, if desired. Yield: 1 (9-inch) cake.

Dried Apple Filling
2 (6-ounce) packages dried apples
4 cups water
¾ cup sugar
1 teaspoon ground cinnamon
½ teaspoon pumpkin pie spice

• **Combine** apples and water in a large saucepan. Bring to a boil; cover, reduce heat, and simmer 35 minutes or until apples are tender. Add sugar and spices; stir well. Remove from heat. Let stand at least 10 minutes or until liquid is absorbed. Yield: about 3½ cups.

Southern Comfort

90s Remember Auntie's Sunday dinner? Mom's Christmas pies and cakes? Picking the first peaches of the season? Step into a memory moment and mix up a classic Southern dessert. The '90s comfort revival reminded us again just how we couldn't live without pecan or chess pies, cobblers, fried pies or baked apple dumplings, carrot cake or strawberry shortcake.

CHOCOLATE PRALINE TORTE

make ahead

This torte will fool people into thinking that you spent hours in the kitchen. Actually, it's a cake mix that's transformed into a torte with crunchy layers of praline.

1½ cups chopped walnuts
1½ cups vanilla wafer crumbs
1 cup firmly packed brown sugar
1 cup butter or margarine, melted
1 (18.25-ounce) package devil's food cake mix without pudding (we tested with Duncan Hines)
1½ cups whipping cream
3 tablespoons powdered sugar
1 teaspoon vanilla extract
Garnishes: chopped walnuts, chocolate shavings

• **Combine** first 4 ingredients. Sprinkle about 1 cup walnut mixture into each of four ungreased 9-inch round cakepans, pressing lightly in pans.
• **Prepare** cake mix according to package directions; pour batter evenly over walnut mixture in prepared pans. Bake at 350° for 18 to 20 minutes or until a wooden pick inserted in center comes out clean. Let layers cool in pans on wire racks 5 minutes; remove from pans. Cool layers completely, nut side up, on wire racks.
• **Beat** whipping cream at medium speed with an electric mixer until foamy; gradually add powdered sugar, beating until soft peaks form. Stir in vanilla.
• **Place** 1 layer, nut side up, on a serving plate. Spread 1 cup whipped cream over layer. Repeat with remaining layers, ending with whipped cream. Garnish, if desired. Serve immediately or cover and chill 1 to 2 hours. To serve, slice torte with a serrated knife. Yield: 1 (9-inch) torte.

STRAWBERRY-ORANGE SHORTCAKE

2 pints fresh strawberries, sliced
2 (11-ounce) cans mandarin oranges, drained
½ cup sugar
1½ tablespoons Triple Sec or other orange-flavored liqueur
2 cups biscuit and baking mix
⅔ cup milk
1 tablespoon sugar
1½ teaspoons ground cinnamon
2 cups whipping cream
½ cup sifted powdered sugar
¼ cup sour cream

• **Combine** first 4 ingredients, stirring until sugar dissolves. Cover and chill 2 hours.
• **Combine** biscuit mix and next 3 ingredients; stir with a fork until dry ingredients are moistened. Turn out onto a lightly floured surface; knead 4 or 5 times. Place dough on a lightly greased baking sheet; press into a 7- x ¾-inch round.
• **Bake** at 425° for 15 minutes or until done. Carefully remove from pan; cool on a wire rack.
• **Beat** whipping cream until foamy; gradually add powdered sugar, beating until soft peaks form. Add sour cream, and beat until stiff peaks form.
• **Split** biscuit round in half horizontally. Place bottom half on a serving dish. Drain fruit, reserving 2 tablespoons liquid. Spoon two-thirds of fruit on bottom round; drizzle with reserved liquid. Spoon half of the whipped cream mixture over fruit. Add top biscuit round. Top mixture with remaining fruit and whipped cream. Yield: 8 servings.

Rainbow Ice Cream Cake

~ make ahead ~

This layered ice cream cake reveals ribbons of color under a whipped cream frosting. Leave out the rum for a great child's birthday cake.

1 quart strawberry ice cream, softened
1 quart pistachio ice cream, softened
1 (18½-ounce) package chocolate cake mix
2 tablespoons light rum (optional)
1 (12-ounce) container frozen whipped topping, thawed
Garnishes: pistachio nuts, chocolate sprinkles

• **Line** an 8-inch cakepan with wax paper, and quickly spread half the strawberry ice cream evenly in pan; cover with more wax paper or plastic wrap, and quickly spread with half of pistachio ice cream. Repeat procedure with remaining ice creams. Freeze until firm.
• **Prepare** cake mix according to package directions. Spoon batter into three well-greased and floured 8-inch cakepans. Bake at 350° for 15 to 20 minutes or until a wooden pick inserted in center comes out clean. Cool in pans on wire racks 10 minutes; remove from pans, and cool completely on wire racks.
• **Gently** fold rum into whipped topping, if desired; chill. Place serving plate in freezer to chill.
• **Place** 1 cake layer on chilled serving plate; top with a layer of strawberry ice cream and a layer of pistachio ice cream; repeat layers, and then top with remaining layer of cake. Frost top and sides of cake with whipped topping. Garnish, if desired. Serve immediately. Cover and freeze any remaining ice cream cake. Yield: 1 (7-layer) cake.

NOTE: You can freeze ice cream layers several days ahead. Bake cake layers and assemble cake, without frosting; then wrap in aluminum foil, and freeze. Remove assembled cake from freezer, and frost just before serving.

White Chocolate Cheesecake

~ make ahead ~

As cheesecakes go, this recipe is as near perfect as one can be. Almonds and oats contribute texture and toasty flavor to the crust; the white chocolate filling is creamy and smooth in your mouth.

¾ cup blanched almonds, ground
¾ cup uncooked quick-cooking oats
¾ cup graham cracker crumbs
¼ cup sugar
¼ cup plus 2 tablespoons butter or margarine, melted
4 (8-ounce) packages cream cheese, softened
1¼ cups sugar
6 large eggs
1 (16-ounce) carton sour cream
1 teaspoon vanilla extract
8 ounces white chocolate, melted

• **Combine** first 5 ingredients in a medium bowl; stir well. Press into bottom and 2 inches up sides of a lightly greased 10-inch springform pan. Bake at 350° for 10 minutes. Cool on a wire rack.
• **Beat** cream cheese at medium speed with an electric mixer until creamy; gradually add 1¼ cups sugar, beating well. Add eggs, 1 at a time, beating just until blended after each addition. Stir in sour cream and vanilla. Stir in melted white chocolate. Pour filling into prepared crust.
• **Bake** at 300° for 1½ hours. Turn oven off, and leave cheesecake in oven with door closed 30 minutes. Partially open oven door, and leave cheesecake in oven 30 more minutes. Remove from oven; cool to room temperature on a wire rack. Cover and chill at least 8 hours. Remove sides of pan before serving. Yield: 1 (10-inch) cheesecake.

BLUEBERRIES 'N' CREAM CHEESECAKE

∽ family favorite, make ahead ∽

*Fresh berry desserts are always a big hit in the summer. This
lavish cheesecake is no exception. We liked the spicy flavor of gingersnaps
in the crust paired with the juicy, sweet blueberries.*

2 cups gingersnap cookie crumbs or
    vanilla wafer crumbs (about 40
    cookies)
⅓ cup butter or margarine, melted
3½ cups fresh blueberries, divided
1 tablespoon cornstarch
3 (8-ounce) packages cream cheese,
    softened
1 cup sugar

5 large eggs
2 tablespoons cornstarch
¼ teaspoon salt
1½ cups sour cream
2 tablespoons sugar
½ teaspoon vanilla extract
¼ cup sugar
¼ cup water
Garnish: fresh blueberries

• **Combine** cookie crumbs and butter. Press into bottom and 1 inch up sides of a light-ly greased 9-inch springform pan. Bake at 325° for 12 minutes. Cool on a wire rack.

• **Process** 2½ cups blueberries and 1 tablespoon cornstarch in container of an electric blender until smooth. Cook blueberry puree in saucepan over medium-high heat 8 min-utes or until slightly thickened, stirring constantly. Set mixture aside to cool. Reserve ½ cup puree for glaze.

• **Beat** cream cheese at medium speed with an electric mixer until light and fluffy. Gradually add 1 cup sugar, beating well. Add eggs, 1 at a time, beating after each addi-tion. Stir in 2 tablespoons cornstarch and salt.

• **Pour** batter into prepared crust. Pour blueberry puree over cheesecake batter; gently swirl with a knife. Bake at 325° for 1 hour and 5 minutes or until almost set in center. Remove from oven, and cool on a wire rack 20 minutes.

• **Combine** sour cream, 2 tablespoons sugar, and vanilla in a small bowl; stir well. Spread sour cream mixture over cheesecake. Bake at 325° for 10 more minutes. Cool completely on wire rack. Cover and chill 8 hours.

• **Combine** reserved ½ cup blueberry puree, ¼ cup sugar, and water in a small saucepan; cook over medium heat, stirring constantly, 8 minutes or until thickened. Gently fold in remaining 1 cup blueberries; remove from heat, and cool.

• **Remove** sides of pan before serving. Spoon blueberry glaze over cheesecake, allow-ing it to drip down sides. Garnish, if desired. Yield: 1 (9-inch) cheesecake.

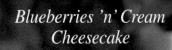
*Blueberries 'n' Cream
Cheesecake*

SOUR CREAM CHEESECAKE

make ahead

1 cup graham cracker crumbs
¼ cup finely chopped pecans
1 tablespoon brown sugar
3 tablespoons butter or margarine, melted
3 (8-ounce) packages cream cheese, softened
1 cup sugar
4 large eggs
2 teaspoons vanilla extract
1 (16-ounce) carton sour cream
⅓ cup red currant jelly
1 pint fresh strawberries, sliced

• **Combine** first 4 ingredients; press mixture into bottom of a 9-inch springform pan. Bake at 325° for 10 minutes. Cool on a wire rack.
• **Beat** cream cheese at medium speed with an electric mixer until creamy; gradually add 1 cup sugar, beating until smooth. Add eggs, 1 at a time, beating until blended after each addition. Stir in vanilla. Gently stir sour cream into cream cheese mixture. Pour into prepared crust.
• **Bake** at 325° for 50 to 55 minutes or until center is almost set. Turn oven off. Carefully run a knife around edge of pan to loosen cheesecake. Let cheesecake stand in oven with door closed 20 minutes. Remove from oven. Cool on a wire rack; cover and chill at least 8 hours.
• **Heat** currant jelly in a small saucepan over low heat until melted; cool. Arrange sliced strawberries on top of cheesecake. Brush melted jelly evenly over strawberries. Remove sides of pan before serving. Yield: 1 (9-inch) cheesecake.

CRÈME DE MENTHE CHEESECAKE

make ahead

5 (8-ounce) packages cream cheese, softened
1½ cups sugar
3 large eggs
1 (16-ounce) carton sour cream
¼ cup white crème de cacao
¼ cup green crème de menthe
2½ teaspoons vanilla extract
Chocolate Cookie Crust
½ cup whipping cream, whipped
Garnish: chocolate-covered mint wafer candy
    shavings

• **Beat** cream cheese at medium speed with an electric mixer until creamy; gradually add sugar, beating well. Add eggs, 1 at a time, beating after each addition. Stir in sour cream and next 3 ingredients. Pour mixture into Chocolate Cookie Crust.
• **Bake** at 350° for 40 minutes. Turn oven off. Let cheesecake stand in oven with door closed 30 minutes. Open oven door; leave cheesecake in oven 30 more minutes. Remove from oven, and carefully run a knife around edge of pan to loosen cheesecake. Cool completely on a wire rack. Cover and chill at least 8 hours. Pipe whipped cream around outer edge of cheesecake, and garnish, if desired. Yield: 1 (10-inch) cheesecake.

Chocolate Cookie Crust

1 (9-ounce) package chocolate wafer cookies,
    crushed (about 2 cups)
⅓ cup butter or margarine, melted

• **Combine** wafer crumbs and butter; firmly press mixture evenly into bottom and 1 inch up sides of a 10-inch springform pan. Bake at 350° for 8 minutes. Yield: 1 (10-inch) crust.

CHOCOLATE MOUSSE CAKE

make ahead

This fine dessert is a cross between a dense cheesecake and chocolate mousse.

8 (1-ounce) squares semisweet
    chocolate
1 (8-ounce) package cream cheese,
    softened
1 (3-ounce) package cream cheese,
    softened

⅔ cup sugar
6 large eggs
⅓ cup whipping cream
1 tablespoon vanilla extract
Chocolate Crust
Whipped Cream Topping

• **Place** chocolate in top of a double boiler; bring water to a boil. Reduce heat to low; cook until chocolate melts. Remove from heat, and cool.

• **Combine** cream cheese and sugar in a large mixing bowl; beat at medium speed with an electric mixer until light and fluffy. Add eggs, 1 at a time, beating until blended after each addition. Add melted chocolate, whipping cream, and vanilla; beat at low speed just until blended. Pour into Chocolate Crust.

• **Bake** at 375° for 35 minutes or just until outside edges are firm but center is still soft. Remove from oven; cool on a wire rack. Cover and chill at least 8 hours.

• **Spread** top of cake with Whipped Cream Topping; sprinkle with reserved ¼ cup Chocolate Crust crumb mixture. Remove sides of pan before serving. Yield: 1 (9-inch) cake.

Chocolate Crust

½ cup butter or margarine
3 (1-ounce) squares semisweet
    chocolate

1½ cups fine, dry breadcrumbs,
    (store-bought)
⅓ cup sugar

• **Combine** butter and chocolate in top of a double boiler; bring water to a boil. Reduce heat to low; cook until chocolate melts. Remove from heat.

• **Add** breadcrumbs and sugar to chocolate mixture, blending well. Reserve ¼ cup crumb mixture. Press remaining mixture into bottom and 2 inches up sides of a lightly greased 9-inch springform pan. Bake at 350° for 5 minutes. Cool on a wire rack. Refrigerate until chilled. Yield: 1 (9-inch) crust.

Whipped Cream Topping

1¼ cups whipping cream
¼ cup sifted powdered sugar

½ teaspoon vanilla extract

• **Beat** whipping cream at high speed with an electric mixer until foamy; gradually add powdered sugar, beating until soft peaks form. Add vanilla; beat well. Yield: 2½ cups.

Cookies and Candies

Cookies are charming food. Whether they're
gooey, chewy, chock-full of chocolate morsels,
filled with jam, or cut into fancy shapes,
cookies are irresistible. And since there never
seems to be enough of them, fill your cookie
jar with a freshly baked batch
from our stellar collection.

Pecan-Butter Cookies and
Walnut Thumbprint Cookies (page 83)

LOADED-WITH-CHIPS COOKIES

family favorite

Chunky with chocolate and nuts, these treats are great for dunking in milk. If you prefer chewy cookies, bake these 10 minutes; if you like them crisp, bake them a minute longer.

½ cup butter or margarine, softened
½ cup shortening
1 cup firmly packed brown sugar
½ cup sugar
2 large eggs
1 teaspoon vanilla extract
1¾ cups all-purpose flour
1½ cups uncooked regular oats
1 teaspoon baking soda
½ teaspoon salt
2 cups (12 ounces) semisweet chocolate morsels
1 cup chopped pecans

• **Beat** butter and shortening at medium speed with an electric mixer until creamy; gradually add sugars, beating well. Add eggs and vanilla, beating well.
• **Combine** flour and next 3 ingredients; gradually add to butter mixture, beating well. Stir in chocolate morsels and pecans.
• **Drop** dough by heaping teaspoonfuls onto ungreased baking sheets. Bake at 350° for 10 to 11 minutes or until golden. Remove to wire racks to cool. Yield: 6 dozen.

RANGER COOKIES

family favorite

Crisp cereal, coconut, and oats flavor these nuggets that are welcome fare for a hike or picnic.

1 cup shortening
1 cup sugar
1 cup firmly packed brown sugar
2 large eggs
1 teaspoon vanilla extract
2 cups all-purpose flour
2 teaspoons baking soda
1 teaspoon baking powder
½ teaspoon salt
2 cups oven-toasted rice cereal
2 cups uncooked regular oats
1 cup flaked coconut
1 cup candy-coated milk chocolate pieces

• **Beat** shortening at medium speed with an electric mixer until creamy; gradually add sugars, beating well. Add eggs, 1 at a time, beating after each addition. Stir in vanilla.
• **Combine** flour and next 3 ingredients; add to shortening mixture, beating well. Stir in cereal, oats, coconut, and candy.
• **Drop** dough by heaping teaspoonfuls onto greased baking sheets. Bake at 350° for 11 to 12 minutes or until golden. Remove to wire racks to cool. Yield: 6 dozen.

JUMBO RAISIN COOKIES

~family favorite~

*These home-style cookies are plump
with raisins and scented with spices.
You'll be glad they're jumbo.*

½ cup boiling water
2 cups raisins
4 cups all-purpose flour
2 teaspoons salt
1 teaspoon baking powder
1 teaspoon baking soda
1½ teaspoons ground cinnamon
¼ teaspoon ground nutmeg
¼ teaspoon ground allspice
1 cup shortening
2 cups sugar
3 large eggs
1 cup chopped pecans
1 teaspoon vanilla extract

• **Pour** boiling water over raisins; let stand until raisins
are plumped and water is absorbed.
• **Combine** flour and next 6 ingredients; set aside.
• **Beat** shortening and sugar at medium speed with an
electric mixer until fluffy. Add eggs to sugar mixture, 1
at a time, beating well after each addition. Gradually
add dry ingredients, beating until blended. Stir in
raisins, pecans, and vanilla.
• **Drop** dough by heaping teaspoonfuls onto lightly
greased baking sheets. Bake at 375° for 9 to 10 minutes. Remove to wire racks to cool. Yield: 5 dozen.

HOLIDAY LIZZIES

*These classic fruitcake cookies are laden
with whiskey. Add them to your holiday
cookie baking repertoire.*

⅓ cup butter or margarine, softened
½ cup sugar
2 large eggs
1½ cups all-purpose flour
1½ teaspoons baking soda
1½ tablespoons milk
1 pound candied cherries, chopped (about 2 cups)
1 pound chopped pecans (about 4½ cups)
1 pound candied pineapple, chopped (about 2
     cups)
2 (8-ounce) packages chopped dates
½ cup bourbon

• **Beat** butter at medium speed with an electric mixer
until creamy; add sugar, beating well. Add eggs, 1 at a
time, beating well.
• **Combine** flour and baking soda; add to butter mixture, blending well. Stir in milk. Add cherries and
remaining ingredients, stirring until blended. Let
dough stand 10 minutes.
• **Drop** dough by heaping teaspoonfuls onto lightly
greased baking sheets. Bake at 325° for 14 to 16 minutes or until lightly browned. Cool on baking sheets 1
minute; remove to wire racks to cool completely. Yield:
about 9 dozen.

FROSTED APRICOT COOKIES

Buttery blonde frosting caps these soft cookies that hint of apricot.

½ cup butter or margarine, softened
1 (3-ounce) package cream cheese, softened
1¼ cups all-purpose flour
¼ cup sugar
1 teaspoon baking powder
¼ teaspoon salt
½ cup apricot preserves
½ cup chopped pecans
½ teaspoon vanilla extract
Apricot Frosting

• **Beat** butter and cream cheese at medium speed with an electric mixer until creamy.
• **Combine** flour, sugar, baking powder, and salt; add to butter mixture, blending well. Stir in preserves, pecans, and vanilla.
• **Drop** dough by rounded tablespoonfuls onto lightly greased baking sheets. Bake at 350° for 15 to 17 minutes. Remove to wire racks, and cool 10 minutes. Spread Apricot Frosting onto warm cookies. Yield: 2 dozen.

Apricot Frosting
1 cup sifted powdered sugar
1 tablespoon butter or margarine, softened
¼ cup apricot preserves

• **Combine** all ingredients; beat at medium speed with an electric mixer until smooth. Yield: ½ cup.

CRISPY OAT COOKIES
family favorite

1 cup butter or margarine, softened
1 cup sugar
1 cup firmly packed brown sugar
1 large egg
1 cup vegetable oil
1 teaspoon vanilla extract
3½ cups all-purpose flour
1 teaspoon baking soda
½ teaspoon salt
1 cup uncooked regular oats
1 cup crushed corn flakes cereal
½ cup flaked coconut
½ cup chopped pecans or walnuts

• **Beat** butter at medium speed with an electric mixer until creamy; gradually add sugars, beating well. Add egg, oil, and vanilla; beat well.
• **Combine** flour, baking soda, and salt; gradually add to butter mixture, mixing well. Stir in oats and remaining ingredients.
• **Shape** dough into 1-inch balls. Place on ungreased baking sheets; flatten cookies with tines of a fork.
• **Bake** at 325° for 15 minutes. Cool 2 minutes; remove to wire racks to cool completely. Yield: 12 dozen.

Oat Cuisine

90s Scientists proved that eating plain Jane oatmeal contributed to lowering cholesterol. Americans embraced the news and ate a whopping 137% more oat products in the early 1990s than in the early 1980s.

PECAN-BUTTER COOKIES

A hint of lemon comes through in these simple butter cookies. They're good plain, and just plain good.

1 cup butter or margarine, softened
1 cup sugar
2 egg yolks
¾ teaspoon vanilla extract
¾ teaspoon almond extract
½ teaspoon lemon extract
2 cups all-purpose flour
1 teaspoon baking powder
¼ teaspoon salt
¾ cup pecan halves

• **Beat** butter at medium speed with an electric mixer until creamy; gradually add sugar, beating well. Add egg yolks, 1 at a time, beating well after each addition. Stir in flavorings.
• **Combine** flour, baking powder, and salt. Add to butter mixture, beating well.
• **Shape** dough into 1-inch balls; place about 2 inches apart on ungreased baking sheets. Press a pecan half into center of each cookie.
• **Bake** at 300° for 17 minutes or until edges are barely golden. Remove cookies to wire racks to cool completely. Yield: 4 dozen.

WALNUT THUMBPRINT COOKIES

Tender impressions in these bumpy walnut cookies secure dollops of brilliantly colored preserves.

½ cup butter or margarine, softened
½ cup sugar
1 large egg, separated
¾ teaspoon grated lemon rind
1 cup all-purpose flour
¼ teaspoon salt
¼ teaspoon ground cinnamon
⅛ teaspoon ground cloves
1¾ cups finely chopped walnuts or pecans, divided
½ cup apricot preserves, red currant jelly, or other preserves

• **Beat** butter at medium speed with an electric mixer until creamy; gradually add sugar, beating well. Add egg yolk and lemon rind; beat well.
• **Combine** flour and next 3 ingredients; gradually add to butter mixture, blending well. Stir in 1 cup walnuts. Cover and chill dough at least 30 minutes.
• **Beat** egg white lightly. Shape dough into 1-inch balls; dip each ball in egg white, and roll in remaining ¾ cup walnuts. Place on lightly greased baking sheets. Press thumb gently into center of each ball, leaving an indentation; fill with preserves.
• **Bake** at 350° for 18 minutes. Remove to wire racks to cool. Add additional preserves or jelly to centers of cookies, if desired. Yield: 2½ dozen.

CHOCOLATE ALMOND FINGERS

This chocolate-tipped butter cookie is ideal for holiday gift giving.

1 cup butter, softened
⅔ cup sugar
3 egg yolks
1 teaspoon vanilla extract
½ teaspoon almond extract
2½ cups all-purpose flour
¼ teaspoon salt
Powdered sugar
1 egg white, lightly beaten
½ cup ground blanched almonds
2 cups (12 ounces) semisweet chocolate morsels, melted

• **Beat** butter at medium speed with an electric mixer until creamy; gradually add sugar, beating well. Add egg yolks, 1 at a time, beating after each addition. Stir in flavorings.
• **Combine** flour and salt; add to butter mixture, beating well. Sift powdered sugar lightly over work surface. Shape 1 tablespoon dough into a 2½-inch log; repeat with remaining dough. Place on lightly greased baking sheets.
• **Brush** each cookie log with egg white, and lightly sprinkle with almonds, reserving remaining almonds. Bake at 400° for 9 to 10 minutes or until barely browned. Remove cookies to wire racks to cool completely.
• **Dip** ends of cookies in melted chocolate, covering about ½ inch on each end. Sprinkle ends with remaining almonds. Place cookies on wire racks until chocolate is firm. Yield: 5 dozen.

CHOCOLATE CHIP-CINNAMON BISCOTTI

⅓ cup butter or margarine, softened
½ cup firmly packed brown sugar
½ cup sugar
1 tablespoon instant coffee or espresso granules
2 large eggs
2 cups all-purpose flour
1½ teaspoons baking powder
½ teaspoon ground cinnamon
⅛ teaspoon salt
1 cup chopped walnuts or pecans
1 cup (6 ounces) semisweet chocolate mini-morsels or regular morsels
2 (2-ounce) squares vanilla-flavored candy coating, melted

• **Combine** first 4 ingredients in a large mixing bowl; beat at medium speed with an electric mixer until creamy. Add eggs, 1 at a time, beating until blended.
• **Combine** flour and next 3 ingredients; add to butter mixture, stirring until blended. Fold in nuts and chocolate morsels.
• **Divide** dough in half; shape each portion into a 10- x 2-inch log on a lightly greased baking sheet.
• **Bake** at 350° for 25 minutes or until firm. Let cool on baking sheet 5 minutes. Remove to wire racks to cool completely.
• **Cut** each log diagonally into ½-inch-thick slices with a serrated knife, using a gentle sawing motion. Place slices on ungreased baking sheets.
• **Bake** at 350° for 10 minutes; turn cookies over, and bake 10 more minutes. Remove to wire racks to cool.
• **Dip** 1 end of each cookie into candy coating; chill until set. Yield: 2½ dozen.

CRESCENT SUGAR COOKIES

1 cup butter or margarine, cut up
2 cups all-purpose flour
1 (8-ounce) carton sour cream
1 egg yolk
¾ cup sugar
¾ cup chopped pecans
1 teaspoon ground cinnamon

• **Cut** butter into flour with a pastry blender until mixture is crumbly. Add sour cream and egg yolk, stirring until flour mixture is moistened. Cover and chill dough several hours.
• **Combine** sugar, pecans, and cinnamon; set aside.
• **Divide** dough into 5 equal portions. Roll each portion into an 8-inch circle; sprinkle with sugar mixture. Cut circle into eighths, using a sharp knife. Roll up each wedge, starting at wide end; seal points firmly. Place on ungreased baking sheets, point side down.
• **Bake** at 350° for 25 minutes or until lightly browned. Remove to wire racks to cool. Yield: 40 cookies.

BOURBON BALLS

make ahead, quick

This is easy holiday food with a short ingredient list that's long on flavor.

2 cups vanilla wafer crumbs
2 cups chopped pecans or walnuts
2 cups sifted powdered sugar
¼ cup cocoa
¼ cup light corn syrup
⅓ cup bourbon
Sifted powdered sugar

• **Combine** first 4 ingredients in a large bowl, and stir well. Combine corn syrup and bourbon; stir into crumb mixture, and shape into 1-inch balls.
• **Roll** each ball in powdered sugar. Store in an airtight container. Reroll in powdered sugar before serving, if desired. Yield: about 4 dozen.

If It Ain't Broke, Don't Fix It

In 1985, decision-makers at Coca-Cola changed their signature soft drink formula. New Coke, their creation, fizzled when outraged Coke lovers blanketed the company's Atlanta headquarters with letters and phone calls. The company got the message: It returned to the original recipe and renamed it Classic Coke. Southerners still prefer the real thing!

Dainty Almond Sandwich Cookies

DAINTY ALMOND SANDWICH COOKIES

These sweet and tender little cookies are great with a sip of tea. You can vary the color of the filling by using different food coloring.

1 cup butter or margarine, softened
2¼ cups all-purpose flour
⅓ cup whipping cream
½ cup sugar
¼ cup butter or margarine, softened
¾ cup sifted powdered sugar
1 teaspoon almond flavoring
1 or 2 drops of food coloring (optional)

• **Beat** butter at medium speed with an electric mixer until light and fluffy. Gradually add flour alternately with whipping cream, beginning and ending with flour. Shape dough into a flat disc; cover and chill 2 hours.
• **Divide** dough into fourths. Work with 1 portion of dough at a time, keeping remaining dough in refrigerator. Let dough stand 2 to 3 minutes or until pliable. On a lightly floured surface, roll dough to ⅛-inch thickness; cut with a 1½-inch round cutter. Dip both sides of each cookie in sugar, and place on an ungreased baking sheet. Repeat procedure with remaining dough. Prick half of the cookies several times with a fork or cut decorative shapes from the centers of cookies, using aspic cutters.
• **Bake** at 375° for 7 to 9 minutes or until barely browned. Gently transfer cookies to wire racks to cool.
• **Combine** ¼ cup butter, powdered sugar, and almond flavoring, mixing well. Add food coloring, if desired. Gently spread each solid cookie with a thin layer of filling; top each with a decorative cookie. Yield: about 3½ dozen.

PINWHEEL COOKIES

family favorite, make ahead

½ cup butter or margarine, softened
1 cup firmly packed brown sugar
1 large egg
1 teaspoon vanilla extract
2 cups all-purpose flour
1 teaspoon baking powder
¼ teaspoon salt
2 tablespoons cocoa

• **Beat** butter at medium speed with an electric mixer until creamy; gradually add brown sugar, beating well. Add egg and vanilla, beating well.
• **Combine** flour, baking powder, and salt; gradually add to butter mixture, mixing well. Divide dough in half; stir cocoa into 1 portion.
• **Roll** each portion into a 12- x 9-inch rectangle on wax paper. Invert chocolate dough onto plain dough; peel off wax paper, and press chocolate dough firmly onto plain dough with a rolling pin. Roll up, jellyroll fashion, starting with long side; cover and chill 8 hours.
• **Cut** dough with an electric knife into ¼-inch-thick slices; place on lightly greased baking sheets. Bake at 350° for 6 to 8 minutes. Remove to wire racks to cool. Yield: about 4 dozen.

NOTE: You can freeze unbaked cookie dough up to one month. Before baking, thaw in refrigerator; then slice and bake as directed.

RUM-CURRANT SHORTBREAD

½ cup currants
¼ cup light rum
1 cup butter, softened
½ cup sifted powdered sugar
1¾ cups all-purpose flour
¼ teaspoon baking powder
¼ teaspoon salt

• **Bring** currants and rum to a boil in a small saucepan. Remove from heat; cover and let stand 30 minutes. Drain currants, discarding rum.
• **Beat** butter at medium speed with an electric mixer until creamy; gradually add powdered sugar, beating well. Combine flour, baking powder, and salt; gradually add to butter mixture, beating at low speed until blended after each addition. Stir in currants. Chill 30 minutes.
• **Roll** dough to ¼-inch thickness on a lightly floured surface. Cut with a 2-inch round cutter; place 2 inches apart on lightly greased baking sheets.
• **Bake** at 375° for 12 to 14 minutes or until edges just begin to brown; cool on baking sheets on wire racks 5 minutes. Remove to wire racks to cool completely. Yield: 2 dozen.

NUTTY BROWNIES

These cakelike brownies are great plain. For a fudgier brownie, shorten the baking time by a few minutes.

1 cup butter or margarine
4 (1-ounce) unsweetened chocolate squares
4 large eggs
2 cups sugar
2 cups all-purpose flour
½ teaspoon salt
1 teaspoon vanilla extract
1½ cups chopped walnuts or pecans

• **Microwave** butter and chocolate in a 1-quart microwave-safe bowl at HIGH 2 minutes or until both are melted, stirring once.
• **Beat** eggs at medium speed with an electric mixer; gradually add sugar, beating well. Add flour, salt, and vanilla to egg mixture, beating well. Stir in chocolate mixture and walnuts. Pour batter into a greased 13- x 9-inch pan.
• **Bake** at 325° for 40 to 45 minutes. Cool in pan on a wire rack. Cut into squares. Yield: 2½ dozen.

NOTE: For added interest, stir 1 cup of any of the following ingredients into the Nutty Brownies batter before baking: butterscotch, peanut butter, or semisweet morsels; candy-coated chocolate pieces; chopped candy bars; almond brickle chips; or dried cherries.

NO-BAKE BROWNIES

2 cups (12 ounces) semisweet chocolate morsels
1 cup plus 2 teaspoons evaporated milk, divided
1 (11-ounce) package vanilla wafers
2 cups miniature marshmallows
1 cup chopped pecans
1 cup sifted powdered sugar
½ teaspoon salt

• **Combine** chocolate morsels and 1 cup evaporated milk in a saucepan; cook over low heat until chocolate melts, stirring occasionally. Set aside.
• **Position** knife blade in food processor bowl; add half of vanilla wafers. Process to make coarse crumbs. Place crumbs in a large bowl. Repeat procedure with remaining vanilla wafers.
• **Stir** marshmallows and remaining 3 ingredients into vanilla wafer crumbs. Reserve ½ cup chocolate mixture. Stir remaining chocolate mixture into crumb mixture. Press mixture evenly into a well-greased 9-inch square pan.
• **Combine** reserved ½ cup chocolate mixture and remaining 2 teaspoons evaporated milk; spread evenly over crumb mixture. Cover and chill at least 1 hour. Cut into squares. Yield: 3 dozen.

DOUBLE CHOCOLATE BROWNIES

Two kinds of chocolate distinguish these brownies from the typical box variety. They sport a white chocolate base laced with chunks of dark chocolate.

1 cup butter or margarine
8 (2-ounce) white chocolate baking bars, coarsely
    chopped
4 large eggs
¼ teaspoon salt
1 cup sugar
1 tablespoon vanilla extract
2 cups all-purpose flour
1 (8-ounce) package semisweet chocolate squares,
    coarsely chopped
1 cup macadamia nuts or pecans, coarsely
    chopped

• **Melt** butter in a heavy saucepan over low heat; remove from heat. Add half of white chocolate (do not stir).
• **Beat** eggs and salt at high speed with an electric mixer until mixture is slightly thickened. Add sugar; beat 2 to 3 minutes or until fluffy. Add butter mixture, vanilla, and flour, beating until smooth.
• **Fold** in remaining chopped white chocolate, semi-sweet chocolate, and nuts. Spoon batter into a lightly greased 15- x 10-inch jellyroll pan.
• **Bake** at 350° for 30 to 35 minutes or until lightly browned. Cool in pan on a wire rack. Cut into squares. Yield: 2½ dozen.

LEMON BARS

~ family favorite ~

Lemon Bars never go out of style, and this version is one of our favorites. The bars have a thick shortbread crust and just the right amount of lemon in the chesslike filling.

2½ cups all-purpose flour, divided
¾ cup sifted powdered sugar, divided
1 cup cold butter or margarine, cut up
½ teaspoon baking powder
4 large eggs, beaten
2 cups sugar
⅓ cup lemon juice
Garnish: fresh mint leaves

• **Combine** 2 cups flour and ½ cup powdered sugar. Cut butter into flour mixture with a pastry blender until mixture is crumbly.
• **Spoon** flour mixture into a 13- x 9-inch pan; press into pan evenly and firmly, using fingertips. Bake at 350° for 20 to 25 minutes or until lightly browned.
• **Combine** ½ cup flour and baking powder; set aside. Combine eggs, 2 cups sugar, and lemon juice; beat well. Stir dry ingredients into egg mixture, and pour over baked crust.
• **Bake** at 350° for 22 to 25 minutes or until lightly browned and set. Cool on a wire rack. Sprinkle with ¼ cup powdered sugar, and cut into bars. Garnish, if desired. Yield: 2 dozen.

MELT AWAYS

Melt Aways have such a tender texture that they'll quickly melt in your mouth. Coffee is a good accompaniment.

1 cup butter or margarine, softened
1 cup sugar
1 large egg, separated
1 teaspoon vanilla extract
2 cups all-purpose flour
1 cup chopped pecans, divided

• **Beat** butter at medium speed with an electric mixer until creamy. Add sugar, beating well. Add egg yolk and vanilla, beating well. Gradually add flour, beating well. Stir in ½ cup pecans. Spread dough evenly in a lightly greased 15- x 10-inch jellyroll pan.
• **Beat** egg white until foamy; brush evenly over dough. Sprinkle with remaining pecans. Bake at 350° for 20 to 25 minutes or until lightly browned. Cool completely. Cut into bars. Yield: 3 dozen.

PECAN SQUARES

2 cups all-purpose flour
½ cup powdered sugar
1 cup cold butter or margarine, cut up
1 (14-ounce) can sweetened condensed milk
1 large egg
1 teaspoon vanilla extract
1 (7.5-ounce) package almond brickle chips
    (we tested with Bits 'O Brickle)
1 cup chopped pecans

• **Combine** flour and powdered sugar in a medium bowl. Cut in butter with a pastry blender until crumbly. Press mixture evenly into a greased 13- x 9-inch pan. Bake at 350° for 15 minutes.
• **Combine** condensed milk and remaining 4 ingredients; pour over crust. Bake at 350° for 25 minutes or until golden. Cool; cut into squares. Yield: 4 dozen.

CHOCOLATE CANDY-OAT BARS

family favorite

If M & M candies are your thing, you'll love them in these fudgy bar cookies.

2 cups uncooked quick-cooking oats
1½ cups all-purpose flour
1 cup chopped pecans
1 cup firmly packed brown sugar
1 teaspoon baking soda
¼ teaspoon salt
1 cup butter or margarine, melted
1½ cups candy-coated chocolate pieces, divided
1 (14-ounce) can sweetened condensed milk

• **Combine** first 6 ingredients, stirring well. Add butter, and stir or beat at low speed with an electric mixer until mixture is crumbly. Reserve 1½ cups crumb mixture; press remaining crumb mixture into a lightly greased 15- x 10-inch jellyroll pan. (Mixture will be thin in pan.) Bake at 375° for 10 minutes. Cool on a wire rack. Reduce oven temperature to 350°.
• **Place** 1 cup chocolate pieces in a microwave-safe bowl; microwave at HIGH 1 to 1½ minutes, stirring after 30 seconds. Press chocolate pieces with back of a spoon to mash them. (The candies will almost be melted with pieces of color coating still visible.) Stir in condensed milk. Spread mixture evenly over crust in pan, leaving a ½-inch border on all sides.
• **Combine** reserved 1½ cups crumb mixture and remaining chocolate pieces; sprinkle evenly over chocolate mixture, and press lightly.
• **Bake** at 350° for 18 to 20 minutes or until golden; cool in pan on a wire rack. Cut into bars. Yield: 4 dozen.

Chocolate Candy-Oat Bars

ALMOND CREAM CONFECTIONS

Cookie crumbs, coconut, and toasted almonds contribute to an incredible crust for these dainty little brownies.

½ cup butter or margarine
¼ cup sugar
2 tablespoons cocoa
2 teaspoons vanilla extract
¼ teaspoon salt
1 large egg, lightly beaten
1 cup slivered almonds, toasted and chopped
1¾ cups vanilla wafer crumbs
½ cup flaked coconut
Cream Filling
2 (1-ounce) squares semisweet chocolate

• **Combine** first 6 ingredients in a heavy saucepan. Cook over low heat, stirring constantly, until butter melts and mixture begins to thicken. Remove from heat; add almonds, vanilla wafer crumbs, and coconut, stirring well. Press crumb mixture firmly into an ungreased 9-inch square pan; cover and chill.
• **Spread** Cream Filling over almond mixture; cover and chill several hours. Cut into 1½-inch squares. Remove from pan, and place squares about ½ inch apart on a baking sheet.
• **Place** chocolate in a heavy-duty zip-top plastic bag; seal bag. Submerge in hot water until chocolate melts. Snip a tiny hole in 1 corner of bag with scissors; drizzle chocolate over cream filling. Yield: 3 dozen.

Cream Filling

⅓ cup butter or margarine, softened
3 to 4 tablespoons milk
½ teaspoon vanilla extract
3 cups sifted powdered sugar

• **Beat** butter at high speed with an electric mixer until creamy. Add milk and vanilla. Slowly add sugar; beat until smooth. Yield: 1½ cups.

CRANBERRY-CARAMEL BARS

1 cup fresh cranberries
2 tablespoons sugar
2 cups all-purpose flour
2 cups uncooked regular oats
½ cup sugar
½ cup firmly packed brown sugar
½ teaspoon baking soda
1 cup butter or margarine, melted
1 (10-ounce) package chopped dates
¾ cup chopped pecans
1 (12-ounce) jar caramel sauce
⅓ cup all-purpose flour

• **Stir** together cranberries and 2 tablespoons sugar in a small bowl; set aside.
• **Combine** 2 cups flour and next 4 ingredients; stir in butter until mixture is crumbly. Reserve 1 cup flour mixture. Press remaining mixture into bottom of a lightly greased 13- x 9-inch baking dish.
• **Bake** at 350° for 15 minutes. Sprinkle with dates, pecans, and cranberry mixture.
• **Stir** together caramel sauce and ⅓ cup flour; spoon over cranberries. Sprinkle with reserved 1 cup flour mixture. Bake 20 more minutes or until lightly browned. Cool completely on a wire rack. Cut into bars. Yield: 2 dozen.

SEVEN-LAYER BARS

~family favorite~

⅓ cup butter or margarine
1½ cups graham cracker crumbs
1 (7-ounce) can flaked coconut
1 cup (6 ounces) semisweet chocolate morsels
1 cup (6 ounces) butterscotch morsels
1 (14-ounce) can sweetened condensed milk
1 cup chopped pecans

• **Place** butter in a 13- x 9-inch pan; bake at 325° for 3 minutes or until melted. Add graham cracker crumbs and remaining ingredients, layering in the order listed. (Do not stir.) Bake at 325° for 30 minutes. Cool completely in pan; cut into bars. Yield: 3 dozen.

CREAM CHEESE-ALMOND BARS

make ahead

½ cup butter or margarine, softened
2 teaspoons sugar
2 tablespoons milk
½ teaspoon grated lemon rind
1⅓ cups all-purpose flour
2 (8-ounce) packages cream cheese, softened
1 cup sugar
1 large egg, lightly beaten
1 teaspoon grated lemon rind
1 cup chopped almonds, toasted
1 cup sifted powdered sugar
1 tablespoon water
1 teaspoon ground cinnamon
Garnish: toasted sliced almonds

• **Combine** first 4 ingredients; beat at medium speed with an electric mixer until creamy. Gradually add flour, beating well. Press dough into a lightly greased 9-inch square pan. Set aside.
• **Combine** cream cheese, 1 cup sugar, egg, and 1 teaspoon lemon rind; beat at medium speed until smooth. Stir in almonds; spoon mixture over prepared dough. Bake at 300° for 1 hour and 10 minutes or until set.
• **Combine** powdered sugar, water, and cinnamon, stirring well. Dollop topping onto uncut warm brownies. Let stand 1 minute; spread topping evenly. Cool in pan on a wire rack. Cover and chill 3 to 4 hours; cut into bars. Garnish, if desired. Yield: 2½ dozen.

CHOCOLATE DREAM BARS

¾ cup butter or margarine
⅓ cup cocoa
¼ cup sugar
1 large egg, lightly beaten
2 cups graham cracker crumbs
1 cup flaked coconut
½ cup chopped pecans
1 teaspoon vanilla extract
Custard Filling
1 cup (6 ounces) semisweet chocolate
    morsels
2 tablespoons butter or margarine

• **Combine** first 4 ingredients in top of a double boiler; bring water to a boil. Reduce heat to low; cook until mixture thickens and registers 160°, stirring constantly. Remove from heat. Add graham cracker crumbs, coconut, pecans, and vanilla; mix well. Press mixture into a lightly greased 9-inch square pan; chill 15 minutes.
• **Spread** Custard Filling over chocolate mixture. Chill 30 minutes or until custard mixture becomes firm.
• **Combine** chocolate morsels and 2 tablespoons butter in a heavy saucepan over low heat; stir until chocolate melts and mixture is smooth. Spread over Custard Filling. Chill 2 hours. Cut into bars. Cover and store in refrigerator. Yield: 2½ dozen.

Custard Filling
¼ cup butter or margarine, softened
3 tablespoons milk
2 tablespoons vanilla instant pudding mix
2 cups sifted powdered sugar

• **Beat** butter at medium speed with an electric mixer until creamy. Add milk and pudding mix; beat well. Gradually add powdered sugar, beating until smooth. Yield: 1 cup.

Marbled Peanut Butter Fudge

MARBLED PEANUT BUTTER FUDGE

⊸ family favorite, make ahead ⊸

The creamy peanut butter layer stays soft in this ultrarich fudge, so keep it chilled for best results.

4 cups sugar
1 (12-ounce) can evaporated milk
1 cup butter or margarine
1 (7-ounce) jar marshmallow cream
3 cups (18 ounces) semisweet chocolate morsels
1 tablespoon vanilla extract
1 cup peanut butter

• **Combine** first 3 ingredients in a large heavy saucepan. Bring mixture to a boil over medium heat; cook 8 minutes, stirring constantly. Add marshmallow cream, chocolate morsels, and vanilla; stir until chocolate melts.
• **Pour** half of mixture into a buttered 13- x 9-inch pan; dollop with peanut butter. Spoon remaining chocolate mixture over peanut butter; swirl with a knife. Cover and chill until firm; cut into 1-inch pieces. Store in refrigerator. Yield: 5 pounds.

CREAMY PEANUT BUTTER FUDGE

⊸ make ahead ⊸

2 cups sugar
⅔ cup milk
¾ cup marshmallow cream
¾ cup creamy peanut butter
¼ cup butter or margarine

• **Combine** sugar and milk in a heavy 3-quart saucepan, stirring well. Cook over medium heat, stirring constantly, until sugar dissolves. Cover and cook over medium heat 2 to 3 minutes to wash down sugar crystals from sides of pan. Uncover and cook, without stirring, until candy thermometer registers 234°, maintaining a rolling boil. Remove from heat; add marshmallow cream, peanut butter, and butter, stirring with a wooden spoon until butter melts and mixture is smooth.
• **Pour** fudge immediately into a buttered 8-inch square pan. Cool and cut into squares. Yield: about 2 pounds.

GERMAN CHOCOLATE FUDGE

⊸ make ahead ⊸

The German chocolate title refers to the type of chocolate bars used in this delectable candy.

4½ cups sugar
1 (12-ounce) can evaporated milk
2 tablespoons butter or margarine
Pinch of salt
2 cups (12 ounces) semisweet chocolate morsels
3 (4-ounce) bars sweet baking chocolate, broken
1 (7-ounce) jar marshmallow cream
2 cups chopped pecans

• **Combine** first 4 ingredients in a heavy 4-quart saucepan, stirring well. Cook over medium heat, stirring constantly, until sugar dissolves. Cover and cook over medium heat 2 minutes to wash down crystals from sides of pan. Uncover, bring to a rolling boil, and continue to cook 6 minutes, without stirring. Remove from heat.
• **Combine** chocolate morsels, baking chocolate, marshmallow cream, and pecans in a large bowl. Pour sugar mixture over chocolate mixture.
• **Beat** mixture with a wooden spoon until it thickens and begins to lose its gloss (3 to 4 minutes). Spread evenly in a buttered 15- x 10-inch jellyroll pan. Cool completely; cut into squares. Yield: 5 pounds.

COFFEE PENUCHE

Penuche is a close cousin to fudge. Coffee adds a new dimension to this old-fashioned candy.

3 cups firmly packed brown sugar
1 cup freshly brewed coffee
2 tablespoons light corn syrup
2 tablespoons butter or margarine
1 teaspoon vanilla extract
⅛ teaspoon salt
1 cup chopped pecans

• **Cook** first 3 ingredients in a large heavy saucepan over low heat, stirring until sugar dissolves. Cover and cook over medium heat 2 to 3 minutes to wash down sugar from sides of pan. Uncover and cook, without stirring, until candy thermometer registers 238° (soft ball stage).
• **Remove** from heat, and add butter, vanilla, and salt (do not stir). Cool to 175°. Stir in pecans, and beat with a wooden spoon until mixture thickens and begins to lose its gloss. Spread into a buttered 8-inch square pan. Cool until firm. Cut into squares. Yield: 2 pounds.

BOURBON PRALINES

If you like bourbon, these are some of the best pralines ever. Two pairs of hands ensure that making them goes smoothly. One person can stir the pralines with a wooden spoon; the other can be ready to spoon them onto wax paper.

2 cups sugar
1 cup buttermilk
⅓ cup bourbon
2 tablespoons butter or margarine
⅛ teaspoon salt
2 cups pecan pieces or chopped walnuts
1 teaspoon baking soda

• **Combine** first 5 ingredients in a large heavy saucepan. Cook over low heat, stirring gently, until sugar

dissolves. Add pecans. Cover and cook over medium heat 2 to 3 minutes to wash down sugar crystals from sides of pan.
• **Uncover** and cook, without stirring, to soft ball stage or until candy thermometer registers 235°. Remove from heat, and stir in soda. Beat with a wooden spoon just until mixture begins to thicken (about 5 to 8 minutes). Working rapidly, drop by tablespoonfuls onto greased wax paper; let stand until firm. Yield: 2 dozen.

DOUBLE ALMOND TOFFEE

This thick toffee tops any candy bar you can buy.

2 cups butter or margarine
2½ cups sugar
1½ cups whole unblanched almonds
1½ cups (9 ounces) semisweet chocolate morsels, melted and divided
1½ cups chopped blanched almonds, lightly toasted and divided

• **Melt** butter over low heat in a 3-quart nonstick heavy saucepan; add sugar. Cook, stirring constantly, over high heat until mixture comes to a boil (about 6 minutes). Reduce heat to medium-high; cook and stir 5 minutes.
• **Add** whole almonds to sugar mixture; cook 7 minutes, stirring constantly. Reduce heat to medium; cook until mixture reaches hard crack stage or a candy thermometer registers 300° (about 10 minutes), stirring occasionally. Pour mixture into a buttered 15- x 10-inch jellyroll pan; cool until firm.
• **Spread** half of melted chocolate over toffee layer. Sprinkle with half of chopped almonds. Press almonds gently into chocolate. Gently turn candy out onto a wax paper-lined baking sheet; spread remaining chocolate over other side. Sprinkle with remaining chopped almonds, pressing almonds gently into chocolate; chill toffee until firm. Break candy into pieces. Store between layers of wax paper in airtight containers. Yield: 3¼ pounds.

Double Almond
Toffee

CHOCOLATE-PRALINE TRUFFLES

make ahead

*Make these luxurious candies ahead,
and chill or freeze them.*

3 (4-ounce) semisweet chocolate bars, broken into
   pieces
¼ cup whipping cream
3 tablespoons butter, cut up
2 tablespoons almond liqueur
Praline Pecans

• **Microwave** chocolate and whipping cream in a 2-quart microwave-safe bowl at MEDIUM (50% power) 3½ minutes.
• **Whisk** until chocolate melts and mixture is smooth. (If chocolate doesn't melt completely, microwave and whisk at 15-second intervals until melted.) Whisk in butter and liqueur; let stand 20 minutes.
• **Beat** at medium speed with an electric mixer 4 minutes or until mixture forms soft peaks. (Do not overbeat.) Cover and chill at least 4 hours.
• **Shape** mixture into 1-inch balls; roll in Praline Pecans. Cover and chill up to 1 week, or freeze up to 1 month. Yield: about 2 dozen.

Praline Pecans
1½ cups chopped pecans
¼ cup firmly packed brown sugar
2 tablespoons whipping cream

• **Stir** together all ingredients; spread in a lightly buttered 9-inch round cakepan.
• **Bake** at 350° for 20 minutes or until coating appears slightly crystallized, stirring once. Remove from oven; stir and cool. Store in an airtight container. Yield: 1½ cups.

White Chocolate-Praline Truffles: Substitute 3 (4-ounce) white chocolate bars for semisweet chocolate bars.

Chocolate Marble Truffles: Prepare 1 recipe each of Chocolate-Praline Truffles and White Chocolate-Praline Truffles. Spoon both mixtures into a 13- x 9-inch pan; swirl with a knife to create a marbled effect. Chill and shape as directed; roll in cream-filled chocolate sandwich cookie crumbs, omitting Praline Pecans.

NOTE: We used Ghirardelli semisweet chocolate bars and Ghirardelli white chocolate bars.

LEMON DIVINITY

One recipe of this fruity divinity will fill several mini tins for gift giving. Store candies layered between sheets of wax paper in tins.

3 cups sugar
¾ cup water
¾ cup light corn syrup
¼ teaspoon salt
2 egg whites
1 (3-ounce) package lemon-flavored gelatin
1 cup chopped pecans or walnuts

• **Cook** first 4 ingredients in a large heavy saucepan over low heat, stirring constantly, until sugar dissolves.
• **Cover** syrup mixture, and cook over medium heat 3 minutes. Uncover; cook over medium heat, without stirring, until mixture reaches hard ball stage or until a candy thermometer registers 258° (about 18 minutes). Remove mixture from heat.
• **Beat** egg whites at high speed with an electric mixer until foamy. Add gelatin, and beat until stiff peaks form.
• **Pour** hot syrup in a heavy stream over egg whites, beating constantly at high speed 4 minutes or until mixture holds its shape. Stir in pecans.
• **Drop** mixture quickly by rounded teaspoonfuls onto wax paper. Cool. Yield: 6 dozen.

Cherry Divinity: Substitute 1 (3-ounce) package cherry-flavored gelatin for lemon-flavored gelatin.

COCONUT-MACADAMIA CARAMELS

~ make ahead ~

1 cup sugar
⅔ cup light corn syrup
1 teaspoon honey
1½ cups half-and-half, divided
½ cup flaked coconut
½ cup chopped macadamia nuts
1 tablespoon minced dried pineapple (optional)
1 teaspoon vanilla extract

• **Cook** first 3 ingredients and ½ cup half-and-half in a large heavy saucepan over low heat, stirring constantly, until sugar dissolves.
• **Cover** and cook over medium-low heat 2 to 3 minutes to wash down sugar crystals from sides of pan.
• **Uncover** and cook, stirring constantly, until a candy thermometer registers 242° (firm ball stage).
• **Add** ½ cup half-and-half, and cook over medium heat, stirring constantly, 12 minutes or until candy thermometer returns to 242°. Repeat procedure with remaining ½ cup half-and-half.
• **Stir** in flaked coconut and remaining ingredients.
• **Pour** into a buttered 9-inch square pan. Cool and cut into 1½-inch pieces (butter your knife to ease cutting). Wrap caramels individually in wax paper. Yield: 1½ pounds.

PECAN CLUSTERS

~ make ahead ~

1 (7-ounce) jar marshmallow cream
1½ pounds milk chocolate kisses
5 cups sugar
1 (12-ounce) can evaporated milk
½ cup butter or margarine
6 cups pecan halves

• **Place** marshmallow cream and chocolate kisses in a large bowl.
• **Bring** sugar, milk, and butter to a boil in a large heavy saucepan, stirring constantly. Boil 8 minutes, stirring constantly. Add milk mixture to marshmallow cream mixture, stirring until chocolate melts. Stir in pecans.
• **Drop** by rounded teaspoonfuls onto wax paper-lined baking sheets; chill until firm. Store in refrigerator. Yield: 12 dozen.

CARAMEL CORN

~ family favorite ~

6 quarts freshly popped corn (about ⅔ cup unpopped corn)
1½ cups pecan halves
1½ cups raw peanuts
1½ cups firmly packed brown sugar
¾ cup butter or margarine
¾ cup light corn syrup
1 teaspoon vanilla extract
½ teaspoon baking soda

• **Combine** popcorn and pecans in a greased large roasting pan; set aside.
• **Combine** peanuts and next 3 ingredients in a large saucepan. Bring to a boil over medium heat, stirring constantly. Boil 5 minutes, stirring occasionally. Remove from heat; stir in vanilla and soda.
• **Pour** peanut mixture over popcorn mixture; stir with a lightly greased long-handled spoon until popcorn mixture is coated.
• **Bake** at 250° for 1 hour, stirring every 15 minutes. Remove from oven, and immediately pour mixture onto wax paper, breaking it apart as it cools. Store in airtight containers at room temperature. Yield: 6½ quarts.

Desserts

Sweet endings have long been a
hallmark for *Southern Living*,
whether it's a recipe for homemade peach ice cream, banana
pudding, or a brownie trifle. You'll
find fabulous finales for every
meal on these pages.

Creamy Peach Ice Cream (page 110)

LEMON-BUTTERMILK CUSTARDS

A soft, golden meringue caps these tangy lemon custards. They make a great dessert choice after a grilled fish dinner.

¾ cup sugar
3 tablespoons cornstarch
1½ cups buttermilk
2 tablespoons butter or margarine
3 large eggs, separated
1½ teaspoons grated lemon rind
¼ cup fresh lemon juice
¼ cup sugar
Garnish: lemon twists

• **Combine** ¾ cup sugar and cornstarch in a 2-quart heavy saucepan; stir well. Add buttermilk; cook over medium heat, stirring constantly, 6 to 8 minutes or until mixture comes to a boil and thickens. Stir in butter.
• **Combine** egg yolks, lemon rind, and juice; beat well. Gradually stir one-fourth of hot mixture into yolks; add to remaining hot mixture, stirring constantly. Cook over medium heat, stirring constantly, 6 to 8 minutes or until smooth and thickened. Spoon mixture into four 10-ounce ungreased custard cups.
• **Beat** egg whites in a large bowl at high speed with an electric mixer until foamy. Gradually add ¼ cup sugar, 1 tablespoon at a time, beating until stiff peaks form. Spread meringue over custards, sealing to edge of each dish.
• **Bake** at 325° for 20 minutes or until meringues are browned. Cool completely before serving. Garnish, if desired. Yield: 4 servings.

SABAYON CREAM FOR FRUIT

Serve this dessert with kiwifruit and fresh berries in wine goblets. The tart fruits provide a nice contrast to the rich cream.

6 egg yolks
Dash of salt
⅔ cup sugar
3 cups whipping cream, divided
½ cup dry white wine
⅔ cup kirsch or other cherry-flavored brandy
Assorted sliced fresh fruit

• **Combine** egg yolks and salt in a large bowl; beat at high speed with an electric mixer until blended. Gradually add sugar, 1 tablespoon at a time; beat 5 minutes or until mixture is thick and pale.
• **Heat** 1 cup whipping cream, white wine, and kirsch in a saucepan until hot, but not boiling. With mixer running on low speed, slowly pour hot cream mixture into beaten egg mixture. Transfer mixture to the top of a double boiler; place over simmering water, and cook 20 minutes, stirring constantly. (Mixture will thicken slightly.) Remove from heat. Place top of double boiler over a bowl of ice water. Stir until mixture is cooled completely.
• **Whip** remaining 2 cups cream at medium speed until stiff. Fold whipped cream into cold egg mixture. Cover and chill. Stir gently before serving. Spoon Sabayon Cream over fresh fruit. Chill until ready to serve. Garnish with fruit, if desired. Yield: 8 servings.

Sabayon Cream for Fruit

Amaretto Crème with Fresh Fruit

Peaches and amaretto are a natural pair for this dessert.

4 egg yolks, lightly beaten
½ cup sugar
2 tablespoons all-purpose flour
1 cup milk
1 tablespoon amaretto
½ teaspoon vanilla extract
Sliced fresh peaches
Fresh raspberries
Garnish: fresh mint sprigs

• **Combine** first 3 ingredients in a medium saucepan; gradually add milk, stirring until smooth. Cook mixture over medium heat, stirring constantly, 10 minutes or until thickened and bubbly.
• **Remove** from heat; stir in amaretto and vanilla. Place pan over a bowl of ice. Chill 10 minutes, stirring often. Serve with peach slices and raspberries or other fresh fruit. Garnish, if desired. Yield: 1½ cups.

A Crock for All Seasons

*70*ˢ The slow cooker, also called the Crock-Pot®, entered the American kitchen in the 1970s. But unlike the fondue pot and the crêpe maker from the same decade, the pea green Crock-Pot didn't always end up at yard sales. Cooks have been relying on the appliance for years.

*90*ˢ The slow cooker is appreciated more than ever in the time-starved '90s when about 58 percent of women work outside the home and everyone comes home just as hungry as always. And now you can buy a slow cooker in a sleek stainless steel design.

Pumpkin Flan

~ make ahead ~

Flan is the custard of choice in Spain. Pumpkin adds a new depth of flavor and texture to this version that's finished with a sprinkle of flaked coconut.

1 cup sugar, divided
2½ cups milk
3 large eggs
3 egg whites
1 cup canned pumpkin
1 teaspoon ground cinnamon
1 teaspoon vanilla extract
¼ cup flaked coconut

• **Sprinkle** ½ cup sugar in a 9-inch round cakepan. Cook over medium-high heat, shaking pan occasionally, using oven mitts, until sugar melts and turns light golden; set aside. (Mixture may crack slightly as it cools.)
• **Heat** milk and remaining ½ cup sugar in a heavy saucepan, stirring constantly, until hot and frothy.
• **Beat** eggs and next 4 ingredients at medium speed with an electric mixer until blended; gradually add hot milk mixture, beating at low speed.
• **Pour** over caramelized sugar. Place cakepan in a roasting pan. Pour hot water into roasting pan to depth of 1 inch.
• **Bake** at 350° for 1 hour or until a knife inserted in center comes out clean.
• **Remove** pan from water; cool on a wire rack. Cover and chill.
• **Bake** coconut in a shallow pan at 350° for 5 to 6 minutes or until toasted, stirring occasionally. Cool.
• **Loosen** edges of flan with a spatula, and invert onto a serving plate, letting caramelized sugar drizzle over flan. Sprinkle with coconut. Yield: 8 servings.

No-Bake Banana Pudding

~ family favorite, make ahead ~

This may well be one of the easiest banana pudding recipes ever. And it's great tasting, too. Sour cream in the filling makes it taste like it's made from scratch.

2 (3.4-ounce) packages vanilla instant
    pudding mix
1 (8-ounce) carton sour cream
3½ cups milk
Vanilla wafers
3 large ripe bananas
1 (8-ounce) carton frozen whipped topping,
    thawed

• **Combine** first 3 ingredients in a large bowl; beat at low speed with an electric mixer 2 minutes or until thickened.
• **Line** bottom and sides of a 3-quart bowl with vanilla wafers. Slice 1 banana, and layer slices over vanilla wafers. Spoon about one-third of pudding mixture over bananas.
• **Repeat** layers two more times, using vanilla wafers, remaining bananas, and remaining pudding. Cover and chill. Spread whipped topping over pudding just before serving. Yield: 10 servings.

Raisin-Rice Pudding

~ family favorite ~

Here's an old-fashioned dessert that warms the spirit. Medium-grain rice is the best choice for creamy-textured results because the grains are plumper and moister when cooked than long-grain rice.

4 large eggs
¾ cup sugar
2 cups milk
1⅓ cups cooked medium-grain rice
⅔ cup raisins
1 tablespoon butter or margarine, melted
1½ teaspoons lemon juice
1½ teaspoons vanilla extract
¼ teaspoon ground nutmeg
¼ teaspoon ground cinnamon

• **Combine** eggs, sugar, and milk; beat at medium speed with an electric mixer 1 to 2 minutes or until sugar dissolves. Add rice and remaining ingredients; stir well. Pour mixture into a greased 1½-quart casserole; place casserole in a larger pan. Pour boiling water into pan to depth of 1 inch.
• **Bake,** uncovered, at 350° for 40 to 45 minutes or until mixture is slightly thickened. Stir and bake 10 to 15 more minutes or until set. Serve pudding warm or at room temperature. Yield: 6 servings.

BREAD PUDDING WITH CUSTARD SAUCE

Croissants make this bread pudding extra buttery.

8 large day-old croissants, torn into small pieces
4 cups milk
3 large eggs, lightly beaten
2 cups sugar
1 cup pecan halves, toasted
1½ tablespoons vanilla extract
1 teaspoon ground cinnamon
½ teaspoon ground nutmeg
Custard Sauce

• **Place** bread in a lightly greased 13- x 9-inch pan.
• **Pour** milk over bread, and let stand 10 minutes. Blend mixture well, using hands. Stir eggs and next 5 ingredients into bread mixture.
• **Bake** at 325° for 40 to 45 minutes or until firm. Serve warm with Custard Sauce. Yield: 15 servings.

Custard Sauce
1 cup sugar
½ cup butter or margarine
½ cup half-and-half
2 tablespoons whiskey or ½ teaspoon vanilla extract

• **Bring** first 3 ingredients to a boil in a heavy saucepan over medium heat, stirring until sugar dissolves. Reduce heat, and simmer 5 minutes. Cool; stir in whiskey. Yield: 1½ cups.

NOTE: Substitute 1 (16-ounce) loaf French bread for croissants, if desired. Bake at 325° for 55 minutes or until firm.

PINEAPPLE UPSIDE-DOWN BREAD PUDDING

⸺ family favorite ⸺

Get out your cast-iron skillet for this favorite comfort food dessert. Instead of a cake batter base, this clever recipe soaks bread in a sweet egg custard before baking.

2 large eggs, beaten
½ cup sugar
1 teaspoon vanilla extract
1 (20-ounce) can pineapple tidbits, undrained
8 cups white bread cubes
½ cup butter or margarine
1 cup firmly packed brown sugar
1 (6-ounce) jar maraschino cherries, drained and halved (about ½ cup)
½ cup coarsely chopped pecans

• **Combine** eggs, ½ cup sugar, and vanilla in a large bowl; stir well. Drain pineapple, reserving juice. Add juice to egg mixture; add bread cubes. Toss gently.
• **Melt** butter in a 9- or 10-inch cast-iron skillet over medium-low heat. Remove 3 tablespoons melted butter, and add to bread mixture.
• **Sprinkle** brown sugar over butter remaining in skillet. Sprinkle cherries and pecans over brown sugar mixture, and arrange pineapple tidbits over cherries. Pour bread mixture over fruit in skillet.
• **Bake** at 350° for 35 to 40 minutes or until bread pudding is set and lightly browned.
• **Place** a platter or large cake plate over skillet, and invert skillet so pudding falls out, upside down, onto plate. Spoon any glaze left in the skillet onto bread pudding. Yield: 9 servings.

CHOCOLATE MOUSSE AU GRAND MARNIER

make ahead

1 (4-ounce) package sweet baking chocolate
4 (1-ounce) squares semisweet chocolate
¼ cup Grand Marnier or other orange-flavored liqueur
2 cups whipping cream
½ cup sifted powdered sugar
Garnishes: orange rind strips, whipped cream

• **Combine** first 3 ingredients in top of a double boiler; bring water to a boil. Reduce heat to low; cook until chocolates melt. Remove from heat, and cool to luke-warm. (Mixture will thicken and appear grainy as it cools.)
• **Beat** whipping cream at medium speed with an electric mixer until foamy; gradually add powdered sugar, beating until soft peaks form. Gently fold about one-fourth of whipped cream mixture into chocolate mixture; fold in remaining whipped cream mixture. Spoon into individual dishes; chill until ready to serve. Garnish, if desired. Yield: 6 servings.

Let Them Eat Dessert

No matter what I serve my guests, it seems they like dessert the best …

In the pursuit of optimum health, we sacrificed salt, whole milk, and fried food. But don't mess with dessert. As the new century opens, Euro style dominates the dessert cart: crème brûlée and tiramisù all around. But, don't count out Ameri-style comfort food. It goes upscale (Pumpkin Flan, page 104, and Pineapple Upside-Down Bread Pudding, left), and continues strongly.

EASY FUDGE BROWNIE TRIFLE

make ahead

This easy fudge brownie dessert is ideal for potluck occasions or supper club crowds.

1 (19.8-ounce) package fudge brownie mix
¼ cup praline or coffee-flavored liqueur (optional)
1 (3.9-ounce) package chocolate fudge instant pudding mix
8 (1.4-ounce) toffee-flavored candy bars, crushed
1 (12-ounce) container frozen whipped topping, thawed
Garnish: chocolate curls

• **Prepare** brownie mix according to package directions. Bake according to package directions in a 13- x 9-inch pan. Prick top of warm brownies at 1-inch intervals with a wooden pick, and brush with liqueur, if desired. Cool; crumble into small pieces.
• **Prepare** pudding according to package directions, omitting chilling procedure.
• **Place** half of crumbled brownies in bottom of a 3-quart trifle bowl; top with half each of pudding, crushed candy bars, and whipped topping. Repeat layers with remaining half of crumbled brownies, pudding, candy bars, and whipped topping. Cover and chill at least 8 hours. Garnish, if desired. Yield: 16 servings.

Fudge Swirl Soufflé

FUDGE SWIRL SOUFFLÉ

A rich swirl of chocolate and vanilla awaits under the puffed hat of this showy soufflé.

¾ cup sugar
½ cup all-purpose flour
¾ teaspoon salt
1⅓ cups milk
1 teaspoon vanilla extract
1 cup (6 ounces) semisweet chocolate morsels
6 large eggs, separated
¼ teaspoon cream of tartar
Garnish: chocolate curls
Crème Anglaise (optional)

• **Combine** first 3 ingredients in a saucepan. Combine milk and vanilla; gradually stir into sugar mixture. Cook over medium heat, stirring constantly, 15 minutes or until mixture thickens. Remove from heat.
• **Transfer** half of mixture to a bowl. Add chocolate morsels to remaining mixture in saucepan; stir until melted.
• **Beat** egg yolks at medium speed with an electric mixer until thick and pale. In another bowl, beat egg whites and cream of tartar at high speed until stiff peaks form, using clean, dry beaters. Stir half of egg yolks and whites into vanilla custard mixture and half into chocolate custard mixture.
• **Pour** mixtures alternately in a zig-zag pattern into an ungreased 3-quart soufflé dish or casserole. Cut through mixture with a knife to create a swirl.
• **Bake** at 325° for 65 to 70 minutes or until set. Serve immediately. Garnish soufflé, and serve with Crème Anglaise, if desired. Yield: 8 servings.

Crème Anglaise
2 cups milk
½ cup sugar, divided
5 egg yolks
½ teaspoon vanilla extract

• Combine milk and ¼ cup sugar in a heavy non-aluminum saucepan. Bring to a simmer over medium heat. Beat remaining ¼ cup sugar and egg yolks at high speed until pale and mixture forms a ribbon.
• Gradually add hot milk mixture to egg mixture, whisking until blended; return to saucepan. Cook over medium-low heat, stirring constantly, until custard thickens slightly and coats a spoon. Remove from heat; strain, if necessary. Stir in vanilla. Cover and chill. Yield: 2 cups.

BUTTER PECAN ICE CREAM

Toasted pecans churned with a rich custard make this ice cream better than any store-bought brand.

1 cup firmly packed brown sugar
½ cup water
⅛ teaspoon salt
2 large eggs, lightly beaten
2 tablespoons butter or margarine
1 cup milk
1 teaspoon vanilla extract
1 cup whipping cream
½ cup chopped pecans, toasted

• **Combine** first 3 ingredients in top of a double boiler over simmering water. Cook until sugar dissolves. Stir about one-fourth of hot mixture into beaten eggs; add to remaining hot mixture.
• **Cook** over hot, not boiling, water until mixture is thickened and reaches 160°, stirring constantly. Stir in butter; remove from heat, and cool. Stir milk and vanilla into egg mixture.
• **Beat** whipping cream at medium speed with an electric mixer until soft peaks form; fold whipped cream into custard mixture. Stir in pecans.
• **Pour** mixture into freezer container of a half-gallon hand-turned or electric freezer. Freeze according to manufacturer's instructions.
• **Pack** freezer with additional ice and rock salt, and let stand 1 hour before serving. Yield: 4 cups.

CREAMY PEACH ICE CREAM

~family favorite ~

Pick fragrant fresh peaches at their peak in the middle of summer for this homemade ice cream shown on page 100.

6 cups mashed ripe peaches (about 2½ pounds)
1 cup sugar
3 large eggs
1½ cups sugar
2 tablespoons all-purpose flour
½ teaspoon salt
4 cups milk
1 cup whipping cream
1 tablespoon vanilla extract
Garnishes: fresh peach slices, thin gingersnaps

• **Combine** peaches and 1 cup sugar; stir well, and set aside.
• **Beat** eggs at medium speed with an electric mixer until frothy. Combine 1½ cups sugar, flour, and salt; stir well. Gradually add sugar mixture to eggs; beat until thickened. Gradually add milk; blend well.
• **Pour** custard mixture into a large saucepan. Cook over medium-low heat, stirring constantly, until mixture thickens and coats back of a metal spoon (about 20 minutes). Remove from heat, and set pan over a bowl of ice water; stir gently until custard cools. Stir in whipping cream, vanilla, and mashed peaches.
• **Pour** mixture into freezer container of a 1-gallon hand-turned or electric freezer. Freeze according to manufacturer's instructions.
• **Pack** freezer with additional ice and rock salt, and let stand 1 hour before serving. Garnish, if desired. Yield: 11 cups.

PEPPERMINT ICE CREAM

Use old-fashioned soft peppermint stick candy for this recipe. The peppermint will dissolve as it's churned with the thick custard.

2 cups sugar
4 large eggs
4 cups milk
2 cups whipping cream
1 pound soft peppermint stick candy, finely crushed (about 20 sticks or 3 cups finely crushed)
1 teaspoon peppermint extract
Additional milk

• **Combine** first 3 ingredients in a large saucepan, stirring gently with a wire whisk. Cook over medium heat, whisking constantly, 15 to 20 minutes or until mixture thickens and coats back of a metal spoon. Remove from heat, and cool completely. Cover and chill thoroughly.
• **Combine** whipping cream, crushed candy, and extract; add to chilled custard.
• **Pour** mixture into freezer container of a 1-gallon hand-turned or electric freezer; add milk to fill line. Freeze according to manufacturer's instructions.
• **Pack** freezer with additional ice and rock salt, and let stand 1 hour before serving. Yield: 1 gallon.

FRANGELICO CREAM

make ahead

Keep the servings small for this divine hazelnut-enhanced ice cream.

⅔ cup hazelnuts or slivered almonds
¾ cup sugar
1¾ cups milk
½ cup sugar, divided
5 egg yolks
¼ cup Frangelico or other hazelnut-flavored liqueur
1 cup whipping cream

• **Place** hazelnuts in an ungreased 15- x 10-inch jellyroll pan. Bake at 350° for 12 to 15 minutes or until skins begin to split. Transfer hot nuts to a colander, and cover with a kitchen towel. Rub nuts briskly with a towel to remove skins. Chop nuts.
• **Sprinkle** ¾ cup sugar in a large heavy skillet. Cook over medium heat, stirring constantly with a wooden spoon, until sugar melts and turns light brown. Remove from heat; add nuts, and stir. Immediately pour mixture into buttered jellyroll pan. Cool 1 hour. Break brittle into small pieces; set aside.
• **Combine** milk and 2 tablespoons sugar in a heavy saucepan; cook over medium heat until mixture comes to a boil.
• **Beat** egg yolks and remaining sugar at medium speed with an electric mixer until thick and pale. Gradually stir about one-fourth of hot mixture into yolks; add to remaining hot mixture, stirring constantly. Add Frangelico. Cook over low heat 5 minutes or until mixture reaches 160°, stirring constantly. (Mixture will not thicken). Do not boil. Cool; cover and chill thoroughly. Stir in whipping cream and brittle.
• **Pour** mixture into freezer container of a half-gallon hand-turned or electric freezer. Freeze according to manufacturer's instructions.
• **Pack** freezer with additional ice and rock salt, and let stand 1 hour before serving. Yield: 4 cups.

PINEAPPLE SHERBET

Pineapple Sherbet makes a refreshing ending to a summer meal. Serve it in champagne flutes, and garnish with fresh herb sprigs.

6 cups milk
2 cups half-and-half
3 cups sugar
Juice of 4 lemons (½ cup)
1 cup whipping cream
1 (15½-ounce) can crushed pineapple, drained

• **Combine** first 3 ingredients, stirring until sugar dissolves. Stir in lemon juice.
• **Beat** whipping cream at medium speed with an electric mixer just until thickened; fold into milk mixture. Fold in pineapple.
• **Pour** pineapple mixture into freezer container of a 1-gallon hand turned or electric freezer. Freeze according to manufacturer's instructions.
• **Pack** freezer with additional ice and rock salt, and let stand 1 hour before serving. Yield: 13 cups.

We've Been Scooped

Southern Living **has a warm spot** for ice cream and it shows in the recipes. In the last 20 years, we've shared nine recipes for strawberry ice cream, 10 versions for vanilla, 11 ways to make peach, and 12 variations of chocolate. For variety, we've made fennel, piña colada, fig, and even scuppernong ice cream. Meanwhile, ice cream makers such as Häagen-Dazs and Ben and Jerry have made top quality blends the industry standard. Cherry Garcia or Chunky Monkey anyone?

HOLIDAY SORBET

make ahead

1½ cups orange juice
1 cup water
⅔ cup sugar
1 (12-ounce) package fresh cranberries
2 tablespoons Grand Marnier or other
    orange-flavored liqueur (optional)
1¾ cups water
⅓ cup sugar
1½ teaspoons lemon juice
1 (6-ounce) can frozen limeade concentrate,
    thawed and undiluted
Garnishes: fresh cranberries, fresh mint sprigs

• **Combine** first 4 ingredients in a large saucepan; bring to a boil. Cover, reduce heat, and simmer 6 to 8 minutes or until cranberry skins pop. Remove from heat, and cool 10 minutes.
• **Process** half of cranberry mixture in food processor until smooth, stopping once to scrape down sides. Repeat procedure with remaining cranberry mixture. Pour cranberry mixture through a large wire-mesh strainer into a bowl, discarding pulp. Stir in liqueur, if desired. Pour mixture into a 13- x 9-inch pan; cover and freeze until mixture is firm.
• **Combine** 1¾ cups water and ⅓ cup sugar in a saucepan; cook over medium heat, stirring constantly, until sugar dissolves. Remove from heat, and stir in lemon juice and limeade concentrate. Pour mixture into an 8-inch square pan; cover and freeze until firm.
• **Process** frozen limeade mixture in food processor until smooth. Set aside. Process half of frozen cranberry mixture until smooth; spread evenly into a 9- x 5-inch loafpan. Spoon limeade mixture over cranberry mixture in pan, spreading evenly. Process remaining frozen cranberry mixture until smooth; spread over limeade mixture. Cover and freeze until firm. Remove from pan; cut into slices. Garnish, if desired. Yield: 8 servings.

STRAWBERRY DELIGHT

quick

Fresh strawberries take center stage in this easy last-minute dessert.

1 quart pineapple sherbet
1½ cups sliced fresh strawberries
¾ cup champagne or sparkling white grape juice

• **Spoon** sherbet evenly into six stemmed glasses. Top each serving with ¼ cup strawberries. Pour champagne over each serving. Serve immediately. Yield: 6 servings.

FROZEN ALMOND-APRICOT SQUARES

make ahead

Quick to make and it serves a crowd—this is one of those trusted desserts that's a guaranteed success.

¼ cup chopped almonds, toasted
1⅓ cups crushed vanilla wafers
2 tablespoons butter or margarine, melted
1 teaspoon almond extract
½ gallon vanilla ice cream, softened
1 (12-ounce) jar apricot preserves

• **Combine** first 4 ingredients; stir well, and set aside ½ cup crumb mixture.
• **Sprinkle** half of remaining crumb mixture into a 9-inch square pan; top with half of ice cream and half of preserves. Repeat layers. Sprinkle reserved ½ cup crumbs on top. Cover and freeze at least 4 hours or until firm. Let stand at room temperature 10 minutes before serving. Yield: 9 servings.

PEACH MELBA BOMBE

make ahead

*Tall desserts make a statement at the table.
This frozen peach ice cream mold is no exception,
especially once you add the brilliantly
colored raspberry sauce.*

1 (16-ounce) package frozen unsweetened sliced
  peaches, thawed and drained
1 (8-ounce) carton sour cream
½ cup grenadine
½ gallon vanilla ice cream, softened
Raspberry Sauce
Garnishes: fresh raspberries, fresh mint sprigs

• **Process** peaches in a food processor until smooth. Add
sour cream and grenadine; process until well blended.
• **Combine** peach mixture and ice cream in a large
bowl; stir until well blended. Pour mixture into a lightly greased 12-cup mold; cover and freeze 8 hours or
until firm.
• **Two** hours before serving, loosen edges of ice cream
from mold, using the tip of a knife. Dip mold halfway
into warm water to loosen, and wrap a warm wet towel
around mold for 30 seconds. Invert mold onto a chilled
serving plate. Remove towel. Shake mold gently, and
slowly remove mold. Immediately return bombe to
freezer.
• **To serve,** cut bombe into slices, and top each with
Raspberry Sauce. Garnish, if desired. Yield: 12
servings.

Raspberry Sauce
1 (14-ounce) package frozen unsweetened
  raspberries, thawed and undrained
¾ cup light corn syrup
¼ cup Grand Marnier

• **Process** raspberries in a food processor until pureed.
Strain raspberries; discard seeds. Stir in corn syrup and
Grand Marnier. Yield: 2 cups.

TOFFEE ICE CREAM DESSERT

family favorite, make ahead

*This layered ice cream dessert is simple to make.
The crunchy cookie crust, brickle filling, and
fudge topping are all hard to resist.*

3 cups cream-filled chocolate sandwich cookie
  crumbs
2 tablespoons butter or margarine, melted
½ gallon vanilla ice cream, softened
1 (7.5-ounce) package almond brickle chips
Commercial fudge sauce, heated
Frozen whipped topping, thawed
Maraschino cherries (optional)

• **Combine** chocolate cookie crumbs and butter, stirring with a fork. Press firmly into bottom of a lightly
greased 13- x 9-inch baking dish. Bake at 350° for 5
minutes. Cool.
• **Spread** half of ice cream over crust; sprinkle with
half of brickle chips. Repeat layers. Cover and freeze
until firm.
• **Cut** ice cream into squares to serve. Top each serving with fudge sauce, a dollop of whipped topping, and
a cherry, if desired. Yield: 15 servings.

*Lemon Meringue
Cream Cups*

LEMON MERINGUE CREAM CUPS

⁓ make ahead ⁓

Wow your friends with these crisp, snow white baked meringues filled with our luscious lemon pudding and decorated with fresh berries. Try commercial lemon curd for a shortcut filling option.

3 egg whites
Pinch of salt
1 teaspoon lemon juice
½ cup sugar
Lemon Cream Filling
Garnishes: fresh berries, lemon verbena sprigs, or
  fresh mint sprigs

• **Place** a sheet of parchment paper on a baking sheet. Draw six 3½-inch circles on parchment paper. Turn parchment paper over; secure with masking tape.
• **Beat** egg whites, salt, and lemon juice at high speed with an electric mixer until foamy. Gradually add sugar, 1 tablespoon at a time, beating until stiff peaks form and sugar dissolves (2 to 4 minutes).
• **Spoon** meringue into a pastry bag fitted with a large round tip, and pipe about 1 tablespoon meringue in center of each circle on parchment paper; spread evenly to edges of circles, using a spoon. Pipe meringue around edges of circles to create cups (sides should be about 2 inches high).
• **Bake** at 200° for 1½ hours. Turn oven off; leave meringues in oven at least 12 hours to dry. Carefully remove meringues from paper.
• **Spoon** Lemon Cream Filling into meringue cups. Garnish, if desired. Yield: 6 servings.

Lemon Cream Filling

3 large eggs
½ cup sugar
3 tablespoons fresh lemon juice
1½ teaspoons grated lemon rind
½ cup whipping cream, whipped (optional)

• **Beat** eggs at medium speed until thick and pale. Add sugar and lemon juice; beat well. Stir in lemon rind. Transfer mixture to a 2-quart saucepan; cook over medium-low heat, stirring constantly, until mixture is thickened and reaches 160°. Cool completely. Fold whipped cream into cooled mixture, if desired. Yield: 1⅔ cups.

NOTE: We've made the whipped cream an option for the filling; if you don't add it, the filling is a deeper yellow and the flavor is slightly more tangy.

BANANAS FOSTER

⁓ quick ⁓

New Orleans is famous for its fabulous food. And it's nice to know some of the classic desserts are still quick and easy, like this favorite from the Crescent City.

½ cup firmly packed brown sugar
¼ cup butter or margarine, melted
¼ teaspoon ground cinnamon
4 bananas, split and quartered
⅓ cup light rum
Vanilla ice cream

• **Combine** first 3 ingredients in a large skillet; cook over medium heat, stirring constantly, until bubbly. Add banana; cook 2 to 3 minutes or until thoroughly heated, basting constantly with syrup mixture.
• **Heat** rum in a small saucepan over medium heat (do not boil). Quickly pour rum over banana mixture; immediately ignite with a long match. Let flames die down; serve immediately over ice cream. Yield: 4 servings.

NOTE: When flambéing a food such as Bananas Foster, use a long-handled match. Hold the lighted match just above the liquid mixture. You want to light the fumes, not the liquid itself. Most important, don't lean over the pan. Stand back to ignite the mixture.

CHOCOLATE DECADENCE

16 (1-ounce) squares semisweet chocolate
⅔ cup butter
5 large eggs
2 tablespoons sugar
2 tablespoons all-purpose flour
2 cups fresh raspberries
2 cups water
¼ cup sugar
2 tablespoons cornstarch
2 tablespoons water
Whipped cream
Garnish: fresh raspberries

• **Line** bottom of a 9-inch springform pan with parchment paper; set aside.
• **Combine** chocolate and butter in a large heavy saucepan. Cook over low heat until chocolate melts. Gradually add chocolate mixture to eggs, beating at medium speed with an electric mixer 10 minutes. Fold in 2 tablespoons sugar and flour. Pour mixture into prepared pan. Bake at 400° for 15 minutes. (Cake will not be set in center.) Remove from oven; cover and chill thoroughly.
• **Combine** 2 cups fresh raspberries, 2 cups water, and ¼ cup sugar in a large saucepan; bring to a boil over medium-high heat. Reduce heat, and simmer 30 minutes, stirring occasionally. Pour raspberry mixture through a wire-mesh strainer into a bowl, discarding seeds. Return raspberry mixture to pan.
• **Combine** cornstarch and 2 tablespoons water; add to raspberry mixture. Cook over medium heat, stirring constantly, until mixture comes to a boil; boil 1 minute, stirring constantly. Cool completely.
• **To serve,** spoon 2 to 3 tablespoons raspberry sauce onto each dessert plate; place wedge of chocolate dessert on sauce. Top each wedge with a dollop of whipped cream. Garnish, if desired. Yield: 12 servings.

BAVARIAN APPLE TORTE

This rustic apple dessert has European flair. Crème fraîche is a smooth accompaniment with the browned almond-topped apples.

½ cup butter or margarine, softened
⅓ cup sugar
1⅓ cups all-purpose flour
¼ teaspoon vanilla extract
1 (8-ounce) package cream cheese, softened
¼ cup sugar
1 large egg
½ teaspoon vanilla extract
⅓ cup sugar
½ teaspoon ground cinnamon
3 Granny Smith apples, peeled and sliced (4 cups)
¼ cup sliced almonds

• **Beat** butter and ⅓ cup sugar in a small mixing bowl at medium speed with an electric mixer until fluffy. Gradually add flour, beating until mixture is blended. Stir in ¼ teaspoon vanilla. (Mixture will be slightly crumbly.)
• **Press** pastry into bottom and 1½ inches up sides of a lightly greased 9-inch springform pan.
• **Beat** cream cheese and ¼ cup sugar at medium speed until smooth. Add egg and ½ teaspoon vanilla, beating well. Spread filling evenly over pastry.
• **Combine** ⅓ cup sugar, cinnamon, and apples, tossing lightly. Arrange apple slices over cream cheese mixture; sprinkle with almonds.
• **Bake** at 400° for 40 minutes. Cool on a wire rack. Remove sides of pan. Serve warm or chilled. Top with crème fraîche, sour cream, or ice cream, if desired. Yield: 1 (9-inch) torte.

NOTE: Look for crème fraîche packaged in small tubs near specialty cheeses at a supermarket deli.

Bavarian Apple Torte

CRANBERRIES JUBILEE

quick

These scarlet jewels are a takeoff on cherries jubilee and are perfect for a Christmas dessert.

1 cup sugar
1 cup water
⅛ teaspoon ground cinnamon
2 cups fresh cranberries
⅓ cup chopped pecans
3 tablespoons rum
Vanilla ice cream

• **Combine** first 3 ingredients in a large saucepan. Bring to a boil over medium heat, stirring occasionally; boil 5 minutes. Add cranberries, and return to a boil; cook 5 minutes, stirring occasionally. Stir in pecans. Remove from heat.
• **Place** rum in a long-handled small saucepan; heat just until warm (do not boil). Remove from heat. Ignite with a long match; pour over cranberries. When flames die down, spoon over ice cream. Yield: 1½ cups.

STRAWBERRIES ROMANOFF

quick

Cointreau is a fine French colorless liqueur, great for splashing over fresh strawberries. If you have other orange-flavored spirits on hand, they'll work, too.

1 quart fresh strawberries
½ cup sifted powdered sugar
¼ cup Cointreau
1 cup whipping cream, whipped
⅓ cup Cointreau
1 pint vanilla ice cream, softened

• **Wash** and hull strawberries; cut into halves. Add sugar and ¼ cup Cointreau; toss gently, and set aside. Fold whipped cream and ⅓ cup Cointreau into softened ice cream.
• **Place** strawberry mixture in chilled stemmed glasses. Top with ice cream mixture. Yield: 6 servings.

TROPICAL FRUIT COMPOTE WITH RASPBERRY PUREE

quick

Showcase the natural beauty and flavor of island fruits in this simple summertime dessert.

3 kiwifruit, peeled and cut into wedges
1 medium pineapple, peeled and cubed
1 papaya, peeled, seeded, and cubed
1 large banana, sliced
¼ cup kirsch or other cherry brandy, divided
1 (10-ounce) package frozen raspberries in syrup, thawed

• **Combine** first 4 ingredients in a large bowl. Add 2 tablespoons kirsch; toss gently. Cover and chill.
• **Process** raspberries in container of an electric blender or food processor until smooth. Strain raspberries; discard seeds. Add remaining 2 tablespoons kirsch, and stir well.
• **To serve,** spoon chilled fruit into compotes; top each serving with raspberry puree. Yield: 8 servings.

CRÊPES FITZGERALD

Sugar and liqueur draw just enough juice from fresh berries for you to spoon over these light crêpes. Tucked inside is a sweet sour cream and cheese filling.

3 cups sliced fresh strawberries
2 tablespoons sugar
2 tablespoons kirsch or other cherry-flavored brandy
1 (8-ounce) package cream cheese, softened
¾ cup sour cream
2 tablespoons sugar
2 teaspoons grated lemon rind
Crêpes

• **Combine** first 3 ingredients in a bowl; toss gently, and set aside.
• **Combine** cream cheese, sour cream, and 2 tablespoons sugar; beat at high speed with an electric mixer until light and fluffy. Stir in lemon rind. Cover and chill.
• **Prepare** crêpes. Spoon about 1 tablespoon cream cheese mixture in center of each crêpe; roll up, place on platter, and keep warm. Just before serving, spoon strawberries over crêpes. Yield: 8 servings.

Crêpes
¾ cup all-purpose flour
Pinch of salt
1¼ cups milk
1 large egg
1 egg yolk
1 tablespoon butter or margarine, melted
Vegetable oil

• **Process** first 6 ingredients in container of an electric blender until smooth.
• **Brush** bottom of a 6-inch crêpe pan or heavy skillet with oil; place over medium heat until hot. Pour 2 tablespoons batter into pan; quickly tilt pan in all directions so batter covers bottom. Cook 1 minute or until crêpe can be shaken loose. Turn crêpe over, and cook about 30 seconds. Place crêpe on a cloth towel to cool. Repeat with remaining batter. Yield: 16 crêpes.

PEACH CARDINALE

3 cups water
1 cup sugar
4 fresh peaches, peeled and halved
1 vanilla bean, split lengthwise
1 (10-ounce) package frozen raspberries in syrup, thawed
¼ cup water
1 tablespoon sugar
2 teaspoons cornstarch
½ cup whipping cream, whipped
Garnish: fresh mint leaves

• **Combine** water and 1 cup sugar in a Dutch oven; bring to a boil. Boil 3 minutes. Reduce heat to medium-low; add peach halves and vanilla bean. Simmer, uncovered, 5 minutes or until peaches are tender. Remove from heat. Chill peaches in sugar syrup at least 1 hour.
• **Process** raspberries and ¼ cup water in a food processor until pureed. Pour raspberry mixture into a wire-mesh strainer; press with back of a spoon against sides of strainer to squeeze out juice and pulp. Discard seeds.
• **Combine** 1 tablespoon sugar and cornstarch; stir into raspberry puree. Bring to a boil over medium heat. Boil 1 minute, stirring constantly. Remove from heat; cool. Chill.
• **Spoon** whipped cream into four dessert dishes. Put 2 peach halves together, and place on top of cream in each dish. Pour ¼ cup raspberry sauce around each peach. Garnish, if desired. Yield: 4 servings.

NOTE: You can substitute 1 tablespoon vanilla extract for the vanilla bean, if desired.

Eggs and Cheese

They're like two old faithful
friends we enjoy routinely at
mealtime. Eggs and cheese bind
and thicken a multitude of foods.
They lend luxurious texture, rich
flavor, and an airy lift to dishes
such as the soufflé opposite.

Corn-and-Cheese Soufflé (page 132)

CLASSIC STUFFED EGGS

family favorite

This classic stuffed egg recipe will dress up a dozen eggs for a brunch. Let fresh herbs from the garden be a simple garnish.

12 large eggs
3 tablespoons mayonnaise
1 tablespoon sugar
1 tablespoon Dijon mustard
1 tablespoon vinegar
1 teaspoon hot sauce
1 teaspoon Worcestershire sauce
⅛ teaspoon salt
Paprika
Garnish: fresh herb sprigs

• **Place** eggs in a large saucepan or Dutch oven. Add enough water to measure at least 1 inch above eggs. Cover and quickly bring to a boil. Remove from heat. Let stand, covered, in hot water 15 minutes. Drain. Immediately run cold water over eggs or place them in ice water until cooled completely.
• **To remove** shell, gently tap each egg all over, and roll between hands to loosen shell; then hold egg under cold running water as you peel the shell.
• **Slice** eggs in half lengthwise, and carefully remove yolks. Mash yolks; add mayonnaise and next 6 ingredients. Stir well. Spoon egg yolk mixture into egg whites. Sprinkle with paprika; garnish, if desired. Yield: 2 dozen.

BACON-STUFFED EGGS

6 large eggs
½ (8-ounce) package cream cheese, softened
2 to 3 tablespoons mayonnaise
2 teaspoons prepared horseradish
1 teaspoon Worcestershire sauce
¼ teaspoon pepper
4 bacon slices, cooked and crumbled

• **Place** eggs in a large saucepan or Dutch oven. Add enough water to measure at least 1 inch above eggs. Cover and quickly bring to a boil. Remove from heat. Let stand, covered, in hot water 15 minutes. Drain. Immediately run cold water over eggs or place them in ice water until cooled completely.
• **To remove** shell, gently tap each egg all over, and roll between hands to loosen egg shell; then hold egg under cold running water as you peel the shell.
• **Slice** eggs in half lengthwise, and carefully remove yolks; mash yolks with a fork. Add cream cheese and next 4 ingredients to yolks, stirring until smooth. Stir in bacon, and spoon into egg whites. Yield: 1 dozen.

HAM AND EGGS À LA SWISS

quick

Set ham, sliced cooked eggs, and cheese high atop crusty English muffins for a filling breakfast.

4 English muffins, split
3 tablespoons butter or margarine, softened
½ pound thinly sliced deli ham
4 hard-cooked eggs, sliced
½ cup sour cream
½ cup mayonnaise
1 cup (4 ounces) shredded Swiss cheese
Paprika
Garnish: pickled jalapeño pepper slices

• **Spread** muffins with butter. Toast muffins until lightly browned. Divide ham evenly among muffin halves. Arrange egg slices evenly over ham. Set aside.
• **Combine** sour cream and mayonnaise, stirring well. Spoon mixture evenly over sandwiches; sprinkle each half with shredded cheese and paprika.
• **Place** sandwiches on a baking sheet. Broil 5½ inches from heat 1 to 2 minutes or until cheese melts and sandwiches are heated. Garnish, if desired. Yield: 4 servings.

Ham and Eggs à la Swiss

POACHED FLORENTINE EGGS

1 (9-ounce) package frozen creamed spinach
3 ripe plum tomatoes
½ teaspoon dried oregano
½ teaspoon dried basil
2 tablespoons butter or margarine
2 tablespoons freshly grated Parmesan cheese
4 large eggs
2 English muffins, split and toasted
¼ teaspoon salt
¼ teaspoon pepper
Freshly grated Parmesan cheese
6 bacon slices, cooked and crumbled

• **Cook** spinach according to package directions, and keep warm.
• **Cut** tomatoes into ¼-inch-thick slices; place in a 15- x 10-inch jellyroll pan. Sprinkle with oregano and basil; dot with butter. Sprinkle with 2 tablespoons cheese. Broil tomato slices 5½ inches from heat 2 minutes.
• **Bring** 2 inches of water to a boil in a large saucepan; reduce heat to maintain a light simmer. Break eggs, 1 at a time, into a saucer; slip eggs, 1 at a time, into water, holding saucer close to water surface. Simmer 5 minutes or until done. Remove with a slotted spoon, and trim edges, if desired.
• **Top** muffin halves with tomato. Place eggs over tomato; sprinkle evenly with salt and pepper. Top with spinach, and sprinkle with cheese. Top with bacon; serve immediately. Yield: 2 servings.

CHEESE-CHIVE SCRAMBLED EGGS

~ quick ~

6 large eggs, lightly beaten
2 tablespoons water
¼ teaspoon seasoned salt
Dash of pepper
2 tablespoons butter or margarine
1 (3-ounce) package cream cheese, cut into ¼-inch cubes and softened
1 tablespoon chopped fresh chives

• **Combine** first 4 ingredients.
• **Melt** butter in a large nonstick skillet over medium heat, tilting pan to coat bottom.
• **Add** egg mixture to pan; top with cream cheese and chives.
• **Cook,** without stirring, until mixture begins to set on bottom. Draw a spatula across bottom of pan to form large curds. Continue cooking until eggs are thickened but still moist; do not stir constantly. Yield: 4 servings.

TEX-MEX EGG BURRITOS

~ quick ~

These breakfast burritos are a nod to the Southwest. Top them with fresh cilantro for extra kick.

4 (8-inch) flour tortillas
½ pound hot ground pork sausage
6 large eggs, lightly beaten
1 (4.5-ounce) can chopped green chiles, undrained
Picante sauce
Shredded Cheddar cheese

• **Heat** tortillas according to package directions.
• **Meanwhile,** brown sausage in a large skillet, stirring until it crumbles; drain and return to skillet. Add eggs

and chiles to sausage. Cook, without stirring, until mixture begins to set on bottom. Draw a spatula across bottom of pan to form large curds. Continue cooking until eggs are thickened but still moist. Do not stir constantly.

• **Spoon** egg mixture evenly down centers of warm tortillas; top each with picante sauce and cheese. Fold opposite sides over filling. Serve immediately. Yield: 4 servings.

SAUSAGE OMELETS

½ pound ground pork sausage
1 cup sliced fresh mushrooms
2 tablespoons butter or margarine
2 tablespoons all-purpose flour
¾ cup milk
2 (3-ounce) packages cream cheese, cubed
¼ teaspoon salt
⅛ teaspoon pepper
8 large eggs, lightly beaten
3 tablespoons water
½ teaspoon salt
¼ teaspoon pepper
1 tablespoon plus 1 teaspoon butter or
   margarine, divided

• **Brown** sausage in a 10-inch omelet pan or nonstick skillet, stirring until it crumbles; drain, reserving drippings in pan. Pat sausage dry with paper towels, and set aside.

• **Cook** mushrooms in drippings over medium-high heat, stirring constantly, until tender. Drain and pat dry with paper towels. Wipe drippings from skillet with a paper towel.

• **Melt** 2 tablespoons butter in a heavy saucepan over low heat; add flour, stirring until smooth. Cook 1 minute, stirring constantly. Gradually add milk, and cook over medium heat, stirring constantly, until mixture is thickened and bubbly. Add cream cheese, ¼ teaspoon salt, and ⅛ teaspoon pepper; stir until cream cheese melts. Stir in sausage and mushrooms. Set aside, and keep warm.

• **Combine** eggs and next 3 ingredients; stir with a wire whisk until blended. Heat omelet pan or nonstick skillet over medium heat until hot enough to sizzle a drop of water. Add 2 teaspoons butter, and tilt pan to coat bottom. Pour half of egg mixture into pan. As mixture starts to cook, gently lift edges of omelet with a spatula, and tilt pan so uncooked portion flows underneath.

• **Spoon** half of sausage mixture evenly over half of omelet. Fold omelet in half; transfer to a serving plate. Repeat procedure with remaining ingredients. Cut omelets in half to serve. Serve immediately. Yield: 4 servings.

SHIITAKE MUSHROOM OMELET

quick

2 ounces large shiitake mushrooms
2 tablespoons butter or margarine, divided
1 small onion, finely chopped
⅔ cup cottage cheese
4 large eggs, lightly beaten
¼ teaspoon salt
¼ teaspoon freshly ground pepper

• **Remove** stems from mushrooms; discard. Slice mushroom caps.

• **Melt** 1 tablespoon butter in a nonstick skillet over medium-high heat; add mushrooms and onion, and cook, stirring constantly, until tender. Transfer to a bowl, and stir in cottage cheese.

• **Combine** eggs, salt, and pepper in a bowl; beat lightly with a fork.

• **Melt** remaining 1 tablespoon butter in a 10-inch omelet pan or nonstick skillet, rotating pan to coat bottom evenly. Add egg mixture. As mixture starts to cook, gently lift edges of omelet with a spatula, and tilt pan so uncooked portion flows underneath.

• **Spoon** mushroom mixture onto omelet; fold in half, and transfer to a serving plate. Cut omelet in half to serve. Serve immediately. Yield: 2 servings.

HUEVOS RANCHEROS

~family favorite~

6 (6-inch) corn tortillas
1 cup chopped onion
1 cup chopped green pepper
2 cloves garlic, minced
3 tablespoons olive oil
1 tablespoon all-purpose flour
2 (16-ounce) cans whole tomatoes, drained and
   chopped
1 (4.5-ounce) can chopped green chiles
¼ cup dry white wine or chicken broth
½ teaspoon dried oregano
½ teaspoon ground cumin
½ teaspoon chili powder
¼ teaspoon salt
⅛ teaspoon pepper
6 large eggs
1 cup (4 ounces) shredded sharp Cheddar cheese
¼ cup sliced ripe olives

• **Wrap** tortillas tightly in aluminum foil; bake at 350° for 15 minutes or until thoroughly heated. Set aside, and keep warm.
• **Cook** onion, green pepper, and garlic in hot oil in a large skillet over medium heat, stirring constantly, 5 to 10 minutes or until vegetables are tender. Add flour; cook 1 minute, stirring constantly. Add tomatoes and next 7 ingredients; stir well. Bring to a boil over medium heat, stirring constantly; cook, uncovered, 10 minutes or until mixture is thickened, stirring often.
• **Line** a lightly greased 11- x 7-inch baking dish with warm tortillas, letting tortillas extend up sides of dish. Pour tomato mixture into dish; spread evenly over tortillas. Make 6 indentations in tomato mixture, using back of a spoon; carefully break 1 egg into each indentation. Bake, uncovered, at 350° for 20 minutes or just until eggs are set. Sprinkle with cheese and olives; bake 5 more minutes or until cheese melts. Yield: 6 servings.

GREEK SPINACH QUICHE

Feta and oregano give this quiche Grecian flair.

Pastry for 9-inch pie
3 large eggs, lightly beaten
1 cup milk
¼ cup butter or margarine, melted
2 tablespoons all-purpose flour
2 tablespoons grated Parmesan cheese
¼ teaspoon salt
¼ teaspoon dried oregano
Dash of ground nutmeg
1 (10-ounce) package frozen chopped spinach,
   thawed and well drained
1 cup crumbled feta cheese

• **Line** a 9-inch quiche dish with pastry; trim excess pastry around edges. Prick bottom and sides of pastry with a fork. Bake at 400° for 3 minutes; remove from oven, and gently prick with a fork. Bake 5 more minutes. Set aside.
• **Combine** eggs and next 7 ingredients; stir with a wire whisk until blended. Stir in spinach and feta cheese; pour into pastry shell. Bake at 350° for 35 minutes or until quiche is set and golden. Let stand 10 minutes. Yield: 1 (9-inch) quiche.

SWISS ALPINE QUICHE

Pastry for 9-inch pie
1 (10-ounce) package frozen chopped broccoli
2 cups chopped cooked ham
2 cups (8 ounces) shredded Swiss cheese
3 tablespoons minced onion
3 large eggs, lightly beaten
1½ cups milk
⅛ teaspoon salt
⅛ teaspoon pepper

• **Line** a 9-inch quiche dish with pastry; trim excess pastry around edges. Prick bottom and sides of pastry

with a fork. Bake at 400° for 3 minutes; remove from oven, and gently prick with a fork. Bake 5 more minutes. Set aside.
• **Cook** broccoli according to package directions, omitting salt; drain well. Layer half each of broccoli, ham, and cheese in pastry shell; repeat layers. Sprinkle onion evenly over top.
• **Combine** eggs and remaining 3 ingredients; stir with a wire whisk until blended. Pour over layers in pastry shell. Bake at 450° for 10 minutes. Reduce oven temperature to 325°, and bake 30 minutes or until set and golden. Let stand 10 minutes. Yield: 1 (9-inch) quiche.

CHILE CHEESE QUICHE

Pastry for 9-inch pie
1 **cup (4 ounces) shredded Cheddar cheese**
1½ **cups (6 ounces) shredded Monterey Jack cheese, divided**
1 **(4.5-ounce) can chopped green chiles, drained**
3 **large eggs, lightly beaten**
1 **cup half-and-half**
⅛ **teaspoon salt**
⅛ **teaspoon pepper**

• **Line** a 9-inch quiche dish with pastry; trim excess pastry around edges. Prick bottom and sides of pastry with a fork. Bake at 400° for 3 minutes; remove from oven, and gently prick pastry again. Bake 5 more minutes. Set aside.
• **Layer** Cheddar cheese, ¾ cup Monterey Jack cheese, green chiles, and remaining ¾ cup Monterey Jack cheese in pastry shell. Combine eggs and remaining ingredients; pour into pastry shell. Bake at 350° for 50 minutes or until set. Let stand 10 minutes before serving. Yield: 1 (9-inch) quiche.

Sealed with a Quiche

We learned to pronounce quiche and loved every bite of it.

80ˢ During the '80s, the decade of quiche, *Southern Living* published more than 50 recipes for the savory egg custard pie including tempters such as Pizza Quiche, Green Chile Quiche, and even Spinach Quichelets and Eggless Quiche. Every restaurant worthy of the name offered quiche and *real* men (and women) didn't hesitate to order it.

90ˢ The quiche craze crumbled in the '90s with all but die-hard aficionados labeling the term *passe*. But what's in a name anyway? Savory Summer Pie, a tomato-herb egg custard baked in a shapely crust, graced the cover of *Southern Living* in 1999, updating our beloved quiche for the twenty-first century.

HAM AND GRITS CRUSTLESS QUICHE

½ **cup water**
¼ **teaspoon salt**
⅓ **cup quick-cooking yellow grits, uncooked**
1 **(12-ounce) can evaporated milk**
1½ **cups chopped cooked ham**
1 **cup (4 ounces) shredded sharp Cheddar cheese**
1 **tablespoon chopped fresh parsley**
1 **teaspoon dry mustard**
1 to 2 **teaspoons hot sauce**
3 **large eggs, lightly beaten**

• **Bring** water and salt to a boil in a large saucepan; stir in grits. Remove from heat; cover and let stand 5 minutes (mixture will be thick). Stir in milk and remaining ingredients. Pour into a greased 9½-inch quiche dish or deep-dish pieplate. Bake at 350° for 30 to 35 minutes. Let stand 10 minutes before serving. Yield: 1 (9-inch) quiche.

Salmon Quiche

SALMON QUICHE

Salmon and fresh dill flavor the filling for this brunch quiche, and an almond-cheese mixture forms a complementary crust.

1 cup whole wheat flour
⅔ cup (3 ounces) shredded Cheddar cheese
½ cup chopped almonds
¼ teaspoon salt
¼ teaspoon paprika
¼ cup vegetable oil
3 large eggs, beaten
1 (8-ounce) carton sour cream
½ cup (2 ounces) shredded Cheddar cheese
¼ cup mayonnaise
1 tablespoon grated onion
1 teaspoon chopped fresh dill or ¼ teaspoon
      dried dillweed
⅛ teaspoon hot sauce
1 (14¾-ounce) can salmon, undrained
½ teaspoon chopped fresh dill
Garnishes: slivers of smoked salmon, fresh dill
      sprigs

• **Combine** first 6 ingredients in a medium bowl, stirring until well blended. Press crust mixture in bottom and up sides of a 9-inch quiche dish. Bake at 400° for 10 minutes. Remove from oven; reduce heat to 325°.
• **Combine** eggs and next 6 ingredients in a large bowl; stir well. Drain and flake salmon, reserving liquid. Remove and discard bones and skin from salmon, if desired. Add salmon to egg mixture. Add water to reserved liquid to measure ½ cup; add to salmon mixture, stirring well. Spoon salmon mixture into crust.
• **Bake** at 325° for 45 to 50 minutes. Sprinkle with ½ teaspoon fresh dill. Garnish, if desired. Yield: 1 (9-inch) quiche.

PIZZA QUICHE

1 unbaked 9-inch pastry shell
¾ cup (3 ounces) shredded Swiss cheese
¾ cup (3 ounces) shredded mozzarella cheese
½ cup chopped pepperoni
1 green onion, chopped
3 large eggs, lightly beaten
1 cup half-and-half
½ teaspoon salt
¾ teaspoon dried oregano

• **Line** a 9-inch quiche dish with pastry; trim excess pastry around edges. Prick bottom and sides of pastry with a fork. Bake at 325° for 5 minutes. Cool.
• **Combine** cheeses, pepperoni, and onion; sprinkle into pastry shell. Combine eggs, half-and-half, salt, and oregano; mix well, and pour over cheese mixture in pastry shell. Bake at 325° for 45 minutes. Let stand 10 minutes before serving. Yield: 1 (9-inch) quiche.

BREAKFAST PIZZA

1 (8-ounce) can refrigerated crescent rolls
1 pound ground pork sausage, cooked and drained
1 cup (4 ounces) shredded sharp Cheddar cheese
1 cup (4 ounces) shredded mozzarella cheese
5 large eggs, lightly beaten
½ cup milk
¾ teaspoon dried oregano
⅛ teaspoon pepper

• **Unroll** crescent rolls, separating into 8 triangles. Place triangles with elongated points toward center on a greased 12-inch pizza pan. Press perforations together to form a crust. Bake at 375° for 8 minutes on lower rack of oven. (Crust will be puffy when removed from oven.) Reduce oven temperature to 350°. Spoon sausage over dough; sprinkle with cheeses.
• **Combine** eggs and remaining 3 ingredients; pour over sausage mixture. Bake at 350° on lower rack of oven 30 to 35 minutes or until crust is golden. Yield: 6 servings.

ASPARAGUS-AND-BACON FRITTATA

Plum tomatoes, onion, and asparagus lend garden-fresh flavor to this Italian omelet.

6 large plum tomatoes
1 (12-ounce) package bacon
1 medium onion, chopped
2 garlic cloves, crushed
2 cups (1-inch) fresh asparagus pieces
10 large eggs, lightly beaten
½ teaspoon seasoned salt
¼ teaspoon pepper
½ cup sour cream
¼ cup chopped fresh parsley
2 cups (8 ounces) shredded Cheddar cheese,
     divided

• **Cut** tomatoes into thin slices. Drain well, pressing between layers of paper towels to remove excess moisture; set aside.
• **Cook** bacon in a 12-inch ovenproof skillet until crisp; remove bacon, reserving 1 tablespoon drippings in skillet. Crumble bacon, and s~~e~~ ~~as~~ide.
• **Sauté** onion and garlic in ~~reserved hot~~ drippings 4 to 5 minutes or until tender. Add ~~asparagus~~, and sauté 1 minute.
• **Beat** eggs, seasoned salt, and pepper at medium-high speed with an electric mixer until foamy; stir in sour cream. Pour over vegetables in skillet. Reserve ¼ cup bacon; stir in remaining bacon, parsley, and 1 cup cheese.
• **Cook** over medium-low heat 3 to 4 minutes or until eggs begin to set around edges.
• **Bake** at 350° for 15 minutes. Remove frittata from oven, and top with tomato slices, reserved ¼ cup bacon, and remaining 1 cup cheese.
• **Bake** 10 to 15 more minutes or until frittata is set. Yield: 8 servings.

TWO-PEPPER FRITTATA

This recipe will capture your attention–it's delicious and beautiful. A baking sheet will catch any liquid that leaks from the springform pan during baking.

3 cloves garlic, minced
1 large purple onion, sliced
2 sweet red peppers, cut into thin strips
1 yellow pepper, cut into thin strips
3 tablespoons olive oil, divided
2 yellow squash, thinly sliced
2 zucchini, thinly sliced
½ pound fresh mushrooms, sliced
6 large eggs
¼ cup whipping cream
2½ to 3 teaspoons salt
2 teaspoons freshly ground pepper
8 slices sandwich bread, cubed
1 (8-ounce) package cream cheese, cubed
2 cups (8 ounces) shredded Swiss cheese such as
     Gruyère

• **Cook** first 4 ingredients in 1 tablespoon oil in a large skillet until tender. Drain and pat dry; set aside.
• **Cook** squash and zucchini in 1 tablespoon oil in skillet until tender. Drain and pat dry; set aside.
• **Cook** mushrooms in remaining tablespoon oil in skillet until tender. Drain and pat dry; set aside.
• **Whisk** together eggs and next 3 ingredients in a large bowl; stir in vegetables, half of bread cubes, cream cheese, and Swiss cheese. Press remaining bread cubes in bottom of a lightly greased 10-inch springform pan, and place on a baking sheet. Pour vegetable mixture into pan.
• **Bake** at 325° for 1 hour, covering with aluminum foil after 45 minutes to prevent excessive browning. Serve warm. Yield: 8 servings.

CHEDDAR STRATA

make ahead

3 large eggs, lightly beaten
1¼ cups milk
½ cup minced onion
¼ teaspoon salt
¼ teaspoon dry mustard
¼ teaspoon black pepper
¼ teaspoon ground red pepper
⅛ teaspoon paprika
¼ teaspoon Worcestershire sauce
Butter or margarine
8 slices white bread
3 cups (12 ounces) shredded Cheddar cheese

• **Combine** first 9 ingredients; set aside. Butter bread; cut off crusts, and cut each slice into small squares. Arrange a single layer of bread squares in a lightly greased 9-inch square pan; top with 1 cup cheese. Repeat layers until all bread and cheese are used. Pour egg mixture over all. Cover and chill 8 hours.

• **Remove** from refrigerator; let stand at room temperature 30 minutes before baking. Bake, uncovered, at 325° for 1 hour. Serve hot. Yield: 6 servings.

What's a Strata?

You won't find *strata* **as a food term** in most dictionaries, but you will find it in the pages of *Southern Living.* Our first strata, similar to the recipe above, debuted in 1970. It resembled a cheese soufflé, but was more forgiving. You simply layered bread and cheese, covered it with a milk and egg mixture, and stashed it in the fridge until ready to cook, usually the next morning. The '80s brought flavor inspiration as we varied the cheese and tossed in sausage and other favorite foods. The recipe, above right, features very '90s ingredients—fresh mushrooms and artichoke hearts. Stratas remain popular with our audience for their flavor and convenience.

ARTICHOKE-CHEESE STRATA

make ahead

Mushrooms and marinated artichoke hearts pack flavor and texture into this easy do-ahead dish.

½ cup sliced fresh mushrooms
3 green onions, chopped
1 tablespoon butter or margarine, melted
3 slices white bread, cubed
¾ cup (3 ounces) shredded sharp Cheddar cheese
      or Monterey Jack cheese
1 (14-ounce) can artichoke hearts, drained and
      quartered, or 1 (12-ounce) jar marinated
      quartered artichoke hearts, drained
1 (4-ounce) jar diced pimiento, drained
4 large eggs, lightly beaten
1½ cups milk
½ teaspoon dry mustard
¼ teaspoon salt
⅛ teaspoon white pepper

• **Sauté** mushrooms and green onions in butter in a skillet over medium heat 2 minutes or until tender. Set aside.

• **Layer** half each of bread, mushroom and green onion mixture, cheese, artichoke hearts, and pimiento in a lightly greased 9-inch quiche dish, 9½-inch deep-dish pieplate, or 1½ quart baking dish. Repeat layers.

• **Combine** eggs and remaining 4 ingredients; stir well. Pour mixture into quiche dish; cover and chill 3 to 8 hours.

• **Remove** from refrigerator, and let stand 30 minutes before baking. Bake, uncovered, at 350° for 45 to 55 minutes or until set. Let stand 10 minutes before serving. Yield: 6 servings.

BRUNCH FOR A BUNCH

The title tells it all. Just add some chunks of fresh melon and a carafe of coffee.

1 pound ground hot pork sausage
3 cups frozen hash brown potatoes, thawed
3 cups (12 ounces) shredded Cheddar cheese
½ cup chopped green pepper
12 large eggs, lightly beaten
2 cups milk
½ teaspoon salt
Garnishes: celery leaves, tomato wedges

• **Brown** sausage in a medium skillet, stirring until it crumbles; drain. Place hash browns in a lightly greased shallow 3-quart baking dish. Layer cooked sausage, cheese, and chopped green pepper evenly over hash browns.
• **Combine** eggs, milk, and salt in a large bowl, stirring with a wire whisk or fork until blended; pour egg mixture over chopped green pepper layer. Bake at 350° for 50 minutes or until golden. Garnish, if desired. Yield: 8 servings.

SAUSAGE BREAKFAST CASSEROLE

family favorite, make ahead

6 slices white bread
Butter or margarine
1 pound ground pork sausage
1½ cups (6 ounces) shredded Longhorn cheese
6 large eggs, lightly beaten
2 cups half-and-half
½ teaspoon salt
⅛ teaspoon pepper

• **Trim** crust from bread slices. Spread butter over 1 side of each bread slice. Place bread slices, buttered side up, in a lightly greased 13- x 9-inch baking dish. Set aside.
• **Brown** sausage in a large skillet, stirring until it crumbles; drain. Spoon sausage over bread; sprinkle with cheese. Combine eggs, half-and-half, salt, and pepper; pour over cheese. Cover and chill 8 hours or overnight.
• **Remove** casserole from refrigerator; let stand 30 minutes. Bake, uncovered, at 350° for 45 minutes or until golden. Yield: 8 servings.

CORN-AND-CHEESE SOUFFLÉ

A soufflé has a brief moment of puffed glory; see it captured in the photograph on page 120.

⅓ cup butter or margarine
¼ cup all-purpose flour
⅓ cup milk
1½ cups (6 ounces) shredded sharp Cheddar cheese
½ cup (2 ounces) shredded provolone cheese
1 (16½-ounce) can cream-style corn
⅛ teaspoon garlic powder
⅛ teaspoon ground red pepper
5 large eggs, separated
¼ teaspoon cream of tartar

• **Lightly** butter the bottom of a 2-quart soufflé dish. Set aside.
• **Melt** ⅓ cup butter in a heavy saucepan over low heat. Add flour, stirring until smooth. Cook 1 minute, stirring constantly. Gradually add milk; cook over medium heat, stirring constantly, until thickened. Add cheeses, stirring until melted. Stir in corn, garlic powder, and ground red pepper. Beat egg yolks at medium speed with an electric mixer until thick and pale. Stir into corn mixture.
• **Combine** egg whites and cream of tartar; beat at high speed until stiff peaks form; fold into soufflé mixture. Spoon into prepared dish. Bake at 350° for 55 to 60 minutes. Serve immediately. Yield: 8 servings.

CHEESE SOUFFLÉ ROLL

Vegetable oil
⅓ cup butter or margarine
⅓ cup all-purpose flour
1¼ cups milk
1 cup (4 ounces) shredded Cheddar cheese, divided
½ cup grated Parmesan cheese
¾ teaspoon salt
⅛ teaspoon ground red pepper
7 large eggs, separated
¼ teaspoon cream of tartar
2 tablespoons grated Parmesan cheese
Spinach-Mushroom Filling
Fresh spinach leaves

• **Lightly** oil bottom and sides of a 15- x 10-inch jellyroll pan; line with wax paper, allowing paper to extend beyond ends of pan. Lightly oil wax paper. Set aside.
• **Melt** butter in a heavy saucepan over low heat; add flour, stirring until smooth. Cook 1 minute, stirring constantly. Gradually add milk; cook over medium heat, stirring constantly, until mixture is very thick. Add ½ cup Cheddar cheese, ½ cup Parmesan cheese, salt, and pepper, stirring until cheeses melt. Transfer mixture to a large bowl.
• **Beat** egg yolks at high speed with an electric mixer until thick and pale. Gradually stir about one-fourth of hot cheese mixture into egg yolks; add to remaining cheese mixture, stirring well.
• **Beat** egg whites and cream of tartar at high speed until stiff peaks form. Stir a small amount of cheese mixture into beaten egg whites. Gradually fold egg white mixture into remaining cheese mixture.
• **Spread** batter evenly in prepared pan. Bake at 350° for 18 minutes or until puffy and firm in center (do not overcook). Loosen edges of soufflé with a knife blade or metal spatula. Turn soufflé out onto a double layer of wax paper sprinkled with 2 tablespoons Parmesan cheese. Carefully peel wax paper off top of soufflé. Spread soufflé evenly with Spinach-Mushroom Filling. Starting with long side, and using wax paper for support, carefully roll up soufflé, jellyroll fashion.
• **Carefully** slide roll, seam side down, onto a large baking sheet; sprinkle with remaining ½ cup Cheddar cheese. Broil 5½ inches from heat 1 minute or until cheese melts. Carefully transfer roll to a spinach leaf-lined serving platter. Yield: 8 servings.

Spinach-Mushroom Filling

1 (10-ounce) package frozen chopped spinach
3 cups chopped fresh mushrooms
¼ cup finely chopped green onions
2 tablespoons butter or margarine, melted
½ cup sour cream
½ teaspoon garlic salt

• **Cook** spinach according to package directions; drain well, pressing between layers of paper towels to remove excess moisture. Set aside.
• **Cook** mushrooms and green onions in butter in a large skillet over medium-high heat, stirring constantly, until tender; stir in spinach, sour cream, and garlic salt. Cook 3 minutes or until mixture is thoroughly heated. Remove from heat, and keep warm. Yield: 2½ cups.

Eggs-tra, Eggs-tra

80s Cholesterol concerns clipped egg popularity in the 1980s, but omelets, scrambled eggs, and the devilish Southern family reunion favorite, stuffed eggs, never submitted to banishment.

90s Even the salmonella scare of the '90s did not end it all for the infamous egg. *Southern Living* adapted recipes for frosting, fillings, ice creams, and more to make sure any eggs included were thoroughly cooked. Southern family favorites can't do without the incredible, edible egg.

Blintz Soufflé

BLINTZ SOUFFLÉ

Cream cheese and cottage cheese give this casserole soufflé ultrarich taste. The blueberry sauce adorns it beautifully.

1 (8-ounce) package cream cheese, softened
2 cups small-curd cottage cheese
2 egg yolks
2 tablespoons sugar
1 teaspoon vanilla extract
6 large eggs
1½ cups sour cream
½ cup orange juice
½ cup butter or margarine, softened
1 cup all-purpose flour
⅓ cup sugar
2 teaspoons baking powder
1 teaspoon grated orange rind
Blueberry Sauce

• **Combine** first 5 ingredients in a small bowl; beat at medium speed with an electric mixer until smooth. Set mixture aside.
• **Blend** eggs and next 3 ingredients in container of an electric blender until smooth. Add flour, ⅓ cup sugar, baking powder, and orange rind; blend until smooth. Pour half of batter into a lightly greased 13- x 9-inch baking dish. Spoon cream cheese mixture evenly over batter, and spread gently with a knife. Pour remaining batter over cream cheese mixture.
• **Bake** at 350° for 50 to 55 minutes or until puffed and golden. Serve immediately with warm Blueberry Sauce. Yield: 8 servings.

Blueberry Sauce
⅔ cup sugar
2 tablespoons cornstarch
Dash of ground cinnamon
Dash of ground nutmeg
Pinch of salt
1 cup water
2 cups fresh blueberries
2 tablespoons lemon juice

• **Combine** first 5 ingredients in a small heavy saucepan. Gradually stir in water. Cook over medium-high heat, stirring constantly, until mixture comes to a boil; boil 1 minute. Stir in blueberries and lemon juice, and boil 1 minute, stirring constantly. Remove from heat. Yield: 2½ cups.

THREE-CHEESE AND CHILE CASSEROLE

One pantry staple that comes in handy for a multitude of dishes is canned green chiles. Here they add a Western accent to a favorite cheesy egg casserole.

8 large eggs, lightly beaten
½ cup all-purpose flour
1 teaspoon baking powder
1 (16-ounce) carton small-curd cottage cheese
2 cups (8 ounces) shredded Monterey Jack cheese
2 cups (8 ounces) shredded Cheddar cheese
2 (4.5-ounce) cans chopped green chiles
¼ cup butter or margarine, melted
½ teaspoon garlic powder
½ teaspoon chili powder

• **Combine** eggs, flour, and baking powder, stirring well. Stir in cheeses and remaining ingredients. Pour mixture into a lightly greased 13- x 9-inch baking dish.
• **Bake,** uncovered, at 325° for 35 minutes. Yield: 8 servings.

Chiles Rellenos with Red Sauce

CHILES RELLENOS WITH RED SAUCE

family favorite

8 canned whole mild green chiles (about four 4-ounce cans) or 8 fresh poblano or Anaheim chiles
1 (8-ounce) package Monterey Jack cheese with peppers
½ cup all-purpose flour
¼ teaspoon salt
⅛ teaspoon pepper
4 large eggs, separated
¼ cup all-purpose flour
Vegetable oil
Red Sauce
Tomatillo salsa (store-bought) (optional)
Garnish: fresh cilantro

• **If using** canned chiles, rinse chiles, and remove seeds; pat dry. If using fresh chiles, place on a baking sheet. Broil 5½ inches from heat 5 to 10 minutes on each side or until chiles look blistered. Place chiles in a zip-top plastic bag; seal and let stand 10 minutes. Peel off skins; remove seeds.
• **Cut** block of cheese into 8 crosswise strips; place a strip of cheese inside each chile. (If chiles tear, overlap torn sides; batter will hold chiles together.)
• **Combine** ½ cup flour, salt, and pepper in a shallow bowl; set aside. Beat egg yolks until thick and pale. Beat egg whites in a large bowl at high speed of an electric mixer until stiff peaks form. Gently fold yolks and ¼ cup flour into beaten egg white.
• **Pour** oil to depth of 2 inches into a Dutch oven; heat to 375°. Dredge each stuffed chile in dry flour mixture; dip in egg batter.
• **Fry** chiles, a few at a time, in hot oil until golden, turning once; drain on paper towels. Serve warm with Red Sauce, and tomatillo salsa, if desired. Garnish, if desired. Yield: 4 servings.

Red Sauce
4 cloves garlic, crushed
¼ cup butter or margarine, melted
¼ cup all-purpose flour
1 cup beef broth
1 (8-ounce) can tomato sauce
1 tablespoon chili powder
1 teaspoon rubbed sage
1 teaspoon ground cumin

• **Cook** garlic in butter in a medium saucepan over medium heat 3 minutes, stirring constantly; add flour, stirring until smooth. Cook 1 minute, stirring constantly. Gradually add beef broth and tomato sauce, stirring constantly. Add chili powder, sage, and cumin; cook, stirring constantly, until mixture is thickened and bubbly. Yield: 2 cups.

CREAMY PIMIENTO CHEESE

family favorite, quick

Sharp cheese has impact when you're making homemade pimiento cheese for sandwiches or snacking.

1 (8-ounce) package cream cheese, softened
2 cups (8 ounces) shredded sharp Cheddar cheese, softened
⅓ cup mayonnaise
Dash of garlic powder
1 (4-ounce) jar diced pimiento, drained

• **Beat** cream cheese at medium speed with an electric mixer until creamy; add Cheddar cheese, and continue beating until light and fluffy. Add mayonnaise and garlic powder; mix well. Stir in pimiento. Cover and chill. Serve at room temperature. Yield: 2½ cups.

EGG ROULADE WITH MUSHROOM FILLING

An herbed mushroom filling gets rolled up inside this savory brunch roulade.

Vegetable oil
¼ cup butter
¼ cup all-purpose flour
¼ teaspoon salt
⅛ teaspoon ground nutmeg
⅛ teaspoon pepper
¾ cup milk
6 large eggs, separated
¼ teaspoon cream of tartar
Mushroom Filling
¼ cup freshly grated Parmesan cheese
1 cup (4 ounces) shredded Swiss cheese, divided

• **Grease** bottom and sides of a 15- x 10-inch jellyroll pan with oil; line with wax paper. Lightly oil wax paper.
• **Melt** butter in a heavy saucepan over low heat; add flour, salt, nutmeg, and pepper, stirring until smooth. Gradually add milk. Cook over medium heat, stirring constantly, until thickened and bubbly.
• **Lightly** beat egg yolks in a large mixing bowl; gradually add white sauce. Set aside.
• **Beat** egg whites until foamy; add cream of tartar, beating until stiff but not dry. Stir a small amount of beaten egg white into sauce mixture; fold in remaining egg white. Spread batter into prepared pan. Bake at 350° for 15 to 18 minutes or until puffy and firm in center.
• **Cover** a baking sheet with aluminum foil; coat with vegetable cooking spray. Turn out roulade onto aluminum foil; carefully remove wax paper. Spread with Mushroom Filling; sprinkle with Parmesan cheese and ½ cup Swiss cheese. Starting at short end, roll up roulade, ending with seam side down. Sprinkle remaining ½ cup Swiss cheese over roulade. Broil 3 inches from heat 1 to 2 minutes or until cheese melts. Yield: 8 servings.

Mushroom Filling
1 tablespoon butter or margarine
¾ pound mushrooms, finely chopped
¼ cup sliced green onions
1 clove garlic, minced
1 teaspoon all-purpose flour
1 teaspoon chopped fresh tarragon or ¼ teaspoon dried tarragon
¼ cup milk

• **Melt** butter in a large skillet over medium-high heat. Add mushrooms, green onions, and garlic; sauté until vegetables are tender and liquid is absorbed.
• **Combine** flour, tarragon, and milk in a small bowl; stir well. Add to mushroom mixture; cook 1 minute, stirring constantly. Remove from heat. Yield: 1¼ cups.

FRUITED CREAM CHEESE

⁓ make ahead, quick ⁓

Even though you can buy flavored cream cheese at the supermarket, making it yourself is easy and fun.

1 (8-ounce) package cream cheese, softened
Choice of prepared fruit
2 tablespoons powdered sugar

• **Combine** cream cheese, prepared fruit, and powdered sugar; beat at medium speed with an electric mixer until mixture is well blended. Cover and chill. Yield: about 1¼ cups.

Strawberry Cream Cheese: Coarsely chop 6 medium strawberries. Proceed with recipe above.
Pineapple Cream Cheese: Drain 1 (8-ounce) can crushed pineapple. Gently press pineapple between paper towels to remove excess moisture. Proceed with recipe above.

Orange Cream Cheese: Combine ¼ cup chopped fresh orange sections and 1½ teaspoons Grand Marnier or other orange-flavored liqueur. Proceed with recipe at bottom left.

Peach Cream Cheese: Combine 2 canned peach halves, drained and coarsely chopped, and ½ teaspoon almond extract. Proceed with recipe at bottom left.

Cherry Cream Cheese: Combine ¼ cup drained and chopped maraschino cherries and ¼ teaspoon almond extract. Proceed with recipe at bottom left.

CHEESE KUCHEN

Kuchen is a wonderful German dish usually served for breakfast; this cheese version also makes a great dessert.

1   cup all-purpose flour
¼   cup sugar
3   tablespoons butter or margarine, melted
1   large egg, lightly beaten
2   cups small-curd cottage cheese
½   cup sugar
⅓   cup golden raisins
2   large eggs, lightly beaten
2   tablespoons all-purpose flour
2   tablespoons butter or margarine, melted
½   teaspoon vanilla extract
¼   teaspoon salt
¼   teaspoon almond extract
¼   teaspoon ground cinnamon

• **Combine** first 4 ingredients; press mixture into bottom and 1 inch up sides of an 8-inch square pan.
• **Combine** cottage cheese and next 8 ingredients; stir well. Pour mixture into pan; sprinkle with cinnamon. Bake at 425° on bottom rack of oven 10 minutes. Reduce heat to 350°; bake 36 to 38 more minutes or until knife inserted in center comes out clean. Yield: 9 servings.

SWISS CHEESE FONDUE

~ quick ~

This fondue will feed a crowd. Sliced apples and pears make great dippers.

6   cups (1½ pounds) shredded Swiss cheese
2   cups (8 ounces) shredded Gruyère cheese
2   tablespoons cornstarch
2   cloves garlic, halved
2   cups dry white wine
2   tablespoons lemon juice
⅓   cup dry sherry
1   teaspoon salt
¼   teaspoon white pepper
French bread, cut into cubes

• **Combine** first 3 ingredients, stirring well; set aside.
• **Rub** inside of a large heavy saucepan with cut garlic; discard garlic. Add wine; cook over medium heat until hot, but not boiling. Add lemon juice.
• **Gradually** add cheese mixture; cook, stirring constantly, until cheese melts. Stir in sherry, salt, and pepper. Pour mixture into a fondue pot, keeping warm. Serve with bread cubes, sliced fruit, and nuts. Yield: about 4 cups.

PUB FONDUE

~ quick ~

1   (10¾-ounce) can Cheddar cheese soup, undiluted
¾   cup beer
2   cups (8 ounces) shredded Cheddar cheese
2   teaspoons prepared mustard
1   teaspoon Worcestershire sauce

• **Combine** soup and beer in a heavy saucepan; bring to a boil over medium heat, stirring constantly. Gradually add shredded cheese, mustard, and Worcestershire sauce, stirring constantly, until cheese melts.
• **Spoon** into fondue pot or chafing dish. Yield: 2½ cups.

Garlic and Wine Braised
Mussels

Fish and Shellfish

When in the mood for simple,
fresh-tasting, healthy entrées, reel
in some of our fish and shellfish
recipes. The key to success is
selecting the freshest fish available
and keeping an eye on the
cooking time.

Garlic and Wine Braised Mussels (page 159)

SOUTHERN FRIED CATFISH

family favorite

1¹/₃ cups cornmeal
²/₃ cup all-purpose flour
1 tablespoon salt
1 teaspoon ground red pepper
4 (1-pound) pan-dressed catfish
1 cup buttermilk
Peanut oil or vegetable oil

• **Combine** first 4 ingredients in a large shallow dish. Dip each catfish in buttermilk, allowing excess to drip off. Dredge in cornmeal mixture.

• **Pour** oil to depth of 2 inches into an electric skillet or Dutch oven. Heat oil to 375° over medium-high heat. Increase heat to high; immediately add 2 catfish; adjust heat as needed to maintain 375° oil. Fry catfish 3 to 4 minutes on each side or until fish flakes easily when tested with a fork. Drain on paper towels. Remove large bits of crust from oil with a slotted spoon, if necessary, and immediately repeat frying procedure with remaining fish. Serve immediately. Serve with tartar sauce. Yield: 4 servings.

CAJUN-STYLE GRILLED CATFISH

quick

1 teaspoon lemon-pepper seasoning
1 teaspoon white pepper
1 teaspoon Creole seasoning
1 teaspoon blackened fish seasoning (we tested with Prudhomme's Blackened Redfish seasoning)
4 catfish fillets (1½ to 2 pounds)
2 tablespoons lemon juice
Garnish: lemon wedges

• **Combine** first 4 ingredients; rub seasoning on catfish. Sprinkle lemon juice on both sides of catfish. Grill, covered with grill lid, over medium-hot coals (350° to 400°) 5 minutes on each side or until fish flakes easily when tested with a fork. Garnish, if desired. Yield: 4 servings.

CRACKERMEAL CATFISH FINGERS

¹/₂ cup all-purpose flour
¹/₄ teaspoon salt
¹/₄ teaspoon coarsely ground pepper
2 large eggs, beaten
2 tablespoons water
1 cup round buttery cracker crumbs
    (24 crackers; we tested with Ritz)
¹/₄ cup fine, dry breadcrumbs (store-bought)
Vegetable oil
1 pound catfish fillets, cut into 16 strips

• **Combine** flour, salt, and pepper in a medium bowl. Combine eggs and water; stir well. Combine cracker crumbs and breadcrumbs in a medium bowl.

• **Pour** oil to depth of 1½ inches into a heavy skillet; heat to 375°. Dredge fish strips in flour mixture; dip in egg mixture, and coat with crumb mixture. Fry strips, a few at a time, 1 to 2 minutes or until golden. Drain on paper towels. Serve with tartar sauce. Yield: 4 servings.

Cajun Craze

80s Louisiana Chef Paul Prudhomme presented his spicy Cajun food to the world, and the world couldn't get enough of his blackened redfish. The popularity of the redfish dish may have dwindled by the end of the decade, but not the desire for all things Cajun. Cayenne continues strong and regional cooking is hotter than ever.

BLACKENED CATFISH

quick

2 tablespoons paprika
2½ teaspoons salt
2 teaspoons lemon pepper
1½ teaspoons garlic powder
1½ teaspoons dried basil
1½ teaspoons ground red pepper
1 teaspoon onion powder
1 teaspoon dried thyme
4 catfish fillets (1½ pounds)
1 cup unsalted butter, melted

• **Combine** first 8 ingredients in a large shallow dish. Dip fish in butter; dredge in spice mixture. Place on wax paper.
• **Heat** a large cast-iron or heavy aluminum skillet over medium-high heat 10 minutes.
• **Cook** fish, 2 at a time, 2 to 3 minutes on each side or until fish is blackened and flakes easily with a fork. Serve with lemon wedges. Yield: 4 servings.

GROUPER WITH PECAN SAUCE

quick

4 (1-inch-thick) grouper or flounder fillets (1½ to 2 pounds)
1 tablespoon soy sauce
¼ cup all-purpose flour
3 tablespoons vegetable oil
1 cup whipping cream
1 tablespoon dark corn syrup or molasses
1 teaspoon soy sauce
½ cup pecan pieces, toasted

• **Place** fillets in a shallow baking dish. Brush with 1 tablespoon soy sauce; cover and chill 10 minutes.

• **Dredge** fish in flour, shaking off excess flour. Heat oil in a large nonstick skillet over medium-high heat until hot. Add fish; cook 6 to 8 minutes on each side or until browned and fish flakes easily when tested with a fork. Remove fish from skillet, and keep warm.
• **Wipe** skillet dry with a paper towel. Add whipping cream and corn syrup to skillet; bring to a boil over medium heat. Boil until mixture is reduced to ¾ cup (about 5 minutes). Stir in 1 teaspoon soy sauce and pecans; spoon sauce over fish. Yield: 4 servings.

GRILLED MARINATED GROUPER

1 teaspoon grated lemon rind
⅓ cup fresh lemon juice
2 teaspoons prepared horseradish
2 cloves garlic, halved
1 tablespoon chopped fresh oregano or 1 teaspoon dried oregano
1 tablespoon chopped fresh basil or 1 teaspoon dried basil
¾ teaspoon salt
¼ teaspoon pepper
⅓ cup olive oil
2 pounds grouper fillets
Vegetable cooking spray

• **Process** first 8 ingredients in an electric blender or food processor 20 seconds. With motor running, gradually add olive oil in a slow, steady stream. Set marinade aside.
• **Cut** fish into serving size portions. Arrange fish in a 13- x 9-inch baking dish. Pour ½ cup marinade over fish, turning to coat both sides. Cover and marinate in refrigerator 1 hour, turning fish once. Remove fish from marinade, discarding marinade.
• **Coat** grill rack with cooking spray; place rack on grill over medium-hot coals (350° to 400°). Place fish on rack. Grill, covered with grill lid, 7 to 8 minutes on each side or until fish flakes easily when tested with a fork, basting often with remaining marinade. Yield: 6 servings.

PEPPERED SNAPPER

A medley of peppers and onions tops these fillets and keeps them moist as they bake.

2 medium onions, cut into ½-inch slices
1 sweet red pepper, seeded and cut into ½-inch slices
1 or 2 jalapeño peppers, seeded and cut into thin strips
2 tablespoons vegetable oil or olive oil
½ teaspoon salt, divided
¼ cup rice vinegar
1½ teaspoons chopped fresh oregano or ½ teaspoon dried oregano
6 red snapper fillets (2½ to 3 pounds)
½ teaspoon pepper
Garnish: lemon wedges (optional)

• **Cook** onion, sliced red pepper, and jalapeño pepper strips in oil in a skillet over medium-high heat 10 minutes or until tender, stirring often. Add ¼ teaspoon salt, vinegar, and oregano. Cook 1 minute; set aside.
• **Sprinkle** fish fillets with remaining salt and pepper; place fillets in a lightly greased 13- x 9-inch baking dish. Top with vegetable mixture. Bake, uncovered, at 350° for 20 minutes or until fish flakes easily when tested with a fork. Garnish, if desired. Yield: 6 servings.

RED SNAPPER LOUISIANE

A buttery artichoke and almond topping smothers this skillet-fried snapper. It's a rich dish and great for company. Just add sliced tomatoes and crisp salad greens to the meal.

4 red snapper fillets (2 to 2½ pounds)
¼ teaspoon salt
¼ teaspoon pepper
1 large egg, lightly beaten
1 cup milk
½ cup all-purpose flour
Vegetable oil
1 (14-ounce) can quartered artichoke hearts, drained
1 cup sliced fresh mushrooms
¼ cup butter or margarine, melted
⅓ cup sliced almonds, toasted
1 teaspoon Worcestershire sauce
1 teaspoon lemon juice
1 teaspoon white wine vinegar or tarragon vinegar

• **Sprinkle** fillets with salt and pepper. Combine egg and milk in a shallow bowl, mixing well. Dip fillets in milk mixture, and dredge in flour.
• **Pour** oil to depth of 2 inches into a Dutch oven or large deep skillet; heat to 350°.
• **Fry** fillets in 2 batches in hot oil 5 minutes or until golden, turning to brown both sides. Drain on paper towels. Remove to a serving platter, and keep warm.
• **Cook** artichoke hearts and mushrooms in butter in a large skillet over medium-high heat, stirring gently, until mushrooms are tender. Add almonds and remaining 3 ingredients; cook 1 minute. Spoon over fish; serve immediately. Yield: 4 servings.

NOTE: You can substitute other white fillets such as grouper, flounder, Mingo snapper or other types of snapper, if desired.

Red Snapper Louisiane

Valencian Orange Roughy

This dish is reminiscent of a common way seafood is prepared in Valencia and other coastal towns in Spain. Tomatoes, olive oil, lemon juice, and herbs are characteristic flavors.

¼ pound sliced fresh mushrooms
1 small onion, chopped
2 cloves garlic, minced
2 tablespoons olive oil, divided
¾ cup chopped, peeled tomato
3 tablespoons lemon juice
1½ teaspoons chopped fresh basil or ½ teaspoon dried basil
2 orange roughy fillets (about 1 pound)
½ teaspoon salt, divided
½ teaspoon pepper, divided
1 clove garlic, minced
1 (10-ounce) package fresh spinach
Garnish: lemon slices

• **Sauté** mushrooms, onion, and 2 cloves garlic in 1 tablespoon oil over medium-high heat 5 minutes or until onion is lightly browned. Stir in tomato, lemon juice, and basil. Simmer 1 minute. Remove from heat. Set aside.
• **Sprinkle** orange roughy with ¼ teaspoon salt, and ¼ teaspoon pepper. Place in a lightly greased 13- x 9-inch baking dish. Top with vegetable mixture; cover and bake at 350° for 20 to 25 minutes or until fish flakes easily when tested with a fork.
• **Heat** remaining tablespoon oil in a large skillet over medium heat. Add remaining garlic. Sauté just until garlic is lightly browned. Add spinach, remaining ¼ teaspoon salt, and ¼ teaspoon pepper. Cover and cook 5 minutes or until spinach is wilted, stirring occasionally. Transfer spinach to a serving platter. Gently transfer fish and vegetables to platter. Garnish, if desired. Yield: 2 servings.

Teriyaki-Glazed Salmon

A tangy-sweet marinade bathes these salmon fillets with flavor before cooking and again when they're served.

⅓ cup orange juice
⅓ cup soy sauce
¼ cup dry white wine
2 tablespoons vegetable oil
1 tablespoon grated fresh ginger
1 teaspoon dry mustard
1 teaspoon lemon juice
Pinch of sugar
1 garlic clove, minced
½ teaspoon freshly ground pepper
4 (6-ounce) salmon fillets

• **Combine** first 10 ingredients in a shallow dish or large heavy-duty, zip-top plastic bag; add salmon fillets. Cover or seal; chill 30 minutes, turning once.
• **Remove** fillets from marinade, reserving marinade. Place fillets in a lightly greased 13- x 9-inch pan.
• **Bake,** uncovered, at 450° for 10 minutes or until fish flakes easily when tested with a fork. Remove from oven; keep warm.
• **Bring** reserved marinade to a boil in a small heavy saucepan; cook 6 to 8 minutes or until reduced by half, stirring often. Pour over fillets. Yield: 4 servings.

Salmon Steaks with Herb Butter

~ quick ~

¼ cup butter or margarine, softened
1 tablespoon chopped fresh tarragon or
   1 teaspoon dried tarragon
1 tablespoon chopped fresh chives
1 tablespoon chopped fresh parsley
1 tablespoon Dijon mustard
⅛ teaspoon freshly ground pepper
1 shallot, minced
4 (1½-inch-thick) salmon steaks

• **Combine** first 7 ingredients.
• **Brush** salmon steaks with half of butter mixture. Grill steaks, uncovered, over medium-hot coals (350° to 400°) 8 minutes on each side or until fish flakes easily when tested with a fork, brushing often with remaining butter mixture. Yield: 4 servings.

Trout Amandine

~ family favorite ~

Buttery toasted almonds are the traditional topping for this classic panfried trout.

¼ cup butter or margarine
½ cup slivered blanched almonds
¾ teaspoon salt, divided
1 tablespoon fresh lemon juice
¾ cup all-purpose flour
½ teaspoon pepper
½ teaspoon chopped fresh thyme
¾ cup vegetable oil
6 trout or bass fillets (8 ounces each)
Milk
2 tablespoons chopped fresh parsley
Garnish: lemon wedges

• **Melt** butter in a saucepan over medium heat. Sauté almonds in butter until golden. Add ¼ teaspoon salt and lemon juice; remove from heat. Set aside.
• **Combine** remaining ½ teaspoon salt, flour, pepper, and thyme. Heat oil in a large skillet over medium-high heat. Dip fillets in milk; dredge in flour mixture.
• **Fry** fillets, 2 at a time, until browned on both sides; drain on paper towels. Remove to a serving dish; drizzle with almond butter sauce, and sprinkle with chopped parsley. Garnish, if desired. Yield: 6 servings.

Tuna Steaks with Sautéed Vegetables

½ cup olive oil
¼ cup white wine
2 tablespoons soy sauce
4 tuna steaks (1 pound)
1 small onion, chopped
1 green bell pepper, chopped
1 medium tomato, chopped
1 clove garlic, minced
¼ teaspoon dried crushed red pepper
1 tablespoon olive oil

• **Combine** first 3 ingredients in a shallow dish; add tuna. Cover; chill 1 hour, turning tuna occasionally. Remove tuna from marinade, discarding marinade.
• **Grill,** uncovered, over medium-hot coals (350° to 400°) 3 to 4 minutes on each side or until fish flakes easily when tested with a fork. Sauté onion and next 4 ingredients in 1 tablespoon hot oil in a large skillet until tender. Serve with tuna. Yield: 4 servings.

Garlic Shrimp

GARLIC SHRIMP

family favorite, quick

A crusty Parmesan-breadcrumb topping is dusted over these big garlicky shrimp before serving. Grill or toast some French bread for sopping up the aromatic juices.

2 dozen large fresh shrimp
¼ cup olive oil
¼ cup chopped fresh parsley
3 cloves garlic, minced
½ teaspoon dried crushed red pepper
¼ teaspoon pepper
¼ cup butter or margarine, melted
½ cup French breadcrumbs (homemade), toasted
½ cup freshly grated Parmesan cheese

• **Peel** shrimp; devein, if desired. Arrange in a 11- x 7-inch baking dish; pour oil over shrimp. Combine parsley and next 3 ingredients; sprinkle over shrimp. Cover and bake at 300° for 15 minutes.
• **Turn** shrimp over; drizzle with butter, and sprinkle with breadcrumbs and cheese. Bake, uncovered, 5 to 10 more minutes. Yield: 2 servings.

SZECHUAN SHRIMP

A glaze with dried crushed red pepper gives these shrimp their pow.

2 pounds unpeeled medium-size fresh shrimp
½ cup ketchup
¼ cup soy sauce
2 tablespoons dry sherry
1 to 1½ teaspoons dried crushed red pepper
1 teaspoon sugar
½ teaspoon ground ginger
¼ teaspoon salt
2 green peppers, seeded and cut into 1-inch pieces
2 tablespoons vegetable oil or peanut oil
2 bunches green onions, sliced (2 cups)
4 cloves garlic, minced
1 (6-ounce) package frozen snow pea pods, thawed and drained
Hot cooked rice

• **Peel** shrimp; devein, if desired.
• **Combine** ketchup and next 6 ingredients in a small bowl, stirring well.
• **Stir-fry** green pepper in hot oil in a large skillet over medium-high heat 1 minute; add shrimp, and stir-fry 2 minutes or until shrimp turn pink. Add green onions, garlic, and snow peas; stir-fry 1 minute. Stir in ketchup mixture. Stir-fry 1 minute or until thoroughly heated. Serve over rice. Yield: 6 servings.

Shrimp Tales

How does a Southerner most likely enjoy his shrimp?

70s Shrimp was most commonly fried, with hush puppies served on the side.

80s Shrimp joined the health craze and was stirred into stir-fries, curries, or creoles.

90s The proliferation of pasta shaped the shrimp of the '90s, that is, until *Forrest Gump* met *Southern Living* and enumerated the endless ways to cook shrimp. *Forrest Gump* may be the first novel turned screenplay turned cookbook, as Forrest's friend Bubba published 75 of his favorite shrimp recipes in the instant best-seller, *The Bubba Gump Shrimp Company Cookbook*, published in collaboration with *Southern Living*.

Sweet-and-Sour Shrimp

family favorite

1 pound unpeeled large fresh shrimp
$^1/_2$ cup all-purpose flour
$^1/_3$ cup plus 1 tablespoon water
$^1/_4$ cup cornstarch
1 teaspoon vegetable oil
$^1/_2$ teaspoon salt
$^1/_2$ teaspoon baking powder
1 large egg, lightly beaten
Vegetable oil
Sweet-and-Sour Sauce
Hot cooked rice

• **Peel** shrimp; devein, if desired. Combine flour and next 6 ingredients.
• **Pour** oil to depth of 3 inches into a Dutch oven; heat to 375°. Dip shrimp into batter; fry shrimp, a few at a time, in hot oil until golden. Drain on paper towels. Arrange shrimp on a baking sheet; place in a 200° oven to keep warm while frying remaining shrimp. Combine shrimp and Sweet-and-Sour Sauce; serve hot over rice. Yield: 6 servings.

Sweet-and-Sour Sauce
$^1/_2$ cup sliced carrot
$^1/_2$ cup coarsely chopped green pepper
$^3/_4$ cup sugar
$^1/_3$ cup ketchup
1 tablespoon soy sauce
$^1/_4$ teaspoon salt
1 (15$^1/_4$-ounce) can pineapple chunks, undrained
3$^1/_2$ tablespoons cornstarch
$^1/_3$ cup water
$^1/_2$ cup white vinegar

• **Cook** carrot in a small amount of boiling water 2 minutes. Add green pepper; cook 1 minute. Drain; rinse with cold water. Drain; set aside.

• **Combine** sugar and next 3 ingredients in a medium saucepan; stir well. Drain pineapple, reserving juice; stir pineapple juice into sugar mixture. Bring to a boil.
• **Combine** cornstarch and water, stirring until smooth; add cornstarch mixture and vinegar to juice mixture. Cook over medium heat, stirring constantly, until mixture is thickened and bubbly. Stir in vegetables and pineapple chunks. Yield: about 4 cups.

Broiled Shrimp 'n' Bacon

14 unpeeled jumbo fresh shrimp (1 pound)
2 ounces Monterey Jack cheese, cut into 14 (1$^1/_2$-inch) strips
7 bacon slices, cut in half lengthwise
$^1/_4$ cup butter or margarine, melted
1 tablespoon grated Parmesan cheese
1 clove garlic, crushed
1 teaspoon lemon juice

• **Peel** shrimp, leaving tails on; devein, if desired. Butterfly shrimp by making a deep slit down back, from large end to tail, cutting to, but not through, inside curve of shrimp. Place a Monterey Jack cheese strip inside each slit; wrap sides of shrimp around cheese.
• **Wrap** each shrimp in a bacon slice, and secure each with two wooden picks. Stir together butter and remaining 3 ingredients; brush on shrimp. Place shrimp on a baking sheet.
• **Broil** 5$^1/_2$ inches from heat 4 minutes on each side or until bacon is crisp. Yield: 2 servings.

SHRIMP EGG ROLLS

Two or three of these savory shrimp rolls can quickly fill you up as an entrée or you can serve them individually as appetizers.

Vegetable cooking spray
½ pound ground raw chicken
2 cups shredded cabbage
1 cup finely chopped cooked shrimp
½ cup shredded carrot
¼ cup chopped bean sprouts
2 tablespoons finely chopped onion
2 teaspoons sugar
½ teaspoon salt
¼ teaspoon pepper
10 egg roll wrappers
Vegetable oil

• **Coat** a large skillet with cooking spray; add chicken. Cook over medium-high heat until chicken crumbles, stirring often. Add shredded cabbage and next 7 ingredients; cook 2 minutes, stirring often.
• **Spoon** ⅓ cup vegetable mixture into center of each egg roll wrapper. For each roll, fold 1 corner of wrapper over filling; fold left and right corners of wrapper over filling. Lightly brush exposed corner of wrapper with water. Tightly roll filled end toward exposed corner; lightly press corner to seal securely.
• **Pour** oil to depth of 2 inches into a wok or Dutch oven; heat to 375°. Fry egg rolls, a few at a time, until golden, turning once; drain. Serve with soy sauce, hot mustard, or sweet and sour sauce. Yield: 10 egg rolls.

NOTE: You won't need a whole package of egg roll wrappers for this recipe. Just freeze the extras.

LEMON-PEPPER SHRIMP

These shrimp swim in a spicy butter sauce laden with pepper and Worcestershire. It's a great dish for entertaining a crowd in the summer. Serve with corn on the cob and roasted potatoes.

3 pounds unpeeled large fresh shrimp
3 stalks celery with leaves, coarsely chopped
4 cloves garlic, chopped
1 small onion, thinly sliced
6 lemons, cut in half
1 cup butter
1 (2¼-ounce) jar cracked black pepper
½ cup Worcestershire sauce
½ cup lemon juice
1 tablespoon salt
2 to 3 teaspoons hot sauce
French bread

• **Place** shrimp in a 13- x 9-inch pan. Add celery, garlic, and onion. Squeeze lemons over shrimp; add squeezed lemon halves to pan. Melt butter in a small saucepan; stir in pepper and next 4 ingredients. Pour mixture over shrimp in pan.
• **Bake,** uncovered, at 400° for 25 to 28 minutes or until shrimp are done, stirring several times. Serve with French bread to sop up the juices. Yield: 6 servings.

SHRIMP VERSAILLES

2 pounds unpeeled large fresh shrimp
2 green onions, sliced
3 tablespoons butter or margarine, melted
1 (8-ounce) package cream cheese, cubed
¼ cup milk
½ cup (2 ounces) shredded Swiss cheese
¼ cup dry white wine
Dash of ground red pepper
¼ cup fine, dry breadcrumbs (store-bought)
2 tablespoons butter or margarine, melted
12 ounces dried angel hair pasta, cooked

• **Peel** shrimp; devein, if desired.
• **Cook** green onions in 3 tablespoons butter in a large skillet over medium heat until tender. Add shrimp. Cook over medium heat 5 minutes or until shrimp turn pink, stirring occasionally. Remove shrimp with a slotted spoon.
• **Add** cream cheese and milk to skillet; cook over low heat, stirring constantly, until cheese melts. Stir in Swiss cheese and wine. Add shrimp and red pepper; cook, stirring constantly, just until heated. Pour shrimp mixture into a lightly greased 1½-quart casserole.
• **Combine** breadcrumbs and 2 tablespoons butter; sprinkle over casserole. Broil 5½ inches from heat 3 to 5 minutes or until golden. Serve shrimp mixture over hot cooked pasta. Yield: 6 servings.

SHRIMP WITH WILD RICE

4 cups water
2 teaspoons salt
1½ pounds unpeeled large fresh shrimp
1 (6-ounce) package long-grain-and-wild rice (we tested with Uncle Ben's)
½ cup butter or margarine
½ cup thinly sliced onion
½ cup sliced fresh mushrooms
¼ cup chopped green pepper
¼ cup all-purpose flour
1¾ cups chicken broth
⅛ teaspoon ground white pepper
1 tablespoon Worcestershire sauce
Dash of hot sauce

• **Bring** 4 cups water and salt to a boil; add shrimp, and cook 2 to 3 minutes or until shrimp are almost done. Drain; rinse with cold water. Peel shrimp; devein, if desired.
• **Cook** rice according to package directions, adding seasoning packet but omitting butter.
• **Melt** ½ cup butter in a large skillet. Add onion, mushrooms, and green pepper; sauté until tender. Gradually add flour; cook over low heat 1 minute, stirring constantly. Gradually add broth; cook, stirring constantly, until thickened and bubbly. Add white pepper, Worcestershire, and hot sauce; simmer 2 minutes.
• **Combine** shrimp, rice, and vegetable mixture; spoon into a lightly greased shallow 2-quart baking dish. Bake, uncovered, at 350° for 20 to 30 minutes or until bubbly. Yield: 4 servings.

SHRIMP AND CHICKEN CASSEROLE

1 (3-pound) broiler-fryer
1 teaspoon salt
4 cups water
1 pound unpeeled medium-size fresh shrimp
2 (16-ounce) packages frozen broccoli cuts, thawed and drained
1 (10³/₄-ounce) can cream of chicken soup, undiluted
1 (10³/₄-ounce) can cream of celery soup, undiluted
1 cup mayonnaise
2 tablespoons lemon juice
¹/₄ teaspoon ground white pepper
1 cup (4 ounces) shredded Cheddar cheese
¹/₂ cup soft breadcrumbs (homemade)
1 tablespoon butter or margarine, melted
Paprika

• **Combine** chicken and salt in a Dutch oven; add enough water to cover. Bring to a boil; cover, reduce heat, and simmer 45 minutes or until chicken is tender. Remove chicken from broth; reserve broth for another use, if desired. Let chicken cool to touch; skin, bone, and cut chicken into bite-size pieces. Set aside.
• **Bring** 4 cups water to a boil; add shrimp, and cook 3 to 5 minutes or until shrimp turn pink. Drain well; rinse with cold water. Chill. Peel shrimp, and devein, if desired.
• **Spread** broccoli in a lightly greased 13- x 9-inch baking dish. Combine cream of chicken soup and next 4 ingredients; spread about one-third of soup mixture over broccoli. Sprinkle chicken and shrimp evenly over soup mixture in dish. Spread remaining soup mixture over chicken and shrimp.
• **Cover** and bake at 350° for 30 minutes. Uncover and sprinkle with cheese. Combine breadcrumbs and butter; sprinkle over cheese. Bake, uncovered, 15 minutes or until thoroughly heated and bubbly. Sprinkle with paprika. Yield: 8 servings.

SEAFOOD BROCHETTES

Large buttery-tasting sea scallops and crispy bacon are the highlights on these skewers.

1 pound unpeeled large fresh shrimp
1 pound grouper fillets, cut into 1-inch pieces
¹/₂ pound sea scallops
4 slices bacon, quartered
8 medium-size fresh mushroom caps
1 large green pepper, seeded and cut into 1-inch pieces
Citrus-Ginger Sauce
Hot cooked rice

• **Peel** shrimp; devein, if desired. Alternately thread shrimp, grouper, and next 4 ingredients onto 8 (12-inch) skewers. Place skewers, in batches, on a lightly greased rack of a broiler pan. Broil 5½ inches from heat 12 to 15 minutes or until shrimp turn pink and fish flakes easily when tested with a fork, turning and basting with Citrus-Ginger Sauce. Serve brochettes over rice. Yield: 4 servings.

Citrus-Ginger Sauce
¹/₂ cup butter or margarine, melted
¹/₂ cup pineapple juice
2 tablespoons lemon juice
2 tablespoons Dijon mustard
1 teaspoon ground ginger
Freshly ground pepper to taste

• **Combine** all ingredients; stir well. Yield: 1¹/₄ cups.

*Chesapeake Bay
Crab Cakes*

CHESAPEAKE BAY CRAB C

~ family favorite ~

The secret to great crab cakes is buying very fresh lumps of cra
and not overstirring the crab mixture before shaping it.

$1/4$ cup minced onion
2 tablespoons minced green pepper
$1/4$ cup butter or margarine, melted
1 pound fresh lump crabmeat,
    drained
$1^1/4$ cups soft breadcrumbs
    (homemade), toasted and divided
1 tablespoon chopped fresh parsley
1 tablespoon mayonnaise

1 tablespoon lemon juice
1 teaspoon Old Bay seasoning
1 teaspoon dry mustard
1 teaspoon Worcestershire sauce
Dash of ground red pepper
1 large egg, lightly beaten
Vegetable oil
Garnishes: fresh parsley, lemon
    wedges

• **Cook** onion and green pepper in butter in a large skillet over medium-high heat, stirring constantly, until tender. Remove from heat; stir in crabmeat, $3/4$ cup breadcrumbs, parsley, and next 7 ingredients. Shape mixture into 8 patties; dredge patties in remaining breadcrumbs.

• **Pour** oil to depth of $1/4$ inch into a large heavy skillet. Fry patties in hot oil over medium-high heat 3 minutes on each side or until golden. Drain on paper towels. Garnish, if desired. Serve hot with cocktail sauce and tartar sauce. Yield: 4 servings.

TRIPLE SEAFOOD CASSEROLE

Loaded with scallops, shrimp, and crab, this casserole feeds the whole family.

1 pound unpeeled medium-size fresh shrimp
1 cup dry white wine
1 tablespoon chopped fresh parsley
1 tablespoon butter or margarine
1 teaspoon salt
1 medium onion, thinly sliced
1 pound fresh bay scallops
3 tablespoons butter or margarine
3 tablespoons all-purpose flour
1 cup half-and-half
$^{1}/_{2}$ cup (2 ounces) shredded Swiss cheese
2 teaspoons lemon juice
$^{1}/_{8}$ teaspoon pepper
$^{1}/_{2}$ pound fresh crabmeat or crab-flavored
    seafood product, flaked
1 ($4^{1}/_{2}$-ounce) can sliced mushrooms, drained
1 cup soft breadcrumbs (homemade)
$^{1}/_{4}$ cup grated Parmesan cheese

• **Peel** and devein shrimp. Combine wine and next 4 ingredients in a large Dutch oven; bring to a boil. Add shrimp and scallops. Cook 3 to 5 minutes or until shrimp turn pink, stirring often. Drain, reserving $^{2}/_{3}$ cup cooking liquid.

• **Melt** 3 tablespoons butter in Dutch oven over low heat; add flour, stirring until smooth. Cook 1 minute, stirring constantly. Gradually add half-and-half; cook over medium heat, stirring constantly, until thickened and bubbly. Stir in Swiss cheese. Gradually stir in reserved cooking liquid, lemon juice, and pepper. Stir in shrimp mixture, crabmeat, and mushrooms.

• **Spoon** mixture into a lightly greased 11- x 7-inch baking dish. Cover and bake at 350° for 40 minutes or until bubbly. Combine breadcrumbs and Parmesan cheese; sprinkle over casserole. Bake, uncovered, 5 more minutes. Let stand 10 minutes before serving. Yield: 6 servings.

FRIED SOFT-SHELL CRABS

You don't have to do much to enhance the naturally sweet flavor of soft shell crabs. This particular coating is a bit peppery—and we liked it that way. Serve the crabs hot alongside French rolls and slaw.

8 fresh or frozen soft-shell crabs, thawed
1 cup all-purpose flour
3 tablespoons Old Bay seasoning
2 teaspoons black pepper
1 teaspoon ground red pepper
1 teaspoon garlic powder
1 large egg, lightly beaten
$^{1}/_{2}$ cup milk
Vegetable oil

• **To clean** crabs, remove spongy substance (gills) that lie under the tapering points on either side of back shell. Place crabs on back, and remove the small piece at lower part of shell that terminates in a point (the apron). Wash crabs thoroughly; drain well.

• **Combine** flour and next 4 ingredients; set aside. Combine egg and milk; stir well.

• **Pour** oil to depth of 1 inch into a large Dutch oven; heat oil to 350°. Dip crabs into egg mixture; dredge in flour mixture. Fry crabs 1 to 2 minutes or until golden; drain on paper towels. Serve hot. Yield: 4 servings.

CRABMEAT IMPERIAL

Baking shells contain this creamy crabmeat filling as it bakes. Pair this imperial entrée with a crisp white wine for dinner.

¼ cup butter or margarine
2 tablespoons all-purpose flour
1 cup milk
1 teaspoon dry mustard
½ teaspoon salt
⅛ teaspoon pepper
1 teaspoon Worcestershire sauce
1 pound fresh lump crabmeat, drained
½ cup diced green pepper
½ cup soft breadcrumbs (homemade)
1 tablespoon butter or margarine, melted
Paprika (optional)

• **Melt** ¼ cup butter in a heavy saucepan over low heat; add flour, stirring until smooth. Cook 1 minute, stirring constantly. Gradually add milk; cook over medium heat until thickened and bubbly, stirring constantly.
• **Stir** in mustard and next 3 ingredients. Stir in crabmeat and green pepper. Spoon mixture into lightly greased baking shells.
• **Mix** breadcrumbs and butter; sprinkle over crabmeat mixture. Sprinkle with paprika, if desired. Bake at 425° for 18 to 20 minutes or until lightly browned. Yield: 6 servings.

CRABMEAT WITCHERY

◦ quick ◦

1 pound fresh lump crabmeat, drained
1½ cups half-and-half
½ cup dry sherry
¼ cup butter or margarine, melted
1 teaspoon salt
½ teaspoon ground mace
¼ teaspoon ground red pepper
1 teaspoon grated lemon rind
1 teaspoon fresh lemon juice
2 tablespoons all-purpose flour
2 tablespoons water
Puff pastry patty shells or toast points

• **Combine** first 9 ingredients in a large saucepan; cook over low heat 5 minutes, stirring constantly.
• **Combine** flour and 2 tablespoons water; stir into crabmeat mixture. Cook over low heat until thickened and bubbly, stirring constantly. Serve over patty shells or toast points. Yield: 4 servings.

An Insatiable Thirst

Water was first bottled for general consumption in 1976 amid much skepticism about why anyone would buy a bottle of something so readily available in every home. By the mid '90s, Americans consumed over three billion gallons of bottled water a year and seemed driven by an unquenchable quest for better water quality as sales of home water purifiers proliferated.

FRIED OYSTERS

Enjoy these crusty oysters as an entrée or appetizer or pile them high on a hoagie roll with tartar sauce.

2 (12-ounce) containers oysters
½ teaspoon salt
½ teaspoon pepper
3 large eggs, lightly beaten
¼ teaspoon hot sauce
3 cups finely crushed saltine crackers
Vegetable oil

• **Drain** oysters, and press between paper towels to remove excess moisture. Sprinkle oysters with salt and pepper. Combine eggs and hot sauce. Dip oysters in cracker crumbs, egg mixture, and again in cracker crumbs.
• **Pour** oil to depth of 2 inches into a large deep skillet; heat to 375°. Fry oysters, in batches, about 2 minutes or until golden, turning to brown both sides. Drain on paper towels. Serve with tartar sauce. Yield: 6 servings.

NOTE: Cut any extralarge oysters in half before breading and frying them.

OYSTERS ROCKEFELLER

1 (10-ounce) package frozen chopped spinach, thawed and well drained
1 cup Italian-seasoned breadcrumbs
¼ cup butter or margarine, melted
¼ cup grated Parmesan cheese
2 large eggs, lightly beaten
1 garlic clove, minced
¼ teaspoon salt
¼ teaspoon pepper
¼ teaspoon hot sauce
2 dozen oysters on the half shell, drained
6 slices bacon, each cut crosswise into
    4 pieces

• **Combine** first 9 ingredients. Place oysters in shells on a baking sheet. Spoon spinach mixture onto oysters; top with bacon. Bake at 350° for 15 minutes. Broil 5½ inches from heat 3 minutes. Yield: 6 servings.

STEAMED CLAMS CHESAPEAKE

Wash clams under cold running water with a stiff brush to remove dirt. Discard any cracked clams.

2 dozen cherrystone clams
1½ tablespoons Old Bay seasoning
½ teaspoon salt
¼ teaspoon freshly ground black pepper
1 cup water
2 tablespoons butter or margarine, melted
Lemon wedges (optional)
Freshly ground black pepper

• **Scrub** clams with a brush; place in a large Dutch oven. Sprinkle with seasonings. Add 1 cup water; cover and bring to a boil. Reduce heat, and steam 8 minutes or until shells open. Discard unopened clams.

• **Drain** clams, reserving liquid. Arrange clams on serving plates. Drizzle with clam liquid and melted butter. Serve with lemon wedges, if desired, and sprinkle with freshly ground pepper. Yield: 2 servings.

CRAWFISH ÉTOUFFÉE

2 pounds fresh or frozen peeled crawfish tails, thawed
$^{1}/_{2}$ teaspoon hot sauce
$^{1}/_{2}$ teaspoon ground red pepper
1 cup vegetable oil
1 cup all-purpose flour
4 stalks celery, chopped
4 large onions, chopped
4 large green peppers, seeded and chopped
1 bunch green onions, chopped
1 cup water
2 teaspoons salt
1 teaspoon black pepper
$^{1}/_{2}$ teaspoon ground red pepper
$^{3}/_{4}$ cup chopped fresh parsley
Hot cooked rice

• **Sprinkle** crawfish with hot sauce and $^{1}/_{2}$ teaspoon red pepper; set aside.
• **Combine** oil and flour in a Dutch oven; cook over medium heat, stirring constantly, until roux is chocolate colored (about 20 minutes).
• **Stir** in celery and next 3 ingredients; cook, stirring constantly, until vegetables are tender. Add crawfish tails and water; cook, uncovered, over low heat, 15 minutes, stirring occasionally. Stir in salt, black pepper, and $^{1}/_{2}$ teaspoon red pepper. Simmer, uncovered, 5 minutes; stir in parsley. Serve étouffée over rice. Yield: 8 servings.

GARLIC AND WINE BRAISED MUSSELS

The beauty of mussels in their slick black shells is on display over a bed of pasta in this dish worthy of company. Don't miss the aromatic, flavorful broth of wine, garlic, and a sprinkling of cilantro. See this dish on page 140.

2 pounds raw mussels in shells
5 cloves garlic, minced
3 tablespoons butter or margarine
3 tablespoons olive oil
$^{1}/_{2}$ cup dry white wine
$^{1}/_{2}$ teaspoon freshly ground pepper, divided
8 ounces dried linguine, cooked
$^{1}/_{2}$ cup chopped fresh cilantro

• **Scrub** mussels with a brush; remove beards. Discard cracked or heavy mussels (they're filled with sand), or opened mussels that won't close when tapped.
• **Sauté** garlic in butter and oil in a Dutch oven over medium heat 1 to 2 minutes or until golden. Stir in wine and $^{1}/_{4}$ teaspoon pepper. Add mussels. Cover and cook 6 to 7 minutes or until mussels open, shaking pan several times.
• **Place** linguine on a warm platter. Transfer mussels to platter with a slotted spoon, discarding any unopened mussels. Pour butter mixture over mussels; sprinkle with remaining pepper and chopped cilantro. Yield: 4 servings.

Lobster Newburg

LOBSTER NEWBURG

A special occasion calls for lobster. Try this unique presentation—a tower of rice in a pool of rich lobster sauce. To do it, we packed hot cooked rice into a measuring cup and unmolded it onto each serving plate.

3 (8- to 10-ounce) fresh or frozen lobster tails, thawed
¼ cup butter or margarine
¼ cup all-purpose flour
½ teaspoon dry mustard
½ teaspoon paprika
1 cup sliced fresh mushrooms
1 cup milk
½ cup whipping cream
¼ cup dry sherry
1 teaspoon salt
Hot cooked rice
Garnishes: fresh tarragon and thyme sprigs

• **Cook** lobster tails in boiling water 5 to 6 minutes. Drain; split tails lengthwise on underside of shell. Remove meat, and coarsely chop. Set aside.
• **Melt** butter in a large skillet over medium-low heat. Add flour, mustard, and paprika, stirring until smooth. Cook 1 minute, stirring constantly. Add mushrooms, and cook 3 minutes, stirring constantly. Gradually add milk and cream; cook over medium heat, stirring constantly, until mixture is thickened and bubbly. Add sherry and salt; simmer 10 minutes. Stir in lobster meat, and cook just until thoroughly heated. Serve over rice. Garnish, if desired. Yield: 4 servings.

LOBSTER MEDAILLONS IN GARLIC-CHIVE BUTTER SAUCE

2 quarts water
3 (8- to 10-ounce) lobster tails
Garlic-Chive Butter Sauce
Garnish: fresh chives

• **Bring** 2 quarts water to a boil; add lobster tails. Cover, reduce heat, and simmer 6 to 8 minutes. Drain; rinse with cold water, and drain again.
• **Split** tails lengthwise. Remove meat, and cut into ¼-inch slices. Arrange lobster medaillons on individual serving plates; spoon warm Garlic-Chive Butter Sauce over lobster. Garnish, if desired. Yield: 3 servings.

Garlic-Chive Butter Sauce
½ cup butter
¼ cup whipping cream
2 tablespoons lemon juice
1 tablespoon chopped fresh chives
1 clove garlic, minced
¼ teaspoon salt
⅛ teaspoon pepper

• **Melt** butter in a heavy saucepan. Add whipping cream, whisking until blended; cook over medium heat 1 minute. Stir in lemon juice and remaining ingredients; remove from heat. Yield: ³/₄ cup.

Meats

~

Some would say that a meal without
meat isn't really a meal. Center your
menu around one of these beef,
pork, veal, lamb, or venison recipes.
They partner easily with a broad
range of flavors and will fit
into any lifestyle.

Crumb-Crusted Rack of Lamb (page 178)

STANDING RIB ROAST

Some of the simple luxuries in life can't be improved upon, such as this rib roast with its salt and pepper crust. Serve mashed potatoes or Yorkshire pudding to soak up the jus.

1 (6-pound) standing rib roast
1 teaspoon kosher salt
1 teaspoon freshly ground pepper

• **Sprinkle** roast with salt and pepper. Place roast, fat side up, on a lightly greased rack in an aluminum foil-lined roasting pan.
• **Bake,** uncovered, at 350° for 2 hours or until meat thermometer inserted in thickest part, making sure it does not touch fat or bone, registers 145° (medium-rare) or to desired degree of doneness.
• **Remove** roast to a serving platter, reserving ½ cup drippings to serve as au jus, if desired. Let rib roast rest 10 minutes before carving. Yield: 8 servings.

PEPPERED BEEF TENDERLOIN BUNDLES

1 zucchini, finely chopped
1 cup chopped fresh mushrooms
½ cup chopped onion
1 clove garlic, minced
3 tablespoons butter or margarine, melted
¼ teaspoon salt
8 (4-ounce) beef tenderloin steaks
2 tablespoons cracked pepper
Vegetable cooking spray
16 sheets frozen phyllo pastry, thawed

• **Cook** first 4 ingredients in butter in a large skillet over medium-high heat until tender, stirring constantly. Stir in salt. Remove mixture from skillet; set aside. Sprinkle both sides of steaks with pepper. Coat skillet with cooking spray; place over high heat until hot. Add steaks, and cook 1½ to 2 minutes on each side or until lightly browned. Set aside.
• **Place** 1 phyllo sheet on a towel. (Keep remaining phyllo covered.) Coat phyllo sheet with cooking spray; fold in half lengthwise. Place 1 steak 3 inches from end of sheet. Spoon 2 tablespoons zucchini mixture onto steak; fold short end of sheet over stuffing. Fold sides of sheet over steak, and roll up.
• **Place** a second phyllo sheet on a towel; cut into a 12-inch square, and coat with cooking spray. Place wrapped steak, vegetable side up, in center of phyllo square. Bring corners of square to the middle, gently pressing together in center. Pull ends up and out to resemble a package. Coat bundle with cooking spray, and place on a baking sheet coated with cooking spray. Repeat procedure with remaining phyllo sheets, steaks, and zucchini mixture.
• **Bake** at 400° for 17 minutes for medium-rare (145°) or 20 minutes for medium (160°). Serve hot. Yield: 8 servings.

BEEF MEDAILLONS WITH HORSERADISH CREAM

¼ cup red wine vinegar
2 tablespoons vegetable oil
¾ teaspoon chopped fresh thyme or ¼ teaspoon dried thyme
¼ teaspoon salt
¼ teaspoon pepper
4 (4-ounce) beef tenderloin steaks
½ pound carrots, scraped and cut into very thin strips
2 tablespoons butter or margarine
¼ teaspoon salt
¼ teaspoon ground nutmeg
⅛ teaspoon ground white pepper
Horseradish Cream
Garnish: fresh thyme sprigs

• **Combine** first 5 ingredients in a shallow dish. Add steaks, turning to coat both sides. Cover and marinate in refrigerator 4 hours, turning once.
• **Cook** carrot strips in boiling water to cover 4 minutes or until crisp-tender; drain.
• **Combine** carrot strips, butter, and next 3 ingredients; toss to coat. Set aside; keep warm.
• **Remove** steaks from marinade, reserving marinade. Broil steaks 3 inches from heat 3 to 4 minutes on each side or to desired degree of doneness, basting with marinade just before turning.
• **Place** 1 steak in center of each of four dinner plates. Spoon 3 tablespoons Horseradish Cream along 1 side of each steak; spoon carrot mixture evenly along other side of each steak. Garnish, if desired. Yield: 4 servings.

Horseradish Cream
1¼ cups whipping cream
2½ tablespoons prepared horseradish
⅛ teaspoon salt
⅛ teaspoon pepper
Pinch of ground nutmeg

• **Cook** whipping cream in a medium saucepan over medium heat until reduced to ¾ cup (about 15 minutes), stirring often. Stir in horseradish, salt, pepper, and nutmeg. Cook, stirring constantly, just until mixture is thoroughly heated. Yield: ¾ cup.

POT ROAST JARDINIERE

This tender roast simmers several hours with no attention needed. Just remember to add the vegetables the last hour of cooking. They make it a one-dish meal.

1 (3- to 4-pound) boneless chuck roast
1 teaspoon salt
¼ teaspoon pepper
1 tablespoon vegetable oil or olive oil
1 (10½-ounce) can beef broth, undiluted
4 carrots, scraped, cut in half crosswise, and sliced lengthwise
2 medium turnips, peeled and quartered
8 boiling onions or 2 small onions, quartered
1 teaspoon fresh or dried rosemary
¼ cup all-purpose flour
¼ cup water
Garnish: fresh herbs

• **Rub** roast with salt and pepper. Brown roast in hot oil over medium heat in a Dutch oven. Add broth; bring mixture to a boil. Cover, reduce heat, and simmer 2½ hours.
• **Add** vegetables and rosemary to Dutch oven. Cover and cook 1 more hour or until meat and vegetables are tender. Remove roast and vegetables with a slotted spoon to a serving platter, reserving liquid in pan.
• **Whisk** together flour and water until smooth. Whisk into reserved liquid in Dutch oven; cook over medium heat until thickened, stirring constantly. Serve gravy with roast and vegetables. Garnish, if desired. Yield: 6 servings.

POT ROAST IN RED SAUCE

This roast simmers in an aromatic red wine and herb mixture, which ultimately becomes a red sauce laden with tangy olives. Spoon it over the roast or mashed potatoes.

1 (5-pound) boneless chuck roast
2 cloves garlic, thinly sliced
½ teaspoon salt
¼ teaspoon pepper
¼ cup all-purpose flour
⅓ cup olive oil
1 (15-ounce) can tomato sauce, divided
1 cup dry red wine
2 cloves garlic, crushed
1 large onion, chopped
1 bay leaf
1 teaspoon fresh or dried rosemary
2 (2¼-ounce) cans sliced ripe olives
½ cup cognac
2 tablespoons minced fresh parsley

• **Make** 10 slits in roast, using a sharp knife. Insert a garlic slice into each slit. Rub roast with salt and pepper; dredge in flour.
• **Brown** roast on all sides in hot oil in a Dutch oven over medium heat. Add 1 cup tomato sauce, red wine, and next 4 ingredients; cover, reduce heat, and simmer 2½ hours or until roast is tender. Remove bay leaf.
• **Transfer** roast to a serving platter, reserving cooking liquid in pan. Add remaining tomato sauce, olives, and cognac; cook over medium heat 5 to 10 minutes. Sprinkle with parsley. Serve sauce with roast. Yield: 10 servings.

SAUERBRATEN

3 tablespoons pickling spice
2 onions, sliced
1 carrot, scraped and sliced
1 cup water
1 cup red wine vinegar
1 cup dry red wine
1 tablespoon salt
½ teaspoon pepper
2 bay leaves
1 (4-pound) sirloin tip roast
3 tablespoons vegetable oil
¼ cup all-purpose flour
1 tablespoon sugar
¾ cup crushed gingersnaps (about 12 cookies)

• **Tie** pickling spice in a cheesecloth bag. Combine bag, onion, and next 7 ingredients in a shallow dish; add roast. Cover and marinate in refrigerator 8 hours, turning occasionally.
• **Remove** roast from marinade, reserving marinade. Brown roast on all sides in hot oil in a Dutch oven. Remove roast, reserving drippings. Whisk flour and sugar into drippings; cook over medium-high heat 2 minutes or until browned, whisking constantly. Gradually stir in marinade.
• **Return** roast to pan; bring to a boil. Cover, reduce heat, and simmer 2½ hours.
• **Discard** spice bag and bay leaves. Remove roast, reserving drippings in pan; slice roast, and keep warm. Stir gingersnaps crumbs into reserved drippings; simmer 2 minutes, stirring constantly. Pour mixture through a colander into a bowl. Press vegetables through colander with back of a spoon. Serve gravy with roast. Yield: 8 servings.

SOUTHWESTERN BEEF TIPS AND NOODLES

The wonderful earthy essence of cumin spices this old-fashioned entrée with Southwestern flavor. Using Mexican-style tomatoes kicks up the heat.

¼ cup all-purpose flour
2 pounds boneless top sirloin roast, cut into
　　½-inch cubes
¼ cup vegetable oil
1 (14½-ounce) can diced tomatoes or
　　Mexican-style diced tomatoes, undrained
1 medium onion, chopped
¼ cup chopped green pepper
1 clove garlic, minced
1 teaspoon ground cumin
¼ teaspoon salt
¼ teaspoon pepper
Hot cooked egg noodles

• **Place** flour in a heavy-duty, zip-top plastic bag. Add beef cubes; seal bag, and shake until meat is coated with flour.
• **Brown** beef in hot oil in a Dutch oven, stirring often. Add tomatoes and next 6 ingredients; bring to a boil. Cover, reduce heat, and simmer 30 minutes. Uncover and simmer 30 more minutes or until beef tips are tender, stirring occasionally. Serve over egg noodles. Yield: 6 servings.

CHICKEN-FRIED STEAK

family favorite, quick

¼ cup all-purpose flour
½ teaspoon salt
½ teaspoon pepper
1 pound cubed beef steaks
1 large egg, lightly beaten
2 tablespoons milk
1 cup saltine cracker crumbs
Vegetable oil
3 tablespoons all-purpose flour
1¼ cups chicken broth
½ cup milk
Dash of Worcestershire sauce
Dash of hot sauce
Additional pepper

• **Combine** first 3 ingredients; sprinkle over both sides of steaks. Combine egg and 2 tablespoons milk. Dip steaks in egg mixture; dredge in cracker crumbs.
• **Pour** oil to depth of ½ inch into a large skillet. Brown steaks on both sides over medium heat. Cover, reduce heat, and cook 15 minutes or until tender, turning occasionally. Drain on paper towels.
• **Reserve** 3 tablespoons drippings in skillet; stir in 3 tablespoons flour. Cook over medium heat 1 minute, stirring constantly. Gradually add broth and next 3 ingredients; cook, stirring constantly, until thickened. Serve steaks with gravy and additional pepper. Yield: 4 servings.

PEPPER STEAK

1½ pounds boneless top round steak
2 tablespoons vegetable oil
2 medium tomatoes, peeled and coarsely
   chopped
2 medium-size green peppers, seeded and
   cut into strips
1 small onion, sliced
1 cup water
¼ cup soy sauce
½ teaspoon beef bouillon granules
½ teaspoon pepper
¼ teaspoon salt
¼ teaspoon garlic powder
¼ teaspoon ground ginger
2 tablespoons cornstarch
2 tablespoons water
Hot cooked rice

• **Flatten** steak to ¼-inch thickness with a meat mallet or rolling pin; slice steak across the grain into thin strips. Brown steak on both sides in hot oil in a Dutch oven; drain. Add chopped tomato and next 9 ingredients; cover and simmer 1 hour.
• **Combine** cornstarch and 2 tablespoons water; add to steak mixture. Cook 2 minutes or until thickened, stirring constantly. Serve over rice. Yield: 4 servings.

GRILLED FLANK STEAK

1 (1½-pound) flank steak
½ cup firmly packed brown sugar
½ cup vegetable oil
½ cup soy sauce
¼ cup dry red wine
1 tablespoon minced garlic
1 tablespoon minced fresh ginger

• **Make** shallow cuts in steak diagonally across the grain at 1-inch intervals. Place steak in a shallow dish or heavy-duty, zip-top plastic bag.

• **Combine** brown sugar and remaining 5 ingredients; pour over steak. Cover dish or seal bag. Marinate in refrigerator 8 hours, turning meat occasionally.
• **Remove** steak from marinade, reserving marinade. Place marinade in a small saucepan; bring to a boil, and remove from heat. Grill steak, covered with grill lid, over medium-hot coals (350° to 400°) 5 minutes on each side or to desired degree of doneness, basting twice with marinade. Let stand 5 minutes. Slice steak diagonally across the grain into thin slices. Yield: 6 servings.

FAJITAS WITH PICO DE GALLO

family favorite

1 garlic bulb
1 large sweet yellow pepper
1 large sweet red pepper
1 large green pepper
2 large onions, sliced
1 cup lime juice
1 tablespoon black pepper
2 (1½-pound) flank steaks
16 (8-inch) flour tortillas
Pico de Gallo
Sour cream

• **Separate** garlic bulb into cloves; peel and crush cloves. Cut peppers into lengthwise strips.
• **Combine** garlic, pepper strips, onion, lime juice, and black pepper in a shallow dish or large heavy-duty, zip-top plastic bag; add steaks. Cover or seal; marinate in refrigerator 4 hours, turning occasionally.
• **Remove** steaks and vegetables from marinade; discard marinade.
• **Coat** vegetables with vegetable cooking spray. Place in a grill basket. Grill steaks and vegetables, covered with grill lid, over hot coals (400° to 500°) 4 minutes on each side or until steak reaches desired degree of doneness and vegetables are tender.

• **Cut** steaks diagonally across the grain into very thin slices. Serve steak, peppers, and onion with tortillas, Pico de Gallo, and sour cream. Yield: 8 servings.

Pico de Gallo

6 medium tomatoes, diced
1 medium onion, diced
¼ cup chopped fresh cilantro
1 to 2 serrano chile peppers, seeded and minced
1 tablespoon olive oil
1 teaspoon salt

• **Stir** together all ingredients; chill. Yield: 7 cups.

CORNED BEEF WITH DIJON GLAZE

A thick, golden Dijon glaze dresses up this corned beef for the table.

1 (3-pound) corned beef brisket, trimmed
4 cups water
¼ cup white vinegar
¼ cup Worcestershire sauce
8 whole cloves
3 cloves garlic, split
2 bay leaves
Dijon Glaze

• **Place** brisket in a large Dutch oven. Add water and next 5 ingredients; bring to a boil. Cover, reduce heat, and simmer 2½ to 3 hours or until brisket is tender. Drain. Return corned beef to Dutch oven. Spread with ½ cup Dijon Glaze. Bake, uncovered, at 350° for 20 minutes. Serve with remaining Dijon Glaze. Yield: 6 servings.

Dijon Glaze

½ cup Dijon mustard
½ cup orange marmalade
2 tablespoons prepared horseradish
2 tablespoons Worcestershire sauce

• **Combine** all ingredients in a small saucepan. Cook over medium heat until thoroughly heated, stirring constantly. Yield: 1¼ cups.

CHILI BEEF BRISKET

This well-seasoned brisket needs little attention once in the oven.

1 (4- to 5-pound) boneless beef brisket
1 teaspoon salt
½ teaspoon pepper
2 tablespoons vegetable oil
½ cup chili sauce
⅓ cup beef broth
¼ cup cider vinegar
1 tablespoon Worcestershire sauce
1½ teaspoons liquid smoke
1 bay leaf
¼ teaspoon pepper
1 medium onion, finely chopped
1 cup chili sauce

• **Trim** excess fat from brisket. Rub brisket with salt and ½ teaspoon pepper; cut brisket in half crosswise, if necessary to fit skillet. Brown brisket on both sides in hot oil in a large skillet over medium-high heat.
• **Place** brisket in a roasting pan. Combine ½ cup chili sauce and next 7 ingredients; pour over meat. Cover tightly with lid or aluminum foil, and bake at 350° for 2½ to 3 hours or until meat is very tender. Remove meat to a platter.
• **Skim** fat from pan juices; add 1 cup chili sauce to pan juices while still warm. Slice meat across the grain into thin slices, and serve with sauce. Yield: 10 servings.

NOTE: Brisket will never be quite as tender as a steak, but it should become pleasantly chewy after braising in a flavorful liquid.

HOME-STYLE MEAT LOAF

family favorite

*Meat loaf is one of those main dishes that meets a friend
in every family. And if there's ever any left over, it's
just as good the next day on a sandwich.*

1 large egg, beaten
½ cup soft breadcrumbs
    (homemade)
½ cup finely chopped onion
½ cup finely chopped green pepper
½ cup finely chopped celery
¼ cup finely chopped fresh
    mushrooms

1 teaspoon salt
½ teaspoon pepper
1 clove garlic, minced
1½ pounds ground chuck
½ cup ketchup
1 tablespoon water

• **Combine** first 9 ingredients in a large bowl. Add ground chuck; stir just until blended. Shape into an 8- x 4-inch freeform loaf on a greased rack of a broiler pan. Bake at 350° for 30 minutes. Combine ketchup and water, and spoon over loaf. Bake 45 more minutes or until done. Yield: 6 servings.

NOTE: You can make 6 mini meat loaves, if desired, as shown at right. Prepare meat loaf mixture as above, and divide evenly among 5- x 3-inch lightly greased miniature loafpans or shape into freeform loaves. Place freeform loaves on a greased rack of a broiler pan. Bake at 350° for 45 minutes, adding ketchup after 25 minutes.

Home-Style Meat Loaf

Caramelized Onion Burger

CARAMELIZED ONION BURGERS

family favorite

While you're grilling burgers, throw some corn on, too. You can also serve these caramelized onions with steak, meat loaf, or pork loin.

4 medium onions, sliced
2 teaspoons sugar
2 tablespoons olive oil
¼ cup water
1 tablespoon balsamic vinegar
¾ teaspoon salt, divided
1 pound ground beef
¼ cup chopped fresh parsley
2 tablespoons tomato paste
2 teaspoons Worcestershire sauce
¼ teaspoon freshly ground pepper
4 hamburger buns, toasted
4 tomato slices
Lettuce leaves

• **Cook** onion and sugar in hot oil in a large nonstick skillet over low heat 20 to 25 minutes or until onion is caramel colored, stirring often. Stir in ¼ cup water, vinegar, and ¼ teaspoon salt. Set mixture aside, and keep warm.
• **Combine** ground beef, parsley, tomato paste, Worcestershire sauce, remaining ½ teaspoon salt, and pepper; shape into 4 patties.
• **Grill,** covered with grill lid, over medium-hot coals (350° to 400°) 4 to 5 minutes on each side or until beef is no longer pink. Serve burgers on toasted buns with caramelized onions, tomato slices, and lettuce. Yield: 4 servings.

BURGERS AU POIVRE BLANC

Crushed white peppercorns form a crusty coating on these burgers once they hit a sizzling hot skillet. Then a red wine butter sauce dresses them up.

2 pounds ground round or chuck
½ teaspoon salt
2 tablespoons crushed white peppercorns
1 large shallot, diced
¼ cup dry red wine
2 tablespoons cognac
¼ cup water
¼ teaspoon chicken bouillon granules
2 tablespoons butter or margarine

• **Shape** ground round into 6 patties. Sprinkle with salt, and press peppercorns into both sides of patties.
• **Place** a large nonstick skillet over medium-high heat. Add patties, and cook 8 to 9 minutes on each side or until beef is no longer pink. Remove from skillet, and keep warm.
• **Add** shallot to skillet; sauté over medium heat 1 minute or until tender. Add wine and cognac; simmer 2 minutes. Combine water and bouillon granules; add to skillet, and simmer 3 minutes. Add butter, swirling skillet until butter melts. Spoon sauce over burgers. Yield: 6 servings.

Burger Time, Any Time

Behold the bodacious burgers, the fashion plates of every food fad. We've made them with ground beef, turkey, pork, venison, and veggies, but we've always called them burgers. *Southern Living* has offered burgers in every form; in fact, we've published over 100 burger recipes in the last 20 years alone. We've published Pizza Burgers, Burgundy Burgers, Nutty Burgers, Chili Burgers, Tortilla Burgers, Brie-Mushroom Burgers, Fried Green Tomato Cheeseburgers, and Vegetable Burgers, to name a few. On this page is a pair of our beefed-up favorites.

BAKED SPICY BEEF CHIMICHANGAS

family favorite

1 **pound ground round**
1 **medium onion, chopped**
2 **cloves garlic, crushed**
2 **cups (8 ounces) 4-cheese Mexican blend shredded cheese, divided**
1 **(16-ounce) can refried beans**
1 **(4.5-ounce) can chopped green chiles, drained**
½ **cup picante sauce**
12 **(8-inch) flour tortillas**
Toppings: salsa, sour cream, shredded lettuce

• **Cook** first 3 ingredients in a large skillet over medium-high heat 8 to 10 minutes or until beef is no longer pink, stirring until beef crumbles. Remove from heat, and drain.
• **Stir** 1½ cups cheese, beans, chiles, and picante sauce into beef mixture. Place ¼ cup beef mixture just below center of each tortilla. Fold opposite sides of tortillas over filling, forming rectangles. Secure with wooden picks.
• **Place** on a baking sheet; coat chimichangas with vegetable cooking spray.
• **Bake** at 425° for 8 minutes; turn chimichangas, and bake 5 more minutes. Remove picks; serve immediately with remaining ½ cup cheese and desired toppings. Yield: 12 chimichangas.

Traditional Spicy Beef Chimichangas: Pour vegetable oil to depth of 2 inches into a Dutch oven; heat to 375°. Fry chimichangas, a few at a time, 1½ minutes on each side or until golden. Drain and serve hot.

VEAL CHOPS IN COGNAC CREAM

Serve this elegant veal dish with rice and a mix of baby lettuces tossed with a simple vinaigrette.

6 **(6-ounce) veal chops**
¾ **teaspoon salt**
½ **teaspoon pepper**
½ **cup all-purpose flour**
3 **tablespoons vegetable oil or olive oil**
2 **tablespoons chopped onion**
1 **(8-ounce) package sliced fresh mushrooms**
1 **tablespoon all-purpose flour**
1 **cup half-and-half, divided**
2 **tablespoons cognac**
2 **egg yolks, lightly beaten**

• **Sprinkle** veal chops with salt and pepper; dredge chops in ½ cup flour.
• **Heat** oil in a large skillet over medium-high heat. Brown veal chops 3 to 4 minutes on each side. Cover and cook 3 to 5 more minutes or until chops are done. Remove chops from skillet, and keep warm, reserving drippings in skillet.
• **Add** onion to skillet, and sauté 2 minutes. Add mushrooms; sauté 5 minutes or until tender. Add 1 tablespoon flour, stirring constantly. Gradually add ½ cup half-and-half; bring mixture to a boil. Stir in cognac. Combine egg yolks and remaining ½ cup half-and-half; gradually add to skillet. Cook, stirring constantly, 4 to 5 minutes or until sauce thickens. Spoon sauce over veal chops. Yield: 6 servings.

Veal with Green Peppercorns

Piquant peppercorns bring a little zing to this rich entrée topped with a wine and cream sauce. Look for the peppercorns packed in brine in jars near relish and pickles on the grocery shelf.

1½ pounds veal cutlets
1 teaspoon salt
½ teaspoon pepper
¼ cup all-purpose flour
¼ cup butter, divided
¼ cup olive oil, divided
1 (8-ounce) package sliced fresh mushrooms
1 cup dry white wine
1 cup whipping cream
1½ teaspoons Dijon mustard
1 tablespoon green peppercorns in brine
Hot cooked rice

• **Place** cutlets between two sheets of heavy-duty plastic wrap or wax paper; flatten to ⅛-inch thickness, using a meat mallet or rolling pin. Sprinkle with salt and pepper, and dredge in flour. Set aside.

• **Heat** 1 tablespoon butter and 1 tablespoon oil in a large skillet over medium-high heat. Add mushrooms; sauté 3 to 4 minutes or until tender. Remove mushrooms from skillet.

• **Heat** 1 tablespoon butter and 1 tablespoon oil in skillet over medium-high heat; add one-third of veal; brown 2 minutes on each side. Remove veal from skillet; keep warm. Repeat twice with remaining butter, oil, and veal.

• **Add** wine to skillet; cook over high heat 4 to 5 minutes or until wine is reduced to ½ cup. Add whipping cream, mustard, and peppercorns; cook over high heat 4 to 5 minutes or until sauce is thickened. Stir in mushrooms. Spoon sauce over veal. Serve over rice. Yield: 6 servings.

Wiener Schnitzel

Wiener Schnitzel is a traditional Austrian dish of tender veal that's dipped in egg, breaded, and sautéed. A squeeze of lemon usually tops it off.

2 pounds veal cutlets
1 teaspoon salt
¼ teaspoon pepper
¾ cup all-purpose flour
4 large eggs, lightly beaten
1¾ cups fine, dry breadcrumbs (commercial)
¼ cup plus 2 tablespoons butter or margarine, divided
3 tablespoons olive oil or vegetable oil, divided
Garnish: lemon wedges

• **Place** cutlets between two sheets of heavy-duty plastic wrap or wax paper, and flatten to ¼-inch thickness, using a meat mallet or rolling pin. Sprinkle cutlets with salt and pepper. Dredge cutlets in flour; dip in beaten eggs, and dredge in breadcrumbs.

• **Heat** 2 tablespoons butter and 1 tablespoon oil in a large deep skillet. Add one-third of veal; brown 2 minutes on each side. Remove veal from skillet; keep warm. Repeat twice with remaining butter, oil, and veal. Garnish, if desired. Yield: 6 servings.

Child—Mother of Food TV

Julia Child started it all in the early '60s. She stepped before the television cameras to reveal French cooking secrets to Americans. Child's ease and exuberance led the American palate where it had never been before. Food lovers honor her, and hundreds of TV cooks who followed, including popular Southern chefs Emeril Lagasse, Justin Wilson, and Nathalie Dupree, owe her a debt. The Food Network, launched in 1993, along with its wildly popular Web site, now feeds America's food obsession. Bon appétit!

MUSHROOM-VEAL MARSALA

~ quick ~

1 teaspoon chopped fresh or dried rosemary
½ teaspoon salt
½ teaspoon freshly ground pepper
1 pound (¼-inch-thick) veal scaloppine
2 tablespoons olive oil
1 (8-ounce) package sliced fresh mushrooms
2 cloves garlic, minced
2 teaspoons cornstarch
1 teaspoon chicken bouillon granules
⅔ cup water
⅓ cup dry Marsala

• **Combine** and rub first 3 ingredients over veal. Heat oil in a large nonstick skillet over medium heat. Add half of veal; cook 2 minutes on each side or until lightly browned. Remove veal from skillet; keep warm. Repeat with remaining veal.

• **Add** mushrooms and garlic to skillet; cook over medium-high heat, stirring constantly, 3 minutes or until tender.

• **Combine** cornstarch and remaining 3 ingredients; add to skillet. Cook, stirring constantly, 1 minute or until thick and bubbly. Serve over veal. Yield: 4 servings.

GARLIC ROASTED LAMB

Garlic, lemon, and oregano are standard Greek flavors that enhance the robust taste of lamb.

1 (6- to 7-pound) bone-in leg of lamb
5 cloves garlic, thinly sliced
⅓ cup fresh lemon juice
¼ cup butter or margarine, melted
1 tablespoon dried oregano
1½ teaspoons salt
½ teaspoon pepper

• **Remove** all fell (tissue-like covering) from lamb. Make slits in lamb at 2- to 3-inch intervals, using a sharp knife. Insert garlic into slits. Place lamb on a rack in a roasting pan.

• **Combine** lemon juice and remaining 4 ingredients; stir well. Brush lamb with lemon juice mixture. Roast at 325° for 2 hours and 45 minutes or until meat thermometer inserted in thickest part of roast, making sure it does not touch fat or bone, registers 150° (medium-rare), basting often. Let stand 10 minutes before serving. Yield: 10 servings.

ROAST LAMB ROSEMARY

Rub a fragrant rosemary seasoning over this leg of lamb before roasting. A rich gravy accumulates in the pan as the meat cooks. Spoon gravy over the lamb or mashed potatoes—or both!

2 medium leeks
1 carrot, scraped and sliced
1 stalk celery, chopped
1 tablespoon butter or margarine, melted
1 tablespoon chopped fresh rosemary, divided
1½ teaspoons salt
½ teaspoon freshly ground pepper
1 (6-pound) bone-in leg of lamb, trimmed
3½ cups water, divided
3 tablespoons all-purpose flour

• **Remove** roots, tough outer leaves, and tops from leeks, leaving 4 inches of dark leaves. Wash leeks thoroughly. Cut into 1-inch slices.

• **Sauté** leeks, carrot, and celery in butter in a large skillet over medium heat 5 minutes or until lightly browned. Set aside.

• **Combine** 2 teaspoons rosemary, salt, and pepper. Rub rosemary mixture into lamb. Place lamb in a greased roasting pan; insert meat thermometer into thickest part of roast, making sure it doesn't touch fat or bone. Add sautéed vegetables and 1½ cups water to roasting pan. Roast, uncovered, at 325° for 1 hour and 35 to 45 minutes or until thermometer registers 150° (medium-rare). Remove lamb from roasting pan; place on a serving platter, and cover with aluminum foil.

• **Add** 1¾ cups water and remaining 1 teaspoon rosemary to vegetables in roasting pan. Scrape any browned bits that have accumulated. Bring to a boil; simmer 1 minute. Strain mixture into a medium saucepan.

• **Combine** flour and remaining ¼ cup water, stirring until smooth. Add to saucepan. Cook over medium-high heat 5 minutes or until thickened, stirring often. Serve gravy and vegetables with lamb. Yield: 10 servings.

CRANBERRY LEG OF LAMB

1 (3- to 4-pound) shank-half leg of lamb
1 clove garlic, sliced
1 teaspoon ground ginger
1 teaspoon dry mustard
½ cup whole-berry cranberry sauce
¼ cup cherry preserves
1 tablespoon port wine
2 tablespoons all-purpose flour
¼ cup water
¼ teaspoon salt
⅛ teaspoon pepper

• **Cut** several ½-inch slits in top of lamb; insert garlic slices into slits. Combine ginger and mustard; rub over

lamb. Place lamb, fat side up, on a lightly greased rack in a shallow roasting pan; insert meat thermometer into thickest part, making sure it does not touch fat or bone. Bake at 325° for 45 minutes.

• **Combine** cranberry sauce and preserves in a saucepan; cook over low heat until mixture melts, stirring occasionally. Stir in wine. Spoon mixture over lamb; bake 1 hour and 15 minutes or until thermometer registers 150° (medium-rare), 160° (medium), or to desired degree of doneness. Transfer lamb to a serving platter, reserving drippings. Let stand 10 minutes before carving.

• **Skim** fat from drippings; add enough water to drippings to measure 1¼ cups. Pour into a saucepan. Combine flour and ¼ cup water; add to drippings. Cook over medium heat, stirring constantly, until thickened and bubbly; stir in salt and pepper. Serve sauce with lamb. Yield: 8 servings.

TERIYAKI LAMB CHOPS

These little chops are painted with Asian flavors while they sizzle on the grill.

6 (4-ounce) lamb loin chops (1 inch thick)
½ cup finely chopped onion
¼ cup soy sauce
¼ cup cider vinegar
2 cloves garlic, sliced
2 tablespoons honey
2 teaspoons ground ginger
¼ teaspoon dry mustard
¼ teaspoon pepper

• **Trim** excess fat from lamb chops; place in a large heavy-duty, zip-top plastic bag. Combine onion and remaining 7 ingredients; pour over chops. Seal bag; marinate in refrigerator 8 hours, turning occasionally.

• **Remove** chops from marinade, reserving marinade. Bring marinade to a boil in a small saucepan; set aside.

• **Grill** chops, uncovered, over medium-hot coals (350° to 400°) 8 minutes on each side or to desired degree of doneness, basting often with marinade. Yield: 3 servings.

CRUMB-CRUSTED RACK OF LAMB

A mustard coating and crusty breadcrumbs dress this rack of lamb. See it pictured on page 162.

¼ cup olive oil
3 tablespoons Dijon mustard
1 clove garlic, minced
1 teaspoon chopped fresh thyme
½ teaspoon salt
2 (8-rib) lamb rib roasts (2½ pounds each)
1½ cups soft breadcrumbs (homemade)
¼ cup butter or margarine, melted
Vermouth Sauce
Garnishes: fresh herbs, assorted baby vegetables

• **Whisk** together first 5 ingredients in a small bowl.
• **Trim** and discard exterior fat on lamb roasts. Remove sinew, and scrape bones clean. Spread mustard mixture over meaty portion of lamb racks. Combine breadcrumbs and butter in a small bowl; pat onto mustard-coated lamb.
• **Place** racks, fat side out with ribs crisscrossed, on a rack in a roasting pan; insert meat thermometer into thickest part of roast, making sure it does not touch fat or bone.
• **Roast** lamb racks at 375° for 40 to 45 minutes or until thermometer registers 150° (medium rare), 160° (medium), or to desired degree of doneness. Serve with Vermouth Sauce. Garnish, if desired. Yield: 8 servings.

Vermouth Sauce
1 (14½-ounce) can beef broth
¼ cup diced onion
¼ cup diced carrot
¼ cup diced celery
2 fresh parsley sprigs
1 bay leaf
1½ teaspoons chopped fresh rosemary or dried rosemary
1½ teaspoons chopped fresh thyme or ½ teaspoon dried thyme
1 tablespoon tomato paste
1 tablespoon cornstarch
1 tablespoon water
½ cup dry vermouth

• **Combine** first 8 ingredients in a saucepan; bring to a boil over medium-high heat. Reduce heat to low; simmer, uncovered, 20 minutes. Strain broth; discard vegetables. Return broth to saucepan.
• **Combine** tomato paste, cornstarch, and water in a small bowl, stirring until smooth. Add tomato mixture to broth. Stir in vermouth. Cook over medium heat, stirring constantly, until thickened and bubbly. Yield: 1¼ cups.

STUFFED CROWN ROAST OF PORK

1 (12-rib) crown roast of pork (about 6 pounds)
½ teaspoon salt
½ teaspoon pepper
1 (6-ounce) package long-grain-and-wild rice mix
2 cups chicken broth
1 cup raisins
4 green onions, sliced
2 tablespoons butter or margarine
½ cup canned garbanzo beans (chickpeas), drained
½ cup chopped pecans, toasted
Garnishes: spiced crabapples

• **Sprinkle** roast on all sides with salt and pepper. Place roast, bone ends up, on a lightly greased rack in a shallow roasting pan. Bake at 325° for 1 hour.

• **Combine** rice mix, contents of seasoning packet, chicken broth, and next 3 ingredients in a medium saucepan. Bring to a boil; cover, reduce heat, and simmer 25 minutes or until liquid is absorbed and rice is tender. Add garbanzo beans and pecans, tossing gently to combine.

• **Spoon** rice mixture into center of roast. Cover stuffing and exposed ends of ribs with aluminum foil. Insert meat thermometer into roast, making sure it does not touch fat or bone. Bake at 325° for 1½ hours or until thermometer registers 160°.

• **Transfer** roast to a large serving platter, and remove foil. Spoon half of rice mixture around roast, leaving center of roast filled with remaining rice mixture. Let stand 10 minutes before carving. Garnish, if desired. Yield: 8 servings.

Livin' High on the Lean Hog

Southerners know their pork ribs, sausage, bacon, chops, and ham with red-eye gravy. It's our tradition, and it's in our blood. And part of the reason we've always loved pork was precisely the reason health-conscious consumers started taking it off their plates in the '80s—its high-fat content. But then pork itself "went on a diet" and even got its own national ad campaign—Pork: the other white meat. We've had to learn new cooking techniques for leaner chops and roasts all over again. And we still love 'em all! Less really is more when it comes to enjoying lean meats cooked to perfection.

MARGARITA PORK KABOBS

1 **cup frozen margarita mix concentrate, thawed**
1 **teaspoon ground coriander**
3 **garlic cloves, minced**
2 **teaspoons grated lime rind**
2 **pounds pork tenderloin, cut into 1-inch cubes**
3 **ears fresh corn**
1 **tablespoon water**
1 **large onion, quartered**
1 **large green pepper, cut into 1-inch pieces**
1 **large sweet red pepper, cut into 1-inch pieces**

• **Combine** first 4 ingredients in a shallow dish; add pork. Cover and marinate in refrigerator 30 minutes, turning occasionally.

• **Cut** each ear of corn into 4 pieces. Place corn and 1 tablespoon water in an 8-inch square microwave-safe dish. Cover with heavy-duty plastic wrap, folding back one corner to allow steam to escape. Microwave at HIGH 4 minutes, giving dish a half turn after 2 minutes.

• **Remove** pork from marinade, discarding marinade. Thread pork, corn, onion, and peppers onto skewers.

• **Coat** grill rack with cooking spray; place on grill over medium-hot coals (350° to 400°). Place kabobs on rack; grill, covered with grill lid, 5 minutes on each side or until pork is done. Yield: 4 servings.

PEPPERCORN PORK ROAST

2 tablespoons olive oil
1 (4½-pound) rolled boneless pork loin roast
1 tablespoon mustard seeds
3 tablespoons cracked black peppercorns or
    multicolored peppercorns
2 tablespoons all-purpose flour
1 tablespoon dry mustard
2 teaspoons dried thyme
1 teaspoon brown sugar
¼ cup butter, softened
2 tablespoons Dijon mustard
1 tablespoon all-purpose flour
1½ cups apple cider, divided
1 tablespoon cider vinegar
1 teaspoon Dijon mustard
3 tablespoons apple brandy
½ teaspoon salt
¼ teaspoon ground black pepper

• **Heat** oil in a heavy skillet over medium-high heat. Add roast; brown on all sides. Place roast in a roasting pan, and cool slightly.
• **Combine** mustard seeds and peppercorns in a heavy-duty, zip-top plastic bag; seal. Crush spices with a meat mallet or rolling pin.
• **Combine** crushed spices, 2 tablespoons flour, and next 3 ingredients; stir in ¼ cup butter and 2 tablespoons Dijon mustard. Spread mixture on top and sides of roast.
• **Bake** at 475° for 20 minutes; reduce heat to 325°. Loosely cover with aluminum foil; bake 1 hour and 10 minutes or until a meat thermometer inserted into thickest portion registers 160°. Remove roast from pan, reserving 2 tablespoons drippings; keep roast warm.
• **Combine** reserved drippings, 1 tablespoon flour, 2 tablespoons apple cider, cider vinegar, and 1 teaspoon Dijon mustard; set aside.
• **Bring** remaining apple cider to a boil in a saucepan over medium-high heat; boil 8 minutes or until reduced to ¾ cup. Stir in brandy; boil 1 minute.
• **Whisk** in flour mixture, salt, and pepper; cook over medium-high heat until thickened. Serve with roast. Yield: 10 servings.

PORK MEDAILLONS IN MUSTARD SAUCE

3 tablespoons vegetable oil
1 tablespoon coarse-grained mustard
½ teaspoon salt
½ teaspoon pepper
2 (¾-pound) pork tenderloins
¼ cup dry white wine
Mustard Sauce

• **Combine** first 4 ingredients; rub over tenderloins. Place tenderloins in a large heavy-duty, zip-top plastic bag. Seal bag; marinate in refrigerator 8 hours, turning bag occasionally.
• **Place** tenderloins on a lightly greased rack in a shallow roasting pan; brush with half of wine. Insert meat thermometer into thickest part of 1 tenderloin. Bake at 400° for 25 minutes or until thermometer registers 160°, brushing with remaining half of wine after 10 minutes. Let stand 10 minutes before slicing. Cut tenderloins into ¼-inch slices; arrange slices evenly on four dinner plates. Spoon Mustard Sauce evenly around slices. Yield: 4 servings.

Mustard Sauce
1¾ cups whipping cream
¼ cup coarse-grained mustard
¼ teaspoon salt
⅛ teaspoon ground white pepper

• **Cook** whipping cream in a medium saucepan over medium heat until reduced to 1¼ cups (about 15 minutes), stirring often. Add mustard, salt, and pepper; cook just until mixture is heated, stirring constantly. Yield: 1⅓ cups.

HERB-CRUSTED PORK WITH NEW POTATOES

2 pounds new potatoes
¼ cup butter or margarine, melted
2 tablespoons prepared horseradish
½ teaspoon salt
½ teaspoon freshly ground pepper
½ cup fine, dry breadcrumbs (store-bought)
⅓ cup chopped fresh basil
3 tablespoons olive oil
1 tablespoon freshly ground pepper
1 teaspoon kosher salt
3 tablespoons chopped fresh thyme
1½ pounds pork tenderloins
2 tablespoons chopped fresh parsley

• **Peel** a 1-inch strip around center of each potato. Place potatoes in a large bowl. Add butter and next 3 ingredients, tossing gently. Place potatoes on a lightly greased rack in a broiler pan.
• **Bake** at 425° for 20 minutes; remove from oven.
• **Stir** together breadcrumbs and next 5 ingredients. Moisten pork tenderloins with water; press crumb mixture over tenderloins, and place on rack with potatoes.
• **Bake** at 425° for 25 more minutes or until potatoes are tender and a meat thermometer inserted in thickest part of tenderloins registers 160°.
• **Sprinkle** potatoes with parsley, and slice tenderloins. Yield: 4 servings.

SWEET-AND-SOUR PORK

family favorite

½ cup all-purpose flour
¼ cup cornstarch
½ teaspoon salt
½ cup water
1 large egg, lightly beaten
1½ pounds boneless pork, cut into ¾-inch pieces
Vegetable oil
1 (20-ounce) can pineapple chunks, undrained
½ cup firmly packed brown sugar
½ cup white vinegar
1 tablespoon soy sauce
2 tablespoons cornstarch
2 tablespoons water
2 tablespoons vegetable oil
2 large carrots, scraped and thinly sliced
1 green pepper, seeded and cut into ¾-inch pieces
1 small onion, cut into thin wedges
1 clove garlic, minced
Hot cooked rice

• **Combine** first 5 ingredients in a bowl; stir with a wire whisk until well blended. Add pork, stirring mixture well.
• **Pour** oil to depth of 2 inches into a large heavy saucepan; heat to 375°. Carefully drop pork into hot oil, and fry 5 minutes or until golden. Drain on paper towels. Arrange pork in a single layer on a baking sheet; place in a 200° oven to keep warm while frying remaining pork.
• **Drain** pineapple, reserving juice. Set pineapple aside. Add enough water to juice to make 1 cup. Combine juice, brown sugar, vinegar, and soy sauce; stir until sugar dissolves. Set aside. Combine 2 tablespoons cornstarch and 2 tablespoons water, stirring until smooth; set aside.
• **Pour** 2 tablespoons oil around top of a preheated wok (or in a large skillet), coating sides; heat at medium-high (375°) for 2 minutes. Add carrot and next 3 ingredients; stir-fry 3 to 5 minutes or until crisp-tender. Stir in juice mixture. Bring to a boil, and boil 1 minute. Stir in cornstarch mixture; cook, stirring constantly, until thickened. Add pork and pineapple; stir-fry until thoroughly heated. Serve over rice. Yield: 6 servings.

Oven-Barbecued Pork Ribs

OVEN-BARBECUED PORK RIBS

family favorite

Country-style ribs are long and chunky, providing ample meat for hearty eaters. They make great picnic food, and you don't even need a grill.

2 tablespoons vegetable oil, divided
4 pounds country-style pork ribs
½ cup dry sherry
½ cup water
½ cup firmly packed brown sugar
1 teaspoon salt
1 teaspoon celery seeds
1 teaspoon chili powder
⅛ teaspoon pepper
2 cups water
¼ cup white vinegar
¼ cup Worcestershire sauce
1 (12-ounce) bottle chili sauce
1 medium onion, chopped

• **Add** 1 tablespoon oil to a large nonstick skillet; place over medium-high heat until hot. Brown half of ribs in skillet; set aside. Brown remaining ribs in remaining 1 tablespoon oil. Return ribs to skillet; add sherry and ½ cup water. Bring to a boil. Cover, reduce heat, and simmer 1½ hours.
• **Meanwhile,** combine brown sugar and remaining 9 ingredients in a 2-quart saucepan. Bring to a boil; simmer, uncovered, over medium heat 1 hour.
• **Transfer** ribs to a 13- x 9-inch pan; pour sauce over ribs. Bake, uncovered, at 300° for 1 hour, basting occasionally. Yield: 4 servings.

SMOKED RIBS

You can use spareribs or baby back ribs in this versatile recipe. Baby back is the smallest cut; it's not necessarily more tender, just more manageable. If you choose the larger spareribs, they may take a little longer to cook. Either way, what you end up with is fall-off-the-bone tender results.

Mesquite chunks
Vegetable cooking spray
1 teaspoon Creole seasoning
½ teaspoon freshly ground pepper
3½ pounds pork ribs

• **Soak** mesquite chunks in water 30 minutes; drain. Pile charcoal on each side of grill, leaving center empty. Place a drip pan between coals. Prepare fire; let burn 10 to 15 minutes. Place mesquite chunks on hot coals. Coat grill rack with cooking spray, and place over coals. Open air vents halfway.
• **Sprinkle** Creole seasoning and pepper on ribs. Arrange ribs on rack over drip pan; cover and cook 2½ to 3 hours or until ribs are very tender. Place additional mesquite chunks on coals during cooking, if necessary. Yield: 4 servings.

Planet Barbecue

Southern barbecue varies as much as our accents. Agreement ends there. North Carolinians brush pork with a peppery-vinegary sauce. Georgians like their BBQ sauce sweeter and red on pork ribs or on chicken. In South Carolina, mustard-based sauces are mopped on pork or chicken. Alabamians prefer a thin, tangy tomato-based sauce on pork. Tennessee BBQers guard their top secret recipes for spices rubbed over pork. Texans claim there's no point to BBQ if beef isn't the base. Don't let us start on the side dishes!

SWEET-AND-TANGY RIBS

⤳ make ahead ⤳

These delectable ribs cook in two stages. First you apply a seasoning rub and bake them; then finish them on the grill the next day, basting with a tangy-sweet sauce.

4 pounds country-style ribs
1 (12-ounce) can beer
1 teaspoon black pepper
½ teaspoon seasoned salt
½ teaspoon garlic powder
¼ teaspoon dried crushed red pepper
2 green onions, chopped
1 tablespoon vegetable oil
1 cup barbecue sauce
½ cup peach preserves
2 tablespoons white wine vinegar

• **Place** ribs on two layers of heavy duty aluminum foil. Pour beer over ribs. Combine black pepper and next 3 ingredients; sprinkle over ribs. Seal foil packet tightly. Bake at 350° for 1 hour. Cool. Cover and chill ribs overnight.
• **Sauté** green onions in oil in a large skillet over medium-high heat until tender. Add barbecue sauce, preserves, and vinegar; stir well. Simmer 1 minute; remove from heat.
• **Grill** ribs, uncovered, over medium-hot coals (350° to 400°) 20 to 30 minutes, basting heavily with barbecue sauce mixture the last 5 minutes. Serve ribs with remaining barbecue sauce mixture. Yield: 4 servings.

We don't need scientific studies to tell us what we've observed in our own backyards: Men are born to grill. Guess they like playing with fire.

MARINATED BAKED HAM

⤳ family favorite ⤳

Ham traditionally makes great holiday fare. Slice it thinly and it goes a long way.

1 (7- to 8-pound) fully cooked ham half
2 cups orange juice
2 cups ginger ale
⅓ cup firmly packed brown sugar
¼ cup orange marmalade
1 teaspoon dry mustard

• **Place** first 3 ingredients in a large heavy-duty, zip-top plastic bag. Seal bag; marinate in refrigerator 8 hours, turning bag occasionally.
• **Remove** ham from marinade, reserving marinade. Place ham, fat side up, in a shallow roasting pan lined with heavy-duty aluminum foil. Bake, uncovered, at 325° for 1½ hours, basting often with marinade.
• **Remove** ham from oven; reduce oven temperature to 300°. Slice skin from ham; score fat in a diamond design. Combine brown sugar, marmalade, and mustard; spread over scored fat. Bake ham, uncovered, 30 more minutes. Let stand 10 minutes before carving. Yield: 16 servings.

SMOKED FRESH HAM

Fresh ham is the hind leg of pork that hasn't been smoked or cured. This recipe lets you smoke it and then brush it with a sweet mustard glaze before serving.

1 bag hickory chunks
1 (10-pound) pork leg (fresh ham)
Brown Sugar-Mustard Glaze

• **Soak** hickory chunks in water 30 minutes. Prepare charcoal fire in smoker; let burn 15 minutes. Drain chunks; place chunks on hot coals. Place water pan in smoker; fill with water.
• **Place** ham on grill rack. Insert meat thermometer, making sure it does not touch fat or bone. Cook ham, covered with smoker lid, 7 hours or until meat thermometer registers 160° (ham will develop a hard black outer layer). Refill water pan, and add more charcoal as needed.
• **Remove** ham from grill rack; let stand 10 minutes to cool slightly. Carve away blackened skin, and discard. Brush ham with Brown Sugar-Mustard Glaze. Carve ham into thin slices, and transfer to a serving platter. Serve with remaining glaze. Yield: 20 servings.

Brown Sugar-Mustard Glaze
1 cup firmly packed brown sugar
2 tablespoons dry mustard
⅛ teaspoon ground cloves
⅓ cup cola beverage

• **Combine** all ingredients in a small saucepan. Bring to a simmer over medium heat, stirring constantly. Yield: ¾ cup.

VENISON WITH SOUR CREAM

3 tablespoons vegetable oil
2 pounds boneless venison loin, cut into 1½-inch cubes
1 clove garlic, minced
1 cup sliced celery
½ cup chopped onion
1 cup sliced carrot
2 cups water
1 teaspoon salt
½ teaspoon pepper
1 bay leaf
¼ cup butter or margarine
¼ cup all-purpose flour
1 (8-ounce) carton sour cream
Garnish: fresh parsley sprigs
Hot cooked egg noodles

• **Heat** oil in large skillet over medium-high heat. Place venison and garlic in skillet; brown meat on all sides. Remove meat to a shallow 2½-quart baking dish.
• **Add** celery, onion, and carrot to drippings in skillet; sauté 2 minutes. Stir in water, salt, pepper, and bay leaf; pour over venison.
• **Cover** and bake at 350° for 30 minutes; remove from oven. Drain, reserving broth. Discard bay leaf.
• **Melt** butter in a heavy saucepan over low heat; add flour, stirring until smooth. Cook 1 minute, stirring constantly. Gradually add reserved broth; cook over medium heat, stirring constantly, until thickened. Stir in sour cream. Pour sauce over venison and vegetables. Garnish, if desired. Serve over noodles. Yield: 8 servings.

Pasta, Rice and Grains

Pasta is easy food. It's healthy, affordable, has a long shelf life, and can be an entrée or a side dish. And the same's true of rice and other grains. The fun is deciding what you'll pair with them or spoon over them for dinner.

Linguine Carbonara (page 188)

LINGUINE WITH FRESH TOMATO SAUCE

◦ quick ◦

Summer-ripened tomatoes make all the difference in this dish. Use a flavored feta for extra punch.

4 large tomatoes, chopped
3 tablespoons chopped fresh basil
2 cloves garlic, minced
1 tablespoon olive oil
½ teaspoon salt
¼ teaspoon freshly ground pepper
1 (12-ounce) package dried linguine, cooked
1 (2¼-ounce) can sliced ripe olives, drained
¾ cup crumbled feta cheese

• **Combine** first 6 ingredients. Drain pasta, and place in a large serving bowl. Top with tomato mixture, and sprinkle with olives and cheese. Yield: 6 servings.

PESTO PASTA

◦ family favorite ◦

Fresh herbs give pesto its classic color, and olive oil helps it cling to hot cooked pasta. Stir in grilled chicken strips to make this a main dish.

½ cup tightly packed fresh basil leaves
¼ cup minced fresh parsley
¼ cup grated Parmesan cheese
2 tablespoons pine nuts or chopped walnuts
¼ cup olive oil
¼ teaspoon salt
¼ teaspoon pepper
1 clove garlic, halved
6 ounces dried linguine, cooked

• **Process** all ingredients except linguine in container of an electric blender until smooth, stopping once to scrape down sides.
• **Combine** pesto mixture and linguine; toss gently. Serve immediately. Yield: 4 servings.

LINGUINE CARBONARA

Strips of prosciutto ham and crisp bacon toss meaty flavor into this creamy, rich pasta dish pictured on page 186.

½ pound bacon, cut into 1-inch pieces
¼ cup olive oil
1 medium onion, chopped
1 cup chopped fresh parsley (about 1 bunch)
4 ounces fontina cheese, cubed
3 ounces prosciutto, cut into strips
1 (1-pound) package dried linguine or spaghetti
4 eggs yolks, lightly beaten
¾ cup half-and-half, heated
1 teaspoon salt
Freshly ground pepper to taste
1 cup freshly grated Parmesan cheese, divided
Garnish: fresh parsley sprigs

• **Cook** bacon in a large skillet over medium heat until crisp. Drain on paper towels. Pour off drippings; add oil and onion to skillet; sauté until onion is tender. Set aside.
• **Combine** parsley, fontina cheese, and prosciutto in a small bowl; set aside.
• **Cook** linguine in a Dutch oven according to package directions; drain. Return hot linguine to Dutch oven; immediately stir in egg yolks. Add bacon, onion, parsley mixture, heated half-and-half, seasonings, and ½ cup Parmesan cheese. Cook over low heat until thoroughly heated, stirring constantly; transfer to serving dish. Sprinkle with remaining ½ cup Parmesan cheese. Garnish, if desired. Serve immediately. Yield: 8 servings.

PEPPERONI SPAGHETTI

～family favorite, quick ～

*Pepperoni and lots of cheese make this
a dish kids will love.*

1 medium onion, chopped
1 green pepper, chopped
1 pound ground chuck
1 (3.5-ounce) package sliced pepperoni, chopped
1 (28-ounce) jar pasta sauce with mushrooms
½ (16-ounce) package dried spaghetti, cooked
1 cup (4 ounces) shredded mozzarella cheese
1 tablespoon grated Parmesan cheese

• **Combine** onion, green pepper, and ground chuck in a large skillet. Cook over medium heat until meat browns, stirring until it crumbles. Remove from heat; drain. Return meat mixture to skillet. Add pepperoni and pasta sauce; bring to a boil. Cover, reduce heat, and simmer 20 minutes, stirring occasionally.

• **Arrange** spaghetti in a greased 13- x 9-inch baking dish; top with meat sauce. Sprinkle mozzarella cheese over sauce; bake, uncovered, at 400° for 5 minutes. Remove from oven; top with Parmesan cheese. Serve hot. Yield: 8 servings.

THREE-CHEESE SPAGHETTI

1 tablespoon butter or margarine
1 tablespoon all-purpose flour
1 cup milk
½ cup (2 ounces) shredded Swiss cheese
½ cup (2 ounces) shredded Gouda cheese
¼ teaspoon salt
1 (4½-ounce) jar sliced mushrooms, drained
1 (7-ounce) package dried spaghetti, cooked
2 tablespoons butter or margarine, melted
½ cup grated Parmesan cheese

• **Melt** 1 tablespoon butter in a heavy saucepan over low heat; add flour, stirring until smooth. Cook 1 minute, stirring constantly. Gradually add milk; cook over medium heat, stirring constantly, until mixture is thickened and bubbly. Remove from heat; add Swiss cheese, Gouda cheese, salt, and mushrooms, stirring until cheeses melt.

• **Combine** spaghetti, 2 tablespoons melted butter, and Parmesan cheese; toss well. Combine cheese sauce and spaghetti mixture, stirring well. Yield: 3 servings.

SPINACH-PASTA PIE

Pasta forms a crisp shell for this spinach-custard side dish. It's an ideal complement to roast chicken or turkey.

1 (10-ounce) package frozen chopped spinach, thawed
2 tablespoons butter or margarine, melted
¾ cup grated Parmesan cheese, divided
4 ounces dried vermicelli, cooked
2 large eggs, lightly beaten
3 large eggs, lightly beaten
1 cup (4 ounces) shredded mozzarella cheese
⅓ cup milk
½ teaspoon salt
¼ teaspoon freshly ground pepper
¼ teaspoon onion powder
⅛ teaspoon ground nutmeg

• **Press** spinach between layers of paper towels; squeeze to remove excess moisture.

• **Stir** butter and ½ cup Parmesan cheese into hot vermicelli. Add 2 beaten eggs, stirring well. Spoon mixture into a greased 9-inch pieplate. Use a spoon to shape vermicelli into a pie shell. Cover and bake at 350° for 10 minutes.

• **Combine** spinach, 3 beaten eggs, mozzarella cheese, milk, and seasonings, stirring well. Spoon spinach mixture into baked pasta shell.

• **Cover** and bake at 350° for 35 minutes; uncover and sprinkle with remaining ¼ cup Parmesan cheese. Bake, uncovered, 5 more minutes. Let stand 10 minutes before slicing. Yield: 6 servings.

SHRIMP AND FETA VERMICELLI

*Crumbled feta, crushed garlic, herbs, and
wine give these strands great flavor.
The shrimp is just a bonus.*

1 pound unpeeled medium-size fresh shrimp
⅛ teaspoon dried crushed red pepper
¼ cup olive oil, divided
1 cup (4 ounces) crumbled feta cheese
2 cloves garlic, crushed
1 (14½-ounce) can diced tomatoes, undrained
¼ cup dry white wine
2 teaspoons chopped fresh basil or ¾ teaspoon
   dried basil
1½ teaspoons chopped fresh oregano or
   ½ teaspoon dried oregano
¼ teaspoon salt
¼ teaspoon black pepper
8 ounces dried vermicelli, cooked
Garnish: fresh basil

• **Sauté** shrimp and red pepper in 2 tablespoons oil in a
large skillet over medium-high heat 2 to 3 minutes or
until shrimp turn slightly pink. Arrange shrimp in a
greased 11- x 7-inch baking dish; sprinkle with feta
cheese, and set aside.
• **Add** remaining 2 tablespoons oil to skillet; cook garlic over medium heat 1 minute. Add tomatoes and
juice; cook 1 minute. Stir in wine and next 4 ingredients; simmer, uncovered, 10 minutes. Spoon tomato
mixture over shrimp. Bake, uncovered, at 400° for 10
minutes. Serve over vermicelli. Garnish, if desired.
Yield: 3 servings.

FETTUCCINE WITH POPPY SEEDS

~ quick ~

½ cup sour cream
⅓ cup butter or margarine, melted
1 tablespoon chopped fresh parsley
¾ teaspoon garlic salt
½ teaspoon poppy seeds
⅛ teaspoon pepper
6 ounces dried fettuccine, cooked
½ cup freshly grated Parmesan cheese
Garnish: fresh parsley sprigs

• **Combine** first 6 ingredients; stir well. Combine sour
cream mixture and hot cooked fettuccine; add cheese,
and toss until fettuccine is coated. Spoon into a bowl, and
garnish, if desired. Serve immediately. Yield: 4 servings.

CHICKEN-TOMATO FETTUCCINE

1 (8-ounce) jar dried tomatoes in oil, undrained
1 small onion, chopped
2 garlic cloves, minced
4 skinned and boned chicken breast halves, cut
   into strips
3 tablespoons chopped fresh basil or 1 tablespoon
   dried basil
1 cup half-and-half
½ teaspoon salt
¼ teaspoon pepper
6 ounces dried fettuccine, cooked

• **Drain** tomatoes, reserving ¼ cup oil; coarsely chop
tomatoes.
• **Sauté** onion and garlic in 2 tablespoons reserved oil
over medium-high heat until tender. Add chicken; cook 6
minutes or until done, stirring occasionally. Add tomato

and basil; cook 2 minutes, stirring occasionally. Stir in remaining oil, half-and-half, salt, and pepper. Toss with hot cooked fettuccine. Yield: 4 servings.

SMOKED SALMON-DILL PASTA

⋟ make ahead ⋞

½ cup vegetable oil
1 (8-ounce) carton sour cream
2 tablespoons lemon juice
⅓ cup chopped fresh dill
2 teaspoons minced onion
¼ teaspoon salt
¼ teaspoon pepper
12 ounces dried bow tie pasta, cooked
2 cucumbers, peeled, seeded, and chopped
6 cherry tomatoes, halved
5 ounces smoked salmon, cut into small pieces
¼ cup chopped fresh chives
¼ cup capers

• **Whisk** together first 7 ingredients in a large bowl. Toss with cooked pasta and remaining ingredients. Cover and chill. Yield: 4 servings.

Pasta-tive Attitude

90s In 1992, the U.S. Department of Agriculture (USDA) retired the Basic Four Food Groups and built the Food Guide Pyramid with a foundation of complex carbohydrates. Pasta led the carb party, and we experimented with every shape from mostaccioli to fusilli to rotini to capellini. Southern confidential: In 1997, Florida and Arkansas rated among the top 14 pasta-eating states.

PASTA ANTIPASTO

⋟ make ahead ⋞

Serve this colorful antipasto as a summer salad, entrée, or appetizer.

2 (6½-ounce) jars marinated artichoke hearts, undrained
¾ cup Italian dressing
¼ teaspoon freshly ground pepper
1 pint cherry tomatoes, halved
½ cup pimiento-stuffed olives
½ cup ripe olives or kalamata olives, pitted
½ pound fresh mushrooms
1 medium-size green pepper, seeded and cut into strips
8 ounces dried rotini (corkscrew pasta), cooked
3 to 4 ounces sliced pepperoni
3 to 4 ounces sliced salami
Freshly grated Parmesan cheese

• **Drain** artichoke hearts, reserving ½ cup artichoke liquid. Add Italian dressing and pepper to artichoke liquid; stir well.
• **Combine** artichoke hearts, tomatoes, olives, mushrooms, and green pepper in a bowl. Add three-fourths of marinade to vegetable mixture, tossing gently. Cover and marinate in refrigerator 8 hours. Add remaining marinade to cooked pasta, tossing gently. Cover and marinate in refrigerator 8 hours.
• **Arrange** pepperoni and salami slices around outer edges of a serving platter. Spoon pasta in a ring within meat, using a slotted spoon. Spoon vegetable mixture in center of platter, using a slotted spoon. Top with cheese. Yield: 8 servings.

Pasta Provençale

Pasta Provençale

quick

This ridged pasta dish highlights some of the finest ingredients used daily in Mediterranean cuisine.

2 medium zucchini, halved lengthwise and sliced, or 3 large yellow squash, sliced, or 1 of each
1 (8-ounce) package sliced fresh mushrooms
3 cloves garlic, minced
1 green pepper, chopped
¼ cup chopped onion
2 tablespoons olive oil
1 (14 ½-ounce) can diced tomatoes, undrained
1 tablespoon chopped fresh basil or ¼ teaspoon dried basil
1 tablespoon fresh oregano leaves or ⅛ teaspoon dried oregano
¼ teaspoon salt
¼ teaspoon pepper
5 ounces dried penne pasta, cooked
¼ cup freshly grated Parmesan cheese
Garnish: fresh herbs

• **Sauté** first 5 ingredients in olive oil in a large skillet or Dutch oven over medium-high heat 3 minutes. Add tomatoes, basil, oregano, salt, and pepper; stir well. Bring mixture to a boil; reduce heat, and simmer 1 minute. Remove from heat; transfer to a serving bowl. Add pasta and Parmesan cheese; toss gently. Garnish, if desired. Serve hot. Yield: 6 servings.

Three-Cheese Tortellini with Tomatoes

quick

Here's a simple pasta dish for any night of the week. Make it a meatless entrée for two or an easy side for six. Look for cheese-filled tortellini in the refrigerated section of the supermarket.

1 (9-ounce) package refrigerated cheese-filled tortellini, uncooked
2 cloves garlic, minced
1 jalapeño pepper, seeded and chopped
½ medium-size green pepper, chopped
2 tablespoons chopped onion
2 tablespoons olive oil
2 large tomatoes, chopped
1 teaspoon salt
½ teaspoon dried oregano
½ teaspoon dried basil
½ cup freshly grated Parmesan cheese
Freshly ground pepper

• **Cook** tortellini according to package directions; drain. Keep warm.
• **Sauté** garlic and next 3 ingredients in oil 3 minutes or until crisp-tender. Add tomato, salt, oregano, and basil. Cook 3 minutes, stirring constantly. Spoon mixture over tortellini, and toss gently. Sprinkle with Parmesan cheese and freshly ground pepper. Serve hot. Yield: 6 servings.

PASTA SHELLS STUFFED WITH FIVE CHEESES

1 (14½-ounce) can stewed tomatoes, undrained
1 (8-ounce) can mushroom stems and pieces, drained
1 (8-ounce) can tomato sauce
1 (6-ounce) can tomato paste
½ cup dry white wine
1 teaspoon dried oregano
1 teaspoon dried thyme
1 clove garlic, minced
1 (8-ounce) package cream cheese, softened
1 large egg, lightly beaten
1 cup (4 ounces) shredded mozzarella cheese
1 cup low-fat cottage cheese
¼ cup grated Parmesan and Romano cheese blend
2 teaspoons dried basil
½ teaspoon dried oregano
½ teaspoon dried thyme
⅛ teaspoon grated lemon rind
Pinch of ground nutmeg
16 jumbo dried pasta shells, cooked

• **Process** tomatoes in container of an electric blender or food processor until smooth. Pour pureed tomatoes into a Dutch oven; stir in mushroom stems and pieces and next 6 ingredients. Bring to a boil; reduce heat, and simmer, uncovered, 20 minutes or until thickened. Spoon mushroom mixture into a lightly greased 11- x 7-inch baking dish.

• **Combine** cream cheese and next 9 ingredients. Stuff shells evenly with cheese mixture; arrange over mushroom mixture in baking dish. Cover and bake at 350° for 25 to 30 minutes or until thoroughly heated. Yield: 4 servings.

OLD-FASHIONED MACARONI AND CHEESE

family favorite

Sometimes the simplest recipe brings the greatest pleasure. Macaroni and cheese proves the point again and again.

1 (8-ounce) package dried elbow macaroni, cooked
3 cups (12 ounces) shredded Cheddar cheese, divided
2 large eggs, lightly beaten
1½ cups milk
¾ teaspoon salt
⅛ teaspoon ground white pepper
Freshly ground black pepper (optional)

• **Layer** one-third of macaroni in a lightly greased 2-quart casserole; sprinkle with 1 cup cheese. Repeat layers with remaining two-thirds macaroni and 1 cup cheese, ending with macaroni layer. Reserve remaining 1 cup cheese.

• **Combine** eggs and next 3 ingredients, stirring with a wire whisk or fork until blended. Pour egg mixture over macaroni. Cover and bake at 350° for 45 minutes or until thoroughly heated. Uncover and sprinkle with remaining 1 cup cheese. Cover and let stand 10 minutes before serving. Sprinkle with freshly ground pepper, if desired. Yield: 8 servings.

Old-Fashioned
Macaroni and
Cheese

MOZZARELLA-AND-OLIVE ORZO

Orzo is a pearl-colored, rice-shaped pasta that cooks quicker than most rice. This Greek-inspired side dish will serve a crowd.

1 (12-ounce) block mozzarella cheese
16 ounces dried orzo, uncooked
2 tablespoons butter or margarine
2 tablespoons olive oil
1½ cups chopped onion
2 cups chopped celery
2 tablespoons all-purpose flour
1 cup chicken broth
1 (28-ounce) can plum tomatoes, drained
1 tablespoon fresh basil or 1 teaspoon dried basil
½ teaspoon dried crushed red pepper
2 (2¼-ounce) cans sliced ripe olives, drained
¼ teaspoon salt

• **Cut** 4 ounces mozzarella into thin strips; cut remaining cheese into cubes. Set aside.
• **Cook** orzo in a large saucepan according to package directions; drain and transfer to a large bowl.
• **Heat** butter and oil in saucepan over medium heat until butter melts; add onion, and sauté until tender. Add celery; sauté 5 minutes.
• **Stir** in flour, and sauté 3 minutes. Stir in broth and next 3 ingredients. Cook 5 minutes, stirring constantly.
• **Stir** broth mixture, cheese cubes, olives, and salt into orzo; spoon into a lightly greased shallow 3-quart baking dish. Arrange cheese strips on top.
• **Bake,** uncovered, at 350° for 45 minutes or until slightly crisp on top. Yield: 10 servings.

MEATY MANICOTTI

~ family favorite ~

This manicotti earned high marks in our Test Kitchens. The slow simmered tomato sauce produces delicious results that make this manicotti a great company dish. Just add a salad and garlic bread.

½ pound Italian link sausage
1 pound ground chuck
2 medium onions, chopped
5 cloves garlic, minced
2 (15-ounce) cans tomato sauce
1 (14½-ounce) can plum tomatoes, undrained and chopped
1 (12-ounce) can tomato paste
1½ teaspoons dried oregano
1¼ teaspoons dried basil
1 teaspoon sugar
½ teaspoon salt
½ teaspoon pepper
½ teaspoon dried thyme
½ teaspoon dried rosemary
¼ teaspoon dried marjoram
⅛ teaspoon ground red pepper
1 (15-ounce) carton ricotta cheese
1 (8-ounce) package cream cheese, softened
½ (8-ounce) tub cream cheese with chives, softened
½ cup grated Parmesan cheese
4 cloves garlic, crushed
½ teaspoon pepper
½ teaspoon dried thyme
½ teaspoon dried oregano
4 cups (16 ounces) shredded mozzarella cheese, divided
1 (8-ounce) package dried manicotti shells, cooked

• **Remove** sausage from casings. Cook sausage, beef, onion, and garlic in a large Dutch oven until beef is browned, stirring until meats crumble; drain well. Return meats to Dutch oven.

• **Add** tomato sauce and next 11 ingredients; bring to a boil. Cover, reduce heat, and simmer 1½ hours, stirring occasionally.

• **Combine** ricotta cheese and next 7 ingredients in a large bowl; stir in 3 cups mozzarella. Stuff mixture evenly into manicotti shells.

• **Spoon** half of meat sauce into a lightly greased lasagna pan or two lightly greased 2½-quart shallow casseroles. Arrange stuffed shells over sauce. Spoon remaining sauce over shells.

• **Cover** and bake at 350° for 35 minutes or until thoroughly heated. Sprinkle with remaining 1 cup mozzarella cheese. Let stand 5 minutes before serving. Yield: 7 servings.

What's Old Is New Again

90s Americans' love affair with Italian food isn't ending any time soon. We'll be celebrating well into the 2000s with risotto, the creamy dish made from short-grain Arborio rice; orzo, the rice-shaped pasta; and corn-based polenta dishes. Hmmmm. Sounds like rice and grits, eh?

SPINACH-STUFFED MANICOTTI

family favorite

1 (10-ounce) package frozen chopped spinach, thawed
½ (8-ounce) package cream cheese, softened
1 cup ricotta cheese
1 cup (4 ounces) shredded mozzarella cheese
½ cup freshly grated Parmesan cheese
1 teaspoon dried Italian seasoning
¼ teaspoon salt
8 dried manicotti shells, cooked
2 cups pasta sauce
½ cup freshly grated Parmesan cheese

• **Press** spinach between layers of paper towels to remove excess moisture. Combine spinach, cream cheese, and next 5 ingredients, stirring well. Stuff mixture evenly into manicotti shells.

• **Pour** ½ cup pasta sauce into a lightly greased 11- x 7-inch baking dish; arrange stuffed shells over sauce. Spoon remaining 1½ cups pasta sauce over shells.

• **Cover** and bake at 350° for 30 minutes or until thoroughly heated. Sprinkle with ½ cup Parmesan cheese; bake, uncovered, 5 more minutes or until cheese melts. Yield: 4 servings.

LASAGNA MARIA

family favorite

*Sausage and pepperoni add chunks of flavor to this
favorite multilayered casserole.*

1 pound ground pork sausage
1 (28-ounce) jar spaghetti sauce
½ cup water
1 large egg, lightly beaten
1 (15-ounce) carton ricotta cheese
¼ cup grated Parmesan cheese
1 tablespoon dried parsley flakes
½ teaspoon dried oregano
¼ teaspoon pepper

1 (8-ounce) package lasagna noodles,
    cooked
2 cups (8 ounces) shredded mozzarella
    cheese, divided
1 (7-ounce) jar sliced mushrooms,
    drained
1 (3½-ounce) package sliced
    pepperoni

• **Brown** sausage in a skillet over medium heat, stirring until it crumbles; drain. Stir in spaghetti sauce and water; set aside. Combine egg and next 5 ingredients, stirring well.
• **Spread** about ½ cup meat sauce in a lightly greased 13- x 9-inch pan. Layer 3 lasagna noodles, half of the ricotta cheese mixture, one-third of mozzarella cheese, and one-third of remaining meat sauce; repeat layers. Top with remaining noodles. Arrange mushrooms and pepperoni slices on top. Spoon remaining meat sauce on top.
• **Bake,** uncovered, at 375° for 20 minutes. Sprinkle with remaining mozzarella cheese, and bake 5 more minutes. Yield: 6 servings.

*NOTE: If desired, sauté 2 cups sliced fresh mushrooms in 1 tablespoon olive oil
3 minutes over medium-high heat instead of using mushrooms in a jar.*

Lasagna Maria

CHICKEN LASAGNA

1 (2½- to 3-pound) broiler-fryer
6 cups water
1 teaspoon salt
1 clove garlic, minced
2 tablespoons butter or margarine, melted
1 (10¾-ounce) can cream of celery soup,
    undiluted
½ teaspoon dried oregano
¼ teaspoon pepper
8 lasagna noodles, uncooked
1 (8-ounce) loaf process American cheese, cut into
    ¼-inch slices, divided
2 cups (8 ounces) shredded mozzarella cheese,
    divided
2 tablespoons grated Parmesan cheese

• **Place** chicken in a Dutch oven; add water and salt, and bring to a boil. Cover, reduce heat, and simmer 45 minutes or until chicken is tender. Drain, reserving broth; cool slightly.
• **Remove** chicken from bone, cutting meat into bite-size pieces; set aside.
• **Cook** garlic in butter in a skillet over medium-high heat 2 minutes, stirring constantly. Add soup, ¾ cup reserved chicken broth, oregano, and pepper.
• **Cook** lasagna noodles according to package directions in remaining reserved chicken broth, adding more water, if necessary; drain.
• **Spoon** a small amount of sauce into a lightly greased 11- x 7-inch baking dish. Layer with half each of noodles, sauce, chicken, and American and mozzarella cheeses. Repeat procedures with noodles, sauce, and chicken, reserving remaining American and mozzarella cheeses.
• **Bake** at 350° for 25 minutes; top with remaining American and mozzarella cheeses and Parmesan cheese. Bake 5 more minutes. Let stand 10 minutes. Yield: 6 servings.

VEGETABLE LASAGNA

2 cups sliced fresh mushrooms
5 medium carrots, scraped and shredded (1 cup)
½ cup chopped onion
1 tablespoon vegetable oil
1 (18-ounce) can tomato paste
1 (15-ounce) can tomato sauce
1 (4-ounce) can sliced ripe olives, drained
1½ teaspoons dried oregano
1 teaspoon dried fennel
12 lasagna noodles, cooked
2 cups cottage cheese, divided
1 (10-ounce) package frozen chopped spinach,
    thawed and well drained
2 (8-ounce) packages sliced mozzarella cheese,
    divided
Grated Parmesan cheese

• **Sauté** mushrooms, carrot, and onion in oil in a large skillet over medium heat until tender. Stir in tomato paste and next 4 ingredients; bring to a boil. Remove skillet from heat.
• **Arrange** half of noodles in a lightly greased 13- x 9-inch baking dish. Layer half each of cottage cheese, spinach, vegetable mixture, and mozzarella in dish. Repeat layers with remaining noodles, cottage cheese, spinach, and vegetable mixture.
• **Bake** at 375° for 40 minutes. Add remaining mozzarella slices, and bake 5 more minutes. Let stand 10 minutes; serve with Parmesan cheese. Yield: 8 servings.

PARSLIED RICE

quick

3 cups water
1 tablespoon chicken bouillon granules
1½ cups uncooked long-grain rice
3 green onions, sliced
2 tablespoons butter or margarine, melted
½ cup chopped fresh parsley

• **Combine** water and bouillon granules in a large saucepan; bring to a boil. Stir in rice; return to a boil. Cover, reduce heat, and simmer 25 minutes or until liquid is absorbed and rice is tender.
• **Sauté** green onions in melted butter in a small skillet over medium heat until tender. Combine cooked rice, green onions, and parsley; toss gently. Yield: 6 servings.

ORANGE-HERB RICE

2 **tablespoons chopped onion**
2 **tablespoons butter or margarine, melted**
2 **cups water**
½ **teaspoon grated orange rind**
½ **cup orange juice**
1 **teaspoon salt**
⅛ **teaspoon dried marjoram or oregano**
⅛ **teaspoon dried thyme**
1 **cup uncooked long-grain rice**

• **Cook** onion in butter in a large saucepan over medium-high heat until tender, stirring constantly. Add water and next 5 ingredients; bring to a boil. Stir in rice. Cover, reduce heat, and simmer 25 minutes or until liquid is absorbed and rice is tender. Yield: 4 servings.

Read "Oil" About It

*70*ˢ Vegetable oil and shortening replaced lard in most recipes as we sought a lighter taste.

*80*ˢ Polyunsaturated fats (safflower, soybean, and corn oils) rose to favor among cholesterol-conscious consumers.

*90*ˢ Olive oil, a monounsaturated fat, oozed into the spotlight with nutritionists' blessings. Interest in the Mediterranean style of cooking soared and olive oil poured.

BEER RICE

A good all-purpose rice dish is essential to any cook's repertoire. Add this one to your collection.

½ **cup chopped onion**
½ **cup chopped green pepper**
½ **cup butter or margarine, melted**
2 **chicken bouillon cubes**
2 **cups boiling water**
1 **cup uncooked long-grain rice**
¾ **cup beer**
¼ **teaspoon salt**
¼ **teaspoon pepper**
¼ **teaspoon dried thyme**

• **Sauté** onion and green pepper in butter in a saucepan over medium heat until tender. Dissolve bouillon cubes in boiling water; add bouillon mixture to onion and green pepper mixture. Stir in rice, beer, and seasonings. Bring to a boil; cover, reduce heat, and simmer 30 to 40 minutes or until liquid is absorbed and rice is tender. Yield: 4 servings.

RICE PILAF

1½ **cups uncooked long-grain rice**
2 **tablespoons butter or margarine, melted**
3¼ **cups chicken broth**
⅓ **cup chopped fresh parsley**
⅓ **cup chopped celery**
⅓ **cup chopped carrot**
⅓ **cup sliced almonds**
¼ **teaspoon pepper**

• **Cook** rice in butter in a large skillet over medium-high heat until rice is lightly browned, stirring often. Stir in chicken broth and remaining ingredients. Bring to a boil, and remove from heat. Pour rice mixture into a lightly greased 2-quart casserole. Cover and bake at 375° for 30 minutes or until liquid is absorbed and rice is tender. Yield: 6 servings.

CURRIED RICE WITH RAISINS INDIENNE

Indienne is a French term referring to a dish flavored with curry and served with rice. This version pairs well with grilled pork.

1 cup uncooked long-grain rice
2 tablespoons butter or margarine, divided
1 to 1½ teaspoons curry powder
2 cups chicken broth
⅔ cup raisins
⅓ cup chopped green onions
⅓ cup chopped green pepper
⅓ cup chopped celery
2 tablespoons diced pimiento
1 tablespoon chutney
1 tablespoon cider vinegar
1 tablespoon brown sugar
½ teaspoon seasoned salt
2 tablespoons pine nuts, toasted (optional)

• **Combine** rice, 1 tablespoon butter, and curry powder in a saucepan. Cook over medium-low heat 5 minutes, stirring often. Add chicken broth, and bring to a boil. Cover tightly, and cook over low heat 15 minutes or until liquid is absorbed and rice is tender. Keep warm.
• **Heat** remaining 1 tablespoon butter in a skillet over medium-high heat. Add raisins and next 3 ingredients; sauté 2 minutes or just until tender. Stir in pimiento and next 4 ingredients; add pine nuts, if desired. Spoon hot rice onto a serving platter; spoon raisin mixture over top. Yield: 4 servings.

ARMENIAN RICE

Bits of broken pasta and rice become partners in this simply flavored side dish. Serve it with a pork roast or pot roast.

½ cup butter or margarine
1 medium onion, chopped
1 cup dried vermicelli, broken
2 cups uncooked long-grain rice
¼ teaspoon salt
¼ teaspoon pepper
4 cups beef consommé

• **Melt** butter in a Dutch oven over medium heat. Add onion and vermicelli; sauté until onion is tender. Stir in rice and remaining ingredients; bring to a boil. Cover, reduce heat, and simmer 30 minutes or until liquid is absorbed and rice is tender. Yield: 10 servings.

SAVANNAH RED RICE

family favorite

5 slices bacon
1¼ cups chopped onion
½ cup chopped celery
½ cup chopped green pepper
1 (14½-ounce) can whole tomatoes, undrained and chopped
1 cup uncooked long-grain rice
¾ cup water
½ teaspoon salt
¼ teaspoon black pepper
¼ teaspoon ground red pepper
⅛ teaspoon hot sauce

• **Cook** bacon in a large skillet until crisp; remove bacon, reserving 2 tablespoons drippings in skillet. Crumble bacon, and set aside.
• **Sauté** onion, celery, and green pepper in drippings over medium-high heat until tender. Stir in bacon, tomatoes,

and remaining ingredients. Spoon rice mixture into a lightly greased 2-quart casserole. Cover and bake at 350° for 1 hour or until liquid is absorbed and rice is tender. Yield: 6 servings.

BROWN RICE CASSEROLE

make ahead

Make this brown rice casserole ahead to serve with pork roast, chicken, or turkey.

½ cup butter or margarine, divided
1 bunch green onions, chopped (about 1½ cups)
3 medium carrots, scraped and chopped (about 1½ cups)
2 cups uncooked brown rice
4½ cups chicken broth
½ cup dry white wine
2 cloves garlic, minced
1 (8-ounce) package sliced fresh mushrooms
¾ cup chopped fresh parsley
¼ teaspoon freshly ground black pepper
1 cup freshly grated Parmesan cheese
2 large eggs, beaten
1 cup half-and-half
⅛ teaspoon ground nutmeg

• **Melt** ¼ cup butter in a large skillet over medium-high heat. Add green onions and carrot; sauté 5 minutes. Add rice, and cook 1 minute, stirring constantly. Add chicken broth and wine. Bring to a boil; cover, reduce heat, and simmer 45 minutes or until liquid is absorbed and rice is tender.
• **Sauté** garlic in remaining ¼ cup butter 1 minute; add mushrooms, and cook 5 minutes or until mushrooms are tender. Stir in parsley and pepper.
• **Layer** half of rice mixture in a greased 13- x 9-inch baking dish. Spoon mushroom mixture over rice; top with ½ cup Parmesan cheese. Spread remaining rice

mixture on top. Sprinkle with remaining ½ cup Parmesan cheese.
• **Combine** eggs, half-and-half, and nutmeg. Pour over rice. Cover and chill up to 24 hours.
• **Remove** casserole from refrigerator, and let stand 20 minutes. Bake, uncovered, at 350° for 30 minutes or until thoroughly heated. Yield: 8 servings.

JAMBALAYA

family favorite

2 cups uncooked long-grain rice
1 pound smoked sausage, cut into ½-inch slices
½ pound cooked ham, chopped
½ cup vegetable oil
½ cup all-purpose flour
1 cup chopped onion
1 cup chopped celery
1 medium-size green pepper, chopped
1 bunch green onions, chopped and divided
4 cloves garlic, minced
1 (28-ounce) can stewed tomatoes
1 teaspoon garlic salt
½ teaspoon pepper
½ teaspoon paprika
½ teaspoon dried thyme
¼ teaspoon ground red pepper

• **Cook** rice according to package directions. Brown sausage and ham in a large skillet; drain well.
• **Heat** oil in a large Dutch oven. Add flour, and cook over medium-high heat, stirring constantly, until mixture turns copper colored (about 8 minutes). Stir in onion, celery, green pepper, half of green onions, and garlic.
• **Cook** over medium heat 15 minutes, stirring often. Add tomatoes and seasonings. Reduce heat, and simmer 5 minutes, stirring occasionally. Stir in meat and remaining green onions; cook until thoroughly heated. Add rice, and stir well. Serve immediately. Yield: 6 servings.

Hopping John

HOPPING JOHN

~family favorite~

This New Year's day recipe of good luck peas and rice is a universal favorite.

1 cup sliced celery
⅔ cup chopped onion
1 clove garlic, minced
1 tablespoon vegetable oil
1 (16-ounce) package frozen black-eyed peas
¾ pound cubed cooked ham
2½ cups chicken broth
¼ teaspoon dried crushed red pepper
1 bay leaf
1 cup uncooked long-grain rice
Freshly ground pepper
Garnish: celery leaves

• **Cook** first 3 ingredients in hot oil in a Dutch oven over medium-high heat, stirring constantly, until tender. Stir in peas and next 4 ingredients. Bring to a boil; cover, reduce heat, and simmer 30 minutes. Stir in rice; cover and cook 20 to 25 minutes or until liquid is absorbed and rice is tender. Discard bay leaf before serving. Sprinkle with freshly ground pepper. Garnish, if desired. Yield: 4 servings.

GOURMET WILD RICE

⅔ cup currants
¼ cup brandy
1⅓ cups uncooked wild rice
3 cups chicken broth
2 tablespoons olive oil
½ cup pine nuts, toasted

• **Combine** currants and brandy; set aside. Combine wild rice and chicken broth in a medium saucepan; bring to a boil. Cover, reduce heat, and simmer 55 to 60 minutes or until liquid is absorbed and rice is tender. Stir in currant mixture, olive oil, and pine nuts. Yield: 6 servings.

WILD AND DIRTY RICE

Before you roast your next turkey, remove the giblets. You can freeze them for several months. And then when you want to make dirty rice, you'll have them on hand.

1 quart water
2 skinned, boned chicken breast halves (½ pound)
10 ounces chicken gizzards and hearts (1½ cups)
½ pound chicken livers (1 cup)
4 stalks celery, chopped
1 green pepper, chopped
1 large onion, chopped (about 2¾ cups)
5 green onions, chopped
3 cloves garlic, minced
3 tablespoons chopped fresh parsley
⅓ cup olive oil
2 (2.75-ounce) packages quick-cooking wild rice, uncooked
¼ cup uncooked long-grain rice
1 (7-ounce) can sliced mushrooms, drained
3 cups chicken broth
2 teaspoons salt
1 teaspoon black pepper
½ teaspoon poultry seasoning
¼ teaspoon ground red pepper
½ cup slivered almonds

• **Combine** water, chicken breast halves, and gizzards and hearts in a Dutch oven; bring to a boil. Cover, reduce heat, and simmer 15 minutes; add livers, and cook 10 more minutes or until tender. Drain; finely chop chicken breasts, gizzards, hearts, and livers. Set chopped meat aside.
• **Sauté** celery and next 5 ingredients in oil in a large skillet until tender; add rices and next 6 ingredients. Pour rice mixture into a lightly greased 13- x 9-inch baking dish.
• **Cover** and bake at 350° for 50 minutes. Uncover, sprinkle with slivered almonds, and bake 20 more minutes. Yield: 10 servings.

SAFFRON RISOTTO WITH PISTACHIOS

¼ cup unsalted butter
1 medium-size yellow onion, chopped
1 teaspoon saffron threads
1¾ cups uncooked Arborio rice
1 cup dry white vermouth or chicken broth
5 cups chicken broth
1 cup grated Parmesan cheese
3 tablespoons coarsely chopped pistachios

• **Melt** butter in a skillet over medium-high heat; add onion. Sauté 5 minutes. Add saffron; sauté 1 minute. Add rice; cook 2 minutes, stirring constantly. Reduce heat to medium; add vermouth and 2 cups broth. Cook, stirring constantly, until liquid is absorbed.
• **Repeat** procedure with remaining broth, ½ cup at a time. (Cooking time is 30 to 45 minutes.) Remove from heat; stir in cheese and pistachios. Yield: 8 servings.

True Grits

True grits lovers know how to convert the uninitiated: Cheese Grits. Stir in Cheddar, Swiss, or blue cheese. We like to add green chiles and crumbled sausage. The final touch— garlic! And, don't be shy about it. Here were some other captivating gritty Southern Living *recipe titles:*

70ˢ Mexican Grits Soufflé

80ˢ Grits Patties and Fried Grits

90ˢ Grilled Grits, Southwestern Grits Cakes, Redneck Risotto, and Spoonbread Grits with Savory Mushroom Sauce

SPINACH-PARMESAN COUSCOUS

⌁ *quick* ⌁

Couscous cooks in mere minutes. It's simple and healthy food, combined here with some of the best flavors of the Mediterranean—garlic, olive oil, lemon, and Parmesan.

1 medium onion, chopped
1 garlic clove, crushed
2 tablespoons olive oil
1 (14½-ounce) can chicken broth
1 (10-ounce) package frozen chopped spinach
1 (10-ounce) package couscous
¾ cup freshly grated Parmesan cheese
½ cup chopped pecans, toasted
2 tablespoons lemon juice
½ teaspoon salt
½ teaspoon freshly ground pepper

• **Sauté** onion and garlic in hot oil in a large saucepan until tender. Add broth and spinach; cook until spinach thaws, stirring occasionally. Bring to a boil, stirring occasionally.
• **Stir** in couscous; cover, remove from heat, and let stand 5 minutes or until liquid is absorbed.
• **Stir** in cheese and remaining ingredients. Serve immediately. Yield: 8 servings.

SERRANO CHILE POLENTA

~ quick ~

Serve this polenta just as you would mashed potatoes.

3 cups water
1 cup white cornmeal
½ cup butter or margarine, cut up
1 cup shredded Parmesan cheese
2 serrano chiles, seeded and chopped or jalapeño peppers
1 tablespoon chopped fresh cilantro
¼ teaspoon salt
¼ teaspoon pepper

• **Bring** 3 cups water to a boil in a large heavy saucepan; gradually add cornmeal, whisking until smooth. Cook 3 to 5 minutes or until thickened. Remove from heat.
• **Whisk** in butter and remaining ingredients. Serve warm or spread polenta into a lightly greased 9-inch square pan. Cool slightly. Cut into desired shapes. Yield: 4 servings.

GARLIC-CHEESE GRITS

~ quick ~

4 cups water
1 cup uncooked quick-cooking grits
½ teaspoon salt
1 (6-ounce) roll process cheese food with garlic
⅛ teaspoon ground red pepper

• **Bring** water to a boil in a large saucepan or Dutch oven; stir in grits and salt.

• **Return** to a boil; cover, reduce heat, and simmer 5 minutes, stirring occasionally. Remove from heat; add cheese and pepper, stirring until cheese melts. Serve hot. Yield: 6 servings.

CHEESE GRITS CASSEROLE

~ family favorite ~

4 cups water
1 teaspoon salt
1 cup quick-cooking grits
2 cups (8 ounces) shredded sharp Cheddar cheese
⅔ cup milk
⅓ cup butter or margarine
1 teaspoon Worcestershire sauce
¼ teaspoon ground red pepper
4 large eggs, lightly beaten
Paprika

• **Bring** water and salt to a boil in a large saucepan; stir in grits. Return to a boil. Cover, reduce heat, and simmer 5 minutes, stirring occasionally.
• **Remove** from heat. Add cheese and next 4 ingredients, stirring until cheese and butter melt. Add eggs; stir well.
• **Spoon** mixture into a lightly greased 2-quart casserole; sprinkle with paprika.
• **Bake,** uncovered, at 350° for 1 hour or until thoroughly heated and lightly browned. Let stand 5 minutes before serving. Yield: 8 servings.

Pies and Pastries

An assortment of prizeworthy
pies and pastries abounds on these
pages. While there is nothing as
American as apple pie, there is
nothing more Southern than
pie of any kind.

Coconut Cream Pie (page 216)

APPLE STREUSEL PIE

~family favorite~

A crunchy golden streusel topping adorns tender spiced apples for this all-American dessert.

¾ cup sugar
3 tablespoons all-purpose flour
1 teaspoon ground coriander
½ teaspoon ground cinnamon
¼ teaspoon salt
⅛ teaspoon ground nutmeg
7 cups peeled, sliced Granny Smith apples
1 unbaked 10-inch deep-dish pastry shell
Streusel Topping
Ice cream or sweetened whipped cream

• **Combine** first 6 ingredients in a large bowl; add apple slices, stirring until coated. Let stand 30 minutes. Spoon apple mixture into pastry shell. Sprinkle Streusel Topping over apples. Bake at 375° for 50 to 55 minutes or until golden.
• **Serve** warm with ice cream or sweetened whipped cream. Yield: 1 (10-inch) pie.

Streusel Topping
1 cup all-purpose flour
½ cup firmly packed brown sugar
½ cup butter or margarine, cut into small pieces

• **Combine** flour and brown sugar; stir well. Cut in butter with a pastry blender until mixture is crumbly. Yield: about 2 cups.

APPLESAUCE PIE

Enjoy homemade chunky applesauce sweetened and spooned into a flaky crust. Dollop spiced ice cream onto each warm serving.

10 large Granny Smith apples, peeled and chopped
1 large lemon, sliced and seeded
2½ cups sugar
3 tablespoons butter or margarine
1 teaspoon vanilla extract
1 (15-ounce) package refrigerated piecrusts
Spiced Ice Cream

• **Cook** first 3 ingredients in a Dutch oven over medium heat 35 minutes or until thickened, stirring often. Remove from heat. Discard lemon. Add butter and vanilla, stirring until butter melts. Cool.
• **Unfold** piecrusts. Fit 1 piecrust into a 9-inch pieplate according to package directions. Pour applesauce mixture into crust.
• **Roll** remaining piecrust to press out fold lines; cut into ½-inch strips. Reserve 4 strips. Arrange remaining strips in a lattice design over filling; fold edges under, and crimp.
• **Cut** reserved pastry strips in half lengthwise. Lay halves side by side, and twist; arrange around inner edge of pie.
• **Bake** on lowest oven rack at 425° for 30 to 35 minutes or until golden, shielding with aluminum foil to prevent excessive browning, if necessary. Serve with Spiced Ice Cream. Yield: 1 (9-inch) pie.

Spiced Ice Cream
2 pints vanilla ice cream, softened
1 teaspoon ground cinnamon
½ teaspoon ground nutmeg

• **Stir** together all ingredients. Freeze. Yield: 2 pints.

BAKED APPLE TURNOVERS

～ quick ～

Refrigerated piecrusts make these fruit turnovers ultraeasy.

1 cup apple pie filling
¼ teaspoon apple pie spice (optional)
1 (15-ounce) package refrigerated piecrusts
1 cup sifted powdered sugar
1 tablespoon plus 1 teaspoon milk
½ teaspoon vanilla extract

• **Chop** pie filling. Stir apple pie spice into chopped pie filling, if desired. Set aside.
• **Unfold** piecrusts, pressing lightly to remove fold lines; cut into 8 (4½-inch) circles.
• **For** each turnover, spoon 2 tablespoons pie filling mixture onto half of pastry circle. Moisten edges of circle with water; fold dough over filling, pressing edges to seal. Crimp edges with a fork. Place turnovers on a lightly greased baking sheet. Bake at 425° for 13 to 15 minutes or until golden.
• **Combine** powdered sugar, milk, and vanilla, stirring until smooth. Drizzle glaze over warm turnovers. Yield: 8 turnovers.

BLACKBERRY PIE

～ family favorite ～

Here's a great use for fresh-picked berries. Dress up the pie with a woven top crust.

1 cup sugar
3 tablespoons all-purpose flour
Pinch of salt
4 cups fresh blackberries, washed and capped
1 (15-ounce) package refrigerated piecrusts
2 tablespoons butter or margarine
1 tablespoon sugar

• **Combine** first 3 ingredients in a large bowl, stirring well. Add berries, and toss gently; set aside.
• **Unfold** piecrusts. Fit 1 piecrust into a 9-inch pieplate according to package directions. Spoon berry mixture into crust; dot with butter.
• **Roll** remaining piecrust to press out fold lines; cut into ½-inch strips. Arrange strips in a lattice design over filling; fold edges under, and crimp. Sprinkle lattice with remaining tablespoon sugar.
• **Bake** at 400° for 40 minutes, shielding pie with aluminum foil near end of baking, if necessary. Serve with ice cream. Yield: 1 (9-inch) pie.

PEACHES 'N' CREAM PIE

~ make ahead ~

½ (15-ounce) package refrigerated piecrusts
6 medium peaches, peeled and thinly sliced
1 (8-ounce) carton sour cream
½ cup sugar
3 tablespoons all-purpose flour
½ teaspoon grated lemon rind
¼ teaspoon ground nutmeg

• **Unfold** piecrust. Fit piecrust into a 9-inch pieplate according to package directions; fold edges under, and crimp.
• **Bake** piecrust at 400° for 8 minutes; set aside. Combine peaches and remaining 5 ingredients in a large bowl, stirring well. Spoon into pastry shell.
• **Bake** at 400° for 10 minutes. Reduce heat to 350°; bake 10 more minutes. Shield pie with aluminum foil, and bake 20 more minutes. Cool completely on a wire rack. Chill 2 hours before serving. Yield: 1 (9-inch) pie.

Easy as Pie

***Southern Living* has created** piecrusts made with chocolate, nuts, graham crackers, and gingersnaps. We've filled them beyond the brim with apples, blackberries, pecans, ice cream, coconut cream, chocolate amandine, and many other filling choices. But *Southern Living* didn't invent the easiest piecrust solution of all. Pillsbury did in 1981 with refrigerated piecrusts. We won't tell if you're tempted to call them your own—we frequently do, and we usually get away with it!

EASY BLUEBERRY PIE

Nutmeg enhances the tangy blueberry flavor in this easy summer pie.

¾ to 1 cup sugar
¼ cup all-purpose flour
¼ teaspoon ground nutmeg
⅛ teaspoon salt
4 cups fresh blueberries
1 (15-ounce) package refrigerated piecrusts
1 tablespoon lemon juice
2 tablespoons butter or margarine
1 large egg, lightly beaten
Sugar

• **Combine** first 4 ingredients in a large bowl, stirring well. Add blueberries, and toss gently; set aside.
• **Unfold** piecrusts. Fit 1 piecrust into a 9-inch pieplate according to package directions. Spoon berry mixture into crust; sprinkle with lemon juice, and dot with butter.
• **Roll** remaining piecrust to press out fold lines; transfer to top of pie. Fold edges under, and crimp. Cut slits in top of pastry to allow steam to escape. Brush pastry with beaten egg; sprinkle with sugar.
• **Bake** at 425° for 10 minutes; reduce oven temperature to 375°, and bake 30 more minutes, shielding pie with aluminum foil to prevent excessive browning, if necessary. Yield: 1 (9-inch) pie.

*Easy Blueberry
Pie*

CRANBERRY STREUSEL PIE

The crimson-colored holiday berry debuts in this pretty pie. Fresh or frozen berries work well, too.

½ (15-ounce) package refrigerated piecrusts
2 cups fresh or frozen cranberries
¼ cup sugar
¼ cup firmly packed light brown sugar
½ cup chopped walnuts
½ teaspoon ground cinnamon
1 large egg
⅓ cup sugar
¼ cup butter or margarine, melted
3 tablespoons all-purpose flour

• **Unfold** piecrust. Fit piecrust into a 9-inch pieplate according to package directions; fold edges under, and crimp.
• **Stir** together cranberries and next 4 ingredients, and spoon into piecrust.
• **Whisk** together egg and remaining 3 ingredients; pour over cranberry mixture.
• **Bake** at 400° for 20 minutes. Reduce oven temperature to 350°, and bake 30 more minutes. Yield: 1 (9-inch) pie.

PEAR-MINCEMEAT PIE

3 pounds pears, peeled and diced
1 (15-ounce) package raisins
3½ cups sugar
⅓ cup cider vinegar
½ teaspoon salt
1½ teaspoons ground nutmeg
1½ teaspoons ground cinnamon
1½ teaspoons ground allspice
1½ teaspoons ground cloves
1 (15-ounce) package refrigerated piecrusts
½ cup chopped pecans, toasted
1 large egg, lightly beaten

• **Bring** first 9 ingredients to a boil over high heat in a large heavy saucepan, stirring often. Reduce heat to medium-high, and cook 25 to 30 minutes or until thickened, stirring often. Cool.
• **Unfold** piecrusts. Fit 1 piecrust into a 9-inch deep-dish pieplate according to package directions.
• **Stir** pecans into pear mixture; spoon filling into prepared piecrust.
• **Roll** remaining piecrust to press out fold lines. Cut out leaf shapes from center of piecrust, using a leaf-shaped cookie cutter and leaving a 3-inch border around edges.
• **Place** piecrust carefully over filling, and fold edges under. Make diagonal cuts into edge at ¼-inch intervals, and fold every other piece inward. Brush piecrust and leaves with beaten egg. Arrange leaves on pie.
• **Bake** on lowest oven rack at 350° for 1 hour or until golden, shielding with aluminum foil to prevent excessive browning, if necessary. Yield: 1 (9-inch) pie.

FRESH PEACH CRISP

family favorite

1 cup all-purpose flour
½ cup sugar
½ cup firmly packed brown sugar
¼ teaspoon salt
½ teaspoon ground cinnamon
½ cup butter or margarine, cut up
4 cups sliced fresh peaches (3½ pounds)
1 tablespoon lemon juice
2 tablespoons water

• **Combine** flour, sugars, salt, and cinnamon; cut in butter with a pastry blender until mixture is crumbly.
• **Combine** peaches, lemon juice, and water; toss gently. Spoon mixture into a greased 8-inch square pan. Sprinkle flour mixture over peaches.
• **Bake** at 350° for 1 hour or until bubbly and crust begins to crisp. Serve warm. Yield: 6 servings.

CREAM CHEESE TARTS

family favorite, make ahead

2 (8-ounce) packages cream cheese, softened
1 cup sugar
2 large eggs
1 teaspoon vanilla extract
12 vanilla wafers
Blueberry or cherry pie filling

• **Beat** cream cheese at medium speed with an electric mixer until creamy; add sugar, beating well. Add eggs, 1 at a time, beating after each addition. Stir in vanilla.
• **Place** a vanilla wafer in each paper-lined cup of a muffin pan. Spoon cream cheese mixture over wafers, filling cups full. Bake at 350° for 20 minutes. Cool. Leave in pan, and chill tarts overnight.
• **To serve,** top each tart with 1 level tablespoon fruit pie filling. Yield: 1 dozen.

CHOCOLATE-CHERRY TART

make ahead

This rich, dense dessert is a great choice for easy entertaining.

1½ cups chocolate cookie crumbs
2 tablespoons sugar
¼ cup butter or margarine, melted
1 cup sugar
½ cup butter or margarine, melted
2 large eggs
½ teaspoon vanilla extract
¼ teaspoon almond extract
⅔ cup all-purpose flour
1 teaspoon baking powder
3 tablespoons cocoa
1 (16-ounce) can pitted tart water-packed red cherries, well drained
½ cup chopped pecans, toasted
1 cup whipping cream
2 tablespoons powdered sugar
2 tablespoons cherry liqueur (optional)

• **Combine** first 3 ingredients; press firmly into bottom and 1 inch up sides of a greased and floured 9-inch springform pan. Set crust aside.
• **Beat** 1 cup sugar and ½ cup melted butter at medium speed with an electric mixer until smooth. Add eggs and flavorings, beating well.
• **Combine** flour, baking powder, and cocoa; add to egg mixture, beating until well blended. Stir in cherries and pecans; pour into prepared crust.
• **Bake** at 325° for 1 hour and 10 minutes or until center springs back when touched. Cool on a wire rack.
• **Cover** tart, and chill 8 hours.
• **Beat** whipping cream until foamy; gradually add powdered sugar, beating until soft peaks form. Gently fold in liqueur, if desired.
• **Remove** sides of springform pan; slice tart into wedges. Serve whipped cream mixture with tart. Yield: 1 (9-inch) tart.

COCONUT CREAM PIE

family favorite

Toasted coconut blankets a whipped cream-covered coconut pudding—this pie will be a hit in any household. See it on page 208.

¾ cup sugar
¼ cup cornstarch
¼ teaspoon salt
2 cups milk
3 egg yolks
2 tablespoons butter or margarine
1 teaspoon vanilla extract
1 cup flaked coconut
1 baked 9-inch pastry shell
1 cup whipping cream
¼ cup sifted powdered sugar
Garnish: toasted flaked coconut

• **Combine** first 3 ingredients in a heavy saucepan; gradually stir in milk. Cook over medium heat, stirring constantly, until thickened and bubbly. Cook 1 minute.
• **Beat** egg yolks; gradually stir about one-fourth of hot mixture into yolks; add to remaining hot mixture, stirring constantly. Cook, stirring constantly, 1 minute or until temperature reaches 160°. Remove from heat; stir in butter, vanilla, and 1 cup flaked coconut. Pour into pastry shell. Cool completely; cover and chill 1 to 2 hours.
• **Beat** whipping cream at high speed with an electric mixer until foamy; gradually add powdered sugar, 1 tablespoon at a time, beating until soft peaks form. Pipe or spoon sweetened whipped cream onto pie. Garnish, if desired. Yield: 1 (9-inch) pie.

LUSCIOUS LEMON PIE

make ahead

A chilled lemon (or lime) pie is a refreshing dessert after a grilled fish dinner. Substitute fresh lime juice and rind for a lime pie.

1 cup sugar
3 tablespoons cornstarch
1 tablespoon grated lemon rind
¼ cup butter or margarine
¼ cup fresh lemon juice
1 cup milk
3 egg yolks, lightly beaten
1 (8-ounce) carton sour cream
1 baked 9-inch pastry shell
Whipped cream
Garnish: grated lemon rind

• **Combine** first 7 ingredients in a heavy saucepan. Cook over medium heat 7 to 8 minutes or until smooth and thickened, stirring constantly. Remove from heat.
• **Fold** sour cream into filling, and pour into pastry shell; cover and chill at least 3 hours before serving. Top pie with whipped cream, and garnish, if desired. Yield: 1 (9-inch) pie.

KEY LIME PIES

family favorite, make ahead

Pucker up. This recipe makes two tangy-sweet pies. You can easily cut ingredients in half if one pie is all you need.

8 large eggs, lightly beaten
2 cups sugar
¼ cup grated lime rind
⅔ cup Key lime juice
Dash of salt
1 cup unsalted butter or margarine, softened
Graham Cracker Crusts
2 cups whipping cream
¼ cup sifted powdered sugar
2 teaspoons vanilla extract
Garnish: lime twists

• **Combine** first 5 ingredients in top of a double boiler, and bring water to a boil. Reduce heat to low; cook, whisking constantly, until thickened. Add butter, and cook, whisking constantly, until butter melts and mixture thickens. Pour into Graham Cracker Crusts.
• **Bake** at 300° for 20 minutes or until set; cool. Cover and chill at least 8 hours.
• **Beat** whipping cream at high speed with an electric mixer until foamy; gradually add powdered sugar, beating until soft peaks form. Stir in vanilla, and spread over filling. Chill. Garnish just before serving, if desired. Yield: 2 (9-inch) pies.

Graham Cracker Crusts
2½ cups graham cracker crumbs
½ cup firmly packed light brown sugar
⅔ cup unsalted butter, melted

• **Combine** all ingredients; press into two 9-inch pieplates.
• **Bake** at 375° for 6 to 8 minutes; cool. Yield: 2 (9-inch) piecrusts.

BUTTERMILK CHESS PIE

family favorite

We gave this simple buttery pie high marks. It's an old-fashioned pie with as much appeal today as ever.

5 large eggs, lightly beaten
2 cups sugar
⅔ cup buttermilk
½ cup butter or margarine, melted
2 tablespoons all-purpose flour
1 teaspoon vanilla extract
1 unbaked 9-inch pastry shell

• **Combine** first 6 ingredients. stirring until blended; pour into pastry shell.
• **Bake** at 350° for 45 minutes or until set. Cool on a wire rack. Yield: 1 (9-inch) pie.

ANGEL PIE

~ quick ~

Graham cracker crumbs and pecans become the delicious base for this easy old-fashioned pie.

3 egg whites
1 teaspoon vanilla extract
1 cup sugar
1 cup graham cracker crumbs
1 cup chopped pecans
1 teaspoon baking powder
Sweetened whipped cream
Maraschino cherries or toasted pecans

• **Beat** egg whites and vanilla at high speed with an electric mixer until foamy. Gradually add sugar, 1 tablespoon at a time, beating until stiff peaks form and sugar dissolves (2 to 4 minutes).
• **Combine** graham cracker crumbs, 1 cup pecans, and baking powder; fold into egg white mixture. Spread evenly in a well-greased and floured 9-inch pieplate. Bake at 325° for 25 minutes. Cool.
• **Top** each serving with a dollop of whipped cream and a cherry or toasted pecans. Yield: 1 (9-inch) pie.

BUTTERMILK- LEMON PIES

This recipe makes a pair of pies when you want to serve a crowd.

2 cups sugar
¼ cup plus 3 tablespoons cornstarch
5 cups buttermilk
1 (3-ounce) package cream cheese, softened
7 large eggs, separated
2 teaspoons grated lemon rind
¼ cup lemon juice
2 tablespoons butter or margarine
1 teaspoon lemon extract
¾ teaspoon cream of tartar
¼ cup plus 3 tablespoons powdered sugar
¼ teaspoon lemon extract
2 baked 9-inch pastry shells

• **Combine** 2 cups sugar and cornstarch in a heavy saucepan; gradually add buttermilk, stirring until blended. Add cream cheese, and cook over medium heat, stirring constantly, until mixture thickens and comes to a boil. Boil 1 minute.
• **Beat** egg yolks until thick and pale. Gradually stir about one-fourth of hot mixture into yolks; add to remaining hot mixture, stirring constantly. Cook over medium heat 3 minutes, stirring constantly. Remove from heat; stir in lemon rind and next 3 ingredients; set aside.
• **Beat** egg whites and cream of tartar at high speed with an electric mixer 1 minute. Gradually add powdered sugar, 1 tablespoon at a time, beating until stiff peaks form. Beat in ¼ teaspoon lemon extract. Spoon hot filling into pastry shells. Spread meringue over hot filling, sealing to edge.
• **Bake** at 325° for 25 minutes or until browned. Cool completely. Chill thoroughly. Yield: 2 (9-inch) pies.

COFFEE ICE CREAM PIE

make ahead

1 (7-ounce) can flaked coconut
½ cup butter or margarine, melted
½ cup chopped pecans
2 tablespoons all-purpose flour
½ gallon coffee ice cream, softened
1 cup whipping cream
¼ cup sifted powdered sugar
Chocolate curls
½ cup Kahlúa or other coffee-flavored liqueur
    (optional)

• **Combine** first 4 ingredients; press mixture in bottom and up sides of a 10-inch pieplate. Bake at 375° for 10 to 12 minutes or until lightly browned; cool completely on a wire rack. Spoon ice cream into prepared crust, and freeze until firm.
• **Beat** whipping cream until foamy; gradually add powdered sugar, beating until soft peaks form. Spread whipped cream over ice cream layer; top with chocolate curls. Cut into wedges; drizzle each serving with 1 tablespoon Kahlúa, if desired. Yield: 1 (10-inch) pie.

BUTTER PECAN ICE CREAM PIE

make ahead

Butter pecan ice cream and crushed toffee candy make this frozen pie great. Other flavors of ice cream would work as well.

2 cups butter pecan ice cream, softened
1 (9-ounce) graham cracker crust
3 (1.4-ounce) English toffee-flavored candy bars, crushed, divided
2 cups vanilla ice cream, softened
Caramel sauce

• **Spread** butter pecan ice cream in crust; sprinkle with half of crushed candy bars. Cover and freeze 1 hour.
• **Spread** vanilla ice cream over top; sprinkle with remaining crushed candy bars. Cover and freeze 4 hours or until pie is firm. Serve with caramel sauce. Yield: 1 (9-inch) pie.

The Kitchen Appliance Hall of Fame

Chop, chop: Cuisinart introduced food processors to the American kitchen in 1973. By the late '90s, 37 percent of kitchens had at least one food processor from a choice of sizes. More power and deluxe design features fueled the food processor market through the '90s.

Ride the wave: In 1979, almost a third of *Southern Living* subscribers owned a microwave oven, so the magazine began a monthly column on the new timesaving appliance. We were eager to learn the fine points of cooking *everything* in the microwave. By the early '90s, more than 90% of our readers owned microwaves, but they rarely used them to cook complete recipes. As a result, we discontinued the column devoted to recipes cooked exclusively in the microwave and zapped microwave instructions into conventional recipes wherever possible.

Knead this: Homemade yeast bread was close to extinction in the average household when the bread machine came on the scene in the early '90s. By century's end about one-third of all households owned a bread machine. About a third of the owners used the machine once or twice a month. Among the latest machines are those that turn out dense Euro-style breads. Other models produce baking powder-raised loaves that look yeast raised, but they mix and bake in less than an hour.

Frozen Chocolate Pie with Pecan Crust

FROZEN CHOCOLATE PIE WITH PECAN CRUST

~ make ahead ~

The key to success with this toasty pecan crust is to finely chop the pecans for pressing into the pieplate.

6 (1-ounce) squares semisweet chocolate
½ teaspoon instant coffee granules
2 large eggs, beaten
3 tablespoons Kahlúa or other coffee-flavored liqueur
¼ cup powdered sugar
¾ cup whipping cream
1 teaspoon vanilla extract
Pecan Crust
¾ cup whipping cream
1 tablespoon Kahlúa
Grated chocolate

• **Place** chocolate squares and coffee granules in top of a double boiler; bring water to a boil. Reduce heat to low; stir until chocolate melts. Gradually stir about one fourth of melted chocolate mixture into eggs, mixing well; add to remaining chocolate mixture in double boiler. Gradually stir in Kahlúa and powdered sugar. Cook, stirring constantly, until mixture reaches 160°. Remove from heat. Cool to room temperature.
• **Beat** ¾ cup whipping cream until soft peaks form; fold into chocolate mixture. Stir in vanilla. Spoon into Pecan Crust; cover and freeze. Transfer pie from freezer to refrigerator 1 hour before serving.
• **Beat** ¾ cup whipping cream until foamy; gradually add 1 tablespoon Kahlúa, beating until soft peaks form. Pipe or dollop whipped cream around edge of pie. Sprinkle with grated chocolate. Yield: 1 (9-inch) pie.

Pecan Crust
2 cups finely chopped pecans
⅓ cup firmly packed brown sugar
¼ cup butter or margarine, melted
2 teaspoons Kahlúa
Vegetable cooking spray

• **Combine** first 4 ingredients, mixing well. Firmly press mixture into bottom and up sides of a 9-inch pieplate coated with cooking spray. Bake at 350° for 12 to 14 minutes or until pecans are toasted. Press sides of crust with back of a spoon. Cool completely. Yield: 1 (9-inch) crust.

DECADENT MUD PIE

~ make ahead, quick ~

The title says it all. Five ingredients become a decadent dessert.

1 (11¾-ounce) jar hot fudge sauce, heated and divided
1 (9-ounce) graham cracker crust
½ gallon coffee ice cream, softened
Frozen whipped topping, thawed
Blanched slivered almonds, toasted

• **Spread** ⅓ cup fudge sauce over crust. Spread ice cream over fudge sauce; cover and freeze until firm.
• **Let** pie stand at room temperature 5 minutes before slicing. Cut into wedges. Top each serving with remaining fudge sauce, whipped topping, and almonds. Serve immediately. Yield: 1 (9-inch) pie.

MISSISSIPPI MUD PIE

✤ family favorite, make ahead ✤

Chocolate sandwich cookie crumbs make the crust for this coffee lovers' ice cream pie.

Chocolate Sandwich Cookie Pastry Shell
½ cup whipping cream
3 (1-ounce) squares unsweetened chocolate, chopped
1½ cups sifted powdered sugar
⅓ cup butter or margarine
3 tablespoons light corn syrup
Dash of salt
1 tablespoon vanilla extract
3 cups coffee ice cream, softened and divided
1 cup chopped toasted pecans, divided
Sweetened whipped cream

• **Prepare** pastry shell; set aside.
• **Combine** whipping cream and chocolate in a heavy saucepan over low heat; cook until chocolate melts. Add powdered sugar and next 3 ingredients. Cook, stirring constantly, until mixture is smooth. Remove from heat; stir in vanilla. Cool.
• **Spread** ½ cup chocolate sauce into pastry shell. Freeze 10 minutes. Remove from freezer, and spread 1 cup ice cream over chocolate sauce. Sprinkle with ⅓ cup pecans; freeze 20 minutes. Repeat layers twice.
• **Cover** and freeze at least 8 hours. Drizzle remaining chocolate sauce over pie. Pipe whipped cream onto pie. Yield: 1 (9-inch) pie.

Chocolate Sandwich Cookie Pastry Shell
2 cups cream-filled chocolate sandwich cookie crumbs (about 40 cookies)
2 tablespoons butter or margarine, melted

• **Process** cookies in batches in an electric blender or food processor until smooth. Combine crumbs and melted butter in a medium bowl. Firmly press mixture evenly into bottom and up sides of a well-greased 9-inch pieplate. Yield: 1 (9-inch) pastry shell.

COCONUT-CARAMEL PIES

✤ make ahead ✤

You'll be glad this recipe makes two pies. Plan on it as part of a holiday menu.

¼ cup butter or margarine
1 (7-ounce) package flaked coconut
½ cup chopped pecans
1 (8-ounce) package cream cheese, softened
1 (14-ounce) can sweetened condensed milk
1 (16-ounce) container frozen whipped topping, thawed
2 baked 9-inch pastry shells
1 (12-ounce) jar caramel ice cream topping

• **Melt** butter in a large skillet. Add coconut and chopped pecans; cook until coconut is golden, stirring often. Set mixture aside.
• **Combine** cream cheese and condensed milk; beat until smooth. Fold in whipped topping.
• **Layer** one-fourth of cream cheese mixture in each pastry shell. Drizzle one-fourth of caramel topping on each pie. Sprinkle one-fourth of coconut mixture evenly over each pie. Repeat layers with remaining ingredients; cover and freeze at least 8 hours or until firm.
• **Let** frozen pie stand at room temperature 5 minutes before slicing. Yield: 2 (9-inch) pies.

PEANUT PIE

make ahead

1 (8-ounce) package cream cheese, softened
1 cup sifted powdered sugar
1 cup chunky peanut butter
½ cup milk
1 (8-ounce) container frozen whipped topping, thawed
1 (9-ounce) graham cracker crust or chocolate cookie crust
¼ cup coarsely chopped peanuts, toasted

• **Combine** first 4 ingredients in a large mixing bowl; beat at medium speed with an electric mixer until blended. Fold in whipped topping; spoon into crust, and sprinkle with peanuts. Cover and chill 8 hours. Yield: 1 (9-inch) pie.

Hail to the Peanut

Southerners are no strangers to peanuts. The double-nut legume has inspired over 100 recipes since *Southern Living* was born. We love 'em in cookies, candies, snacks, pies, (crust, too!), stir-fries, salads, sauces, and even ice cream. Nope, we didn't forget peanut soup, either. Georgia ranks as the top peanut producing state in the United States. The state stood proud when its favorite son, Peanut Farmer Jimmy Carter, was elected President in 1976.

CINNAMON-ALMOND-PECAN PIE

You'll enjoy this almond-inspired twist on traditional pecan pie.

½ (15-ounce) package refrigerated piecrusts
⅔ cup sugar
1 tablespoon ground cinnamon
4 large eggs, lightly beaten
1 cup light corn syrup
2 tablespoons butter or margarine, melted
1 tablespoon vanilla extract
1 to 1½ teaspoons almond extract
1 cup coarsely chopped pecans
½ cup slivered almonds
1 large egg white, lightly beaten (optional)

• **Unfold** piecrust. Fit piecrust into a 9-inch pieplate according to package directions; trim excess pastry even with pieplate.
• **Stir** together sugar and next 6 ingredients in a medium bowl until blended. Stir in pecans and almonds.
• **Pour** filling into piecrust. Brush edges of piecrust with beaten egg white, if desired.
• **Bake** at 350° for 40 minutes or until filling is set, shielding pie with aluminum foil after 25 minutes to prevent excessive browning. Yield: 1 (9-inch) pie.

NOTE: You can use a whole package of piecrusts, cutting shapes from remaining pastry with a cookie cutter and attaching to edges of crust in pieplate before filling and baking pie.

RUM PECAN PIE

Brandied Butter Pastry and a splash of dark rum earn rave reviews for this pecan pie.

¾ cup light corn syrup
½ cup sugar
⅓ cup butter or margarine
¼ cup maple syrup
4 large eggs, lightly beaten
1 cup coarsely chopped pecans
3 tablespoons dark rum
Brandied Butter Pastry
¾ cup pecan halves

• **Cook** first 4 ingredients in a medium saucepan over medium heat until butter melts and sugar dissolves; cool slightly. Gradually add eggs to syrup mixture, beating constantly with a wire whisk. Stir in chopped pecans and rum.
• **Line** a 9-inch pieplate with Brandied Butter Pastry. Pour filling into pastry, and top with pecan halves. Bake at 325° for 48 minutes or until filling is set. Yield: 1 (9-inch) pie.

Brandied Butter Pastry
1¼ cups all-purpose flour
½ teaspoon salt
¼ cup plus 2 tablespoons cold butter
3 to 4 tablespoons cold brandy

• **Combine** flour and salt; cut in butter with a pastry blender until mixture is crumbly. Sprinkle cold brandy (1 tablespoon at a time) evenly over surface; stir with a fork until dry ingredients are moistened. Shape into a ball before rolling out.
• **Roll** pastry to ⅛-inch thickness on a lightly floured surface. Place in a 9-inch pieplate; trim off excess pastry along edges. Fold edges under, and crimp. Yield: 1 (9-inch) pastry shell.

PRALINE PECAN TART

Add a small scoop of cinnamon ice cream alongside a slice of this tart, and drizzle melted chocolate over both just before serving.

½ (15-ounce) package refrigerated piecrusts
1 cup sugar
1 cup light corn syrup
⅓ cup butter or margarine
4 large eggs, lightly beaten
1 teaspoon vanilla extract
¼ teaspoon salt
1 cup pecan halves
1 quart vanilla ice cream, slightly softened
1½ teaspoons ground cinnamon
½ cup semisweet chocolate morsels

• **Unfold** piecrust. Roll piecrust into a 12-inch circle on a lightly floured surface. Place in a 9-inch round tart pan with removable bottom; roll over top of tart pan with a rolling pin to trim excess pastry. Prick bottom of piecrust with a fork. Line bottom of piecrust with parchment paper; fill with pie weights or dried beans. Bake at 450° for 5 minutes. Carefully remove beans and paper; bake 2 more minutes. Set aside.
• **Combine** 1 cup sugar, corn syrup, and butter in a saucepan; cook over medium heat, stirring constantly, until sugar dissolves and butter melts. Cool slightly. Add eggs, 1 teaspoon vanilla, and salt; stir well. Pour into prepared piecrust; top with pecan halves. Bake at 325° for 55 minutes or until set.
• **Combine** ice cream and cinnamon; stir. Cover and freeze until firm.
• **Place** chocolate morsels in a small heavy-duty, zip-top plastic bag; seal bag. Submerge bag in hot water until chocolate melts. Snip a tiny hole in one corner of bag, using scissors; drizzle chocolate in a decorative design over each serving. Serve cinnamon ice cream with tart. Yield: 1 (9-inch) tart.

Praline Pecan Tart

PECAN PIE

family favorite

Try this buttery pecan pie and you may deem it worthy of becoming your Thanksgiving dessert.

½ (15-ounce) package refrigerated piecrusts
4 large eggs
1 cup dark corn syrup
¾ cup sugar
⅓ cup butter or margarine, melted
Pinch of salt
1 teaspoon vanilla extract
1 cup chopped pecans
¾ cup pecan halves

• **Unfold** piecrust. Fit piecrust into a 9-inch pieplate according to package directions; fold edges under, and crimp.
• **Beat** eggs and next 5 ingredients at medium speed with an electric mixer until smooth. Stir in chopped pecans; pour into crust. Arrange pecan halves on top.
• **Bake** at 350° for 50 minutes, shielding edges with aluminum foil after 30 minutes to prevent excessive browning. Yield: 1 (9-inch) pie.

EASY PECAN TARTS

quick

Package these tarts for gift giving. They're good using almonds or walnuts, too.

2 large eggs, lightly beaten
1 cup chopped pecans
¾ cup firmly packed brown sugar
2 tablespoons butter or margarine, melted
1 teaspoon vanilla extract
Pinch of salt
8 (2-inch) unbaked tart shells
Garnishes: whipped cream, pecan halves

• **Combine** first 6 ingredients; stir well.
• **Spoon** pecan mixture into tart shells. Place filled shells on a baking sheet. Bake at 425° for 16 to 18 minutes or until filling is set. Cool completely on a wire rack. Garnish, if desired. Yield: 8 tarts.

SWEET POTATO PIE

Cooking fresh sweet potatoes for this pie makes a big flavor difference.

2 large sweet potatoes (1½ pounds)
½ (15-ounce) package refrigerated piecrusts
¾ cup sugar
¼ cup firmly packed light brown sugar
2 tablespoons all-purpose flour
2 large eggs
½ cup evaporated milk
1 teaspoon ground nutmeg
½ teaspoon ground allspice
¼ teaspoon salt
Dash of ground cinnamon
1 teaspoon vanilla extract

• **Cook** sweet potatoes in boiling water to cover 45 to 50 minutes or until tender; drain. Cool.
• **Unfold** piecrust. Fit piecrust into a 9-inch pieplate according to package directions; fold edges under, and crimp. Line pastry with aluminum foil or parchment paper, and fill with pie weights or dried beans.
• **Bake** at 450° for 8 minutes. Remove weights and foil; bake 4 more minutes.
• **Peel** sweet potatoes, and place in a mixing bowl; beat at medium speed with an electric mixer until smooth. Add sugars and remaining ingredients, beating until blended. Pour into piecrust.
• **Bake** at 375° for 45 to 50 minutes or until a knife inserted in center comes out clean; shield edges with strips of aluminum foil the last 15 minutes to prevent excessive browning. Serve warm or at room temperature. Yield: 1 (9-inch) pie.

PUMPKIN PIE

family favorite

This pumpkin pie is well spiced.

3 cups canned pumpkin
1 cup sugar
½ teaspoon salt
½ teaspoon ground ginger
½ teaspoon ground allspice
½ teaspoon ground nutmeg
½ teaspoon ground cinnamon
3 large eggs, lightly beaten
1 (12-ounce) can evaporated milk
1 unbaked 10-inch pastry shell
Frozen whipped topping, thawed (optional)

• **Combine** first 9 ingredients in a large bowl; stir well. Pour filling into pastry shell. Bake at 425° for 15 minutes. Reduce oven temperature to 350°, and bake 40 to 45 minutes more or until a knife inserted near center comes out clean. Serve with whipped topping, if desired. Yield: 1 (10-inch) pie.

FUDGE PIE

family favorite

3 large eggs, lightly beaten
1½ cups sugar
¾ cup chopped pecans
⅓ cup all-purpose flour
⅓ cup cocoa
¾ cup butter or margarine, melted
½ teaspoon vanilla extract
1 unbaked 9-inch pastry shell
Vanilla ice cream (optional)

• **Combine** first 7 ingredients. Pour mixture into pastry shell. Bake at 350° for 35 minutes or until set. Serve with ice cream, if desired. Yield: 1 (9-inch) pie.

SWEETHEART FUDGE PIE

You'll enjoy the brownielike top crust and distinct hint of rum in this rich pie. The shorter baking time will yield a more gooey pie.

½ cup butter or margarine, softened
¾ cup firmly packed brown sugar
3 large eggs
2 cups (12 ounces) semisweet chocolate morsels, melted
2 teaspoons instant coffee granules
2 tablespoons dark rum or 1 teaspoon rum extract
½ cup all-purpose flour
1 cup coarsely chopped walnuts
1 unbaked 9-inch pastry shell
Garnishes: unsweetened whipped cream, chopped walnuts

• **Beat** butter at medium speed with an electric mixer until creamy. Gradually add brown sugar, beating well. Add eggs, 1 at a time, beating after each addition. Stir in melted chocolate, coffee granules, and rum. Stir in flour and 1 cup walnuts.
• **Pour** mixture into pastry shell. Bake at 375° for 25 to 28 minutes; cool completely. Chill. Garnish, if desired. Yield: 1 (9-inch) pie.

Country Peach Dumpling

COUNTRY PEACH DUMPLINGS

Inside tender pastry hides a fresh peach seasoned with earthy spices.
A drizzle of honey takes it to marvelous.

3 cups all-purpose flour
2 teaspoons baking powder
½ teaspoon salt
1 cup butter or shortening
⅓ cup milk
¼ cup sugar
¼ cup firmly packed brown sugar
½ teaspoon ground cinnamon

¼ teaspoon ground allspice
¼ teaspoon ground nutmeg
⅛ teaspoon ground cloves
6 medium ripe peaches, peeled
Milk
2 tablespoons butter or margarine, melted
Honey (optional)

• **Combine** flour, baking powder, and salt; cut in 1 cup butter with a pastry blender until mixture is crumbly. Sprinkle ⅓ cup milk, 1 tablespoon at a time, evenly over surface; stir with a fork until dry ingredients are moistened. Divide dough into 6 portions.
• **Roll** each portion of dough into a 7-inch square on a lightly floured surface. Trim edges of dough with a fluted pastry cutter, if desired.
• **Combine** sugar and next 5 ingredients. Reserve 2 tablespoons mixture, and set aside. Coat each peach with remaining sugar mixture, and place in center of a pastry square. For each dumpling, moisten edges of dough with milk; pull corners of square over peach. Pinch dough together, sealing all seams. Freeze dumplings 30 minutes.
• **Place** dumplings in a lightly greased 13- x 9-inch baking dish. Drizzle each dumpling with 1 teaspoon butter; sprinkle with reserved sugar mixture. Bake at 425° for 35 minutes. Drizzle with honey before serving, if desired. Yield: 6 servings.

OLD-FASHIONED BLACKBERRY COBBLER

family favorite

Place an aluminum foil-lined baking sheet under cobbler to catch any juices that bubble over during baking.

4 cups fresh blackberries or 2 (16-ounce) packages frozen blackberries, thawed
¾ cup sugar
3 tablespoons all-purpose flour
1½ cups water
1 tablespoon lemon juice
Pastry
2 tablespoons butter or margarine, melted
Whipping cream
Sugar

• **Place** berries in a lightly greased 2-quart baking dish. Combine ¾ cup sugar and flour; add water and lemon juice, mixing well. Pour sugar mixture over berries; bake at 350° for 15 minutes. Place Pastry over hot berries; brush with butter.

• **Bake** at 425° for 20 minutes or until Pastry is golden. Serve warm with whipping cream, and sprinkle each serving with sugar. Yield: 8 servings.

Pastry

1¾ cups all-purpose flour
2 to 3 tablespoons sugar
2 teaspoons baking powder
1 teaspoon salt
¼ cup shortening
⅓ cup whipping cream
⅓ cup buttermilk

• **Combine** flour, sugar, baking powder, and salt; cut in shortening with a pastry blender until mixture is crumbly; stir in whipping cream and buttermilk. Knead dough 4 or 5 times; roll to ¼-inch thickness on a lightly floured surface. Cut dough to fit baking dish. Yield: pastry for 1 cobbler.

RASPBERRY-NUT STRUDEL

1 cup butter or margarine, softened
1 (8-ounce) package cream cheese, softened
3 cups all-purpose flour
Powdered sugar
1 cup raisins
1 (12-ounce) jar red raspberry preserves
1 cup finely chopped walnuts
1 cup firmly packed brown sugar
1 cup flaked coconut

• **Beat** butter and cream cheese at medium speed with an electric mixer until creamy; stir in flour. Divide dough into 4 equal portions. Wrap each in plastic wrap, and chill at least 8 hours.

• **Sift** powdered sugar lightly over work surface. Work with 1 portion of dough at a time. (Keep remaining portions in refrigerator.) Roll dough into a 12- x 8-inch rectangle.

• **Combine** raisins, preserves, walnuts, brown sugar, and coconut; spread one-fourth of mixture over dough. Roll up jellyroll fashion, starting at short side.

• **Pinch** seam and ends together. Place roll, seam side down, on an ungreased baking sheet. Repeat procedure with remaining dough and filling mixture.

• **Bake** at 325° for 55 minutes. Serve warm or at room temperature. Sprinkle lightly with powdered sugar. Yield: 16 servings.

AUTUMN APPLE STRUDEL

This German pastry dessert contains layers of buttery cookie crumbs.

1 cup hot water
½ cup golden raisins
6 large Granny Smith apples, peeled and each cut into 8 wedges
2 cups sugar, divided
2 tablespoons grated orange rind
1 tablespoon vanilla extract
¼ cup butter or margarine
1 (7¼-ounce) package butter cookies, finely crumbled (we used Pepperidge Farm Chessmen Butter Cookies)
2 cups chopped pecans, toasted
12 frozen phyllo pastry sheets, thawed
¾ cup butter or margarine, melted
Powdered sugar

• **Pour** 1 cup hot water over raisins; let stand 20 minutes. Drain raisins; set aside.
• **Stir** together apple wedges, 1 cup sugar, orange rind, and vanilla.
• **Melt** ¼ cup butter in a large skillet over medium-high heat; add apple mixture, and cook 15 to 20 minutes or until mixture thickens, stirring occasionally. Remove from heat; stir in raisins. Cool.
• **Stir** together cookie crumbs, remaining 1 cup sugar, and pecans. Set aside.
• **Unfold** phyllo, and cover with a damp towel to prevent it from drying out.
• **Stack** 4 sheets on a flat surface covered with wax paper, brushing each sheet with melted butter. Sprinkle with one-third of crumb mixture. Repeat procedure 2 times with remaining phyllo, butter, and crumb mixture. Top with apple mixture, leaving a 2-inch border around edges. Fold in short sides 2 inches.
• **Roll** up, starting at long side. Place, seam side down, on a greased baking sheet. Cut ¼-inch-deep slits, 1 inch apart, across top. Brush strudel with melted butter. Bake at 375° for 25 minutes or until golden. Cool 10 minutes. Sprinkle with powdered sugar. Yield: 10 servings.

BAKLAVA

⁓ make ahead ⁓

Pronounced BAHK-lah-vah, this Greek dessert has a delicate flavor and flaky texture. It freezes well stored in an airtight container.

2¼ cups sugar
1 cup water
½ cup honey
1 tablespoon fresh lemon juice
1 (3-inch) stick cinnamon
12 cups finely chopped pecans (3 pounds, shelled)
1 cup sugar
1 tablespoon ground cinnamon
1 teaspoon ground cloves
1 (16-ounce) package frozen phyllo pastry, thawed
1 pound unsalted butter, melted

• **Combine** first 5 ingredients in a saucepan; bring to a boil over medium-high heat, stirring constantly. Immediately remove from heat; cool syrup completely.
• **Combine** pecans and next 3 ingredients in a bowl, stirring well.
• **Cut** phyllo sheets in half crosswise; keep covered with a slightly damp towel.
• **Brush** two 13- x 9-inch pans with butter. Place 8 phyllo sheets in one pan, brushing each sheet with melted butter; top with 2 cups pecan mixture.
• **Place** 3 phyllo sheets over pecan mixture, brushing each sheet with melted butter; top with 2 cups pecan mixture. Repeat with 3 more phyllo sheets and 2 cups pecan mixture; top with 6 more phyllo sheets, brushing all but the top sheet with melted butter.
• **Repeat** procedure with remaining phyllo sheets, butter, and pecan mixture in second pan.
• **Cut** layers diagonally into ¾-inch diamonds; gently brush with remaining butter.
• **Bake** at 300° for 1 hour. Remove from oven, and pour syrup evenly over baklava. Cool completely in pans on wire racks. Cut again diagonally; remove from pans, and store in airtight containers at room temperature. Yield: about 10 dozen pieces.

*Apricot and Strawberry
Pinwheels*

APRICOT AND STRAWBERRY PINWHEELS

Use different colors of preserves and jelly for these fanciful pastries. They're good for dessert, an afternoon coffee break, or even breakfast.

1 (17¼-ounce) package frozen puff pastry sheets, thawed
½ cup apricot or strawberry preserves
1 egg yolk, beaten
1 tablespoon water
1 cup sifted powdered sugar
1½ tablespoons water
¼ cup finely chopped pistachios or pecans

• **Place** 1 portion of pastry on top of other portion. Roll on a lightly floured surface into a 17½-x 15½-inch rectangle. Cut pastry into 20 (3½-inch) squares, using a sharp knife. Leave remaining strip of pastry uncut.

• **Cut** each square of pastry diagonally from the corners to the center, leaving center of pastry uncut.

• **Spoon** about 1 teaspoon apricot preserves onto center of each square. Fold every other point of cut corners to the center to make a pinwheel. Press down firmly to seal seam of points.

• **Cut** 20 (¾-inch) rounds from remaining strip of uncut pastry. Combine egg yolk and 1 tablespoon water. Brush 1 side of small pastry round with egg yolk mixture. Place pastry round in center of each pinwheel, brushed side down, pressing gently to seal. Brush entire pinwheel with additional egg yolk mixture. Place on lightly greased baking sheets. Chill 10 minutes. Bake at 400° for 10 minutes or until lightly browned.

• **Combine** powdered sugar and 1½ tablespoons water, stirring until smooth. Drizzle over warm pastries. Sprinkle with pistachios. Serve warm or cold. Yield: 20 pastries.

COFFEE NAPOLEONS

1 (3.4-ounce) package chocolate pudding and pie filling mix (not instant)
1 cup milk
2 teaspoons instant coffee granules
1 (8-ounce) package cream cheese, cut into pieces and softened
½ cup whipping cream, whipped
1 (17¼-ounce) package frozen puff pastry sheets, thawed
¼ cup whipping cream
2 teaspoons instant coffee granules
6 (1-ounce) squares semisweet chocolate, chopped
Powdered sugar

• **Combine** pudding mix and milk in a saucepan, stirring well; stir in 2 teaspoons coffee granules. Bring to a boil over medium heat, stirring constantly; remove from heat. Stir in cream cheese; cool completely.

• **Fold** whipped cream into pudding mixture; cover and chill.

• **Unfold** 1 pastry sheet on a lightly floured baking sheet. Roll into a 12-inch square. Cut into 2 (12- x 6-inch) rectangles. Cut each rectangle into 6 (6- x 2-inch) strips. Prick each strip several times with a fork. Place another baking sheet directly on pastry strips (to prevent overpuffing).

• **Bake** at 425° for 10 minutes. Remove top baking sheet; bake 5 more minutes or until golden. Cool on wire racks. Repeat with remaining pastry.

• **Combine** ¼ cup whipping cream, 2 teaspoons coffee granules, and chocolate in a heavy saucepan; cook over low heat, stirring constantly, until chocolate melts. Cool slightly; spoon mixture into a heavy-duty, zip-top plastic bag, and snip a tiny hole in one corner of bag. Drizzle over 12 pastry strips.

• **Pipe** or spoon filling evenly on remaining 12 pastry strips; top with chocolate-drizzled pastry strips. Sprinkle with powdered sugar, and serve immediately. Yield: 12 servings.

Poultry

～

Chicken and other types of poultry
are ideal choices for dinner. You can
always count on them to be favorites
with family and friends. Poultry has
a mild, delicate flavor that teams well
with fruits and vegetables and takes
naturally to many seasonings and
cooking methods.

Pesto Chicken with Basil Cream (page 255)

HERB-ROASTED CHICKEN

Tarragon is a slender herb that has a peppery scent and a hint of anise. It's used here as the predominant flavor in a marinade for brushing on the bird as it cooks.

2 tablespoons butter or margarine, melted
⅓ cup white vinegar
3 tablespoons lemon juice
3 tablespoons chopped fresh tarragon
2 tablespoons olive oil
1 clove garlic, minced
1 teaspoon salt
1 teaspoon freshly ground pepper
1 pound round red potatoes, unpeeled
1 cup diagonally sliced celery
1 (2-ounce) jar sliced pimiento, drained
¼ cup chopped fresh parsley
1 (5- to 6-pound) whole chicken
Garnishes: fresh parsley, fresh tarragon

• **Combine** first 8 ingredients in a small bowl, mixing well. Set aside.
• **Cover** potatoes with water in a saucepan; cook, covered, over medium heat 15 minutes or until tender. Drain potatoes; cool.
• **Cut** potatoes into bite-size pieces. Add celery, pimiento, and ¼ cup parsley, tossing gently. Add 2 tablespoons tarragon-oil mixture, tossing to coat. Set aside.
• **Remove** giblets from cavity of chicken, and reserve for another use. Rinse chicken with cold water; pat dry with paper towels. Fold neck skin over back; secure with a wooden pick. Tuck wings under chicken.
• **Stuff** chicken cavity with potato mixture. Close cavity with wooden picks or skewers; tie legs together with string. Place chicken, breast side up, on a rack in a roasting pan. Brush entire chicken with remaining tarragon-oil mixture.
• **Insert** a meat thermometer into meaty part of thigh, making sure it does not touch bone. Bake at 375° until thermometer registers 180° (about 2 hours), basting often with tarragon-oil mixture. Cool 10 to 15 minutes before slicing. Place on a serving platter; garnish, if desired. Yield: 6 servings.

ROASTED STUFFED CHICKEN

A well-seasoned vegetable and brown rice mixture roasts inside this chicken.

¼ cup chicken broth
2 tablespoons olive oil
1 teaspoon lemon juice
1 clove garlic, minced
1 teaspoon salt
1 teaspoon freshly ground pepper
1 cup cooked brown rice
1 carrot, scraped and chopped
1 celery rib, chopped
1 small onion, chopped
1 (6-pound) whole chicken

• **Stir** together first 6 ingredients.
• **Stir** together rice and next 3 ingredients. Toss with half of chicken broth mixture, reserving remaining broth mixture.
• **Spoon** rice mixture into chicken cavity. Tuck wings under, and tie legs together with string, if desired. Place chicken, breast side up, on a rack in a roasting pan; brush with reserved broth mixture.
• **Bake** at 375° for 2 hours or until a meat thermometer inserted in chicken thigh registers 180° and in stuffing registers 165°. Let stand 15 minutes before slicing chicken. Yield: 6 servings.

SLOW-ROASTED CHICKEN

This easy entrée first bakes covered and then uncovered for even browning. The broth in the pan helps keep the meat moist.

1 (4- to 4½-pound) whole chicken
1 onion, cut into 1-inch pieces
6 cloves garlic
½ teaspoon salt
¼ teaspoon pepper
2 tablespoons olive oil
1 cup chicken broth

• **Remove** giblets from chicken. Place giblets, onion, and garlic in a shallow roasting pan.
• **Tuck** wings under; tie legs together with string, if desired. Place chicken, breast side up, over giblets and vegetables; sprinkle with salt and pepper. Drizzle chicken and giblet mixture with oil. Add broth to roasting pan.
• **Cover** and bake at 350° for 1 hour. Uncover and bake 1 more hour or until a meat thermometer inserted in chicken thigh registers 180°. Yield: 6 servings.

GREEK BAKED CHICKEN

⅓ cup olive oil
¼ cup lemon juice
1 teaspoon salt
½ teaspoon dried oregano
¼ teaspoon pepper
1 (2½- to 3-pound) broiler-fryer

• **Stir** together first 5 ingredients.
• **Place** chicken in a shallow dish or large heavy-duty, zip-top plastic bag; pour oil mixture over chicken. Cover or seal; marinate in refrigerator 8 hours.

• **Remove** chicken from marinade, discarding marinade. Tuck wings under, and tie legs together with string, if desired. Place chicken, breast side up, on a rack in a shallow roasting pan.
• **Bake** at 450° for 45 minutes or until a meat thermometer inserted in chicken thigh registers 180°. Yield: 3 servings.

CITRUS CHICKEN

1 medium onion, sliced
8 cloves garlic, minced
¼ cup olive oil
½ cup orange juice
⅓ cup fresh lime juice
3 tablespoons white wine or chicken broth
1 teaspoon sugar
1 teaspoon salt
¼ teaspoon pepper
1 teaspoon white vinegar
1 (3- to 3½-pound) broiler-fryer
Garnishes: lime slices, orange slices, fresh
    cilantro

• **Cook** onion and garlic in olive oil in a medium saucepan over medium-high heat 2 minutes. Add orange juice and next 6 ingredients.
• **Bring** to a boil. Remove from heat; cool. Reserve ¼ cup marinade, and refrigerate it.
• **Place** chicken in a shallow dish or heavy-duty, zip-top plastic bag. Pour remaining marinade over chicken. Cover or seal; marinate in refrigerator 8 hours, turning chicken occasionally.
• **Remove** chicken from marinade; discard marinade. Dry chicken with a paper towel. Place on a lightly greased rack, and place rack in a broiler pan.
• **Bake** at 400° for 15 minutes; reduce heat to 350°, and bake 1 hour to 1 hour and 15 minutes, basting with reserved ¼ cup marinade.
• **Cover** chicken with aluminum foil after 1 hour to prevent excessive browning. Place on a serving platter, and garnish, if desired. Yield: 4 servings.

WHOLE POACHED CHICKEN

Court-bouillon (koor bwee-YAWN) is a flavored cooking liquid made by simmering vegetables and herbs in water. It's used here to poach chicken to tender results. For a shortcut, you can substitute canned low-sodium, fat-free chicken broth.

1 (5-pound) whole chicken, skinned
4 to 5 cups court-bouillon
1 teaspoon salt
2 carrots, chopped
4 stalks celery, chopped
1 onion, chopped
2 bay leaves
4 fresh parsley sprigs
16 small new potatoes
4 carrots, scraped and diagonally sliced
16 boiling onions
1 teaspoon salt
1 teaspoon pepper
2 large tomatoes, peeled, seeded, and diced
¼ cup chopped fresh parsley

• **Simmer** first 8 ingredients in a Dutch oven 1 to 1½ hours or until chicken is done. Remove chicken; cool slightly. Cut into serving-size pieces, and place on a serving platter. Keep warm.
• **Pour** broth through a wire-mesh strainer into a large bowl, discarding solids; return broth to Dutch oven. Skim fat from broth. Boil broth 20 minutes or until reduced by half.
• **Remove** a strip of peel around middle of each potato. Add potatoes, sliced carrot, and next 3 ingredients to broth; cook 20 minutes or until tender. Remove and discard bay leaves. Stir in tomato and chopped parsley, and spoon over chicken. Yield: 6 servings.

Court-Bouillon

12 whole cloves
1 onion, peeled
2 carrots, sliced
2 stalks celery, sliced
½ cup chopped fresh parsley
6 cloves garlic, crushed
2 quarts water
2 cups dry white wine
¼ cup white wine vinegar
1 teaspoon dried thyme
1 bay leaf
1 teaspoon cracked pepper

• **Insert** cloves evenly into onion.
• **Bring** onion, carrot, and remaining ingredients to a boil in a Dutch oven. Reduce heat, and simmer 30 minutes, stirring occasionally; cool completely.
• **Pour** mixture through a wire-mesh strainer into a large bowl, discarding solids. Yield: 2 quarts.

CHICKEN BLONDE

~ family favorite ~

Microwaving is a shortcut that cuts the cooking time in half for this chicken that finishes on the grill.

1½ cups mayonnaise
⅓ cup apple cider vinegar
¼ cup lemon juice
2 tablespoons sugar
2 tablespoons freshly ground pepper
2 tablespoons white wine Worcestershire sauce
1 (3-pound) broiler-fryer, quartered

• **Combine** first 6 ingredients in a small bowl; stir well. Place chicken in a large heavy-duty, zip-top plastic bag. Pour 1 cup sauce over chicken. Cover and chill remaining sauce. Seal bag securely, and marinate chicken in refrigerator 6 to 8 hours. Remove chicken, discarding marinade, and arrange in a large baking dish with skin side down and thicker portion of chicken toward outside of dish. Cover with wax paper, and microwave at HIGH 10 to 12 minutes; turn and rearrange chicken after 5 minutes.

• **Grill** chicken, uncovered, over medium-hot coals (350° to 400°) 20 minutes or until done, turning once and basting with reserved sauce. Yield: 4 servings.

COUNTRY-STYLE CHICKEN AND DUMPLINGS

~ family favorite ~

Chicken and dumplings make a soul-satisfying meal. This recipe features rolled (or slick) dumplings.

1 (3½- to 4-pound) broiler-fryer
2 quarts water
1 carrot, halved
1 stalk celery, halved
1 medium onion, quartered
1½ teaspoons salt
½ teaspoon pepper
2 cups all-purpose flour
2 teaspoons baking powder
¾ teaspoon salt
⅓ cup shortening

• **Combine** first 7 ingredients in a Dutch oven. Bring to a boil; cover, reduce heat, and simmer 1 hour or until chicken is tender. Remove chicken from broth, reserving broth in Dutch oven. Let chicken cool. Skin, bone, and coarsely chop chicken; set aside. Remove vegetables from broth, and discard vegetables. Skim fat from broth, if desired. Reserve and set aside ⅔ cup broth. Return chopped chicken to broth in Dutch oven.

• **Combine** flour, baking powder, and ¾ teaspoon salt; cut in shortening with a pastry blender until mixture is

crumbly. Add reserved ⅔ cup broth, stirring with a fork just until dry ingredients are moistened. Turn dough out onto a lightly floured surface, and knead lightly 30 seconds. Roll dough to ⅛-inch thickness; cut dough into ¾- x 2-inch strips or 2-inch squares.

• **Bring** broth in Dutch oven to a boil; drop dumplings, 1 at a time, into boiling broth. Cover, reduce heat, and simmer 10 minutes. Yield: 4 servings.

LEMON-BARBECUED CHICKEN

Squeeze lemon wedges over this grilled chicken just before serving.

3 (2½- to 3-pound) broiler-fryers
2 cups vegetable oil
1 cup lemon juice
2 tablespoons salt
1½ tablespoons dried basil
1½ tablespoons onion powder
2 teaspoons paprika
2 teaspoons dried thyme
6 cloves garlic, crushed
1 lemon, thinly sliced
Lemon wedges

• **Split** chickens in halves or quarters; place in two shallow baking dishes. Combine oil and next 8 ingredients; stir well. Set aside 1 cup marinade for basting. Pour remaining marinade over chicken; cover and marinate in refrigerator 6 to 8 hours, turning chicken occasionally.

• **Remove** chicken, discarding marinade. Grill, covered with grill lid, skin side up, over medium coals (300° to 350°) 20 to 25 minutes. Turn chicken, and grill 20 more minutes, basting often with reserved 1 cup marinade. Serve with lemon wedges. Yield: 10 servings.

COUNTRY CAPTAIN CHICKEN

A captain deserves only the best, and this chicken dinner delivers.

½ cup all-purpose flour
1 teaspoon salt
½ teaspoon pepper
1 (2½- to 3-pound) broiler-fryer, cut up
Vegetable oil
2 medium onions, chopped
2 medium-size green peppers, chopped
¼ cup chopped celery
1 clove garlic, minced
2 (16-ounce) cans whole tomatoes, undrained and chopped
¼ cup currants
2 teaspoons curry powder
¾ teaspoon salt
½ teaspoon ground white pepper
½ teaspoon ground thyme
3 cups hot cooked rice
1½ tablespoons minced fresh parsley
3 tablespoons cornstarch
¼ cup cold water
¼ cup sliced natural almonds, toasted

• **Combine** first 3 ingredients; stir well. Dredge chicken in flour mixture.
• **Pour** oil to depth of ½ inch into a large heavy skillet. Fry chicken in hot oil (350°) until browned.
• **Arrange** chicken in a 13- x 9-inch baking dish; set aside. Drain pan drippings, reserving 2 tablespoons drippings in skillet.
• **Cook** onion, green pepper, celery, and garlic in pan drippings until vegetables are tender. Add tomatoes and next 5 ingredients; stir well. Spoon sauce over chicken in baking dish.
• **Cover** and bake at 350° for 40 to 50 minutes or until chicken is tender.
• **Transfer** chicken to a large serving platter with a slotted spoon; reserving sauce in baking dish. Combine rice and parsley, tossing gently to combine; spoon around chicken. Set aside, and keep warm.
• **Transfer** sauce to a medium saucepan. Combine cornstarch and water, stirring until smooth; stir into sauce. Bring sauce to a boil; cook, stirring constantly, 1 minute or until slightly thickened. Spoon sauce over chicken. Sprinkle almonds over chicken. Serve immediately. Yield: 4 servings.

BALSAMIC MARINATED CHICKEN

Honey and balsamic vinegar create incredible pan drippings for basting this bird.

¼ cup balsamic vinegar
¼ cup honey
¼ cup olive oil
2 tablespoons chopped fresh rosemary
1 teaspoon salt
3 pounds chicken breasts, thighs, and legs

• **Combine** first 5 ingredients in a large heavy-duty, zip-top plastic bag; add chicken. Seal and marinate in refrigerator 2 hours, turning occasionally.
• **Remove** chicken, and place in a lightly greased 13- x 9-inch baking dish; pour marinade over chicken.
• **Bake** at 375° for 45 minutes or until done, basting often with pan drippings. Yield: 4 servings.

CRISPY FRIED CHICKEN

family favorite

3 cups all-purpose flour
2 teaspoons paprika
1½ teaspoons salt
3 large eggs
⅓ cup milk
2 tablespoons lemon juice
2 (2- to 3-pound) broiler-fryers, cut up
Vegetable oil

• **Stir** together first 3 ingredients in a shallow dish.
• **Whisk** together eggs, milk, and lemon juice in a bowl. Dredge chicken in flour mixture, dip in egg mixture, and dredge again in flour mixture. Chill coated chicken 2 hours.
• **Pour** oil to depth of ½ inch into an electric skillet; heat to 375°.
• **Fry** chicken, in batches, 10 minutes on each side or until golden. Reduce heat to 250°; cover and cook 25 minutes or until done. Drain chicken pieces on paper towels. Yield: 8 servings.

Southern Comfort

90s Comfort food went trendy in the '90s, but Southerners never abandoned such tummy warmers as chicken with dumplings, so-called, "feather beds of the South," chicken pot pie, and fried chicken. In fact, 45 fried chicken recipe titles have graced the pages of *Southern Living* over the years, including Spicy Fried, Buttermilk Fried, Mexican Fried, Lemon Fried, Garlic Fried, Cheese Stuffed, Spinach Stuffed, and, of course, Fried Chicken with Cream Gravy.

CHICKEN FRICASSEE

Fricassee is a dish of sautéed chicken stewed with vegetables and enhanced with wine. The results are thick, chunky, and filling.

1 teaspoon salt
½ teaspoon ground nutmeg
½ teaspoon pepper
½ teaspoon paprika
2 to 3 pounds chicken pieces
3 tablespoons vegetable oil
3 tablespoons all-purpose flour
2 cups water
1 cup dry white wine
3 tablespoons butter or margarine
1 onion, chopped
2 cups small fresh mushrooms
1 tablespoon chopped fresh sage
1 tablespoon chopped fresh parsley
1 cup half-and-half
Hot cooked rice

• **Combine** first 4 ingredients. Sprinkle chicken pieces with seasonings.
• **Brown** chicken in hot oil over high heat in a Dutch oven; remove chicken. Reduce heat to medium; add flour, and cook, whisking constantly, until lightly browned.
• **Whisk** in water and wine until smooth. Return chicken to Dutch oven; bring to a boil. Cover, reduce heat, and simmer 50 minutes or until chicken is done. Remove chicken, reserving broth; keep chicken warm. Cool broth.
• **Pour** broth through a strainer into a 4-cup liquid measuring cup; discard particles.
• **Melt** butter in Dutch oven over medium-high heat; add onion, and sauté until tender.
• **Add** reserved broth, chicken, mushrooms, and next 3 ingredients to Dutch oven. Cook over medium heat, stirring occasionally, until thoroughly heated. Serve over rice. Yield: 4 servings.

Chili-Barbecued Chicken

This tender grilled chicken gets its smoky flavor from wood chips.

2 cups hickory or mesquite wood chips
¼ cup water
3 tablespoons ketchup
2 tablespoons butter or margarine, melted
2 tablespoons cider vinegar
2 tablespoons Worcestershire sauce
1 tablespoon lemon juice
1 teaspoon salt
1 teaspoon dry mustard
1 teaspoon paprika
2 teaspoons chili powder
¼ teaspoon dried crushed red pepper
3 to 4 pounds chicken pieces

• **Soak** wood chips in water to cover 30 minutes.
• **Stir** together ¼ cup water and next 10 ingredients; set aside.
• **Drain** wood chips. Place in center of a large square of aluminum foil, and fold edges to seal. Punch several holes in top of packet.
• **Prepare** fire by piling charcoal or lava rocks on sides of grill, leaving center empty. Place foil packet on 1 side of coals; place drip pan between coals. Coat food rack with vegetable cooking spray; place rack on grill.
• **Arrange** chicken, skin side up, over drip pan; grill, covered with grill lid, over medium-high coals (350° to 400°) 10 minutes on each side. Brush chicken with sauce; grill 20 to 25 more minutes or until done, basting and turning often. Yield: 6 servings.

Chicken Bundles with Bacon Ribbons

Serve this crowd-pleasing entrée with hot cooked rice, green beans, and mixed greens. The recipe can be easily cut in half for a smaller meal.

12 whole chicken breasts, skinned and boned
1 cup molasses
¼ cup olive oil
¼ cup lemon juice
¼ cup soy sauce
2 tablespoons Worcestershire sauce
½ teaspoon ground ginger
¼ teaspoon garlic powder
½ cup butter or margarine, divided
4 (8-ounce) packages sliced fresh mushrooms, divided
20 green onions, sliced and divided
24 slices bacon

• **Place** chicken breast between two sheets of heavy-duty plastic wrap; pound to ¼-inch thickness, using a meat mallet or rolling pin. Place chicken in a large shallow baking dish; set aside.
• **Combine** molasses and next 6 ingredients; stir well. Pour mixture over chicken; cover and marinate in refrigerator 8 hours, turning chicken occasionally.
• **Melt** ¼ cup butter in a large skillet; add half each of mushrooms and green onions. Cook over medium-high heat until liquid evaporates, stirring constantly. Repeat process with remaining mushrooms, green onions, and ¼ cup butter.
• **Partially** cook bacon in a large skillet over medium-high heat until limp but not crisp.
• **Remove** chicken from dish, reserving marinade. Pour marinade into a small saucepan; bring to a boil. Remove from heat, and set aside.
• **Place** 2 slices bacon in a crisscross pattern on a flat surface for each chicken bundle. Place a chicken breast in center of bacon. Top with 3 tablespoons mushroom mixture.Fold sides and ends of chicken over mushroom mixture to make a square-shaped pouch. Pull bacon

around chicken, and tie ends of bacon together; secure with wooden picks.

• **Place** chicken bundles on grill, tied side up; grill, covered with grill lid, over low coals (under 300°) 45 to 50 minutes or until done, turning and basting with reserved marinade every 15 minutes. Remove wooden picks before serving. Yield: 12 servings.

PARMESAN BAKED CHICKEN

◦ quick ◦

Here's an easy ovenfried recipe.

½ cup fine, dry breadcrumbs (store-bought)
¼ cup grated Parmesan cheese
½ teaspoon dried basil
½ teaspoon dried thyme
¼ teaspoon salt
4 skinned and boned chicken breast halves
¼ cup butter or margarine, melted

• **Combine** first 5 ingredients in a heavy-duty, zip-top plastic bag; seal bag, and shake well.
• **Dip** chicken in butter. Add 1 piece of chicken at a time to breadcrumb mixture; seal bag, and shake until well coated. Place chicken on a greased baking sheet. Bake at 400° for 25 to 30 minutes or until done. Yield: 4 servings.

TOASTED ALMOND CHICKEN

◦ quick ◦

A mixture of cream, mustard, and orange marmalade becomes a tasty sauce for this chicken sprinkled with almonds.

6 skinned and boned chicken breast halves
⅛ teaspoon salt
⅛ teaspoon black pepper
3 tablespoons butter or margarine, divided
1½ cups whipping cream
2 tablespoons orange marmalade
1 tablespoon Dijon mustard
⅛ teaspoon ground red pepper
1 (2.25-ounce) package sliced almonds, toasted

• **Place** each chicken breast half between two sheets of heavy-duty plastic wrap, and flatten to ¼-inch thickness, using a meat mallet or rolling pin. Sprinkle with salt and black pepper.
• **Melt** 1½ tablespoons butter in a large skillet over medium-high heat. Add half of chicken, and cook 2 minutes on each side or until golden. Remove chicken from skillet. Repeat procedure with remaining butter and chicken.
• **Reduce** heat to medium; add whipping cream and next 3 ingredients to skillet, stirring well. Add chicken; sprinkle with almonds, and cook 8 minutes or until sauce thickens. Yield: 6 servings.

Chicken Rellenos

CHICKEN RELLENOS

This dish is a meaty twist on the traditional Mexican chiles rellenos. Relleno is Spanish for stuffed.

4 skinned and boned chicken breast halves
¼ teaspoon salt
2 canned whole green chiles, halved
4 ounces Monterey Jack cheese with peppers, cut crosswise into 16 slices
½ cup all-purpose flour
1 large egg, beaten
1 tablespoon milk
1¼ cups soft breadcrumbs (homemade)
Vegetable oil
Salsa
Garnish: fresh cilantro sprigs

• **Place** each chicken breast half between two pieces of heavy-duty plastic wrap. Flatten each breast to ¼-inch thickness, using a meat mallet or rolling pin. Sprinkle with salt.
• **Place** a green chile half and 4 slices cheese in center of each piece of chicken; roll up lengthwise, tucking edges inside. Secure roll with wooden picks.
• **Dredge** chicken in flour. Combine egg and milk; dip chicken in egg mixture. Roll in breadcrumbs.
• **Fry** chicken in 2 inches of hot oil (375°) in a deep skillet or Dutch oven 10 minutes or until golden, turning once. Drain well on paper towels. Serve immediately. Serve with salsa. Garnish, if desired. Yield: 4 servings.

CHICKEN AND MUSHROOM MARSALA

◦ quick ◦

Marsala is a slightly sweet, smoky flavored wine that enhances many chicken and veal dishes.

½ cup all-purpose flour
½ teaspoon salt
½ teaspoon freshly ground pepper
1½ pounds skinned and boned chicken breast halves
¼ cup olive oil
½ pound sliced fresh mushrooms
⅔ cup chopped green onions
6 medium tomatoes, seeded and chopped
½ teaspoon salt
½ teaspoon dried basil
1½ cups Marsala
½ cup freshly grated Parmesan cheese
¼ cup chopped fresh parsley

• **Combine** first 3 ingredients in a large heavy-duty, zip-top plastic bag. Add chicken to flour mixture, a few pieces at a time; seal bag, and shake until chicken is well coated.
• **Heat** oil in a large skillet over medium heat. Add chicken, and cook 5 minutes on each side or until done; remove chicken, and drain on paper towels.
• **Add** mushrooms to skillet; cook over medium-high heat, stirring constantly, until tender. Remove mushrooms from skillet, and set aside; reserve pan drippings in skillet.
• **Add** green onions to drippings; cook, stirring constantly, until tender. Stir in tomato, salt, and basil; cook 4 to 5 minutes or until most of liquid evaporates. Add Marsala, and simmer, uncovered, 8 minutes or until thickened.
• **Return** chicken and mushrooms to skillet, and cook until thoroughly heated. Sprinkle with Parmesan cheese and parsley. Yield: 6 servings.

SHERRIED CHICKEN WITH ARTICHOKES

6 skinned and boned chicken breast halves
1 teaspoon paprika
½ teaspoon pepper
2 tablespoons butter or margarine, melted
1 (14-ounce) can artichoke hearts, halved
1⅓ cups sliced fresh mushrooms
2 green onions, sliced
2 tablespoons butter or margarine, melted
1 tablespoon cornstarch
1 teaspoon chicken bouillon granules
½ teaspoon fresh or dried rosemary
⅔ cup water
¼ cup dry sherry

• **Sprinkle** chicken on both sides with paprika and pepper. Cook chicken in 2 tablespoons butter in a large skillet over medium-high heat 2 minutes on each side or until lightly browned. Place chicken in a greased 11- x 7-inch baking dish. Arrange artichoke hearts around chicken.
• **Cook** mushrooms and green onions in 2 tablespoons butter in a skillet over medium heat, stirring constantly, until tender. Combine cornstarch and remaining 4 ingredients; add to skillet. Bring to a boil, and cook 1 minute, stirring constantly. Pour mixture over chicken and artichokes. Cover and bake at 375° for 30 minutes or until chicken is done. Yield: 6 servings.

CHICKEN ALOUETTE

1 (17¼-ounce) package frozen puff pastry sheets, thawed
1 (4-ounce) container garlic-and-spice-flavored Alouette cheese
6 skinned and boned chicken breast halves
½ teaspoon salt
⅛ teaspoon pepper
1 large egg, beaten
1 tablespoon water

• **Unfold** pastry sheets, and roll each into a 14- x 12-inch rectangle on a lightly floured surface. Cut first sheet into 4 (7- x 6-inch) rectangles; cut second sheet into 2 (7- x 6-inch) rectangles and 1 (12- x 7-inch) rectangle. Set large rectangle aside. Shape each small rectangle into an oval by trimming off corners; spread pastry ovals evenly with cheese.
• **Sprinkle** chicken breast halves with salt and pepper; place 1 in center of each pastry oval. Lightly moisten pastry edges with water. Fold ends over chicken; fold sides over, and pinch to seal. Place bundles, seam side down, on a lightly greased baking sheet.
• **Cut** large pastry rectangle crosswise into 36 strips (about ¼ inch wide). Braid 3 strips together, and place crosswise over 1 chicken bundle, tucking ends under bundle and trimming any excess length. Braid 3 more strips, and place lengthwise over bundle, tucking ends under. Repeat procedure with remaining strips and chicken bundles. Cover and chill up to 2 hours, if desired.
• **Combine** egg and 1 tablespoon water. Brush egg mixture over pastry bundles. Bake at 400° on lower oven rack 25 minutes or until golden. Yield: 6 servings.

BIRD'S NEST CHICKEN

family favorite

Delicate pasta nests create 8 servings in this casserole of chicken and spinach in a cheesy cream sauce.

8 nested angel hair pasta bundles
8 skinned and boned chicken breast halves
1 teaspoon salt
½ teaspoon pepper
1 (6-ounce) jar sliced mushrooms, drained
1 (10-ounce) package frozen chopped spinach, thawed and well drained
1 (10¾-ounce) can cream of chicken soup, undiluted
⅔ cup water
¾ cup (3 ounces) shredded Monterey Jack cheese
¾ cup (3 ounces) shredded Cheddar cheese

- **Gently** boil pasta according to package directions, keeping nests intact; drain well.
- **Sprinkle** chicken with salt and pepper; arrange in a lightly greased 13- x 9-inch baking dish. Spoon mushrooms and chopped spinach over chicken. Arrange cooked pasta nests over spinach.
- **Combine** soup and water in a small saucepan; bring to a boil, stirring often. Pour sauce evenly over pasta nests. Cover and bake at 375° for 1 hour.
- **Combine** Monterey Jack and Cheddar cheeses; sprinkle over chicken. Uncover and bake 5 more minutes. Yield: 8 servings.

CHAMPAGNE CHICKEN

quick

2 tablespoons all-purpose flour
1 teaspoon salt
¼ teaspoon pepper
4 skinned and boned chicken breast halves
2 tablespoons butter or margarine, melted
1 tablespoon olive oil
1 cup champagne or dry white wine
½ cup sliced fresh mushrooms
½ cup whipping cream

- **Combine** flour, salt, and pepper in a shallow dish. Dredge chicken in flour mixture. Heat butter and oil in a large skillet; add chicken, and sauté 3 to 4 minutes on each side. Add champagne; cook over medium heat about 12 minutes or until chicken is done. Remove chicken, and set aside. Add mushrooms to skillet, and sauté 1 to 2 minutes. Add whipping cream to skillet; cook over medium heat, stirring constantly, just until thickened. Add chicken, and cook until thoroughly heated. Serve warm. Yield: 4 servings.

SESAME SEED CHICKEN

A thick white gravy drapes these crispy fried chicken pieces. Just add green beans and mashed potatoes for a perfect Sunday supper.

1 teaspoon salt
½ teaspoon pepper
1 cup all-purpose flour, divided
8 skinned and boned chicken breast halves
4 large eggs, lightly beaten
¼ cup milk
1 teaspoon salt
½ cup sesame seeds
Vegetable oil
White Chicken Gravy

- **Combine** 1 teaspoon salt, pepper, and ¼ cup flour in a zip-top plastic bag. Add chicken, and shake to coat. Combine eggs and milk in a small bowl; set aside. Combine remaining ¾ cup flour, 1 teaspoon salt, and sesame seeds in a small bowl.
- **Dip** each chicken breast in egg mixture; coat with sesame seed mixture.
- **Pour** oil to depth of 1 inch into a heavy 10- to 12-inch skillet; heat to 350°. Fry chicken in hot oil over medium heat 15 minutes or until golden. Serve with White Chicken Gravy. Yield: 8 servings.

White Chicken Gravy
¼ cup plus 2 tablespoons butter or margarine
¼ cup all-purpose flour
3 cups chicken broth
2 egg yolks, lightly beaten

- **Melt** butter in a heavy saucepan over low heat; add flour, stirring until smooth. Gradually add chicken broth; cook until slightly thickened, stirring constantly.
- **Gradually** stir one-fourth of hot mixture into egg yolks; add to remaining hot mixture, stirring constantly. Cook over low heat, stirring constantly, 10 minutes or until thickened and smooth. Yield: about 2 cups.

HEARTS OF PALM CHICKEN ROLLS

6 skinned and boned chicken breast halves
½ teaspoon salt
¼ teaspoon ground white pepper
¼ cup butter or margarine, melted and divided
1 (14.4-ounce) can hearts of palm, drained
Béarnaise Sauce

• **Place** chicken breast halves between two sheets of heavy-duty plastic wrap; flatten to ¼-inch thickness, using a meat mallet or rolling pin. Sprinkle with salt and pepper; brush with 2 tablespoons melted butter.
• **Place** a heart of palm on each chicken breast half; roll up from short side, and secure each with a wooden pick. Place chicken rolls on a lightly greased rack in a roasting pan; brush with remaining 2 tablespoons melted butter. Cover and bake at 325° for 1 hour. Transfer chicken rolls to a serving platter. Serve with Béarnaise Sauce. Yield: 6 servings.

Béarnaise Sauce
3 tablespoons white wine vinegar
2 teaspoons minced shallots
1½ teaspoons chopped fresh tarragon or
   ½ teaspoon dried tarragon
3 egg yolks, lightly beaten
⅛ teaspoon salt
⅛ teaspoon ground red pepper
2 tablespoons lemon juice
½ cup butter or margarine, cut up

• **Combine** vinegar and shallots in a small saucepan; bring to a boil over medium heat. Reduce heat, and simmer until vinegar is reduced by half. Pour mixture through a wire-mesh strainer into a bowl, discarding shallots. Let vinegar cool slightly; stir in tarragon. Set aside.
• **Combine** egg yolks, salt, and pepper in top of a double boiler; gradually add lemon juice, stirring constantly. Add one-third of butter to egg mixture; cook over hot (not boiling) water, stirring constantly with a wire whisk until butter melts. Add another third of butter, stirring constantly. As sauce thickens, stir in remaining third of butter. Cook, stirring constantly, until mixture is thickened. Remove from heat immediately. Add vinegar mixture to sauce, stirring well. Serve immediately. Yield: ¾ cup.

ITALIAN FRIED CHICKEN

Shake chicken pieces in a zip-top bag to coat them for frying. It makes cleanup a snap.

6 bone-in chicken breast halves
1 (8-ounce) bottle zesty Italian dressing
2 large eggs
¼ cup water
1½ cups all-purpose flour
1½ tablespoons paprika
1½ teaspoons curry powder
1½ teaspoons salt
1 teaspoon pepper
Vegetable oil

• **Place** chicken in a large heavy-duty, zip-top plastic bag. Pour dressing over chicken. Shake well; seal bag securely, and marinate in refrigerator 8 hours.
• **Combine** eggs and water; stir well. Combine flour and next 4 ingredients in a large zip-top plastic bag; shake well.
• **Drain** chicken, discarding salad dressing. Place 2 or 3 pieces of chicken in flour mixture; shake well. Dip in egg mixture; return to flour mixture, and shake again. Repeat with remaining chicken breast halves.
• **Heat** ½ inch oil to 350° in a large deep skillet; add chicken, and fry 20 to 25 minutes or until golden, turning to brown both sides. Drain on paper towels. Yield: 6 servings.

GREEK CHICKEN BREASTS

Tuck garlic under the skin of these chicken breast halves for a flavor surprise in each bite. A sprinkling of olives and feta cheese adds to the Greek accent.

4 bone-in chicken breast halves
8 cloves garlic, crushed
2 tablespoons olive oil
1 teaspoon salt
1 teaspoon freshly ground pepper
2 teaspoons dried oregano
4 lemons, thinly sliced
16 to 20 kalamata olives, pitted
1 (4-ounce) container crumbled feta cheese
Garnishes: lemon slices, fresh oregano sprigs

• **Lift** skin gently from each chicken breast without detaching it; place 2 garlic cloves under skin of each chicken breast. Replace skin.
• **Rub** chicken breasts evenly with oil; sprinkle with salt, pepper, and dried oregano.
• **Place** lemon slices in a 13- x 9-inch baking dish, and arrange chicken breasts over lemon. Sprinkle olives around chicken.
• **Bake** at 350° for 45 minutes or until done. Remove from oven, and sprinkle with feta cheese. Garnish, if desired. Yield: 4 servings.

CHICKEN BEER BAKE

Toasted almonds and beer contribute flavor to this easy weeknight dish.

⅓ cup all-purpose flour
½ teaspoon salt
½ teaspoon pepper
6 split chicken breast halves
Vegetable oil
2 (10¾-ounce) cans cream of chicken soup, undiluted
1 tablespoon soy sauce
¼ cup toasted slivered almonds, divided
1 cup beer
1 cup sliced fresh mushrooms

• **Combine** flour, salt, and pepper; dredge chicken in flour mixture. Brown chicken in hot oil in a large skillet over medium-high heat. Remove chicken, and place in a 13- x 9-inch baking dish.
• **Combine** soup, soy sauce, 2 tablespoons almonds, beer, and mushrooms; pour over chicken. Bake, uncovered, at 350° for 1 hour, basting occasionally. Sprinkle with remaining almonds before serving. Yield: 6 servings.

CHICKEN DIVAN

~family favorite~

Chicken Divan nestles broccoli spears next to chicken in a subtle curried cream sauce.

4 bone-in chicken breast halves, skinned
½ teaspoon salt
¼ teaspoon pepper
2 tablespoons butter or margarine
¼ cup all-purpose flour
1 cup milk
1 egg yolk, beaten
1 cup sour cream
½ cup mayonnaise
½ teaspoon grated lemon rind
2 tablespoons lemon juice
½ teaspoon salt
¼ to ½ teaspoon curry powder
2 (10-ounce) packages frozen broccoli spears, thawed and drained
⅓ cup grated Parmesan cheese
Paprika

• **Place** first 3 ingredients in a large saucepan; add water to cover. Bring to a boil. Cover, reduce heat, and simmer 15 to 20 minutes or until chicken is tender. Drain, reserving ½ cup broth. Let chicken cool slightly. Bone and chop chicken; set aside.

• **Melt** butter in a small heavy saucepan over low heat; add flour, stirring until smooth. Cook 1 minute, stirring constantly. Gradually add milk and reserved broth; cook over medium heat, stirring constantly, until thickened and bubbly.

• **Stir** one-fourth of hot mixture into egg yolk; add to remaining hot mixture and cook 1 minute, stirring constantly. Remove from heat; stir in sour cream and next 5 ingredients.

• **Layer** half each of broccoli, chicken, and sauce in a greased 2-quart casserole. Repeat layers. Sprinkle with Parmesan cheese.

• **Bake**, uncovered, at 350° for 30 to 35 minutes. Sprinkle with paprika. Yield: 4 servings.

CHICKEN BREASTS SALTIMBOCCA

Slivers of salty prosciutto and fresh sage flavor this Italian dish of buttery, sautéed chicken (or veal) that's braised in white wine.

4 bone-in chicken breast halves
4 fresh sage leaves or 1 teaspoon dried sage leaves
8 thin slices prosciutto
2 teaspoons olive oil
½ teaspoon salt
½ teaspoon freshly ground pepper
3 tablespoons butter or margarine
½ cup dry white wine
1 cup chicken broth
½ cup (2 ounces) shredded mozzarella cheese
2 tablespoons minced fresh flat-leaf parsley

• **Lift** skin gently from each chicken breast without detaching it; place 1 sage leaf (or ¼ teaspoon dried sage), 2 prosciutto slices, and ½ teaspoon oil under skin of each chicken breast. Replace skin. Sprinkle chicken with salt and pepper.

• **Melt** butter in a heavy skillet over medium-high heat; add chicken, and cook 2 to 3 minutes on each side or until golden.

• **Add** wine and broth; cover, reduce heat, and simmer 20 minutes or until chicken is done. Sprinkle with cheese and parsley. Yield: 4 servings.

SZECHUAN CHICKEN WITH CASHEWS

Dried tiny red peppers qualify this dish as Szechuan. Leave them in for presentation, but don't eat them.

2 tablespoons soy sauce
2 tablespoons water
1 tablespoon cornstarch
1 teaspoon sherry
1 pound skinned, boned chicken breast halves, cut into bite-size pieces
3 tablespoons peanut oil or vegetable oil
2 dried whole red peppers
2 tablespoons chopped fresh ginger
½ cup sliced fresh mushrooms
1 green pepper, cut into thin strips
4 green onions, cut into ½-inch pieces
2 stalks celery, diagonally sliced
2 tablespoons soy sauce
1 tablespoon sherry
⅓ cup water
1 tablespoon cornstarch
1 tablespoon plus 1 teaspoon sugar
1 teaspoon coarsely ground black pepper
2 teaspoons white vinegar
1 teaspoon peanut oil or vegetable oil
1 cup toasted cashews
Hot cooked rice

• **Combine** first 4 ingredients in a heavy-duty, zip-top plastic bag; add chicken. Seal bag securely; marinate in refrigerator 20 minutes.
• **Pour** 3 tablespoons oil around top of a preheated wok, coating sides; heat at medium-high (375°) 2 minutes. Add red peppers; stir-fry 1 minute, and remove. Add ginger; stir-fry 1 minute, and discard. Add chicken; stir-fry 3 minutes or until done; remove and set aside. Add mushrooms, green pepper, green onions, and celery. Stir-fry about 5 minutes or until vegetables are crisp-tender. Return chicken to vegetable mixture in wok.

• **Combine** 2 tablespoons soy sauce, 1 tablespoon sherry, ⅓ cup water, and 1 tablespoon cornstarch, stirring well; stir in sugar, black pepper, vinegar, and 1 teaspoon peanut oil. Pour mixture over chicken; add cashews and reserved red peppers. Stir-fry 1 to 2 minutes or until sauce is thickened. Serve over rice. Yield: 4 servings.

PRINCESS CHICKEN

2 tablespoons cornstarch
2 tablespoons soy sauce
1 pound skinned and boned chicken breast halves, cut into 1-inch pieces
2 tablespoons soy sauce
1 tablespoon sugar
1 tablespoon rice wine or white wine
1 teaspoon cornstarch
1 teaspoon sesame oil
¼ cup peanut oil or vegetable oil
5 or 6 dried whole red peppers
2 teaspoons grated fresh gingerroot
½ cup chopped roasted peanuts

• **Combine** 2 tablespoons cornstarch and 2 tablespoons soy sauce in a medium bowl; stir well. Add chicken, mixing well. Cover and refrigerate 30 minutes.
• **Combine** 2 tablespoons soy sauce and next 4 ingredients; mix well, and set aside.
• **Pour** peanut oil around top of a preheated wok, coating sides; heat at medium-high (375°) 1 minute. Add chicken and red peppers; stir-fry until peppers are dark brown. Add gingerroot; stir-fry 1 minute. Add soy sauce mixture. Cook until slightly thickened. Stir in peanuts. Yield: 4 servings.

CHICKEN FETTUCCINE SUPREME

family favorite

This creamy, rich chicken and pasta dish is guaranteed to become a family favorite.

¼ cup butter or margarine
1¼ pounds skinned and boned chicken breast halves, cut into bite-size pieces
3 cups sliced fresh mushrooms
1 cup chopped green onions
1 small sweet red pepper, cut into thin strips
1 clove garlic, crushed
½ teaspoon salt
½ teaspoon pepper
10 ounces dried fettuccine, cooked
¾ cup half-and-half
½ cup butter or margarine, melted
¼ cup chopped fresh parsley
¼ teaspoon salt
¼ teaspoon pepper
½ cup grated Parmesan cheese
1 cup chopped pecans, toasted

• **Melt** ¼ cup butter in a large skillet over medium heat; add chicken, and cook, stirring constantly, until browned. Remove chicken from skillet, reserving pan drippings in skillet; set chicken aside.
• **Add** mushrooms and next 5 ingredients to pan drippings in skillet, and sauté until vegetables are tender.
• **Add** chicken; reduce heat, and cook 15 minutes or until chicken is tender. Set aside, and keep warm.
• **Place** fettuccine in a large bowl. Add half-and-half and next 4 ingredients to fettuccine; toss gently to combine.
• **Add** chicken mixture and Parmesan cheese to fettuccine; toss gently to combine. Sprinkle with pecans, and serve immediately. Yield: 4 servings.

CHICKEN CURRY

Multiple toppings make this curried dish intriguing.

6 bone-in chicken breasts halves, skinned
2 cloves garlic, halved
2 bay leaves
4 whole peppercorns
1 teaspoon salt
3 tablespoons butter or margarine
1 large carrot, scraped and sliced
½ cup chopped celery
1 onion, chopped
1 Golden Delicious apple, peeled, and chopped
1½ tablespoons curry powder
½ teaspoon hot chili powder
3 tablespoons all-purpose flour
¾ teaspoon salt
¼ teaspoon ground mace
¼ teaspoon ground allspice
¼ teaspoon ground nutmeg
¼ teaspoon ground cinnamon
¼ teaspoon ground cloves
Hot cooked rice
Assorted condiments
Garnish: fresh cilantro

• **Place** first 5 ingredients in a Dutch oven; add water to cover. Bring to a boil; cover, reduce heat, and simmer over medium heat 30 minutes or until chicken is tender. Drain, reserving broth. Bone chicken; cut into bite-size pieces.
• **Melt** butter in Dutch oven over medium heat. Add carrot, celery, onion, and apple; cook 10 to 15 minutes or until tender, stirring often. Add curry and chili powder; cook 5 minutes, stirring occasionally. Stir in 1 cup reserved broth. Remove from heat; cool slightly.
• **Process** mixture in an electric blender until smooth. Add flour; process until blended. Return mixture to Dutch oven; cook over medium heat 5 minutes. Gradually whisk in 2 cups reserved broth; bring to a simmer, and cook 5 minutes. Add salt and next 5 ingredients. Stir in chicken. Serve over rice with the following condiments: flaked coconut, peanuts, chopped green onions, chutney, and currants. Garnish, if desired. Yield: 6 servings.

Chicken
Curry

CHICKEN POT PIE

family favorite

Cheddar pastry puts this pot pie in a class all by itself.

¼ cup butter or margarine
⅓ cup all-purpose flour
2¾ cups chicken broth
½ teaspoon salt
½ teaspoon pepper
3 cups chopped cooked chicken
1 (10-ounce) package frozen mixed vegetables, thawed
½ cup chopped celery
3 hard-cooked eggs, chopped
Cheddar Pastry
1 large egg, lightly beaten
1 teaspoon water

• **Melt** butter in a heavy saucepan over low heat; add flour, stirring until smooth. Cook 1 minute, stirring constantly. Gradually add chicken broth; cook over medium heat until mixture is thickened and bubbly, stirring constantly. Stir in salt and pepper. Stir in chicken and next 3 ingredients. Spoon mixture into a lightly greased 11- x 7-inch baking dish.
• **Roll** out pastry to ⅛-inch thickness on a lightly floured surface. Cut into ¾-inch-wide strips, using a fluted pastry wheel. Arrange strips lattice-fashion across top of pot pie. Combine egg and water; lightly brush over pastry. Bake pot pie at 400° for 35 to 40 minutes or until golden. Yield: 6 servings.

Cheddar Pastry
1½ cups all-purpose flour
1 teaspoon salt
½ cup plus 1½ tablespoons shortening
½ cup (2 ounces) shredded sharp Cheddar cheese
4 to 5 tablespoons ice water

• **Combine** flour and salt; cut in shortening with a pastry blender until mixture is crumbly. Stir in cheese.

Sprinkle ice water, 1 tablespoon at a time, evenly over surface; stir with a fork until dry ingredients are moistened. Shape into a ball; chill. Yield: pastry for one 11- x 7-inch lattice crust.

NOTE: To get chopped cooked chicken buy a roasted chicken from the grocery deli, ook your own whole chicken in simmering water 1 to ½ hours or until tender. Drain and chop chicken to yield 3 cups.

EASY CHICKEN ENCHILADAS

family favorite

2 cups chopped cooked chicken
2 cups sour cream
1 (10¾-ounce) can cream of chicken soup
1½ cups (6 ounces) shredded Monterey Jack cheese
1½ cups (6 ounces) shredded Colby Jack cheese
1 (4.5-ounce) can chopped green chiles, drained
2 tablespoons chopped onion
¼ teaspoon pepper
⅛ teaspoon salt
10 (10-inch) corn tortillas
Vegetable oil
1 cup (4 ounces) shredded Colby Jack cheese
Salsa

• **Combine** first 9 ingredients; stir well. Fry tortillas, 1 at a time, in 2 tablespoons oil in a skillet 5 seconds on each side or until softened; add additional oil, if necessary. Drain.
• **Place** heaping ½ cup chicken mixture on each tortilla; roll up each tortilla, and place, seam side down, in a 13- x 9-inch baking dish.
• **Cover** and bake at 350° for 20 minutes. Sprinkle with 1 cup cheese, and bake, uncovered, 5 more minutes. Serve with salsa. Yield: 5 servings.

PESTO CHICKEN WITH BASIL CREAM

A fresh basil cream sauce accents these pesto chicken rolls. For a pretty presentation, slice each roll into 4 or 5 pinwheels as shown on page 234.

8 skinned and boned chicken breast halves
8 (1-ounce) slices prosciutto or other ham
Pesto
¼ cup olive oil
2 cloves garlic, minced
¼ teaspoon pepper
Basil Cream
Garnish: fresh basil

• **Place** each chicken breast half between two sheets of plastic wrap; flatten to ¼-inch thickness, using a meat mallet or rolling pin. Place 1 slice prosciutto and 2 tablespoons Pesto in center of each chicken piece. Roll up crosswise; secure with a wooden pick. Place in a 13- x 9-inch pan.

• **Combine** olive oil, garlic, and pepper. Grill chicken, uncovered, over medium coals (300° to 350°) 15 to 20 minutes or until done, turning and basting occasionally with olive oil mixture. Serve with Basil Cream. Garnish, if desired. Yield: 8 servings.

Pesto

2 cups packed fresh basil leaves
½ cup freshly grated Parmesan cheese
½ cup freshly grated Romano cheese
¼ cup chopped walnuts
2 cloves garlic, halved
¼ teaspoon salt
¼ teaspoon freshly ground pepper
½ cup olive oil

• **Process** first 7 ingredients in a food processor until smooth. With processor running, pour oil through food chute in a slow, steady stream until Pesto is well blended. Yield: 1 cup.

Basil Cream

⅓ cup dry white wine
2 shallots, finely chopped
1½ cups whipping cream
1 cup finely chopped tomato
¼ cup shredded fresh basil
¼ teaspoon salt

• **Combine** wine and shallots in a saucepan; bring to a boil, and cook 2 minutes or until liquid is reduced to about ¼ cup.

• **Add** whipping cream; return to a boil, and simmer 8 to 10 minutes or until reduced to about 1 cup, stirring constantly. Stir in tomato, basil, and salt; cook just until heated. Yield: 2 cups.

CHICKEN LIVERS IN WINE

12 slices bacon
4 green onions, finely chopped
½ cup chopped green pepper
1 pound chicken livers
⅓ cup all-purpose flour
1 cup dry white wine
1 teaspoon chopped fresh thyme
¼ teaspoon salt
⅛ teaspoon freshly ground pepper
Hot cooked rice

• **Cook** bacon in a large skillet over medium heat until crisp; remove bacon, reserving 3 tablespoons drippings in skillet. Crumble bacon, and set aside.

• **Cook** green onions and green pepper in reserved bacon drippings over medium heat until tender.

• **Dredge** livers in flour; add to vegetables in skillet, and cook 5 minutes. Add wine and seasonings; cover, reduce heat, and simmer 5 minutes or until livers are done. Serve over rice. Sprinkle with crumbled bacon. Yield: 4 servings.

SAUTÉED CHICKEN LIVERS

◦ quick ◦

¼ cup all-purpose flour
½ teaspoon salt
½ teaspoon pepper
1 pound chicken livers
2 tablespoons vegetable oil or olive oil
¼ cup plus 2 tablespoons butter or margarine, melted
2 medium onions, chopped
2 cups sliced fresh mushrooms
¼ cup dry sherry
¼ cup chopped fresh parsley

• **Combine** flour, salt, and pepper; dredge livers in flour mixture. Heat oil and butter in a large skillet; brown chicken livers over medium-high heat 3 minutes. Remove livers, reserving drippings in skillet. Set livers aside; keep warm.
• **Add** onion to drippings in skillet; cook, stirring constantly, 5 minutes or until tender. Add mushrooms, and cook 3 minutes or until tender. Return livers to pan; add sherry, and simmer 6 minutes. Sprinkle with parsley before serving. Yield: 4 servings.

Turkey: Not Just for the Holidays Anymore

Turkey came along for the ride on the low-cholesterol wave through the '80s. By 1998, Americans ate more than twice as much turkey as they did in 1970. By century's end, we subbed ground turkey for hamburger and reached for prepackaged turkey cutlets, legs, tenderloins, and breasts for everyday dining.

FAST-AND-SAVORY TURKEY

This turkey bakes fast, snugly wrapped in foil for the first hour. Then it's uncovered to finish cooking and to brown nicely surrounded by savory drippings.

Vegetable cooking spray
1 (10- to 12-pound) turkey
2 teaspoons salt
2 teaspoons lemon-pepper seasoning
1 medium onion
6 (4-inch) fresh parsley sprigs
6 (4-inch) fresh rosemary sprigs
1 large carrot, scraped and sliced
1 stalk celery, sliced
1 large onion, sliced
1 (4-inch) sprig fresh rosemary
1 cup dry white wine
½ cup brandy or cognac
1½ cups chicken broth
½ cup tomato juice
3 tablespoons cornstarch
¼ cup whipping cream
¾ teaspoon browning-and-seasoning sauce

• **Line** a large roasting pan with heavy-duty aluminum foil, leaving 3 inches overhang on all sides. Coat foil with cooking spray. Set aside.
• **Remove** giblets and neck from turkey; set aside. Rinse turkey with cold water; pat dry. Sprinkle body cavity with salt and lemon-pepper seasoning. Place medium onion in neck cavity; fold wings under back, and pull neck skin under wings.
• **Place** parsley and 6 rosemary sprigs in body cavity. Tie ends of legs to tail with cord. Place turkey in prepared pan, breast side up; arrange carrot, celery, sliced onion, 1 sprig rosemary, and reserved giblets and neck around turkey.
• **Combine** wine and brandy in a saucepan; cook over low heat until thoroughly heated. (Do not boil.) Pour mixture into cavity and over turkey. Combine chicken broth and tomato juice in a saucepan; cook over medium heat until thoroughly heated. Pour mixture over turkey.

- **Cover** turkey with a sheet of heavy-duty aluminum foil. Fold edges of top and bottom pieces of foil together, and crimp edges to seal, making sure it's airtight. (Do not let foil touch turkey.) Bake at 425° for 1 hour on lowest rack of oven.
- **Remove** roasting pan from oven, and cut top of foil lengthwise. Open foil, folding sides back. Reduce heat to 400°, and bake turkey 1 hour and 15 minutes more or until a meat thermometer inserted in meaty part of thigh registers 180°.
- **Remove** turkey; strain drippings, reserving 3 cups. Place 3 cups drippings in a saucepan. Combine cornstarch and whipping cream, stirring until smooth. Gradually stir cornstarch mixture into drippings, and bring to a boil; cook 1 minute or until thickened, stirring constantly. Stir in browning-and-seasoning sauce. Serve gravy with turkey. Yield: 12 servings.

SMOKED TURKEY BREAST

You won't need a smoker or gas grill for this smoked turkey recipe. Three hours on your charcoal grill give this bird its unbeatable smoky flavor.

1 (5- to 6-pound) bone-in turkey breast
1 teaspoon seasoned salt
1 teaspoon dried crushed red pepper
1 tablespoon seasoned salt
1½ teaspoons dried basil
1 teaspoon paprika
Vegetable cooking spray
Hickory chips

- **Split** turkey breastbone so it will lie flat on grill. Combine 1 teaspoon seasoned salt and crushed red pepper; sprinkle mixture over underside of turkey breast. Combine 1 tablespoon seasoned salt, basil, and paprika; sprinkle mixture over top of turkey breast. Coat both sides of turkey breast with cooking spray.

- **Prepare** charcoal fire in one end of grill; let burn 15 to 20 minutes. Soak hickory chips in water at least 15 minutes; place chips on coals. Place turkey breast on end of grill opposite hot coals; close grill hood. Cook 2½ to 3 hours or until a meat thermometer inserted in thickest part of breast registers 170°. Let stand 10 minutes before carving. Yield: 12 servings.

TURKEY HASH OVER POLENTA

Here's a great use for leftover turkey— an upscale hash with fresh sage and roasted red pepper. Spoon it over panfried polenta or skillet cornbread.

⅓ cup all-purpose flour
1 (8-ounce) package sliced fresh mushrooms
½ chopped green pepper
1 medium onion, chopped
¼ cup butter or margarine, melted
2 cups turkey or chicken broth
1 cup half-and-half
2½ cups chopped cooked turkey
1 teaspoon salt
½ teaspoon ground black pepper
3 tablespoons cooking sherry or dry white wine
⅓ cup chopped roasted red pepper from a jar
½ cup toasted sliced almonds
2 teaspoons chopped fresh sage
Polenta or cornbread

- **Cook** flour in a medium skillet over medium heat until browned, stirring often.
- **Sauté** mushrooms, green pepper, and onion in butter until tender. Add flour, stirring until smooth. Gradually stir in broth and half-and-half; cook until thickened, stirring constantly. Stir in turkey, salt, and black pepper. Simmer 5 minutes.
- **Add** sherry, red pepper, almonds, and sage; cook until thoroughly heated. Serve turkey hash over polenta or cornbread. Yield: 6 servings.

Stuffed Turkey Breast

STUFFED TURKEY BREAST

Spinach and sweet red pepper provide a beautiful ribbon of color as you slice into this rolled turkey. Don't miss the gravy—it's divine. Serve both over rice. Ask your butcher to bone the turkey for you and leave the membrane that attaches the 2 halves intact.

1 (5-pound) skinned, boned turkey breast
1 large sweet red pepper, chopped
1 cup chopped purple onion
1 (8-ounce) can whole water chestnuts, drained and chopped
1 tablespoon olive oil
1 (10-ounce) package frozen chopped spinach, thawed and drained

½ cup dry white wine
½ teaspoon poultry seasoning
½ teaspoon dried savory
½ teaspoon salt
½ teaspoon pepper
¼ cup butter or margarine, melted
¼ cup dry white wine
White Wine Gravy

• **Remove** turkey tendons. Place outer side of turkey breast on heavy-duty plastic wrap. Starting from the center, slice horizontally through thickest part of each side of breast almost to, but not through, outer edges. Flip cut pieces over to enlarge breast. Place heavy-duty plastic wrap on turkey. Pound to a more even thickness, using a meat mallet or rolling pin (place loose pieces of turkey over thinner portions). Set aside.
• **Sauté** chopped pepper, onion, and water chestnuts in oil in a large skillet until tender; add spinach and next 5 ingredients. Cook 2 to 3 minutes or until liquid evaporates, stirring often. Remove from heat.
• **Spread** spinach mixture over center of turkey breast to within 2 inches of sides; roll up, jellyroll fashion, starting with short side. Secure at 2-inch intervals, using heavy string. Place turkey, seam side down, on a greased rack in a roasting pan. Insert meat thermometer into the thickest part of turkey roll.
• **Combine** melted butter and ¼ cup wine; stir well. Brush over turkey roll. Cover and bake at 350° for 1 hour. Uncover and bake 30 more minutes or until meat thermometer registers 170°, basting often with butter mixture. Let stand, covered, 10 minutes. Remove strings.
• **Transfer** turkey to a platter. Slice and serve with White Wine Gravy. Yield: 8 servings.

White Wine Gravy
½ cup dry white wine
1 to 1½ cups chicken broth
½ teaspoon salt

½ teaspoon pepper
2 tablespoons cornstarch
¼ cup water

• **Spoon** drippings from roasting pan into a 2-cup measure. Add ½ cup wine and enough chicken broth to make 2 cups. Combine broth mixture, salt, and pepper in a small saucepan.
• **Combine** cornstarch and water in a small bowl; stir well. Add to broth mixture. Bring to a boil over medium heat. Boil 1 minute or until thickened, stirring constantly. Remove from heat. Yield: 2¼ cups.

CORNISH HENS WITH ORANGE RICE

Surround these golden baked hens with fragrant rice on a serving platter. Grapes make an easy and elegant garnish.

6 (1¼-pound) Cornish hens
½ cup butter or margarine, melted
3 tablespoons cornstarch
1 (10-ounce) jar apple jelly
1⅔ cups Sauternes

1 cup orange juice
½ teaspoon salt
Orange Rice
Garnishes: red or green grapes, celery
    leaves

• **Brown** Cornish hens all over in butter in a large deep skillet over medium-high heat; remove Cornish hens, and place in a greased roasting pan. Add cornstarch to drippings in skillet, blending well. Add apple jelly and next 3 ingredients, stirring with a wire whisk until combined. Cook 2 minutes, stirring constantly, or until smooth and thickened.
• **Pour** ½ cup sauce over Cornish hens in roasting pan; bake, uncovered, at 350° for 1 hour and 10 minutes, basting often.
• **Arrange** Cornish hens and Orange Rice on a serving platter; garnish, if desired. Serve remaining sauce with hens. Yield: 6 servings.

Orange Rice

2 cups diced celery with leaves
½ cup chopped onion
½ cup butter or margarine, melted
2 cups water

1 teaspoon salt
1 tablespoon grated orange rind
1 cup fresh orange juice
1½ cups uncooked long-grain rice

• **Sauté** celery and onion in butter in a large saucepan over medium heat 5 minutes or until tender. Add water, salt, orange rind, and orange juice. Bring to a boil. Add rice; cover, reduce heat, and simmer 20 minutes or until liquid is absorbed and rice is tender. Yield: 6 cups.

Cornish Hens with
Orange Rice

Cajun-Fried Cornish Hens

If you enjoy crispy fried chicken, we think you'll love these seasoned Cornish hens quick-fried in peanut oil.

3 tablespoons Cajun seasoning
1 teaspoon ground red pepper
4 (1¼-pound) Cornish hens
1 cup all-purpose flour
1½ gallons peanut oil

• **Combine** Cajun seasoning and pepper; rub over inside and outside of hens. Tie legs together with one end of a 30-inch string.
• **Place** flour in a large heavy duty, zip-top plastic bag; add hens, 1 at a time, and shake to coat thoroughly.
• **Pour** oil to a depth of 4 inches into a deep pot of a propane cooker; heat to 350°. Carefully lower hens into hot oil, using string.
• **Fry** 18 to 20 minutes or until a meat thermometer inserted in thickest part registers 180°. Remove hens from oil, and drain on paper towels; remove string before serving. Yield: 4 servings.

Cornish Hens with Barley-Mushroom Stuffing

3 (1½-pound) Cornish hens
⅓ cup soy sauce
1½ tablespoons honey
1½ tablespoons dry sherry
½ teaspoon garlic powder
1 cup uncooked barley
2½ cups chicken broth
1½ cups chopped fresh mushrooms
¾ cup chopped water chestnuts
4 green onions, chopped

• **Place** hens in a large heavy-duty, zip-top plastic bag.
• **Stir** together soy sauce and next 3 ingredients; pour into cavities and over hens. Seal bag; marinate in refrigerator 3 to 4 hours, turning often.
• **Bring** barley and chicken broth to a boil in a saucepan; cover, reduce heat, and simmer 45 minutes or until liquid is absorbed. Remove from heat; stir in mushrooms, water chestnuts, and green onions.
• **Remove** hens from marinade, reserving marinade. Stuff hen cavities with barley mixture, reserving extra mixture. Place hens, breast side up, on a rack in a shallow roasting pan.
• **Bake** hens at 375° for 1 hour and 30 minutes or until a meat thermometer inserted into stuffing registers 165°, basting hens occasionally with reserved marinade. Serve hens with reserved barley mixture. Yield: 6 servings.

SPICY FRIED QUAIL

8 quail, dressed
1 cup buttermilk
2 tablespoons Worcestershire sauce
1 tablespoon hot sauce
1 teaspoon dried thyme
1 teaspoon pepper
½ teaspoon salt
1 cup all-purpose flour
1 teaspoon salt
1 teaspoon paprika
½ teaspoon pepper
¼ teaspoon ground red pepper
Vegetable oil
½ cup chicken broth
¼ cup all-purpose flour
2 cups milk
1 tablespoon Worcestershire sauce
½ teaspoon salt
½ teaspoon pepper

• **Split** quail to, but not through, the breastbone. Combine buttermilk and next 5 ingredients in a large shallow dish. Add quail; cover and marinate in refrigerator 8 hours. Remove quail from marinade, reserving marinade.
• **Combine** 1 cup flour and next 4 ingredients; dredge quail in flour mixture, dip in reserved marinade, and dredge again in flour mixture.
• **Heat** ¼ inch oil in a large skillet until hot; add quail, and cook over medium heat 10 minutes or until golden, turning occasionally. Drain on paper towels.
• **Pour** off all but ¼ cup oil in skillet. Add broth and quail; cover and cook over medium heat 15 minutes. Transfer quail to a serving platter. Drain off drippings, reserving ¼ cup drippings in skillet.
• **Add** ¼ cup flour to drippings in skillet; cook over low heat, stirring until smooth. Cook 1 minute, stirring constantly. Gradually add 2 cups milk; cook over medium heat, stirring constantly, until thickened and bubbly. Stir in Worcestershire sauce, ½ teaspoon salt, and ½ teaspoon pepper. Serve quail with brown gravy. Yield: 4 servings.

SMOKED HATCREEK QUAIL

12 quail, dressed
2 cups orange juice
Hickory chips
5 cups cola-flavored beverage
Olive oil
2 oranges

• **Place** quail in a large heavy-duty, zip-top plastic bag; add orange juice. Seal bag; marinate in refrigerator 8 hours, turning bag occasionally.
• **Prepare** charcoal fire in smoker; let burn 20 minutes. Soak hickory chips in water at least 15 minutes; place chips on coals. Place water pan in smoker; add cola-flavored beverage to pan.
• **Drain** quail, and brush with olive oil. Tie legs together with string or cord. Cut each orange into 6 slices; arrange orange slices on rack. Arrange quail on top of orange slices. Cover with smoker lid, and cook 1 to 1½ hours or until quail is done. Clip string holding legs together. Arrange quail on a serving platter over "smoked" orange slices. Yield: 6 servings.

Salads

~

Salads offer abundant options for
mealtime. They display beautiful
color, interesting textures, and flavors
unsurpassed by other foods. Turn the
page to find ruffly mixed greens,
pasta and potato salads, fruit salads,
and meaty main-dish salads.

Curly Endive, Bacon, and Pecan Salad (page 269)

Easy Chef's Salad

Chef salad is typically served as an entrée. Meat, veggies, and cheese top crisp greens, giving you a meal in a bowl.

8 cups mixed salad greens
2 cups chopped mixed fresh vegetables
1 small purple onion, cut in half and sliced
3 cups coarsely chopped cooked chicken or cubed cooked ham
1 cup (4 ounces) cubed Cheddar or mozzarella cheese
1 large avocado, peeled and sliced
6 slices bacon, cooked and crumbled
3 cups croutons
1 (16-ounce) bottle Ranch dressing

• **Toss** together first 3 ingredients. Top with chicken, cheese, and avocado slices. Sprinkle with bacon and croutons. Serve with dressing. Yield: 6 servings.

NOTE: For chopped mixed fresh vegetables, we used yellow squash, broccoli, sweet red pepper, and carrot.

Greek Salad

family favorite

Tangy Greek olives and crumbled feta cheese spread lively and intense flavor onto this popular salad.

6 cups torn iceberg lettuce
4 cups torn romaine lettuce
1 cup pitted ripe olives
2 tomatoes, cut into wedges
1 large cucumber, sliced
½ cup olive oil
3 tablespoons red wine vinegar
1 teaspoon dried oregano
½ teaspoon freshly ground pepper
1 cup crumbled feta cheese

• **Combine** first 5 ingredients in a large bowl; toss well.
• **Combine** olive oil, vinegar, oregano, and pepper in a jar. Cover tightly, and shake vigorously. Pour dressing over salad, tossing to coat. Sprinkle with feta cheese. Serve immediately. Yield: 10 servings.

Bibb Salad with Raspberry Maple Dressing

Blue cheese and pine nuts top this easy green salad along with a delicious dressing.

⅔ cup vegetable oil
¼ cup raspberry vinegar
2 tablespoons maple syrup
5 heads Bibb lettuce, torn
2 small purple onions, sliced and separated into rings
2 cups crumbled blue cheese
½ cup pine nuts, toasted

• **Combine** first 3 ingredients in a jar. Cover tightly, and shake vigorously. Arrange lettuce and onion rings on individual salad plates. Sprinkle each salad with blue cheese and pine nuts, and drizzle with dressing. Yield: 12 servings.

CITRUS-BLUE CHEESE SALAD

make ahead

2 medium-size pink grapefruit
1 (0.7-ounce) envelope Italian dressing mix
½ cup vegetable oil
2 tablespoons water
10 cups mixed salad greens
2 oranges, peeled, seeded, and sectioned
1 (4-ounce) package crumbled blue cheese

• **Peel** and section grapefruit, catching juice in a bowl. Reserve ¼ cup juice; set grapefruit sections aside. Combine reserved juice, dressing mix, oil, and water in a jar. Cover tightly, and shake vigorously. Chill at least 3 hours.
• **Layer** half each of salad greens, grapefruit sections, and orange sections in a large salad bowl. Repeat procedure with remaining greens and fruit sections. Sprinkle with blue cheese. Cover and chill at least 3 hours. Pour dressing over salad, tossing to coat. Serve immediately. Yield: 10 servings.

NOTE: Any combination of lettuces—curly leaf, romaine, and Bibb, and fresh spinach—will work well in this salad.

WALNUT-GOAT CHEESE SALAD

Edible flowers such as pansies make this green salad beautiful. The salad tastes great without them, too.

¼ cup orange juice
3 tablespoons white wine vinegar
⅛ teaspoon salt
⅛ teaspoon ground white pepper
½ cup vegetable oil
¼ cup olive oil
6 cups mixed salad greens
½ cup chopped walnuts, toasted
6 ounces goat cheese, cut into ¼-inch-thick slices
Garnish: edible flowers

• **Combine** first 4 ingredients in container of an electric blender. With blender on high, gradually add oils in a slow, steady stream, processing until blended.
• **Arrange** lettuce, walnuts, and goat cheese slices on individual salad plates. Garnish, if desired. Serve dressing with salad. Yield: 6 servings.

Spinach Salad with Strawberries and Pecans

≈ quick ≈

Strawberries and spinach make an attractive pair in this fresh salad. For a shortcut, buy your favorite brand of poppy seed dressing.

1 (10-ounce) package fresh spinach, torn
1 cup strawberries, halved
1 cup pecan halves, toasted
Poppy Seed Dressing

• **Combine** first 3 ingredients; drizzle with Poppy Seed Dressing. Serve immediately. Yield: 6 servings.

Poppy Seed Dressing
⅓ cup cider vinegar or white vinegar
⅓ cup vegetable oil
¼ cup sugar
1 tablespoon Dijon mustard
1 teaspoon salt
½ teaspoon pepper
1 small onion, coarsely chopped
2 teaspoons poppy seeds

• **Process** first 7 ingredients in container of an electric blender until smooth, stopping once to scrape down sides. Stir in poppy seeds. Yield: about 1⅓ cups.

Honey-Spinach Salad

¼ teaspoon salt
1 clove garlic, crushed
⅓ cup honey
⅓ cup olive oil
1 tablespoon lemon juice
¾ pound fresh spinach
1 (11-ounce) can mandarin oranges, drained
¾ cup coarsely chopped walnuts, toasted

• **Sprinkle** salt in a large bowl; add garlic. Mash garlic and salt to a paste, using back of a spoon. Combine honey, olive oil, and lemon juice in a jar. Cover tightly, and shake vigorously. Add honey mixture to garlic mixture; stir well. Cover and chill at least 2 hours.
• **Remove** stems from spinach; wash leaves thoroughly, and pat dry. Tear leaves into bite-size pieces. Combine spinach, oranges, and walnuts in a large bowl; toss well. Pour honey mixture over salad, tossing to coat. Serve immediately. Yield: 6 servings.

The Greens Revolution

70s Iceberg lettuce alone defined salad days. Your choice: French, Thousand Island or blue cheese dressing?

80s Salad bars sprouted up across the region, with sliced fresh mushrooms, cherry tomatoes, cheese cubes, and bacon bits, among other toppings to adorn the greens. Spinach joined iceberg at the table. (*Southern Living* published a whopping 50 recipes for spinach salad during the decade.)

90s A blend of gourmet greens called *mesclun* hit the marketplace. Frisée, oakleaf, arugula, dandelion, radicchio, and sorrel made up the mesclun mix that filled the salad bowl and bar with fresh flavor. Other popular picks were packages complete with croutons and dressing. Salads were never so easy, so beautiful, so delicious.

ORANGE-WALNUT SPINACH SALAD

family favorite

Sweet-and-Sour Dressing ties the flavors together for this recipe.

1 pound fresh spinach, torn into bite-size pieces
2 small heads Bibb lettuce, torn into bite-size pieces
2 oranges, peeled, seeded, and sectioned
1 small purple onion, sliced and separated into rings
½ cup walnut or pecan pieces
2 teaspoons butter or margarine, melted
Sweet-and-Sour Dressing

• **Place** first 4 ingredients in a large bowl. Sauté walnuts in butter until lightly browned; add to lettuce mixture. Toss with Sweet-and-Sour Dressing. Serve immediately. Yield: 10 servings.

Sweet-and-Sour Dressing
½ teaspoon paprika
½ teaspoon celery seeds
½ teaspoon dry mustard
½ teaspoon salt
½ teaspoon grated onion
¼ cup sugar
½ cup vegetable oil
¼ cup white vinegar

• **Combine** all ingredients in a jar. Cover tightly, and shake vigorously. Chill several hours. Shake again before serving over salad. Yield: 1 cup.

CURLY ENDIVE, BACON, AND PECAN SALAD

quick

Curly endive leaves have frilly edges and a slightly bitter taste. A sweet dressing and Parmesan shavings complement the colorful salad shown on page 264.

3 cups loosely packed curly endive
3 cups loosely packed Boston lettuce
1 small purple onion, thinly sliced
¾ cup pecan halves, toasted
6 slices bacon
¼ cup red wine vinegar
2 teaspoons brown sugar
¼ teaspoon salt
¼ teaspoon pepper
Shaved Parmesan cheese

• **Combine** first 4 ingredients in a large bowl; set aside.
• **Cook** bacon in a large skillet until crisp; remove bacon, reserving 2 tablespoons drippings in skillet. Coarsely crumble bacon; set aside. Add vinegar and next 3 ingredients to skillet; cook over low heat until thoroughly heated. Pour over greens; toss gently. Sprinkle with bacon, and top with cheese. Serve immediately. Yield: 4 servings.

ORANGE SALAD WITH HONEY DRESSING

*This is a wonderful citrus salad
for the holiday season when a bag of oranges is
often on hand. A sweet-and-sour dressing
blends the flavors beautifully.*

¼ cup honey
2½ tablespoons lemon juice
2 tablespoons white vinegar
½ teaspoon dry mustard
⅛ teaspoon salt
⅛ teaspoon celery seeds
½ cup vegetable oil
1 medium-size head romaine lettuce, torn
5 oranges, peeled and sliced
½ small purple onion, thinly sliced

• **Process** first 6 ingredients in container of an electric blender until smooth, stopping once to scrape down sides. With blender on high, gradually add oil in a slow, steady stream; blend until thickened. Cover and chill.
• **Line** individual salad plates with lettuce. Arrange orange and onion slices on lettuce; drizzle dressing over top. Serve immediately. Yield: 6 servings.

CITRUS-AVOCADO SALAD

*Since grapefruit are available year-round, you
can make this tangy salad anytime. The heavier
the grapefruit, the juicier it will be. Be sure to
section fruit over a bowl to catch the juices.*

3 pink grapefruit, peeled and sectioned
3 oranges, peeled and sectioned
2 avocados, peeled and sliced
2 heads Bibb lettuce
Orange French Dressing
⅓ cup coarsely chopped walnuts

• **Combine** first 3 ingredients; toss gently. Arrange fruit over lettuce, and top with Orange French Dressing. Sprinkle with walnuts. Serve immediately. Yield: 8 servings.

Orange French Dressing
1 (6-ounce) can frozen orange juice concentrate, thawed and undiluted
½ cup vegetable oil
¼ cup cider vinegar
3 to 4 tablespoons sugar
½ teaspoon dry mustard
¼ teaspoon salt

• **Combine** all ingredients, stirring well. Cover and chill thoroughly. Yield: 1½ cups.

GREEN SALAD VINAIGRETTE

The combination of bacon, onion, and roasted pecans gives this salad its appeal. The pecans roast in a spicy cinnamon mixture—they're so good you'll be tempted to just nibble them alone. If you're so inclined, we suggest doubling the pecan recipe.

6 cups mixed salad greens
4 slices bacon, cooked and crumbled
1 small purple onion, thinly sliced
Roasted Pecans
¼ cup olive oil
2 tablespoons raspberry vinegar
1½ teaspoons sugar
⅛ teaspoon salt
Freshly ground pepper

• **Combine** first 4 ingredients in a large bowl, and toss well. Combine olive oil and remaining 4 ingredients in a jar. Cover tightly, and shake vigorously. Pour dressing over salad, tossing to coat. Serve immediately. Yield: 6 servings.

Roasted Pecans
1 tablespoon butter or margarine
2 tablespoons sugar
1 tablespoon orange juice
¼ teaspoon ground cinnamon
⅛ teaspoon ground red pepper
1 cup pecan halves

• **Melt** butter in a large skillet over medium heat; stir in sugar and next 3 ingredients. Add pecans to skillet, stirring to coat. Spread pecans on a lightly greased baking sheet. Bake at 325° for 15 minutes, stirring every 5 minutes. Cool completely. Store in an airtight container. Yield: 1 cup.

COMPANY SALAD WITH RASPBERRY VINAIGRETTE

1 head Bibb lettuce, torn
1 Red Delicious apple, unpeeled and thinly sliced
1 kiwifruit, peeled and thinly sliced
2 (11-ounce) cans mandarin oranges, drained
½ pound fresh spinach, torn
½ cup fresh raspberries
½ cup coarsely chopped walnuts, toasted
Raspberry Vinaigrette

• **Combine** first 7 ingredients in a large salad bowl. Drizzle Raspberry Vinaigrette over salad, and toss gently. Serve immediately. Yield: 6 servings.

Raspberry Vinaigrette
¼ cup vegetable oil
2 tablespoons raspberry vinegar
2 teaspoons honey
¼ teaspoon grated orange rind
⅛ teaspoon salt

• **Combine** all ingredients in a jar; cover tightly, and shake vigorously. Chill, if desired. Yield: ⅓ cup.

SALAD RIVIERA

make ahead

1 (14.4-ounce) can hearts of palm, drained and
   sliced
1 (14-ounce) can artichoke hearts, drained and
   quartered
10 pimiento-stuffed olives, halved
10 pitted ripe olives, halved
½ cup chopped green pepper
½ cup chopped sweet red pepper
Dijon Vinaigrette
Boston lettuce leaves
12 teardrop or cherry tomatoes, halved
2 hard-cooked eggs, quartered

• **Combine** first 6 ingredients in a large bowl. Pour
Dijon Vinaigrette over salad, tossing gently to coat.
Cover and chill at least 1 hour.
• **To serve,** arrange salad mixture on a lettuce-lined
platter, and top with tomato and egg. Yield: 4 servings.

Dijon Vinaigrette
3 tablespoons white wine vinegar
3 tablespoons olive oil
3 tablespoons vegetable oil
1 teaspoon Dijon mustard
½ teaspoon salt
½ teaspoon pepper

• **Combine** all ingredients in a small jar. Cover tightly, and shake vigorously. Yield: ½ cup.

MARINATED VEGETABLE PLATTER

make ahead

1 pound fresh asparagus
1 (14-ounce) can artichoke hearts, drained
1 (14-ounce) can hearts of palm, drained and cut
   into thirds
1 (15-ounce) can baby carrots, drained
1 cup small fresh mushrooms
½ cup pitted ripe olives
1 (0.7-ounce) envelope Italian dressing mix
1 (10-ounce) package fresh spinach
1 avocado, peeled, pitted, and sliced into wedges
Horseradish-Sour Cream Sauce
1 cup bakery-style croutons

• **Snap** off tough ends of asparagus. Arrange in a
steamer basket over boiling water. Cover and steam 4
to 5 minutes or until crisp-tender; drain.
• **Place** asparagus, artichoke hearts, and next 4 ingredients in a shallow dish. Prepare dressing mix according to package directions; pour over vegetables. Cover
and chill 3 hours.
• **Drain** vegetables, reserving marinade. Line a serving platter with spinach; arrange marinated vegetables
and avocado on spinach. Drizzle reserved marinade
over salad arrangement. Serve with Horseradish-Sour
Cream Sauce and croutons. Yield: 10 servings.

Horseradish-Sour Cream Sauce
1 (8-ounce) carton sour cream
½ cup mayonnaise
1 tablespoon prepared horseradish
1 tablespoon chopped fresh chives
2 teaspoons grated fresh onion
1 teaspoon lemon juice
¼ teaspoon dry mustard

• **Combine** all ingredients in a small bowl; stir well.
Cover and chill. Yield: 1½ cups.

Marinated Asparagus and Hearts of Palm

~ *make ahead* ~

3 pounds fresh asparagus
2 (14.4-ounce) cans hearts of palm, drained and cut into ½-inch slices
1 pint teardrop or cherry tomatoes
¾ cup vegetable oil
½ cup cider vinegar
1½ teaspoons salt
1 teaspoon pepper
3 cloves garlic, crushed
Bibb lettuce leaves

• **Snap** off tough ends of asparagus. Arrange asparagus, in batches, in a steamer basket over boiling water. Cover and steam 4 to 5 minutes or until crisp-tender. Plunge asparagus into ice water to stop cooking process; drain.
• **Combine** asparagus, hearts of palm, and tomatoes in a large heavy-duty, zip-top plastic bag. Combine oil and next 4 ingredients in a small jar. Cover tightly, and shake vigorously. Pour dressing mixture over vegetable mixture in bag. Seal bag, and marinate in refrigerator 8 hours, turning bag occasionally.
• **To serve,** drain vegetable mixture, discarding marinade. Arrange vegetables on a large lettuce-lined platter. Yield: 12 servings.

Broccoli Salad

~ *make ahead* ~

A thin, slightly sweet dressing coats these fresh broccoli buds.

5 cups broccoli flowerets
1 cup thinly sliced carrot
1 cup (4 ounces) shredded Cheddar cheese
½ cup mayonnaise
2 to 3 tablespoons sugar
1½ tablespoons red wine vinegar
5 slices bacon, cooked and crumbled
Lettuce leaves (optional)

• **Cook** broccoli in boiling water to cover 2 minutes; drain. Plunge into ice water; drain.
• **Combine** broccoli, carrot, and cheese; toss gently.
• **Combine** mayonnaise, sugar, and vinegar; stir well. Add to broccoli mixture; toss well. Cover and chill, if desired. Sprinkle with bacon just before serving. Serve on lettuce leaves, if desired. Yield: 8 servings.

Carrot-Raisin Salad

~ *make ahead* ~

¾ pound carrots, scraped and shredded
½ cup raisins
½ cup chopped walnuts
½ cup mayonnaise
1½ tablespoons cider vinegar
1 tablespoon sugar
⅛ teaspoon lemon juice

• **Combine** carrot, raisins, and walnuts in a bowl. Combine mayonnaise and remaining 3 ingredients, stirring well; add to carrot mixture. Toss gently. Cover and chill. Yield: 4 servings.

Jalapeño Coleslaw

make ahead, quick

⅓ cup sour cream
⅓ cup mayonnaise
2 tablespoons red wine vinegar
2 tablespoons vegetable oil
1 clove garlic, minced
¼ cup chopped pickled jalapeño pepper
¼ teaspoon salt
¼ teaspoon pepper
⅛ teaspoon sugar
1 (16-ounce) bag coleslaw mix

• **Combine** first 9 ingredients in a large bowl; add coleslaw mix, tossing to coat. Cover and chill. Yield: 6 servings.

Sweet Onion Slaw

make ahead

3 large sweet onions (about 3½ pounds)
¼ cup white vinegar
¼ cup water
¼ cup sugar
¼ cup mayonnaise
⅛ teaspoon celery seeds

• **Cut** sweet onions in half; cut halves into thin slices.
• **Stir** together vinegar, ¼ cup water, and sugar in a large bowl until sugar dissolves. Add onion, tossing gently. Cover and chill 8 hours, stirring occasionally.
• **Drain** onion, discarding marinade. Pat dry, and return to bowl. Stir in mayonnaise and celery seeds. Yield: 8 servings.

Asian Slaw

Peanut oil or vegetable oil
4 won ton wrappers, cut into ½-inch strips
1 tablespoon chopped fresh ginger
2 pounds napa cabbage
1 carrot, scraped
4 ounces snow pea pods, trimmed
Sesame-Soy Vinaigrette

• **Pour** oil to depth of ½ inch into a large heavy skillet. Fry won ton strips in batches, in hot oil over medium-high heat until golden. Drain strips on paper towels, reserving drippings in skillet; set strips aside.
• **Sauté** ginger in reserved drippings until crisp; drain on paper towels.
• **Cut** cabbage, carrot, and snow peas into thin strips, and place in a large salad bowl. Add ginger; drizzle with Sesame-Soy Vinaigrette, tossing gently. Serve slaw with won ton strips. Yield: 6 servings.

Sesame-Soy Vinaigrette
1 tablespoon sesame seeds, toasted
½ cup vegetable oil
2 tablespoons sesame oil
¼ cup rice wine vinegar
2 tablespoons soy sauce
¼ cup egg substitute
2 tablespoons chunky peanut butter
2 teaspoons Dijon mustard
1 teaspoon minced fresh ginger

• **Whisk** together all ingredients; cover and chill. Yield: 1¾ cups.

COLORFUL COLESLAW

~ make ahead ~

Red and green pepper, carrot, and fresh herbs make this coleslaw stand out.

1 small cabbage, shredded
1 small onion, chopped
1 carrot, scraped and shredded
½ cup chopped green pepper
½ cup chopped sweet red pepper
3 tablespoons minced fresh parsley or cilantro
½ cup cider vinegar
½ cup vegetable oil
3 tablespoons sugar
½ teaspoon salt
¼ teaspoon ground white pepper

• **Combine** first 6 ingredients in a bowl; set aside.
• **Combine** vinegar, oil, sugar, salt, and white pepper in a small bowl; stir well. Add to cabbage mixture; toss gently. Cover and chill 8 hours or overnight. Yield: 8 servings.

SWEET-AND-SOUR CRISPY SLAW

~ make ahead ~

1 small cabbage, finely shredded
1 medium-size green pepper, seeded and chopped
1 small onion, chopped
½ cup sugar
½ cup white wine vinegar
½ teaspoon salt
½ teaspoon mustard seeds
½ teaspoon celery seeds
⅛ teaspoon ground turmeric

• **Combine** first 3 ingredients in a large bowl; toss and set aside.
• **Combine** sugar and remaining 5 ingredients in a small saucepan; bring to a boil, stirring until sugar dissolves. Pour vinegar mixture over cabbage mixture; toss gently. Cover and chill 8 hours or overnight. Yield: 8 servings.

NOTE: One small cabbage yields about 5 cups. One (10-ounce) bag angel hair slaw yields 4½ cups if you're looking for a shortcut.

HAM AND BLUE CHEESE PASTA SALAD

Bow tie pasta lends interesting shape to this salad. Other pastas, such as penne or even macaroni, will work just fine, too.

3 cups dried bow tie pasta, uncooked
1 cup coarsely chopped pecans, toasted
⅓ cup grated Parmesan cheese
2 tablespoons chopped fresh parsley
1 tablespoon minced fresh rosemary
½ to ¾ teaspoon freshly ground pepper
4 ounces cooked ham, cut into strips
1 (4-ounce) package blue cheese, crumbled
1 clove garlic, minced
¼ cup olive oil

• **Cook** pasta according to package directions. Drain well, and place in a large serving bowl.
• **Add** pecans and next 7 ingredients, tossing gently to combine. Add oil, stirring gently to coat mixture. Serve immediately or cover and chill thoroughly, if desired. Yield: 6 servings.

PLENTIFUL P'S SALAD

⌐ make ahead ⌐

There are at least 6 flavorful "Ps" in this dish. It's a great make-ahead salad for a supper club.

4 cups canned, drained black-eyed peas
2 cups cooked rotelle macaroni
2 tablespoons minced fresh parsley
1 medium-size green pepper, seeded and chopped
1 medium-size sweet red pepper, seeded and chopped
1 medium-size purple onion, chopped
1 (6-ounce) package sliced provolone cheese, cut into strips
1 (4½-ounce) jar sliced mushrooms, drained
1 (3½-ounce) package sliced pepperoni, cut into strips
1 (2-ounce) jar diced pimiento, drained
1 (0.7-ounce) package Italian dressing mix
½ cup white vinegar
¼ cup sugar
¼ cup vegetable oil
¼ teaspoon pepper

• **Combine** first 10 ingredients in a large bowl.
• **Combine** dressing mix and remaining 4 ingredients in a jar. Cover tightly, and shake vigorously; pour dressing over pea mixture. Toss gently. Cover and chill. Yield: 8 servings.

ITALIAN PASTA SALAD

⌐ make ahead ⌐

Artichokes, gutsy olives, roasted red pepper, and basil turn pasta into an Italian feast.

2 (6-ounce) jars marinated artichokes, undrained
1 (12-ounce) package dried fusilli, cooked
2 (4½-ounce) cans sliced ripe olives, drained, or 1 cup whole kalamatas, pitted
1 (7-ounce) jar roasted red pepper, drained and sliced
8 ounces mozzarella cheese, cubed
¼ pound hard salami, cut into ¼-inch strips
½ cup shaved fresh Parmesan
¼ cup finely chopped onion
½ cup chopped flat-leaf parsley
½ cup chopped fresh basil
½ cup zesty Italian dressing

• **Drain** artichokes, reserving liquid. Cut artichokes into fourths. Set aside.
• **Combine** pasta, artichokes, reserved artichoke liquid, olives, and remaining ingredients in a large bowl; toss gently. Serve at room temperature or cover and chill. Yield: 6 servings.

Italian Pasta Salad

CURRY RICE SALAD

Curry dressing makes this rice salad memorable. Serve it warm or cold. Add some chopped cooked chicken, too, if you'd like to turn it into a main dish.

1 (6-ounce) package long-grain-and-wild rice mix
2 cups chicken broth
1 cup raisins
1 cup hot water
½ cup sliced green onions
1 cup chopped pecans, toasted
1 (16-ounce) can garbanzo beans, drained
Lettuce leaves
Curry Dressing

• **Combine** rice mix with seasoning packet and broth in a saucepan. Bring to a boil; cover, reduce heat, and simmer 20 to 25 minutes or until liquid is absorbed and rice is tender.
• **Combine** raisins and water; let stand 10 minutes. Drain. Stir raisins, green onions, pecans, and beans into rice mixture. Serve on lettuce leaves. Drizzle with Curry Dressing. Yield: 8 servings.

Curry Dressing
⅔ cup mayonnaise
1 tablespoon curry powder
1 tablespoon honey
1 tablespoon cider vinegar
⅛ teaspoon ground red pepper
2 teaspoons prepared mustard
1 teaspoon Worcestershire sauce

• **Combine** all ingredients in a bowl; cover and chill. Yield: ¾ cup.

BLACK BEAN SALAD

Serve this fresh, hearty salad as a side dish with burgers when you want a change from the usual potato salad and slaw.

3 ears fresh corn
3 to 4 tablespoons lime juice
2 tablespoons olive oil
1 tablespoon red wine vinegar
1 teaspoon salt
½ teaspoon freshly ground pepper
2 (15-ounce) cans black beans, rinsed and drained
2 large tomatoes, seeded and chopped
3 jalapeño peppers, seeded and chopped
1 small purple onion, chopped
1 avocado, peeled, seeded, and chopped
¼ cup chopped fresh cilantro

• **Cook** corn in boiling water to cover 5 minutes; drain corn, and cool. Cut corn from cob.
• **Whisk** together lime juice and next 4 ingredients in a large bowl.
• **Add** corn, beans, and remaining ingredients; toss to coat. Cover and chill 2 hours. Yield: 6 to 8 servings.

WHITE BEAN-TUNA SALAD

~ *make ahead* ~

Here's an easy and refreshing main-dish summertime salad. Just add a glass of white wine and some crusty French bread.

½ cup olive oil
⅓ cup white wine vinegar
1 clove garlic, crushed
1 tablespoon chopped fresh or ¾ teaspoon dried tarragon
¼ teaspoon ground red pepper
2 (6-ounce) cans solid white tuna in spring water, drained and flaked
1 (15-ounce) can cannellini beans, rinsed and drained
1 large tomato, sliced
6 leaf lettuce leaves

• **Stir** together first 5 ingredients in a medium bowl. Gently stir in tuna and beans. Cover and chill at least 30 minutes.
• **Place** tomato slices on lettuce leaves on individual serving plates. Top each serving with tuna salad. Yield: 3 servings.

HORSERADISH POTATO SALAD

~ *make ahead* ~

Horseradish fans, here's a potato salad you'll love.

5 large red potatoes
½ cup mayonnaise
½ cup sour cream
1 to 2 tablespoons prepared horseradish
1 tablespoon chopped fresh parsley
½ teaspoon salt
½ teaspoon freshly ground pepper
4 hard-cooked eggs, chopped
4 slices bacon, cooked and crumbled
3 green onions, sliced

• **Peel** potatoes, and cut into 1-inch cubes. Cook in boiling salted water to cover 12 minutes or until tender. (Do not overcook.) Drain and cool.
• **Stir** together mayonnaise and next 5 ingredients in a large bowl; add cubed potato, chopped egg, bacon, and green onions, tossing gently. Cover and chill. Yield: 6 servings.

FRENCH POTATO SALAD

make ahead

1½ pounds small round red potatoes
3 tablespoons dry white wine
¼ cup olive oil
2 tablespoons white wine vinegar
2 tablespoons Dijon mustard
1 teaspoon chopped fresh tarragon or
    ¼ teaspoon dried tarragon
¼ teaspoon salt
¼ teaspoon freshly ground pepper
¼ cup thinly sliced chives or green onions
¼ cup chopped fresh parsley

• **Cook** potatoes in boiling water to cover 15 minutes or until tender; drain and cool slightly. Cut potatoes into ¼-inch-thick slices; place in a large bowl. Add wine while potatoes are still warm; toss gently.
• **Combine** olive oil and next 5 ingredients; pour over potato mixture.
• **Add** chives and parsley to potato mixture; toss gently. Cover and chill at least 1 hour. Let stand at room temperature 10 minutes before serving. Yield: 6 servings.

GERMAN POTATO SALAD

5 large red potatoes, unpeeled
4 slices bacon, chopped
1 bunch green onions, chopped
1 tablespoon all-purpose flour
⅔ cup water
¼ cup cider vinegar
1 teaspoon salt
1 teaspoon pepper

• **Cook** potatoes in boiling water to cover 25 to 30 minutes or until tender; drain and cool. Cut into thin wedges.

• **Sauté** bacon in a large skillet over medium-high heat 2 minutes. Add green onions, and sauté 2 minutes.
• **Stir** in flour, and cook 1 minute, stirring constantly. Gradually stir in ⅔ cup water and vinegar; cook, stirring constantly, until thickened. Stir in salt and pepper. Toss with potato wedges. Serve warm. Yield: 4 servings.

WARM POTATO AND SAUSAGE SALAD

quick

3 pounds red potatoes
1 pound kielbasa sausage, sliced
4 green onions, sliced
½ cup dill pickle relish
¼ cup chopped fresh parsley
½ cup olive oil
¼ cup white wine vinegar or white
    vinegar
1 tablespoon chopped fresh tarragon or
    1 teaspoon dried tarragon
1 tablespoon Dijon mustard
1 teaspoon freshly ground pepper
½ teaspoon salt
3 cloves garlic, minced

• **Cook** potatoes in boiling water to cover in a Dutch oven 10 to 15 minutes or until tender; drain and let cool to touch. Peel potatoes, if desired.
• **Meanwhile,** cook sausage in a large nonstick skillet over medium-high heat 4 minutes or until browned. Drain and set aside.
• **Slice** potatoes. Combine potato slices, green onions, pickle relish, and parsley in a large bowl; stir in sausage.
• **Combine** oil and remaining 6 ingredients in a 2-cup liquid measuring cup. Microwave at HIGH 1½ minutes or until mixture comes to a boil. Pour hot dressing over potato mixture; toss to coat. Serve immediately. Yield: 6 servings.

WALDORF SALAD

family favorite, make ahead

*Here's a familiar favorite, and a good use
for a few crisp apples.*

3 Red Delicious apples, chopped
1 cup miniature marshmallows
½ cup chopped pecans, toasted
½ cup chopped celery
½ cup golden raisins
½ cup mayonnaise

• **Combine** all ingredients. Cover and chill at least 1
hour. Yield: 6 servings.

STUFFED APPLE SALAD

make ahead

6 large cooking apples, peeled
2 cups water
1 cup red cinnamon candies
1 cup raisins or currants
½ cup chopped celery
⅓ cup chopped, toasted pecans
⅓ cup mayonnaise

• **Cut** apples in half crosswise; core each with a sharp
knife or melon baller, leaving a 1-inch hole in center.
• **Combine** water and candies in a Dutch oven; bring to
a boil, stirring constantly. Add half of apple halves;
cover and simmer 3 to 4 minutes or until tender.
Remove cooked apples with a slotted spoon, and set
aside. Add remaining apple halves to Dutch oven, and
repeat procedure. Cool.
• **Combine** raisins and remaining 3 ingredients; spoon
into center of apple halves. Cover and chill at least 2
hours before serving. Yield: 12 servings.

FRESH FRUIT SALAD

make ahead

2 oranges, peeled and sectioned
1 medium pineapple, peeled and cut into chunks
    (about 6 cups)
1 small cantaloupe, cut into balls (3 cups)
1 cup sliced strawberries
1 cup seedless red grapes
2 medium bananas, peeled and sliced
1 ripe pear, cored and sliced
1 tablespoon lemon juice
Fruit Dressing

• **Combine** first 5 ingredients in a large bowl. Sprinkle
banana and pear with lemon juice; add to fruit mixture,
and toss gently. Cover and chill thoroughly. Pour Fruit
Dressing over fruit, and toss gently before serving.
Yield: 14 servings.

Fruit Dressing
½ cup orange juice
¼ cup vegetable oil
1 tablespoon sugar
½ teaspoon salt
¼ teaspoon paprika
¼ teaspoon celery seed
1 small clove garlic, crushed

• **Combine** all ingredients in a small jar; cover and
shake gently to blend. Chill thoroughly. Remove garlic
before serving. Yield: ¾ cup.

Frozen Fruit Salad

make ahead

1 (16½-ounce) can pitted dark sweet cherries, drained
1 (15¼-ounce) can pineapple chunks, drained
½ cup chopped pecans, toasted
1 (12-ounce) container frozen whipped topping, thawed
1 (8-ounce) carton lemon yogurt
½ cup mayonnaise
Green leaf lettuce (optional)

• **Combine** first 3 ingredients in a large bowl.
• **Combine** whipped topping, yogurt, and mayonnaise, stirring gently; fold into fruit mixture. Spoon mixture into an 11- x 7-inch dish; cover and freeze at least 8 hours or until firm.
• **Cut** frozen salad into squares, and serve on lettuce leaves, if desired. Yield: 8 servings.

Frozen Cranberry Salad

make ahead

2 (3-ounce) packages cream cheese, softened
2 tablespoons sugar
2 tablespoons mayonnaise
1 (16-ounce) can whole-berry cranberry sauce
1 (8-ounce) can crushed pineapple, drained
½ cup chopped pecans
1 cup whipping cream
½ cup sifted powdered sugar
1 teaspoon vanilla extract
Lettuce leaves
Garnishes: fresh cranberries, fresh mint sprigs

• **Combine** first 3 ingredients, stirring until smooth. Stir in cranberry sauce, pineapple, and pecans.

• **Beat** whipping cream until foamy; gradually add powdered sugar, beating until soft peaks form. Stir in vanilla. Fold whipped cream mixture into cranberry mixture. Spoon mixture into an 8-inch square dish. Cover and freeze until firm. Cut into squares, and serve on lettuce leaves. Garnish, if desired. Yield: 9 servings.

Mimosa Salad

make ahead

3 cups fresh blood orange or navel orange sections
2 envelopes unflavored gelatin
2 cups fresh orange juice, divided
½ cup sugar
2 cups champagne
1 (5-ounce) package mixed salad greens
3 cups sliced fresh strawberries

• **Arrange** orange sections in a lightly oiled 8- to 10-cup ring mold; set aside.
• **Sprinkle** gelatin over ½ cup orange juice in a large bowl; stir and let stand 1 minute.
• **Bring** remaining 1½ cups orange juice and sugar to a boil in a small saucepan, stirring constantly; stir into gelatin mixture. Stir in champagne. Chill until consistency of unbeaten egg white; pour over orange sections in mold. Cover and chill 8 hours.
• **Unmold** salad onto a serving plate lined with salad greens. Place strawberries in center of mold. Yield: 12 servings.

BLOODY MARY SALAD

make ahead

1 envelope unflavored gelatin
½ cup cold water
1 cup Bloody Mary cocktail mix
¼ cup finely chopped onion
½ cup finely chopped celery
¼ teaspoon garlic powder
¼ to ½ teaspoon hot sauce

• **Sprinkle** gelatin over cold water in a small saucepan; let stand 1 minute. Cook over low heat, stirring until gelatin dissolves, about 2 minutes. Stir in cocktail mix; chill 40 minutes or until consistency of unbeaten egg white. Stir in onion and remaining ingredients; pour into a 2-cup mold or 4 individual ½-cup molds. Cover and chill at least 4 hours. Yield: 4 servings.

Salad Bowls Replace Salad Molds

70s This decade solidified the love affair between Southerners and congealed salads, with over 100 variations published in *Southern Living* within a 10-year period. What was a '70s bridge club or ladies' luncheon without congealed salad?

80s In the '80s, pasta and rice salads led the way to heartier mealtime salads. Chilled chicken salad and simple seafood salads (canned tuna and salmon, and boiled shrimp) helped establish salads as main dishes rather than side dishes exclusively.

90s By the '90s, meat-loving men and hungry kids gobbled salads for lunch or dinner: spicy beef taco salad in fried tortilla shells, piles of Asian-style grilled chicken with gourmet greens and sesame dressing, or heaping bowls of pasta salad with salami, roasted veggies, and kalamata olives. Ladies who lunch loved 'em, too, and yet they still stir up trusty congealed salads every now and then.

BLACK CHERRY-WINE MOLD

make ahead

This is a dramatic dark colored salad. Look for a red wine whose label boasts hints of black cherry. It will complement the dark cherries nicely.

2 (16-ounce) cans pitted dark sweet cherries
Water
1 envelope unflavored gelatin
¼ cup water
2 (3-ounce) packages cherry-flavored gelatin
1 cup red wine (such as Pinot Noir or Merlot)
Vegetable cooking spray

• **Drain** cherries, reserving syrup. Set cherries aside. Add enough water (about 1 cup) to syrup to measure 2½ cups liquid. Bring liquid to a boil in a small saucepan.
• **Sprinkle** unflavored gelatin over ¼ cup water in a small bowl or liquid measuring cup; let stand 1 minute.
• **Combine** cherry-flavored gelatin and boiling liquid in a large bowl; stir in unflavored gelatin mixture. Stir 2 minutes or until gelatin dissolves. Stir in wine. Chill mixture 1½ hours or until consistency of unbeaten egg white.
• **Gently** fold in reserved cherries. Pour mixture into a 7-cup mold lightly coated with cooking spray. Cover and chill 8 hours or overnight. Unmold onto a platter, and serve with sour cream, mascarpone, or crème fraîche. Yield: 8 servings.

RASPBERRY RIBBON SALAD

2 (3-ounce) packages raspberry-flavored gelatin
1¼ cups boiling water
2 (10-ounce) packages frozen raspberries in
    syrup, thawed and undrained
1 (15¼-ounce) can crushed pineapple, undrained
½ cup chopped pecans
1 (16-ounce) carton sour cream
Lettuce leaves

• **Combine** gelatin and boiling water, stirring 2 minutes or until gelatin dissolves. Chill until consistency of unbeaten egg white. Fold in raspberries, pineapple, and pecans.
• **Spoon** 1½ cups gelatin mixture into a lightly oiled 9-cup mold; chill until set. (Keep remaining gelatin mixture at room temperature.) Spread half of sour cream over raspberry layer. Spoon half of remaining raspberry mixture over sour cream layer, and chill until set.
• **Spread** remaining sour cream over raspberry layer; top with remaining raspberry mixture. Cover and chill until set. Unmold onto a lettuce-lined serving plate. Yield: 14 servings.

GRILLED TURKEY CAESAR SALAD

4 (¾-inch) slices French bread
¼ cup butter or margarine, melted
1 pound turkey cutlets
¼ teaspoon salt
¼ teaspoon freshly ground pepper
2 cloves garlic
1½ teaspoons anchovy paste
¼ cup olive oil
2 teaspoons lemon juice
2 teaspoons Worcestershire sauce
2 teaspoons Dijon mustard
1 large head romaine lettuce, torn (about 1½
    pounds)
½ cup freshly grated Parmesan cheese
Freshly ground pepper

• **Cut** bread into ¾-inch cubes. Toast bread cubes in butter in a skillet over medium heat until lightly browned, stirring often. Drain on paper towels.
• **Sprinkle** turkey cutlets evenly with salt and ¼ teaspoon pepper. Grill cutlets, covered with grill lid, over medium coals (300° to 350°) 3 minutes on each side or until done. Remove cutlets from grill, and let cool 5 minutes. Slice cutlets diagonally across the grain into thin slices.
• **Press** garlic into a large salad bowl, using a garlic press. Add anchovy paste; mash with back of a spoon to combine. Add olive oil and next 3 ingredients; stir with a wire whisk until well blended. Add sliced turkey; toss to coat. Add lettuce, Parmesan cheese, and bread cubes; toss gently. Sprinkle with freshly ground pepper. Serve immediately. Yield: 4 servings.

FRUITED CHICKEN SALAD

family favorite, make ahead

2 cups chopped cooked chicken
½ cup chopped celery
½ cup sliced almonds, toasted
¼ cup sliced water chestnuts
½ pound seedless red grapes
1 (8-ounce) can pineapple chunks, drained
¾ cup mayonnaise
1 teaspoon curry powder
2 teaspoons lemon juice
2 teaspoons soy sauce
2 avocados, sliced (optional)

• **Combine** first 6 ingredients in a bowl. Combine mayonnaise and next 3 ingredients; spoon over chicken mixture, and toss gently. Cover and chill at least 4 hours. Serve salad with avocado, if desired. Yield: 6 servings.

CHUTNEY ALMOND CHICKEN SALAD

Find chutney on the grocery aisle with jams and jellies. It gives the chicken in this salad zip.

4½ cups chopped cooked chicken
¾ cup mayonnaise
½ cup chutney (we tested with Major Grey)
1 tablespoon lime juice
1½ teaspoons curry powder
¼ teaspoon salt
1½ cups sliced almonds, toasted
Leaf lettuce leaves (optional)

• **Combine** first 6 ingredients; cover and chill. Just before serving, stir in almonds; spoon into a lettuce-lined bowl, if desired. Yield: 4 servings.

GREEK CHICKEN SALAD

¾ cup extra virgin olive oil
¼ cup lemon juice
¼ cup egg substitute
2 cloves garlic, crushed
1 teaspoon dried oregano
¼ teaspoon salt
⅛ teaspoon pepper
3 cups chopped cooked chicken
1 head romaine lettuce, torn
¾ cup kalamata olives, pitted
1 small purple onion, thinly sliced
½ cup crumbled feta cheese
Pita Croutons

• **Whisk** together first 7 ingredients in a small bowl; cover and chill.
• **Combine** chicken and next 4 ingredients; gradually add enough dressing to coat, tossing well. Sprinkle with Pita Croutons, and serve with remaining dressing. Serve with sliced tomato and breadsticks. Yield: 6 servings.

Pita Croutons
2 tablespoons extra virgin olive oil
1 teaspoon dried oregano
1 small clove garlic, crushed
Dash of salt
1 (8-inch) pita bread round, split into 2 circles

• **Stir** together first 4 ingredients, and brush over the inside of each pita circle.
• **Cut** circles into bite-size pieces; place on a baking sheet. Bake at 400° for 5 to 7 minutes or until golden. Yield: 1⅓ cups.

Mexican Chicken Salad

Mexican Chicken Salad

~ family favorite, make ahead ~

4 cups chopped cooked chicken
2 cups (8 ounces) shredded sharp Cheddar cheese
2 tablespoons chopped green pepper
2 tablespoons chopped sweet red pepper
1 (16-ounce) can red kidney beans, rinsed and drained
1 (4.5-ounce) can chopped green chiles, drained
1 medium onion, chopped
½ cup sour cream
½ cup mayonnaise
1 (1.25-ounce) package taco seasoning mix
Corn chips
Shredded iceberg lettuce
2 medium tomatoes, coarsely chopped
2 medium avocados, seeded, and coarsely chopped
1 (2¼-ounce) can sliced ripe olives, drained

• **Combine** first 7 ingredients in a large bowl; toss well. Set aside.
• **Combine** sour cream, mayonnaise, and taco seasoning mix; stir well, and pour over chicken mixture. Toss gently; cover and chill.
• Place corn chips on each plate; top with lettuce. Spoon chicken mixture onto lettuce. Top with tomato, avocado, and olives. Yield: 8 servings.

Greek Lamb Salad

1 pound lean boneless lamb
1 cup olive oil
1 cup red wine vinegar
3 tablespoons chopped fresh mint
3 tablespoons chopped fresh parsley
1½ tablespoons Dijon mustard
1½ teaspoons dried oregano
½ teaspoon salt
½ teaspoon pepper
½ teaspoon dried rosemary, crushed
¼ pound fresh green beans, cut into ½-inch pieces
1 (14-ounce) can artichoke hearts, drained and halved
1 small purple onion, sliced and separated into rings
½ sweet red pepper, seeded and cut into thin strips
⅓ cup pitted ripe olives, halved
4 cups mixed salad greens
2 medium tomatoes, cut into wedges
½ cup crumbled feta cheese

• **Place** lamb on a lightly greased rack of a broiler pan. Broil 5½ inches from heat 6 minutes on each side or to desired degree of doneness. Cool; thinly slice across the grain.
• **Place** lamb in a heavy-duty, zip-top plastic bag. Combine olive oil and next 8 ingredients; pour over lamb. Seal bag; marinate in refrigerator 5 hours, turning bag occasionally.
• **Cook** beans in boiling water to cover 3 minutes. Plunge in ice water; drain well. Add beans, artichoke hearts, and next 3 ingredients to meat mixture. Seal bag; marinate in refrigerator 3 hours, turning bag occasionally.
• **Arrange** mixed greens on a serving platter; top with meat mixture. Arrange tomato wedges around meat mixture; sprinkle with feta cheese. Yield: 4 servings.

Clean Plate Club

One food tradition forges on even after the dizzying changes that occurred in the late twentieth century. The simple words "covered dish dinner" still have the power to pit sister against sister or mother against daughter in the veritable contest of casseroles. All's fair in love and casseroles, so go for the good stuff: hearty lasagna, creamy chicken casserole, or a spicy layered Mexican dish with cheese, meat, and rice. If you don't, your sister will! Dishes scraped clean are at stake here.

GRILLED STEAK SALAD NIÇOISE

All the ingredients of the French classic are here except tuna. Marinated and grilled steak serves up a tasty change of pace.

1½ pounds flank steak
1 (16-ounce) bottle vinaigrette
2 tablespoons Dijon mustard
2 teaspoons anchovy paste (optional)
4 medium-size new potatoes, cut into ¼-inch slices
¼ pound small green beans, trimmed
6 cups salad greens
4 plum tomatoes, each cut into 4 wedges
16 kalamata or niçoise olives
2 hard-cooked eggs, quartered

• **Score** steak diagonally across the grain at ¾-inch intervals.
• **Whisk** together vinaigrette, mustard, and anchovy paste, if desired. Pour ½ cup vinaigrette mixture into a shallow dish or heavy-duty, zip-top plastic bag; reserve remaining vinaigrette mixture.
• **Add** flank steak to dish or bag. Cover or seal; chill 1 hour, turning occasionally.
• **Cook** potato in boiling water to cover in a large saucepan 10 to 12 minutes or until tender; drain and toss with ½ cup reserved vinaigrette mixture. Set aside.
• **Cook** beans in boiling water to cover 3 minutes or until crisp-tender; drain. Plunge beans into ice water to stop the cooking; drain well.
• **Remove** flank steak from marinade, and discard marinade. Grill steak, covered with grill lid, over medium-hot coals (350° to 400°) 5 minutes on each side or to desired degree of doneness. Remove from grill, and let stand 10 minutes. Cut diagonally across the grain into ¼-inch-thick slices.
• **Toss** salad greens with ¼ cup remaining vinaigrette mixture, and place on four serving plates. Arrange steak, green beans, potato, tomato, olives, and egg on salad greens. Drizzle salads with remaining vinaigrette, and serve immediately. Yield: 4 servings.

CRAB LOUIS SALAD

½ cup mayonnaise
½ cup chili sauce
2 tablespoons finely chopped green pepper
2 tablespoons chopped sweet pickle
1 tablespoon minced onion
1 tablespoon lemon juice
½ head iceberg lettuce, shredded
1 pound fresh lump crabmeat, drained
2 plum tomatoes, sliced
2 large hard-cooked eggs, sliced

• **Combine** first 6 ingredients in a small bowl; whisk until well blended. Set aside.
• **Place** shredded lettuce on a platter; arrange crabmeat, tomato slices, and egg slices on lettuce. Serve with dressing. Yield: 4 servings.

CRABMEAT, SHRIMP, 'N' SHELLS

3 cups water
1 pound unpeeled medium-size fresh shrimp
6 ounces small seashell macaroni
1 cup thinly sliced celery
½ medium-size green pepper, finely chopped
½ medium-size sweet red pepper, finely chopped
½ small purple onion, chopped
2 green onions, chopped
1 tablespoon chopped fresh parsley
¼ cup mayonnaise
¼ cup Italian dressing
1 tablespoon lemon juice
1½ teaspoons chopped fresh oregano or ½ teaspoon dried oregano
¾ teaspoon salt
¼ teaspoon pepper
8 ounces fresh lump crabmeat, drained

- **Bring** water to a boil; add shrimp, cook 3 to 5 minutes or until shrimp turn pink. Drain well; rinse with cold water. Peel and devein shrimp; set aside.
- **Cook** macaroni according to package directions, omitting salt; drain. Rinse with cold water, drain again.
- **Add** celery and next 5 ingredients to macaroni in a serving bowl; stir well.
- **Combine** mayonnaise and next 5 ingredients. Add to macaroni mixture. Stir in crabmeat and shrimp. Cover and chill thoroughly. Yield: 6 servings.

SHRIMP SALAD

6 cups water
1¼ pounds unpeeled large fresh shrimp
2 hard-cooked eggs, diced
1 (2-ounce) jar diced pimiento, drained
1 cup sliced celery
¼ cup finely chopped green pepper
¼ cup finely chopped onion
½ cup mayonnaise
½ teaspoon salt
½ teaspoon ground white pepper
1 tablespoon lemon juice
⅛ teaspoon hot sauce
Bibb lettuce leaves

- **Bring** water to a boil; add shrimp, and cook 3 to 5 minutes or until shrimp turn pink. Drain well; rinse with cold water. Chill.
- **Peel** shrimp, and devein, if desired. Combine shrimp, egg, and next 9 ingredients in a large bowl, tossing gently. Serve immediately on lettuce leaves. Yield: 6 servings.

SHRIMP VERMICELLI SALAD

5 cups water
2 pounds unpeeled medium-size fresh shrimp
1 (7-ounce) package dried vermicelli
3 hard-cooked eggs, chopped
1 (10-ounce) package tiny green peas, thawed and drained
1 small green pepper, chopped
6 green onions, chopped (1 bunch)
1 cup chopped dill pickle
2 tablespoons chopped fresh dill
1 (8-ounce) carton sour cream
½ cup mayonnaise
¼ cup lemon juice
2 tablespoons Dijon mustard
1 teaspoon salt
¼ teaspoon pepper
Leaf lettuce (optional)

- **Bring** water to a boil; add shrimp, and cook 3 to 5 minutes or until shrimp turn pink. Drain well; rinse with cold water. Chill.
- **Peel** shrimp, and devein, if desired.
- **Break** vermicelli in half. Cook according to package directions; drain. Add shrimp, eggs, and next 5 ingredients to vermicelli in a large bowl; toss gently.
- **Combine** sour cream and next 5 ingredients; stir well. Pour sour cream mixture over shrimp mixture; toss gently. Serve on a lettuce-lined platter, if desired. Serve immediately or cover and chill. Yield: 6 servings.

Sandwiches

Get delicious results from
stacking your favorite ingredients
on soft or crusty bread. Among
these pages we celebrate a great
assortment of sandwiches
from hoagies to wraps.

The Grinder (page 302)

CORDON BLEU CROISSANTS

ᴖ quick ᴖ

For this recipe look for large croissants, usually four per package, instead of petite croissants with six per package.

2 (6-ounce) packages large croissants
2½ tablespoons prepared horseradish
8 thin slices cooked ham
8 thin slices cooked chicken breast
8 slices Swiss cheese

• **Split** each croissant in half horizontally; spread bottoms of croissants evenly with horseradish. Layer 1 slice each of ham, chicken, and Swiss cheese over horseradish. Cover with croissant tops.
• **Place** croissant sandwiches on a large baking sheet. Bake at 325° for 12 minutes or until thoroughly heated. Yield: 8 servings.

TURKEY CROISSANT MELTS

ᴖ quick ᴖ

Spread a bacon and cream cheese filling on buttery croissants; then top with turkey, avocado, and crunchy sprouts.

4 slices bacon
1 (3-ounce) package cream cheese, softened
1 tablespoon grated Parmesan cheese
1 tablespoon minced onion
1 tablespoon sour cream
4 large croissants, split horizontally
6 ounces thinly sliced deli turkey
2 tomatoes, sliced
1 ripe avocado, sliced
8 slices process American cheese
Alfalfa sprouts

• **Place** bacon on a microwave-safe rack in a baking dish; cover with paper towels. Microwave at HIGH 3 to 4 minutes or until bacon is crisp. Drain and crumble bacon.
• **Combine** bacon, cream cheese, and next 3 ingredients, stirring until blended. Spread on cut sides of croissants.
• **Layer** turkey and next 3 ingredients on bottoms of croissants, and place on a baking sheet. Broil 5½ inches from heat 1 minute or until cheese melts. Top with alfalfa sprouts and croissant tops. Serve immediately. Yield: 4 servings.

BLT Croissant Sandwiches

Goat cheese and tangy sun-dried tomato send this sandwich upscale. Red leaf lettuce provides a pretty ruffly edge.

1 (3-ounce) package cream cheese, softened
1 (3-ounce) package goat cheese, softened
¼ cup chopped oil-packed dried tomatoes
1 tablespoon chopped fresh basil or 1 teaspoon dried basil
6 large croissants, split horizontally
12 slices bacon, cooked
3 plum tomatoes, sliced
6 red leaf lettuce leaves

• **Combine** cream cheese and goat cheese, stirring until smooth; stir in chopped tomato and basil. Cover and chill 8 hours, if desired, to develop stronger flavor. Let mixture stand at room temperature to soften slightly before spreading on bread.
• **Spread** cheese mixture evenly over cut surfaces of croissant halves. Place croissant halves, cheese side up, on an ungreased baking sheet.
• **Bake,** uncovered, at 325° for 5 to 7 minutes or until cheese mixture is thoroughly heated. Place 2 strips bacon on bottom half of each croissant; top evenly with tomato slices, lettuce leaves, and croissant tops. Serve immediately. Yield: 6 servings.

Avocado Crabmeat Sandwiches

Here's a quick and easy way to enjoy crabmeat. The crabmeat spread is also great on crackers.

16 ounces fresh lump crabmeat, drained
¼ cup mayonnaise
2 tablespoons fresh lemon juice
1 tablespoon chopped fresh cilantro
½ teaspoon pepper
6 slices rye bread
3 tablespoons butter or margarine, softened
2 ripe avocados, halved, seeded, peeled, and sliced
6 slices bacon, cooked and crumbled

• **Combine** first 5 ingredients in a small bowl; stir well. Cover and chill.
• **Toast** bread on both sides; lightly butter 1 side of each slice. Spread crab mixture evenly over buttered sides of toast. Top sandwiches with avocado and bacon. Yield: 6 servings.

Toasted Mushroom Sandwiches

Here's a rich-tasting sourdough sandwich that vegetarians will enjoy.

1 (8-ounce) package sliced fresh mushrooms
2 cloves garlic, minced
2 tablespoons butter or margarine
1 (10¾-ounce) can cream of mushroom soup, undiluted
1 (3-ounce) package cream cheese, softened
⅓ cup slivered almonds
1 tablespoon Worcestershire sauce
1½ teaspoons prepared horseradish
2 tablespoons mayonnaise
12 slices sourdough sandwich bread
Freshly ground pepper (optional)
Butter or margarine, softened

• **Sauté** mushrooms and garlic in 2 tablespoons butter in a small skillet over medium-high heat 3 to 4 minutes or until tender. Set aside.
• **Combine** mushroom soup and cream cheese in a small bowl; beat at medium speed with an electric mixer until smooth. Add mushrooms, almonds, Worcestershire sauce, and horseradish to cream cheese mixture; stir until blended. Set aside.
• **Spread** 1 teaspoon mayonnaise over 1 side of 6 slices sourdough bread, and sprinkle with freshly ground pepper, if desired. Spread ⅓ cup mushroom mixture over each of the 6 slices. Top with remaining bread slices.
• **Spread** butter on tops of sandwiches; invert sandwiches onto a hot nonstick griddle or skillet. Cook 2 minutes or until bread is golden. Spread butter on ungrilled sides of sandwiches; turn carefully, and cook until bread is golden. Yield: 6 sandwiches.

Welsh Rarebit

For best results with this classic open-faced sandwich, shred your own cheese instead of using pre-shredded cheese in the rich cheese sauce. After shredding the cheese, let it come to room temperature before proceeding with the recipe. We recommend bakery cheese bread, French bread, or rye bread for this recipe.

1 tablespoon butter or margarine
1 cup beer or milk
1 pound Cheddar cheese, shredded
1 teaspoon Worcestershire sauce
½ teaspoon salt
½ teaspoon paprika
½ teaspoon dry mustard
Dash of ground red pepper
1 large egg, lightly beaten
1 large tomato, cut into 6 slices
6 slices bread
6 slices bacon, cooked

• **Place** butter and beer in top of a double boiler; place over hot water until butter melts and beer is simmering. Gradually add Cheddar cheese, ½ cup at a time, whisking until cheese melts and mixture is smooth (about 15 minutes). Stir in Worcestershire sauce and next 4 ingredients.
• **Gradually** stir one-fourth of hot cheese mixture into beaten egg; add to remaining hot mixture, whisking constantly. Cook mixture over medium-low heat, whisking constantly, until slightly thickened and a thermometer registers 160°. Remove from heat.
• **To serve,** place 1 tomato slice on each slice of bread; top each tomato with 1 slice bacon. Spoon cheese sauce over bacon, and serve immediately. Yield: 6 servings.

Hot Brown Sandwiches

The Hot Brown, a meaty open-faced sandwich, was first served at the old Brown Hotel in Louisville, Kentucky.

¼ cup butter or margarine
¼ cup all-purpose flour
1 cup milk
1 cup turkey or chicken broth
1 cup (4 ounces) shredded Cheddar cheese
¾ teaspoon salt
⅛ teaspoon ground white pepper
8 slices sandwich bread, toasted
¾ pound sliced cooked turkey
8 slices bacon, cooked
Grated Parmesan cheese
Paprika

• **Melt** butter in a saucepan over low heat; add flour, stirring until smooth. Cook 1 minute, stirring constantly. Gradually add milk and broth; cook over medium heat, stirring constantly, until slightly thickened and bubbly. Stir in Cheddar cheese, salt, and pepper; cook, stirring constantly, 2 minutes or until cheese melts. Remove from heat; set aside.

• **Place** 2 bread slices on each of four ovenproof plates; arrange turkey and bacon evenly over bread. Top evenly with cheese sauce, and sprinkle with Parmesan cheese and paprika. Broil 3 inches from heat 4 to 5 minutes or until cheese sauce is golden. Serve immediately. Yield: 4 servings.

Devonshire Sandwiches

These cheesy sandwiches are reminiscent of a Hot Brown, only made in a casserole dish. Use your favorite bakery bread, and slice it fairly thick.

18 slices bacon
½ cup all-purpose flour
2 cups milk
2 cups (8 ounces) shredded sharp Cheddar cheese
1 teaspoon dry mustard
6 slices bread
12 thin slices chicken or turkey breast
½ cup freshly grated Parmesan cheese
Paprika (optional)

• **Cook** bacon in batches in a skillet over medium heat until browned; drain, reserving ¼ cup drippings. Add flour to reserved drippings in skillet; cook over low heat, blending until smooth. Gradually add milk; cook until smooth and thickened, stirring constantly. Add shredded cheese and dry mustard, stirring until cheese melts.

• **Place** 3 slices bacon on each slice of bread, and top with 2 slices of chicken. Place in a 13- x 9-inch baking dish; top with cheese sauce, and sprinkle with Parmesan cheese. Sprinkle with paprika, if desired.

• **Bake,** uncovered, at 350° for 20 minutes or until bubbly. Let stand 5 minutes before serving. Yield: 6 sandwiches.

GRILLED PESTO-PEPPERONI SANDWICHES

family favorite, quick

Make this speedy sandwich on a griddle. It takes only six ingredients, but it tastes like much more.

1 (6-ounce) package sliced mozzarella cheese, cut into thirds
8 (1-inch-thick) slices Italian bread
¼ cup pizza sauce
¼ cup pesto sauce
20 slices pepperoni
2 tablespoons butter or margarine, softened

• **Arrange** 1 cheese slice on each of 4 slices of bread; spread evenly with pizza sauce. Top each with another cheese slice, and spread evenly with pesto sauce. Arrange pepperoni slices over pesto sauce; top with remaining cheese slices and remaining bread slices.

• **Spread** half of butter on tops of sandwiches. Invert sandwiches onto a hot nonstick skillet or griddle; cook over medium heat until browned. Spread remaining butter on ungrilled sides of sandwiches; turn and cook until browned. Serve immediately. Yield: 4 servings.

GRILLED REUBENS

1 (16-ounce) bottle Thousand Island dressing
18 slices rye bread
12 slices Swiss cheese
2 cups canned sauerkraut, drained
2 pounds corned beef, thinly sliced
Softened butter or margarine
Pimiento-stuffed olives (optional)

• **Spread** 1⅓ cups salad dressing evenly on 1 side of 12 bread slices. Layer 1 cheese slice, 2 heaping tablespoons sauerkraut, and about 4 slices corned beef over each prepared bread slice. Stack bread to make 6 (2-layer) sandwiches. Spread 1 side of each of remaining 6 slices with remaining dressing, and place, dressing side down, on sandwiches.

• **Spread** butter over top of each sandwich. Place sandwiches, buttered side down, on a moderately hot griddle or skillet; cook until bread is golden. Spread butter on ungrilled side of sandwiches; turn carefully, and cook until bread is golden. Skewer olives on wooden picks, if desired, and secure sandwiches with wooden picks. Serve immediately. Yield: 6 servings.

ASPARAGUS GRILL SANDWICHES

∽ quick ∽

Asparagus spears lend a healthy note to this open-faced lunch.

16 fresh asparagus spears
4 thin slices onion
8 slices sandwich bread
Butter or margarine
8 slices cooked ham or 16 slices bacon, cooked
4 slices American cheese
4 slices tomato
Cheddar Cheese Sauce
Paprika (optional)

• **Snap** off tough ends of asparagus. Cook asparagus, covered, in a small amount of boiling water 6 to 8 minutes or until crisp-tender. Drain and set aside.
• **While** asparagus is cooking, place onion on a moderately hot griddle; cook 1 minute on each side or until browned. Remove onion from griddle, and set aside.
• **Spread** 1 side of each bread slice with butter. Place 4 slices of bread, buttered side down, on griddle. Layer each bread slice with 2 slices of ham or 4 slices of bacon, and 1 slice of cheese. Place remaining 4 slices bread, buttered side up, on top of cheese. Cook until sandwiches are golden on bottom; turn and cook other side until browned.
• **To serve,** place sandwiches on plates. Top each sandwich with 1 slice each of onion and tomato and 4 asparagus spears. Spoon Cheddar Cheese Sauce over sandwiches. Sprinkle with paprika, if desired, and serve immediately. Yield: 4 servings.

Cheddar Cheese Sauce

2 tablespoons butter or margarine
2 tablespoons all-purpose flour
1 cup milk
1 cup (4 ounces) shredded sharp Cheddar cheese

• **Melt** butter in a heavy saucepan over low heat; add flour, stirring until mixture is smooth. Cook 1 minute, stirring constantly. Gradually add milk; cook over medium heat, stirring constantly, until mixture is thickened and bubbly. Add Cheddar cheese, and stir until cheese melts. Yield: 1½ cups.

TACO PITAS

This recipe stuffs all the taco fixings in a pita pocket. Kids will make a meal out of these pitas that are similar to soft tacos.

1 (10-ounce) can tomatoes and green chiles
1 pound ground chuck
1 small onion, chopped
1 (1¼-ounce) package taco seasoning mix
1 (8¾-ounce) can whole kernel corn, drained
5 (6-inch) pita bread rounds, cut in half
2 cups shredded lettuce
1¼ cups (5 ounces) shredded Cheddar cheese
Taco sauce
Sour cream

• **Drain** tomatoes and green chiles, reserving liquid. Add water to liquid to yield ¾ cup. Set aside.
• **Brown** ground chuck and onion in a large skillet, stirring until beef crumbles; drain. Add tomatoes and green chiles, reserved liquid, taco seasoning, and corn to skillet; bring to a boil. Reduce heat, and simmer, uncovered, 15 to 20 minutes.
• **Place** pita halves on a baking sheet. Bake at 250° for 10 minutes or until warm.
• **Fill** each pita bread half with meat mixture; top with lettuce and cheese. Drizzle with taco sauce, and dollop with sour cream. Yield: 10 sandwiches.

SPINACH-WALNUT PITAS

You won't miss meat in these pitas filled with toasty nuts, artichoke hearts, avocado, and zucchini.

2 (6-ounce) jars marinated artichoke hearts
4 cups torn spinach, lightly packed
1 cup chopped iceberg lettuce
1 small zucchini, thinly sliced
2 green onions, sliced
2 avocados, seeded and coarsely chopped
½ cup toasted chopped walnuts
2 tablespoons toasted sesame seeds
Piquant French Dressing
6 (6-inch) pita bread rounds, cut in half

• **Drain** artichoke hearts, reserving ⅓ cup liquid for dressing.
• **Combine** artichokes, spinach and next 6 ingredients in a large bowl. Toss with Piquant French Dressing. Spoon mixture into pita bread halves. Serve immediately. Yield: 6 servings.

Piquant French Dressing
3 tablespoons lemon juice
3 tablespoons sugar
¾ teaspoon salt
¾ teaspoon paprika
¾ teaspoon dry mustard
¼ teaspoon pepper
¾ teaspoon celery seeds
¾ teaspoon grated onion
2 cloves garlic, halved
⅓ cup reserved artichoke liquid

• **Process** first 9 ingredients in an electric blender until blended, stopping once to scrape down sides. With blender on high, gradually add artichoke liquid in a slow, steady stream; blend until dressing is thickened. Cover and chill at least 1 hour. Stir dressing before serving. Yield: ¾ cup.

CURRIED CHICKEN PITAS

A curry dressing coats the chicken salad for these popular flavored pitas.

4 skinned chicken breast halves
5 cups water
1 bay leaf
6 black peppercorns
1 stalk celery with leaves, cut into pieces
4 medium-size sweet pickles, chopped
2 stalks celery, sliced
1 large carrot, scraped and shredded
1 small onion, chopped
1 medium apple, chopped
½ cup raisins
1 cup mayonnaise
1 tablespoon curry powder
½ teaspoon salt
¼ teaspoon pepper
6 (6-inch) pita bread rounds, cut in half
2 cups alfalfa sprouts

• **Combine** first 5 ingredients in a large saucepan. Bring to a boil; cover, reduce heat, and simmer 20 minutes or until chicken is tender. Drain chicken, and let cool. Debone chicken; cut meat into ½-inch pieces. Combine chicken, pickles, and next 5 ingredients. Set aside.
• **Combine** mayonnaise, curry powder, salt, and pepper, stirring well. Add to chicken mixture, and toss gently. Cover and chill.
• **To serve,** fill each pita bread half with chicken salad, and top with alfalfa sprouts. Yield: 6 servings.

TOSCANA WRAP

This recipe's ingredients are indigenous to the Tuscan area of Italy.

1 (2-pound) eggplant, peeled and cut into 1-inch pieces
1 onion, coarsely chopped
1 green pepper, chopped
1 sweet red pepper, coarsely chopped
1 tablespoon dried Italian seasoning
2 tablespoons balsamic vinegar
1 tablespoon extra virgin olive oil
½ teaspoon dried crushed red pepper
¼ teaspoon salt
½ cup canned cannellini beans or other white beans, drained
4 (10-inch) flour tortillas
2 cups (8 ounces) shredded part-skim mozzarella cheese
1 cup diced tomato

• **Combine** first 9 ingredients in a bowl; toss well. Arrange vegetable mixture in a single layer on a jellyroll pan. Bake at 450° for 40 minutes or until lightly browned, stirring occasionally. Stir in beans.
• **Warm** tortillas according to package directions. Spoon one-fourth of eggplant mixture down center of each tortilla, and sprinkle each with ½ cup cheese and ¼ cup tomato; roll up. Wrap each filled tortilla in foil. Reduce oven temperature to 350°.
• **Bake** at 350° for 5 minutes or until cheese melts. Serve warm. Yield: 4 servings.

It's a Wrap

90s Mid '90s food fad was reborn from classic wrapped food including burritos, egg rolls, crêpes Suzette, and cannoli. The fad fits for soccer moms who welcome easy-to-eat, handheld snacks that kids eat on their way to a practice or a game.

OYSTER-BACON PO' BOYS

Cracker meal and cornmeal combine to give the oysters a crispy coating in these toasted French roll sandwiches.

8 slices bacon
⅓ cup chopped onion
¼ cup chopped green pepper
¼ cup chopped celery
1 tomato, seeded and chopped
2 tablespoons chopped fresh parsley
1 teaspoon garlic powder
½ teaspoon seasoned salt
⅓ cup mayonnaise
¼ teaspoon hot sauce
1 cup cracker meal or finely crushed saltine crackers
½ cup cornmeal
¼ teaspoon seasoned salt
⅛ teaspoon pepper
1 (12-ounce) container fresh Select oysters, drained
2 large eggs, lightly beaten
Vegetable oil
4 (6-inch) French bread rolls, split horizontally and toasted
Leaf lettuce leaves

• **Cook** bacon in a large skillet until crisp; remove bacon, reserving 1 tablespoon drippings in skillet. Set bacon aside.
• **Sauté** onion, green pepper, and celery in drippings until tender. Stir in tomato and next 3 ingredients. Drain well, and transfer to a bowl. Stir in mayonnaise and hot sauce; set aside.
• **Combine** cracker meal, cornmeal, ¼ teaspoon seasoned salt, and pepper in a medium bowl. Dip oysters in egg; dredge in cornmeal mixture.
• **Pour** oil to depth of 2 inches into a Dutch oven; heat to 375°. Fry oysters in batches 1½ to 2 minutes or until golden, turning once. Drain on paper towels.
• **Spread** mayonnaise mixture evenly on cut surfaces of roll halves. Arrange bacon, lettuce, and oysters on bottom halves of rolls; cover with top halves. Yield: 4 servings.

Shrimp Po' Boys

~ family favorite ~

To test the temperature of the oil without a thermometer, sprinkle flour over it; when the flour begins to bubble, add the shrimp.

1½ pounds unpeeled medium-size fresh shrimp
¼ cup mayonnaise
¼ cup lemon juice
¼ teaspoon salt
¼ teaspoon hot sauce
Vegetable oil
1 cup all-purpose flour
Zesty Sauce
4 (6-inch) French rolls, split horizontally and
      toasted
Lettuce leaves

• **Peel** shrimp, and devein, if desired.
• **Combine** mayonnaise and next 3 ingredients in a large shallow dish; add shrimp, stirring to coat.
• **Pour** oil to depth of 2 inches into a Dutch oven, and heat to 375°. Dredge shrimp in flour, and fry, a few at a time, until golden. Drain on paper towels.
• **Spread** ¼ cup Zesty Sauce evenly on cut sides of rolls. Arrange lettuce on bottom halves of rolls; top with shrimp and remaining roll halves. Serve with remaining Zesty Sauce. Yield: 4 servings.

Zesty Sauce
1 cup mayonnaise
2 tablespoons lemon juice
1 tablespoon Creole or Dijon mustard
1 tablespoon sweet pickle relish
1 teaspoon dried parsley flakes
½ to 1 teaspoon dried tarragon
¼ teaspoon hot sauce

• **Combine** all ingredients in a bowl. Cover and chill. Yield: 1¼ cups.

Hot Roast Beef Sandwiches

~ family favorite ~

1 (16-ounce) loaf unsliced Italian bread
½ cup finely chopped purple onion
½ cup chopped ripe olives
¼ cup mayonnaise
2 teaspoons Creole mustard
1 pound thinly sliced deli roast beef
1 (8-ounce) package sliced Swiss cheese

• **Place** bread on a baking sheet; bake at 400° for 5 minutes. Slice bread in half horizontally.
• **Combine** onion and next 3 ingredients; spread mixture on cut surfaces of bread.
• **Layer** half each of beef and cheese on bottom half of bread; repeat layers with remaining beef and cheese. Cover with bread top. Cut sandwich into 4 pieces, and wrap each piece in aluminum foil. Bake at 400° for 20 minutes or until thoroughly heated. Yield: 4 servings.

French Dip Sandwiches

~ family favorite ~

1 (3½- to 4-pound) boneless chuck roast, trimmed
½ cup soy sauce
1 beef bouillon cube
1 bay leaf
4 peppercorns
1 teaspoon fresh or dried rosemary
1 teaspoon dried thyme
1 teaspoon garlic powder
12 French sandwich rolls, split horizontally

• **Place** roast in a 5-quart electric slow cooker. Combine soy sauce and next 6 ingredients; pour over roast. Add water to slow cooker until roast is almost covered.

• **Cook,** covered, on LOW setting 7 hours or until very tender. Remove roast, reserving broth. Discard bay leaf. Shred roast with a fork; place roast in rolls, and serve with reserved broth for dipping. Yield: 12 servings.

PARTY PORK SANDWICHES

Serve these flavorful pork sandwiches as appetizers or slice the pork thicker for entrées. And this horseradish sauce tastes equally good with roast beef, too.

2 (1-pound) pork tenderloins
⅓ cup soy sauce
3 tablespoons rice vinegar
2 tablespoons lemon juice
1 tablespoon molasses
½ teaspoon dried crushed red pepper
2 cloves garlic, crushed
Horseradish Sauce
Party rolls

• **Place** pork tenderloins in an 11- x 7-inch baking dish. Combine soy sauce and next 5 ingredients, stirring well. Pour marinade over pork tenderloins; cover and marinate in refrigerator 3 hours, turning pork occasionally. Remove pork from marinade, discarding marinade.

• **Grill** pork, covered with grill lid, over medium coals (300° to 350°) 25 minutes or until a meat thermometer inserted into thickest part of tenderloin registers 160°, turning occasionally.

• **Thinly** slice pork, and serve with Horseradish Sauce on party rolls. Yield: about 2 dozen appetizer sandwiches.

Horseradish Sauce
2 tablespoons butter or margarine
2 tablespoons all-purpose flour
1 cup milk
2 to 3 tablespoons prepared horseradish
¼ teaspoon salt
Dash of ground white pepper

• **Place** butter in a 2-cup liquid measuring cup. Microwave at HIGH 45 seconds or until butter melts. Add flour, stirring until smooth. Gradually add milk, stirring well. Microwave at HIGH 3 to 4 minutes or until sauce is thickened and bubbly, stirring at 30-second intervals. Stir in horseradish, salt, and pepper. Yield: 1⅓ cups.

NOTE: You can microwave the pork tenderloins for this recipe, if desired. Place pork in a baking dish; cover tightly with heavy-duty plastic wrap. Fold back a small edge of wrap to allow steam to escape. Microwave at HIGH 5 minutes. Reduce to MEDIUM (50% power), and microwave 10 to 12 minutes per pound or until a meat thermometer inserted in pork registers 160°, rotating dish one half-turn every 6 minutes. Let stand 10 to 15 minutes before slicing.

THE GRINDER

The grinder is a huge sandwich that's a cousin to the hoagie and hero. It's so long, you may have to cut it in half to fit in the oven. See it on page 290.

1 green pepper, cut into rings
1 clove garlic, minced
3 tablespoons olive oil
½ teaspoon onion salt
½ pound ham, thinly sliced
2 small tomatoes, thinly sliced
1 (14-ounce) loaf French bread, split horizontally
1½ teaspoons chopped fresh oregano or
      ½ teaspoon dried oregano
Freshly ground pepper
8 ounces sliced mozzarella cheese

• **Sauté** green pepper and garlic in oil until pepper is crisp-tender. Sprinkle with onion salt. Remove green pepper, reserving olive oil mixture.
• **Layer** ham, tomato, and green pepper on bottom half of French bread. Drizzle olive oil mixture over green pepper. Sprinkle with oregano and pepper; top with cheese. Cover with top of bread.
• **Cut** sandwich in half, if necessary; wrap in aluminum foil, and place on a baking sheet. Bake at 350° for 35 minutes or until cheese melts. Slice before serving. Yield: 6 servings.

TURKEY HERO WITH GARLIC SAUCE

A slightly sweet, tangy garlic sauce makes this sandwich taste great.

¼ cup mayonnaise
1 tablespoon minced fresh chives
1 tablespoon vegetable oil
1 tablespoon Dijon mustard
1 teaspoon sugar
1 teaspoon lemon juice
1 large clove garlic, minced
1 (16-ounce) loaf French bread
Lettuce leaves
12 ounces sliced cooked turkey
2 medium tomatoes, sliced
1 small purple onion, sliced and separated into
      rings

• **Process** first 7 ingredients in container of an electric blender until smooth, stopping once to scrape down sides.
• **Slice** bread in half horizontally; spread mayonnaise mixture on cut sides of bread. Layer lettuce leaves, turkey, tomato, and onion on bottom half of bread. Cover with top half of bread.
• **Secure** sandwich with long wooden picks, if necessary. To serve, cut sandwich into 6 portions. Yield: 6 servings.

Open-Faced Jalapeño Heroes

1 pound ground chuck
1 jalapeño pepper, seeded and chopped
1 (15-ounce) can tomato sauce, divided
1½ teaspoons dried oregano
⅛ teaspoon garlic powder
1 (16-ounce) loaf unsliced French bread
1 (8-ounce) jar process cheese spread with
    jalapeños
1 (4-ounce) can sliced mushrooms, drained
1 small onion, thinly sliced and separated into
    rings
1 cup (4 ounces) shredded mozzarella cheese

• **Brown** ground chuck in a large skillet, stirring until it crumbles; drain.
• **Add** jalapeño pepper and half of tomato sauce to beef; bring to a boil. Reduce heat, and simmer, uncovered, 5 minutes, stirring often. Add oregano and garlic powder; simmer 2 more minutes, stirring often. Remove from heat.
• **Slice** bread in half horizontally; place bread halves, cut sides up, on a baking sheet. Spread cut surfaces evenly with cheese spread. Top bread halves evenly with meat mixture, mushrooms, and onion rings. Drizzle remaining half of tomato sauce over both sandwich halves.
• **Bake,** uncovered, at 325° for 15 minutes. Sprinkle with mozzarella cheese; bake 5 more minutes or until cheese melts. Cut each half into 3 pieces, and serve immediately. Yield: 6 servings.

Sausage Sandwiches with Mustard Sauce

Sear sausages in a skillet for this saucy mustard and onion sandwich.

2 tablespoons butter or margarine
1 large onion, sliced
1 clove garlic, minced
1½ tablespoons all-purpose flour
¾ cup chicken broth or beer
2 tablespoons ketchup
2 tablespoons Dijon mustard
1 tablespoon prepared horseradish
4 links Italian or Polish sausage (about 1½
    pounds)
2 tablespoons vegetable oil
4 (8- to 10-ounce) French rolls, split horizontally
    and toasted

• **Melt** butter in a large skillet. Add onion and garlic; cover and cook over medium-high heat 10 minutes, stirring often. Uncover and cook 20 more minutes, stirring occasionally. Stir in flour; cook 1 minute, stirring constantly. Gradually add broth; cook over medium heat, stirring constantly, until thickened and bubbly. Stir in ketchup, mustard, and horseradish. Remove from heat; set aside.
• **Slice** sausage lengthwise to, but not through, other side. Press flat with palm of hand.
• **Brown** sausage in hot oil in a skillet over medium heat 9 to 10 minutes or until done and browned on all sides. Place sausage on roll bottoms. Top with mustard sauce. Cover with roll tops; cut rolls in half. Serve warm. Yield: 8 servings.

Taco Burger

TACO BURGERS

family favorite

Pile this "burger" high with your choice of taco toppings.

1½ pounds ground chuck
1   small onion, chopped
1   (8-ounce) can tomato sauce
1   (1¼-ounce) package taco seasoning mix
6   hamburger buns
1   small onion, sliced and separated into rings
1½ cups shredded lettuce
3   medium tomatoes, chopped
1   cup (4 ounces) finely shredded Cheddar cheese
½   cup sliced pimiento-stuffed olives

• **Brown** beef and chopped onion in a large skillet, stirring until meat crumbles; drain well. Add tomato sauce and taco seasoning to meat mixture; stir well. Bring to a boil; reduce heat, and simmer, uncovered, 5 minutes.
• **Split** and toast hamburger buns. Place onion rings on each sandwich; top with meat mixture. Top each sandwich with lettuce, tomato, cheese, and olives. Replace bun tops. Yield: 6 sandwiches.

HICKORY BURGERS

Barbecue sauce ties beef and ham together in this juicy burger. Ham gives the burgers a smoky pink appearance.

1   pound ground chuck
1   pound ground cooked ham
1   (8-ounce) carton sour cream
¼   cup finely chopped onion
¾   teaspoon salt
¼   teaspoon pepper
Hickory-flavored barbecue sauce (we tested with
      K C Masterpiece)
8   slices American cheese
8   hamburger buns, toasted
Sliced tomato
Sliced sweet pickles
Lettuce
Sliced onion

• **Combine** first 6 ingredients in a large bowl; shape into 8 patties. (Mixture will be sticky.) Grill patties, uncovered, over medium-hot coals (350° to 400°) 4 to 5 minutes on each side or until beef is no longer pink, basting often with barbecue sauce. Top patties with cheese during last 2 to 3 minutes of grilling time.
• **Serve** on buns. Top with tomato slices, pickles, lettuce, and onion. Yield: 8 sandwiches.

GRILLED AMBERJACK SANDWICHES

Other fresh fillets will taste great in this recipe, too. Just be sure the fish is the same thickness or the cook time may vary.

4 (¾-inch-thick) amberjack fillets (about 1½ pounds)
Lemon-Soy Marinade
Vegetable cooking spray
⅓ cup tartar sauce
1½ tablespoons capers
4 whole wheat buns, split and toasted
4 leaf lettuce leaves
4 tomato slices

• **Place** fish in a shallow dish; pour Lemon-Soy Marinade over fish. Cover and marinate in refrigerator 1 hour, turning once. Remove fish from marinade; place marinade in a saucepan. Bring to a boil; remove from heat. Coat a grill basket with cooking spray; place fish in basket. Grill, covered with grill lid, over medium coals (300° to 350°) 8 minutes on each side or until fish flakes easily when tested with a fork, basting occasionally with marinade.
• **Combine** tartar sauce and capers; stir well. Layer bottom halves of buns with lettuce, tomato, tartar sauce mixture, and fish; cover with tops of buns. Yield: 4 servings.

Lemon-Soy Marinade
¼ cup lemon juice
2 tablespoons soy sauce
¼ teaspoon garlic powder
¼ teaspoon pepper
¼ teaspoon hot sauce
¼ cup olive oil

• **Combine** first 5 ingredients in container of an electric blender; cover. With blender running, add oil in a slow, steady stream. Yield: ⅔ cup.

GROUPER HOAGIES WITH ONION RELISH

2½ pounds grouper or other firm-fleshed fish fillets
¾ cup red wine vinegar
¼ cup olive oil
1 tablespoon brown sugar
2 tablespoons honey mustard
4 cloves garlic, minced
½ teaspoon freshly ground pepper
8 (6- to 7-inch) French bread loaves, split horizontally
⅓ cup olive oil
Fresh Herb Mayonnaise
Red leaf lettuce
Onion Relish

• **Cut** fish into 8 serving-size pieces, and place in a shallow dish. Combine vinegar and next 5 ingredients, stirring well. Pour mixture over fish. Cover and marinate in refrigerator 1 hour.
• **Remove** fish from marinade, discarding marinade. Grill fish, covered with grill lid, over medium coals (300° to 350°) 6 to 8 minutes on each side or until fish flakes easily when tested with a fork.
• **Brush** cut sides of French bread loaves with ⅓ cup olive oil. Grill bread, cut sides down, covered, over medium coals 3 to 4 minutes or until toasted. Remove bread from grill, and wrap in aluminum foil. Keep warm until just before serving.
• **To serve,** spread Fresh Herb Mayonnaise evenly on bottom of each French bread loaf. Place lettuce, grilled fish, and Onion Relish on bottom halves; replace tops. Yield: 8 servings.

Fresh Herb Mayonnaise
1 cup mayonnaise
1 tablespoon chopped fresh basil
1 tablespoon chopped fresh oregano
1 tablespoon chopped fresh thyme
1 large clove garlic, crushed

• **Combine** all ingredients in a small bowl, stirring well. Cover and chill at least 1 hour. Yield: 1 cup.

Onion Relish
2 pounds purple onions, sliced
¼ cup butter or margarine, melted
½ cup balsamic vinegar
3 tablespoons brown sugar
½ teaspoon freshly ground pepper

• **Cook** onions in butter in a Dutch oven over medium heat 15 minutes or until very tender, stirring occasionally. Add vinegar, brown sugar, and pepper. Cook, uncovered, over medium heat 12 to 14 minutes or until liquid is absorbed, stirring occasionally. Remove from heat, and let cool to room temperature. Yield: 1½ cups.

MARINATED CHICKEN SANDWICHES

⅔ cup white vinegar
⅔ cup sugar
½ cup dry mustard
1 large egg
8 skinned, boned chicken breast halves
1 cup soy sauce
½ cup pineapple juice
¼ cup firmly packed brown sugar
¼ cup sherry
¾ teaspoon minced garlic
8 slices Monterey Jack cheese
8 kaiser rolls, split horizontally
Leaf lettuce leaves
8 slices tomato (optional)

• **Process** first 4 ingredients in container of an electric blender until smooth. Pour mixture into top of a double boiler; bring water to a boil. Reduce heat to low; cook, stirring constantly, 7 minutes or until smooth and thickened. Cover and chill.
• **Place** chicken in a large heavy-duty, zip-top plastic bag. Combine soy sauce and next 4 ingredients; reserve ¼ cup of mixture for basting. Pour remaining mixture over chicken; seal bag. Marinate in refrigerator 30 minutes.

• **Remove** chicken from marinade, discarding marinade. Grill chicken, covered with grill lid, over medium-hot coals (350° to 400°) 4 minutes on each side, basting with reserved soy sauce mixture. Place 1 slice cheese on each chicken breast, and grill, covered, 2 more minutes or until cheese melts. Remove chicken from grill.
• **Spread** rolls with mustard mixture. Place 1 chicken breast on bottom half of each roll; top with lettuce and a tomato slice, if desired. Cover with roll tops. Yield: 8 servings.

JERK CHICKEN SANDWICHES

1 small onion, quartered
6 green onions, coarsely chopped
2 cloves garlic
2 jalapeño peppers or 1 habanero pepper, seeded
2½ tablespoons fresh thyme
1 tablespoon brown sugar
1 teaspoon salt
1 to 1½ teaspoons freshly ground pepper
1 teaspoon ground allspice
6 skinned, boned chicken breast halves
⅔ cup mayonnaise
1 (16-ounce) unsliced Italian bread loaf, split horizontally

• **Process** first 9 ingredients in a food processor until smooth, stopping to scrape down sides. Reserve ¼ cup mixture. Spread remaining onion mixture on chicken; cover and chill 1 hour.
• **Stir** together reserved ¼ cup onion mixture and mayonnaise. Set aside.
• **Prepare** fire by piling charcoal or lava rocks on 1 side of grill. Place a drip pan on opposite side of grill. Coat food rack with cooking spray, and place on grill. Arrange chicken on food rack over drip pan. Grill, covered, 20 minutes or until done, turning often.
• **Grill** bread, cut sides down, until toasted. Spread bread with mayonnaise mixture. Arrange chicken on bottom half; cover with top. Cut into 6 portions. Yield: 6 servings.

CALZONE

Baked whole, this traditional Italian sandwich resembles a large loaf of bread. Once you slice it into individual servings, it reveals a sausage and cheese filling.

1 package active dry yeast
1 cup warm water (105° to 115°)
1 teaspoon salt
¼ cup vegetable oil
2½ to 3 cups all-purpose flour, divided
½ pound ground pork sausage
1 (6-ounce) can tomato paste
½ cup dry white wine
1 tablespoon chopped fresh basil

1 tablespoon chopped fresh oregano or 1 teaspoon dried oregano
2 cups (8 ounces) shredded mozzarella cheese, divided
1 large egg, lightly beaten
2 tablespoons milk
1 teaspoon sesame seeds
½ teaspoon dried oregano
Freshly ground pepper

• **Combine** yeast and warm water in a 1-cup liquid measuring cup; let stand 5 minutes. Combine yeast mixture, salt, oil, and 1 cup flour in a large bowl; beat at medium speed with an electric mixer until blended. Gradually stir in enough remaining flour to make a soft dough.

• **Turn** dough out onto a well-floured surface, and knead until smooth and elastic (about 5 minutes). Place in a well-greased bowl, turning to grease top. Cover and let rise in a warm place (85°), free from drafts, 1 hour or until doubled in bulk. Punch dough down; roll into a 14- x 10-inch rectangle.

• **Brown** sausage in a large skillet 5 minutes, stirring until it crumbles. Drain well; return to skillet. Add tomato paste and wine; simmer 5 to 6 minutes. Remove from heat; stir in basil, 1 tablespoon fresh oregano, and 1 cup cheese.

• **Spread** mixture in a 12- x 4-inch strip lengthwise down center of dough. Sprinkle with remaining cheese. Fold long sides of dough over filling, overlapping edges. Pinch ends together to seal. Place on a lightly greased baking sheet, seam side down. Cover and let rise in a warm place, free from drafts, 30 minutes.

• **Score** top of loaf to allow steam to escape. Combine egg and milk; beat with a wire whisk. Brush loaf with egg mixture. Sprinkle with sesame seeds, dried oregano, and pepper. Bake at 400° for 25 minutes or until golden. Yield: 4 servings.

Calzone

MUFFULETTA LOAF
～ make ahead ～

⅔ cup olive oil
½ cup chopped pimiento-stuffed olives
½ cup chopped ripe olives
¼ cup chopped fresh parsley
1 teaspoon dried oregano
½ teaspoon pepper
2 teaspoons lemon juice
1 teaspoon minced garlic
1 (20-ounce) round Italian bread loaf
¼ pound sliced salami
¼ pound sliced mozzarella cheese
¼ pound sliced pepperoni

• **Combine** first 8 ingredients, stirring well; cover and chill at least 2 hours.
• **Cut** bread loaf in half horizontally; scoop out bottom, leaving a ½-inch-thick shell.
• **Drain** olive mixture, and spoon half of mixture into bread shell. Top with salami, cheese, pepperoni, and remaining olive mixture. Cover with bread top.
• **Wrap** loaf tightly with plastic wrap, and chill 6 to 8 hours. Cut loaf into wedges. Yield: 8 servings.

STROMBOLI
～ family favorite ～

½ pound ground beef
½ cup chopped onion
1 (32-ounce) package frozen bread dough, thawed and divided
2 tablespoons prepared mustard, divided
12 slices process American cheese, divided
2 cups (8 ounces) shredded mozzarella cheese, divided
2 (3½-ounce) packages sliced pepperoni, divided
2 teaspoons dried Italian seasoning, divided
Vegetable oil

• **Brown** ground beef and onion in a large skillet, stirring until meat crumbles. Drain well, and set aside.
• **For each** stromboli, place 1 loaf bread dough on a lightly floured surface; roll dough into a 12-inch square. Spread 1 tablespoon mustard over dough to within ½ inch of edges. Layer 3 slices American cheese, ½ cup mozzarella cheese, half of pepperoni, and half of beef mixture lengthwise down center third of dough, leaving a ½-inch border at top and bottom of dough; sprinkle with 1 teaspoon Italian seasoning. Top with ½ cup mozzarella cheese and 3 slices American cheese. Fold each side of dough over filling; pinch seam and ends to seal.
• **Transfer** loaves to greased baking sheets; brush loaves with oil. Bake at 350° for 25 minutes or until lightly browned. Cut each loaf into 4 slices. Yield: 8 servings.

DEEP-DISH VEGETARIAN PIZZA

Toss your veggie of choice on top of this cheesy deep-dish pizza. One big slice is like a big Italian open-faced sandwich.

1 (10¾-ounce) can tomato puree
1 clove garlic, crushed
2 tablespoons thinly sliced green onions
1 tablespoon chopped fresh parsley
½ teaspoon dried oregano
¼ teaspoon dried basil
⅛ teaspoon pepper
½ pound sliced fresh mushrooms
1 green pepper, seeded and cut into strips
1 cup broccoli flowerets
1 tablespoon butter or margarine, melted
Pizza Crust
2 tablespoons sliced pimiento-stuffed olives
2 tablespoons sliced ripe olives
¼ cup grated Parmesan cheese
2 cups (8 ounces) shredded mozzarella cheese

• **Combine** first 7 ingredients in a saucepan. Bring to a boil; reduce heat, and simmer, uncovered, 15 minutes, stirring occasionally. Let stand 30 minutes.
• **Sauté** mushrooms, green pepper, and broccoli in butter in a large skillet over medium-high heat until crisp-tender.
• **Spread** tomato mixture over Pizza Crust. Arrange vegetables and olives over tomato mixture; sprinkle with Parmesan cheese. Bake at 425° for 10 minutes. Sprinkle with mozzarella cheese; bake 5 minutes or until cheese melts. Let stand 10 minutes. Yield: 1 (10-inch) pizza.

Pizza Crust
1 package active dry yeast
¼ cup warm water (105° to 115°)
2 cups all-purpose flour
½ cup milk
1 tablespoon vegetable oil
1 teaspoon sugar
1 teaspoon salt

• **Combine** yeast and warm water in a 1-cup liquid measuring cup; let stand 5 minutes. Combine yeast mixture, flour, and remaining ingredients in a large bowl; stir well. Cover and let rise 15 minutes.
• **Turn** dough out onto a floured surface; knead 8 times. Pat dough into bottom and up sides of a greased 10-inch cast-iron skillet. Line crust with aluminum foil; place pie weights or dried beans evenly over foil. Bake at 425° for 8 minutes. Remove foil and pie weights; bake 5 more minutes. Yield: 1 (10-inch) pizza crust.

Reinventing Pizza

80ˢ The Italians may have invented pizza, but Americans have made it their own. In 1982, Wolfgang Puck topped a pizza with duck sausage and called it "gourmet." And two decades later, Puck's culinary pursuits have led to a line of gourmet frozen pizzas, filling supermarket cases across the country. His flair inspired a pizza renaissance. Over the years, *Southern Living* has featured pizza on pita bread, French bread, and bagels, as well as on thin, thick, or whole wheat crusts. Deep-dish pizza? We've done it. Grilled pizza? We've done it. Fruit pizza? We've done it. It's the age of pizza as you like it.

Sauces and Condiments

Whether you're topping a sizzling
grilled steak or a beautiful dessert,
the sauce is the finishing touch.
Sauces and condiments often have
short ingredient lists, but are long
on flavor, complementing food
with tantalizing tastes.

Salsa Cruda (page 319)

CHEESE SAUCE

~ quick ~

Here's a simple sauce for topping a multitude of foods such as steamed vegetables, any number of egg dishes, chicken, or fish.

2 tablespoons butter or margarine, melted
2 tablespoons all-purpose flour
1 cup milk
½ cup (2 ounces) shredded Cheddar cheese
¼ teaspoon salt
⅛ teaspoon dry mustard
Pinch of ground red pepper

• **Melt** butter in a heavy saucepan over low heat; add flour, stirring until smooth. Cook 1 minute, stirring constantly. Gradually add milk; cook over medium heat, stirring constantly, until thickened. Add cheese and remaining ingredients, stirring until cheese melts. Serve over poached eggs or vegetables. Yield: 1 cup.

MUSHROOM SAUCE

~ quick ~

This savory mild, dark sauce is meant for your favorite cut of beef.

1 (8-ounce) package sliced fresh mushrooms
3 tablespoons butter or margarine, melted
1 tablespoon all-purpose flour
¾ cup half-and-half
1 teaspoon soy sauce
¼ teaspoon salt
⅛ teaspoon pepper

• **Sauté** mushrooms in 2 tablespoons butter in a large skillet over medium heat until tender; set aside.
• **Combine** flour and remaining 1 tablespoon butter in a saucepan; place over low heat, stirring until smooth.

Gradually add half-and-half; cook, stirring constantly, until smooth and thickened. Stir in soy sauce and mushrooms. Add salt and pepper. Serve hot with roast or steak. Yield: about 1½ cups.

BALSAMIC SAUCE

~ quick ~

Tangy, aged balsamic vinegar flavors this sauce that pairs perfectly with beef or lamb.

¼ cup dry red wine
¼ cup dry sherry
3 tablespoons balsamic vinegar
1 shallot, chopped
2 cloves garlic, minced
2 egg yolks
⅓ cup unsalted butter, melted

• **Bring** first 5 ingredients to a boil in a small saucepan; cook 2 minutes. Cool.
• **Whisk** egg yolks into wine mixture, and cook over low heat, whisking constantly, until thickened. Slowly whisk in butter until blended. Serve immediately. Yield: ½ cup.

ROASTED GARLIC SAUCE

For kids with adventurous palates and adults who enjoy a change from tomato sauce, this white garlic sauce is a nice option for Italian dishes.

2 garlic bulbs
2 teaspoons olive oil
1 cup whipping cream
¼ cup butter
2 tablespoons all-purpose flour
¾ cup grated Parmesan cheese
¼ teaspoon salt
¼ teaspoon pepper

- **Cut** off pointed end of garlic bulbs; place garlic on a piece of aluminum foil. Drizzle with olive oil. Fold foil to seal.
- **Bake** at 425° for 30 minutes. Remove from oven; cool. Squeeze pulp from garlic cloves. Cook pulp, whipping cream, butter, and flour in a medium saucepan over medium-high heat, stirring constantly, until thickened and bubbly. Remove from heat; add Parmesan cheese, salt, and pepper, stirring until smooth. Yield: 1½ cups.

BEURRE BLANC

◦ quick ◦

Beurre Blanc is French for white butter sauce. It's fairly delicate in color and flavor, and great for topping chicken, veal, or fish.

¼ cup dry white wine
3 small shallots, finely chopped
1 bay leaf
1 pint whipping cream
½ cup butter, softened
1 tablespoon lemon juice
2 teaspoons chopped fresh dill or other fresh
   herb
¼ teaspoon salt
¼ teaspoon pepper

- **Bring** first 3 ingredients to a boil in a large saucepan; reduce heat, and simmer until reduced by half. Discard bay leaf.
- **Process** wine mixture in a blender until smooth, stopping to scrape down sides. Return mixture to saucepan, and whisk in whipping cream. Cook sauce over medium heat 5 minutes, whisking occasionally.
- **Whisk** in butter and remaining ingredients. Yield: 3 cups.

THAI DIPPING SAUCE

◦ quick ◦

Serve little bowls of this sauce with egg rolls or grilled fish.

½ cup fresh lime juice
2½ teaspoons brown sugar
2 teaspoons minced fresh ginger
1 teaspoon minced fresh cilantro
1 teaspoon diced dry-roasted peanuts
1 teaspoon fish sauce
1 green onion, minced

- **Combine** all ingredients, stirring well. Yield: ⅔ cup.

NOTE: You can find fish sauce in large supermarkets and Asian grocery stores.

SHRIMP SAUCE

Try this easy shrimp sauce over steamed broccoli or a baked potato.

1 (3-ounce) package cream cheese, softened
½ cup milk
1 (10¾-ounce) can cream of shrimp soup, undiluted
1 teaspoon chopped chives
2 tablespoons lemon juice
2 tablespoons slivered almonds, toasted

- **Combine** cream cheese and milk in a small saucepan; stir with a wire whisk until smooth. Add soup; cook over medium heat, stirring constantly, until mixture comes to a boil. Remove from heat. Stir in chives and lemon juice. Serve over broccoli, cauliflower, or other vegetables. Sprinkle with almonds before serving. Yield: 1½ cups.

RAISIN SAUCE

～ quick ～

Remember this thick sauce plumped with raisins when the holiday season draws near.

½ cup raisins
½ cup water
½ cup orange juice
⅓ cup currant jelly
½ teaspoon grated orange rind
2 tablespoons brown sugar
1 tablespoon cornstarch
Dash of salt
Dash of ground allspice

• **Combine** first 5 ingredients in a medium saucepan; bring to a boil. Combine brown sugar, cornstarch, salt, and allspice; stir into orange juice mixture. Cook over medium heat 3 to 4 minutes, stirring constantly, until thickened. Serve sauce warm over ham or pork roast. Yield: 1 cup.

CHUNKY CRANBERRY SAUCE

Bake these jeweled berries to develop a thick, sweet sauce; then stir in toasted walnuts, and serve it with turkey or ham.

4 cups fresh cranberries
2 cups sugar
½ teaspoon ground cinnamon
1 (13-ounce) jar orange marmalade
3 tablespoons lemon juice
1 cup coarsely chopped walnuts, toasted

• **Wash** and drain cranberries. Combine sugar and cinnamon; add cranberries, stirring well. Spoon mixture into a lightly greased 9-inch square pan. Cover and

bake at 350° for 45 minutes. Uncover and add orange marmalade, lemon juice, and walnuts, stirring well. Serve sauce warm or chilled. Cover and store in refrigerator. Yield: 4 cups.

HONEY-BUTTER SAUCE

～ quick ～

Use as a basting sauce for grilled chicken or toss with steamed fresh vegetables.

1 cup butter
1 cup white vinegar
¾ cup honey
5 cloves garlic, crushed
1 tablespoon salt
1½ teaspoons dry mustard
¾ teaspoon dried thyme
½ teaspoon pepper

• **Melt** butter in a medium saucepan; stir in vinegar and remaining ingredients. Serve immediately or store in refrigerator up to 1 week. Reheat before serving. Yield: 2½ cups.

ZESTY TOMATO SAUCE

～ quick ～

Use this sauce when you're making pizza at home.

1 (16-ounce) can tomato sauce
2 cloves garlic, crushed
1 teaspoon sugar
¼ teaspoon dried Italian seasoning
¼ teaspoon dried crushed red pepper
1 tablespoon chopped fresh basil or 1 teaspoon
    dried basil

• **Cook** first 5 ingredients in a heavy saucepan over medium-high heat until reduced to 1¼ cups (about 10 minutes), stirring occasionally. Stir in basil. Remove from heat. Yield: 1¼ cups.

BARBECUE SAUCE

Most homemade barbecue sauces have multi-layers of flavor. This sauce is no exception, and the long simmering helps develop and blend the flavors. Serve it with chicken or ribs.

1 medium onion, chopped
2 tablespoons grated orange rind
½ cup molasses
½ cup ketchup
⅓ cup fresh orange juice
2 tablespoons olive oil
1 tablespoon white vinegar
1 tablespoon steak sauce
½ teaspoon Worcestershire sauce
½ teaspoon prepared mustard
¼ teaspoon garlic powder
¼ teaspoon salt
¼ teaspoon ground red pepper
¼ teaspoon hot sauce
⅛ teaspoon ground cloves
¼ cup bourbon

• **Cook** all ingredients except bourbon in a saucepan over low heat 30 minutes. Add bourbon, and simmer 10 minutes. Use to baste poultry, beef, or pork when grilling. Yield: about 2 cups.

DRESSED-UP BARBECUE SAUCE

quick

1 (18-ounce) bottle barbecue sauce with onion bits (we tested with Kraft)
⅔ cup firmly packed brown sugar
½ cup red wine
1 teaspoon Worcestershire sauce
¼ to ½ teaspoon hot sauce

• **Combine** all ingredients, stirring well. Use to baste poultry, beef, or pork when grilling. Yield: 2½ cups.

MEMPHIS-STYLE BARBECUE SAUCE

1 (8-ounce) can tomato sauce
1 cup ketchup
1 cup red wine vinegar
½ cup honey mustard
½ cup hickory-smoked Worcestershire sauce
3 tablespoons butter or margarine
2 tablespoons brown sugar
1 tablespoon paprika
1 tablespoon seasoned salt
1½ tablespoons hot sauce
1 tablespoon lemon juice
1½ teaspoons garlic powder
¼ teaspoon chili powder
⅛ teaspoon ground red pepper
⅛ teaspoon black pepper

• **Combine** all ingredients in a large saucepan. Bring to a boil; cover, reduce heat, and simmer 30 minutes, stirring occasionally. Use to baste poultry, beef, or pork when grilling. Yield: 4 cups.

Pesto Sauce

PESTO SAUCE

make ahead, quick

Pesto's popularity peaked in the '90s. This verdant recipe makes enough pesto for one pound of pasta. The recipe can be doubled easily.

1 cup packed fresh basil leaves (1 large bunch)
¾ cup freshly grated Parmesan cheese
½ cup chopped fresh parsley
¼ cup walnut halves
2 cloves garlic, halved
1 tablespoon lemon juice
½ teaspoon salt
⅛ teaspoon freshly ground pepper
½ cup olive oil

• **Process** first 8 ingredients in a food processor 2 minutes or until smooth, stopping twice to scrape down sides. Gradually pour oil through food chute with processor running, processing until blended. To store sauce, place in an airtight container, and store in refrigerator up to 1 week. (Mixture freezes well in ice cube trays up to 6 months). Yield: 1 cup.

SALSA CRUDA

family favorite, quick

A salsa can be a cooked or fresh mixture. Salsa cruda is an uncooked sauce that lets the fresh, colorful blend of flavors shine through. See it pictured on page 312.

3 large tomatoes, finely chopped
4 green onions, sliced
3 serrano or jalapeño peppers, seeded and diced
1 clove garlic, minced
2 tablespoons diced purple onion
3 tablespoons minced fresh cilantro
½ teaspoon salt
2 tablespoons lime juice

• **Combine** all ingredients; stir well. Cover and chill, if desired. Serve with grilled chicken or fish or serve as a dip with tortilla chips. Yield: 4 cups.

NOTE: You can puree salsa in a food processor or blender for a smoother texture, if desired.

Presto Pesto

80ˢ *Southern Living* answered fresh herb cravings with our first pesto recipe in 1980. It was a primitive recipe by today's standards because it depended on supermarket parsley for the fresh herb texture and dried basil for the traditional flavor, a reflection on herb availability at the time. Five more pesto recipes debuted throughout the decade.

90ˢ The '90s brought a 400% increase in the number of pesto recipes we published, confirming that the aromatic herb sauce had become mainstream. We even took liberties with the traditional basil-garlic-pine nut puree and created Dried Tomato Pesto, Cilantro-Black Walnut Pesto, and Asian Pesto Pasta. We predict pesto's popularity will reach far beyond Y2K.

90s In the early '90s, bottled salsa surpassed ketchup in gross sales figures. Never fear, though, ketchup's flow didn't slow. It still outsells salsa in number of bottles sold, and more ketchup is sold and consumed in the South than any other part of the country.

CHUNKY SALSA

family favorite, make ahead

There are so many chip choices on the market these days. Try red or blue tortillas with this salsa.

1½ cups chopped tomato (about 1 large)
½ cup chopped green onions (about 1 small
     bunch)
1 (4½-ounce) can chopped green chiles
1 (4¼-ounce) can chopped ripe olives
2 cloves garlic, minced
⅔ cup white vinegar
⅓ cup vegetable oil
1 tablespoon sugar
½ teaspoon coarsely ground pepper

• **Combine** first 5 ingredients in a medium bowl. Combine vinegar and remaining 3 ingredients in a jar; cover tightly, and shake vigorously. Pour vinegar mixture over vegetable mixture. Cover and chill at least 3 hours. Drain salsa, if desired, and serve with tortilla chips. Yield: 3 cups.

COCKTAIL SAUCE

family favorite, make ahead, quick

Spoon this familiar sauce into small glasses and drape fresh boiled shrimp over the rims.

1 cup chili sauce
¾ cup ketchup
¼ cup prepared horseradish
2 tablespoons minced celery
2 tablespoons minced onion
2 tablespoons cider vinegar
4 or 5 drops of hot sauce
1 teaspoon Worcestershire sauce

• **Combine** all ingredients; stir well. Cover and chill. Serve with seafood. Yield: 2 cups.

SOUTHWESTERN COCKTAIL SAUCE

make ahead, quick

Jalapeño and cilantro lend Southwestern inspiration to this dipping sauce for shrimp or other seafood.

1 (8-ounce) can tomato sauce
¼ cup chopped fresh cilantro
2 tablespoons diced onion
1½ tablespoons lime juice
1 tablespoon prepared horseradish
¼ teaspoon garlic salt
⅛ teaspoon hot sauce
1 jalapeño pepper, seeded and chopped

• **Combine** all ingredients; stir well. Cover and chill at least 3 hours. Yield: 1 cup.

BLACK BEAN SAUCE

⌒ quick ⌒

*Grilled pork or chicken takes a
turn toward the Southwest when blanketed
with this rustic bean sauce.*

3 slices bacon
½ small sweet red pepper, chopped
½ small purple onion, chopped
2 cloves garlic, crushed
1 (15-ounce) can black beans, undrained
½ cup orange juice
2 tablespoons balsamic vinegar
¼ teaspoon salt
⅛ teaspoon pepper
1 tablespoon chopped fresh cilantro or parsley

• **Cook** bacon in a medium skillet until crisp; remove
bacon, reserving drippings in skillet. Crumble bacon.
• **Sauté** red pepper, onion, and garlic in drippings until
tender.
• **Drain** beans, reserving liquid.
• **Process** red pepper mixture, beans, orange juice, and
next 3 ingredients in a blender until smooth, stopping to
scrape down sides.
• **Stir** in crumbled bacon and cilantro, adding reserved
bean liquid to thin sauce, if desired. Yield: about 2 cups.

EASY HORSERADISH
SAUCE

⌒ make ahead, quick ⌒

1 (8-ounce) carton sour cream
2 tablespoons prepared horseradish
1 tablespoon spicy brown mustard

• **Combine** all ingredients, stirring well. Cover and
chill. Serve with roast beef or pork. Yield: 1¼ cups.

RÉMOULADE SAUCE

⌒ make ahead, quick ⌒

*Capers, gherkins, and anchovies typify
a classic Rémoulade. Serve it chilled with a
fresh catch from the sea.*

1 cup mayonnaise
1 tablespoon chopped onion
1 tablespoon chopped parsley
1 tablespoon chopped gherkin pickles
1 tablespoon capers
1 tablespoon prepared horseradish
1 tablespoon lemon juice or white vinegar
2 tablespoons Dijon mustard
¼ teaspoon salt
⅛ teaspoon hot sauce
¼ cup vegetable oil
½ teaspoon Worcestershire sauce
½ teaspoon anchovy paste

• **Combine** all ingredients in a small bowl; stir until
blended. Cover and chill. Serve with fish or shellfish.
Yield: 1½ cups.

JALAPEÑO TARTAR
SAUCE

*Try this sassy sauce over fried fish,
hush puppies, or onion rings.*

1 cup mayonnaise
1 jalapeño pepper, diced
2 tablespoons sweet pickle relish
1 tablespoon chopped fresh or frozen chives
1 tablespoon capers
1 teaspoon dried dillweed

• **Combine** all ingredients; stir until blended. Cover
and chill. Yield: 1¼ cups.

ANTIPASTO RELISH

1 (14-ounce) can artichoke hearts, drained
2 (4-ounce) cans mushroom stems and pieces, drained
½ cup chopped roasted red pepper
½ cup finely chopped celery
¼ cup finely chopped green pepper
⅓ cup white vinegar or white balsamic vinegar
⅓ cup olive oil
¼ cup instant minced onion
2 cloves garlic, minced
1 teaspoon sugar
1 teaspoon seasoned salt
2½ teaspoons Italian seasoning
½ teaspoon seasoned pepper

• **Finely chop** artichoke hearts and mushrooms; place in a bowl. Add red pepper, celery, and green pepper. Combine vinegar and remaining ingredients in a saucepan. Bring to a boil; remove from heat, and cool slightly. Pour over vegetables, and stir well. Serve at room temperature or cover and chill overnight. Serve with crackers. Yield: 3⅔ cups.

GIBLET GRAVY

~ family favorite ~

Giblets and neck from 1 turkey
1 small onion, coarsely chopped
3 cups water
2 hard-cooked eggs, chopped
2 stalks celery, chopped
¼ teaspoon poultry seasoning
¼ teaspoon rubbed sage
¼ teaspoon dried thyme
¼ teaspoon pepper
1 teaspoon salt
2 tablespoons cornstarch
¼ cup water

• **Combine** first 3 ingredients in a saucepan. Bring to a boil; cover, reduce heat, and simmer 45 minutes or until giblets are fork-tender. Drain, reserving broth. Remove meat from neck; coarsely chop neck meat and giblets. Set aside.
• **Add** enough water to reserved broth to equal 3 cups. Combine broth, chopped neck meat and giblets, eggs, and next 6 ingredients. Bring to a boil; reduce heat, and simmer, uncovered, 30 to 45 minutes.
• **Combine** cornstarch and ¼ cup water; stir into broth mixture. Bring to a boil; boil 1 minute. Serve gravy hot over turkey and dressing. Yield: 2⅔ cups.

SPICY CORN RELISH

Kids will like this colorful sauce that gets a kick from chili sauce and chili powder, especially if you serve it on hot dogs.

1 cup minced onion
½ cup chopped green pepper
1 clove garlic, minced
1 tablespoon vegetable oil
1 (14.5-ounce) can whole tomatoes, drained and chopped
1 (8¾-ounce) can whole kernel corn, drained
1 (4.5-ounce) can chopped green chiles
¼ cup hot chili sauce
1 tablespoon chili powder
1 teaspoon salt
2 teaspoons pepper

• **Cook** onion, green pepper, and garlic in oil until crisp-tender, stirring often. Add tomatoes and remaining ingredients; cook until thoroughly heated, stirring often. Serve warm or at room temperature on chalupas, tacos, hamburgers, hot dogs, or as a dip. Store in refrigerator. Yield: 3 cups.

Spicy Corn Relish

CHOCOLATE SAUCE SUPREME

make ahead, quick

The blend of ingredients gives this sweet sauce a supremely silky consistency for spooning over a variety of desserts.

1 cup (6 ounces) semisweet chocolate morsels
1 cup sifted powdered sugar
¼ cup butter or margarine
Dash of salt
½ cup light corn syrup
¼ cup hot water
¼ cup crème de cacao
1 teaspoon vanilla extract

• **Combine** first 6 ingredients in a heavy saucepan. Cook over low heat, stirring until chocolate melts. Remove from heat; stir in liqueur and vanilla. Serve immediately or cool and store in refrigerator up to 2 weeks. Serve over pound cake or ice cream. Yield: about 2 cups.

HOT FUDGE SAUCE

family favorite, quick

1½ cups (9 ounces) semisweet chocolate morsels
⅔ cup sugar
2 (5-ounce) cans evaporated milk
1 tablespoon butter or margarine
1 teaspoon vanilla extract

• **Combine** first 3 ingredients in a medium saucepan. Bring to a boil over medium heat, stirring often. Boil 1 minute, stirring constantly. Remove from heat; stir in butter and vanilla. Serve warm or cool, and store in refrigerator up to 2 weeks. Serve over ice cream or cake. Yield: 2¼ cups.

BRANDIED CHOCOLATE SAUCE

quick

A little brandy, cinnamon, and coffee give this sauce fancy flavor.

2 cups (12 ounces) semisweet chocolate morsels
½ cup whipping cream
¼ cup brandy
2 tablespoons water
1 tablespoon instant coffee granules
Dash of ground cinnamon

• **Combine** first 4 ingredients in a small saucepan; cook over low heat until chocolate melts and mixture is smooth, stirring often.
• **Add** coffee granules and cinnamon to chocolate mixture, stirring until well blended. Serve warm with fresh fruit over ice cream. Yield: 1¾ cups.

CARAMEL SAUCE

quick

Drizzle warm caramel sauce over your favorite ice cream or freshly baked cake.

¾ cup butter or margarine
1½ cups firmly packed brown sugar
1 cup whipping cream

• **Combine** butter and brown sugar in a heavy saucepan; cook over medium heat, stirring constantly, until sugar dissolves. Gradually add whipping cream; cook, stirring constantly, until mixture comes to a boil. Remove from heat, and cool slightly. Serve warm over ice cream, gingerbread, or pound cake. Store sauce in refrigerator. Yield: 2½ cups.

Rum Sundae Sauce

quick

¾ cup firmly packed brown sugar
⅓ cup water
⅓ cup light corn syrup
2 tablespoons butter or margarine
⅛ teaspoon salt
1 teaspoon rum or ½ teaspoon rum
  extract

• **Combine** first 5 ingredients in a medium saucepan; cook over medium heat, stirring until sugar dissolves. Reduce heat to low; cook, without stirring, until a candy thermometer registers 230° (about 5 minutes). Remove from heat, and cool slightly.
• **Stir** in rum. Serve warm over ice cream. Store sauce in refrigerator up to 2 weeks. Yield: 1 cup.

Praline Sauce

family favorite

Brown sugar and toasty pecans lend the praline flavor to this dessert sauce.

¼ cup butter or margarine
1¼ cups firmly packed brown sugar
¾ cup light corn syrup
3 tablespoons all-purpose flour
1½ cups chopped pecans, toasted
1 (5-ounce) can evaporated milk

• **Melt** butter in a medium saucepan; add brown sugar, corn syrup, and flour, stirring until smooth. Bring to a boil; reduce heat, and simmer 5 minutes, stirring constantly. Remove from heat, and cool 20 minutes. Stir in pecans and evaporated milk. Cool completely. Cover and refrigerate up to 2 weeks. Serve warm over ice cream or plain cheesecake. Yield: 3 cups.

Apple Ice Cream Sauce

quick

½ cup firmly packed brown sugar
1 tablespoon cornstarch
½ teaspoon ground cinnamon
¼ teaspoon ground nutmeg
⅛ teaspoon salt
½ teaspoon grated lemon rind
¾ cup water
1 (21-ounce) can apple pie filling
½ teaspoon vanilla extract
½ cup chopped walnuts

• **Combine** first 8 ingredients in a large saucepan; stir well. Cook over medium heat until thoroughly heated, stirring occasionally. Add vanilla and walnuts; stir well. Serve warm over ice cream. Yield: 3½ cups.

Cinnamon-Honey Butter

quick

We could have called this recipe breakfast butter. It goes well on just about every type of bread you'd enjoy in the morning.

1 cup butter, softened
3 tablespoons honey
½ teaspoon ground cinnamon

• **Beat** butter at medium speed with an electric mixer until creamy. Add honey and cinnamon, beating until blended. Serve with toasted bagel slices, biscuits, French toast, pancakes, or waffles. Store in refrigerator up to 2 weeks. Yield: 1 cup.

RASPBERRY SAUCE

⚬ quick ⚬

1 (14-ounce) package frozen raspberries, thawed
1 tablespoon cornstarch
1 tablespoon water
¼ cup sugar
½ cup red currant jelly
¼ cup Cointreau or other orange-flavored liqueur

• **Process** thawed raspberries in a blender or food processor 10 seconds or until pureed. Pour mixture through a wire-mesh strainer into a bowl; press with back of a spoon against sides of strainer to squeeze out juice, discarding solids.
• **Combine** cornstarch and water; stir well. Combine raspberry puree and cornstarch mixture in a small saucepan; cook over low heat, stirring constantly, until thickened (about 8 minutes). Add sugar and jelly, stirring constantly, until dissolved. Stir in liqueur. Remove from heat; cool. Cover and chill. Serve over vanilla ice cream. Yield: 2 cups.

DARK CHERRY SAUCE

⚬ quick ⚬

We recommend a pinot noir as the wine of choice in this sweet cherry sauce. Serve it over ice cream.

1 (16½-ounce) can pitted dark sweet cherries
2 tablespoons cornstarch
¼ cup sugar
¼ cup dry red wine

• **Drain** cherries, reserving juice.
• **Combine** cornstarch and sugar in a small saucepan; stir well. Gradually stir cherry juice into cornstarch mixture. Cook over medium heat, stirring constantly, until mixture thickens and boils. Boil 1 minute, stirring constantly.
• **Remove** from heat, and stir in wine and cherries. Serve warm over ice cream. Yield: 2½ cups.

LEMON CURD

⚬ family favorite ⚬

Luscious thick lemon curd makes a wonderful gift along with a pan of gingerbread.

2 cups sugar
1 cup butter or margarine
¼ cup grated lemon rind
⅔ cup fresh lemon juice
4 large eggs, lightly beaten

• **Combine** first 4 ingredients in top of a double boiler; bring water to a boil. Reduce heat to low; cook until butter melts. Gradually stir about one-fourth of hot mixture into eggs; add to remaining hot mixture, stirring constantly. Cook over medium-low heat, stirring constantly, until mixture thickens and coats a spoon (about 15 minutes). Remove from heat; cool. Cover and refrigerate up to 2 weeks.
• **Serve** curd chilled as a topping for pound cake, angel food cake, or gingerbread. Yield: 3¼ cups.

BRANDIED FRUIT STARTER

Apricot or peach brandy may be substituted for regular brandy, if desired.

1 (16-ounce) can sliced peaches, drained
1 (16-ounce) can apricot halves, drained
1 (15¼-ounce) can unsweetened pineapple chunks, drained
1 (10-ounce) jar maraschino cherries, drained
1¼ cups sugar
1¼ cups brandy

• **Combine** all ingredients in a large glass bowl, stirring gently. Cover and let stand at room temperature 3 weeks before serving, stirring twice a week. Serve over ice

cream or pound cake. Reserve at least 1 cup starter at all times.
• **To replenish** starter, add 1 cup sugar and 1 of the first 4 ingredients every 1 to 3 weeks, alternating fruit each time. Cover and let stand at room temperature at least 3 days before serving each time starter is replenished. Yield: 6 cups.

JALAPEÑO JELLY

make ahead

We've skipped the canning process to make an easy, small-batch, keep-in-the-fridge jelly.

3 fresh jalapeño peppers, seeded and coarsely
    chopped
½ green pepper, coarsely chopped
3 cups sugar
½ cup cider vinegar
½ (6-ounce) package liquid pectin (one (3-ounce)
    pouch)
2 tablespoons fresh lime juice

• **Position** knife blade in food processor bowl; add jalapeño and green pepper. Process until smooth, stopping once to scrape down sides.
• **Combine** pepper puree, sugar, and cider vinegar in a large nonaluminum saucepan. Bring mixture to a boil over medium-high heat, stirring constantly. Boil 3 minutes; stir in pectin and lime juice. Boil 1 minute, stirring constantly. Remove from heat, and skim off foam with a metal spoon.
• **Spoon** into desired containers. Store in refrigerator. Serve over cream cheese with crackers or toast as an appetizer or with meats as a relish. Yield: 3 cups.

SANGRÍA JELLY

3 cups sugar
1½ cups dry red wine
1 tablespoon grated orange rind
¼ cup orange juice
2 teaspoons Cointreau or other orange liqueur
½ (6-ounce) package liquid pectin (one (3-ounce)
    pouch)

• **Combine** first 5 ingredients in a large Dutch oven; bring to a full rolling boil. Boil 1 to 2 minutes, stirring often. Remove from heat. Stir in pectin, and skim off foam with a metal spoon. Pour hot jelly quickly into hot sterilized jars, leaving ¼ inch headspace; wipe jar rims. Cover at once with metal lids, and screw on bands. Process in boiling water bath 5 minutes. Store in the refrigerator after opening. Yield: 4 half-pints.

CHRISTMAS JAM

Use fresh or frozen cranberries in this holiday recipe.

1 (12-ounce) package fresh or frozen cranberries
2 (10-ounce) packages frozen strawberries in
    syrup, thawed
4 cups sugar
½ (6-ounce) package liquid pectin (one (3-ounce)
    pouch)

• **Process** cranberries in a food processor until coarsely chopped. Combine cranberries, strawberries, and sugar in a Dutch oven. Cook over high heat, stirring constantly, until sugar dissolves. Bring to a boil, stirring often. Cook 1 minute, stirring often. Remove from heat; add pectin. Return to a full rolling boil; boil 1 minute, stirring constantly. Remove from heat, and skim off foam.
• **Pour** hot jam quickly into hot sterilized jars, leaving ¼ inch headspace; wipe jar rims. Cover at once with metal lids, and screw on bands. Process in boiling water bath 5 minutes. Store in refrigerator after opening. Yield: 7 half-pints.

BLUEBERRY JAM

Spread this dark blue jam on biscuits, scones, or toast.

1½ quarts stemmed blueberries, crushed
¼ cup lemon juice
1 (1-inch) stick cinnamon
7 cups sugar
1 (6-ounce) package liquid pectin

• **Combine** first 4 ingredients in a Dutch oven; bring to a boil, and cook until sugar dissolves, stirring often. Boil 2 minutes, stirring often; remove from heat. Discard cinnamon stick. Add pectin, and stir 5 minutes. Skim off foam with a metal spoon.
• **Pour** hot jam quickly into hot sterilized jars, leaving ¼ inch headspace. Remove air bubbles; wipe jar rims. Cover at once with metal lids, and screw on bands. Process in boiling water bath 5 minutes. Store in refrigerator after opening. Yield: 9 half-pints.

HOT-SWEET MUSTARD

Fried foods like egg rolls and chicken fingers taste even better with this tangy mustard.

2 (2-ounce) cans dry mustard
1 cup cider vinegar
1 cup sugar
⅓ cup butter or margarine
3 egg yolks, lightly beaten

• **Combine** mustard and vinegar in a small glass bowl, stirring until smooth. Cover and let stand at room temperature 8 hours.
• **Combine** mustard mixture, sugar, and butter in top of a double boiler; bring water to a boil. Reduce heat to low; cook until butter melts, stirring often. Gradually stir about one-fourth of hot mixture into yolks; add to remaining hot mixture. Cook, stirring constantly, until thickened and thermometer registers 160°. Remove from heat; cool. Spoon into jars. Cover and chill up to 1 month. Yield: 2 cups.

PUMPKIN BUTTER

Pumpkin Butter really isn't butter but a thick, dark spread made by slow-cooking pumpkin, sugar, and spices. Serve it with biscuits or scones.

2¼ cups sugar
3 tablespoons powdered pectin
1 teaspoon ground cinnamon
½ teaspoon ground allspice
1 (16-ounce) can pumpkin

• **Combine** all ingredients in a medium saucepan; bring to a boil over medium heat, stirring constantly. Boil 1 minute, stirring constantly. Remove from heat, and cool; spoon into jars. Cover and refrigerate up to 3 weeks or freeze up to 3 months. Serve with biscuits. Yield: 3 cups.

CRANBERRY-ORANGE CHUTNEY

This citrus-berry chutney complements ham, turkey, or grilled pork tenderloin nicely.

2 oranges, peeled, seeded, and sectioned
1 (16-ounce) can whole-berry cranberry sauce
1 (16-ounce) can pear halves, drained and chopped
1 cooking apple, chopped
1 cup sugar
½ cup raisins
¼ cup chopped pecans
1 tablespoon white vinegar
½ teaspoon ground ginger
½ teaspoon ground cinnamon

• **Chop** orange sections. Combine chopped orange, cranberry sauce, and remaining ingredients in a large saucepan. Cook over medium heat 45 to 50 minutes or until mixture is very thick, stirring often; cool. Store in an airtight container in refrigerator. Yield: 4 cups.

Jeweled Pepper Chutney

Sweet red peppers provide the jewel tone in this condiment that'll look pretty on your shelf, spooned over cream cheese, or on a vegetable plate.

2 cups sugar
2 cups firmly packed brown sugar
2 cups golden raisins
2½ cups cider vinegar
8 large sweet red peppers, seeded and finely chopped
8 cloves garlic, finely chopped
4 jalapeño peppers, seeded and finely chopped
1 (2-ounce) jar crystallized ginger, finely chopped

• **Combine** all ingredients in a large Dutch oven; bring to a boil. Reduce heat, and simmer, uncovered, 1 hour and 45 minutes, stirring occasionally.
• **Pack** hot mixture into hot jars, leaving ½ inch headspace. Remove air bubbles; wipe jar rims. Cover at once with metal lids, and screw on bands. Process in boiling water bath 10 minutes. Store in refrigerator after opening. Yield: 6 half-pints.

Commander's Chutney

⌁ make ahead ⌁

Try this simple fruited chutney over grilled or roasted pork tenderloin.

4 mangoes, peeled and chopped (about 4 cups)
1 cup chopped onion
1 cup raisins
½ cup candied citron
½ cup firmly packed brown sugar
⅔ cup white vinegar
⅔ cup water
2 teaspoons curry powder
1 teaspoon ground ginger
1 teaspoon salt
¼ teaspoon ground cinnamon
¼ teaspoon ground cloves
2 cloves garlic, minced

• **Combine** all ingredients in a large Dutch oven. Bring to a boil; reduce heat, and simmer, uncovered, 1 hour or until very thick, stirring occasionally. Cover and refrigerate up to 2 weeks. Yield: 4 cups.

Sweet on Vinegar

70s Almost every cook kept a jug of apple cider vinegar or white vinegar on the shelf. We used it for pickles, dressings, and in some states, barbecue sauce.

80s We snubbed our old favorites for the trés French red and white wine vinegars. Vinegar glistened through slim green-glass bottles. Herb sprigs and raspberries steeped in vinegar that we used for salads and sauces.

90s Flasks of balsamic vinegar found their way into American kitchens. The Italians have been making the dark nectar from Trebbiano grapes for centuries. We've learned that a little of the sweetly pungent brew weaves magic in soups, dressings, and reduction sauces. Viva Italia! Viva America!

MANGO CHUTNEY

Try this tropical chutney on grilled fish or accompany it with crackers and cream cheese.

4 cups peeled, chopped mangoes (about 4 medium)
3 medium onions, chopped
3 medium-size green peppers, seeded and chopped
1½ cups raisins
2 cloves garlic, minced
1 (2-inch) piece fresh ginger, minced
2 cups cider vinegar (5% acidity)
2 cups sugar
1 (16-ounce) package brown sugar
1 tablespoon salt
1 tablespoon mustard seeds
1½ teaspoons ground cinnamon
¾ teaspoon ground cloves
½ teaspoon ground red pepper

• **Combine** all ingredients in a large glass bowl, stirring well. Cover and chill 8 hours.
• **Pour** mixture into a Dutch oven; cook, uncovered, over medium heat until mixture is the consistency of jam (about 1½ to 2 hours), stirring occasionally.
• **Spoon** hot mixture into hot jars, leaving ½ inch headspace. Remove air bubbles; wipe jar rims. Cover at once with metal lids, and screw on bands. Process in boiling water bath 10 minutes. Store in refrigerator after opening. Yield: 4 pints.

SQUASH PICKLES

Squash pickles are a Southern staple. Pile these pickles up in a bowl to serve family style with a vegetable dinner.

⅔ cup salt
3 quarts water
8 cups thinly sliced yellow squash (2½ pounds)
2½ cups sugar
2 cups white vinegar
2 teaspoons mustard seeds
2 sweet onions, thinly sliced
2 green peppers, thinly sliced
1 (4-ounce) jar sliced pimiento, drained

• **Dissolve** salt in 3 quarts water in a large bowl; add squash. Submerge squash in water, using a plate to hold slices down; cover and let stand 3 hours. Drain and set aside.
• **Bring** sugar, vinegar, and mustard seeds to a boil in a large nonaluminum Dutch oven or stockpot, stirring until sugar dissolves.
• **Add** squash, onion, pepper, and pimiento to Dutch oven; return to a boil. Remove from heat, and cool. Store in airtight containers in refrigerator up to 2 weeks. Yield: 2 quarts.

SWEET PICKLED CANTALOUPE

4 firm ripe cantaloupes (about 14 pounds)
½ cup coarse salt
2 quarts water
2 tablespoons whole allspice
1 tablespoon whole cloves
5 (4-inch) sticks cinnamon
5 cups sugar
2 cups white vinegar (5% acidity)
2 cups water

- **Peel** and seed cantaloupes; cut into bite-size pieces. Dissolve salt in 2 quarts water; add cantaloupe. Let stand 2 hours. Drain and rinse cantaloupe. Set aside.
- **Tie** spices in a cheesecloth bag. Combine spices, sugar, vinegar, and 2 cups water in a large Dutch oven; bring to a boil, and cook 5 minutes. Add cantaloupe; return to a boil. Cook 3 minutes or just until cantaloupe is tender. Remove from heat; cover and let stand 8 hours.
- **Drain** syrup from cantaloupe, and remove spice bag. Return syrup to Dutch oven; bring to a boil. Pack cantaloupe into hot jars; cover with boiling syrup, leaving ½ inch headspace. Remove air bubbles; wipe jar rims.
- **Cover** at once with metal lids, and screw on bands. Process in boiling water bath 15 minutes. Serve as a relish with pork or chicken. Store in refrigerator after opening. Yield: 6 pints.

OKRA DILLS

Bring out these okra dills the next time you have a fish fry.

1 **pound small fresh okra**
3 **small dried red chile peppers**
2 **cloves garlic, minced**
2 **tablespoons fresh celery leaves**
1 **teaspoon dill seeds**
1⅓ **cups water**
⅔ **cup white vinegar**
2½ **tablespoons salt**

- **Combine** first 5 ingredients.
- **Bring** water, vinegar, and salt to a boil in a nonaluminum saucepan, stirring until salt dissolves; pour over okra mixture, and cool.
- **Cover** and marinate in refrigerator 3 days, turning occasionally. Serve immediately or store in an airtight container in refrigerator up to 2 weeks. Yield: about 3 pints.

LIME PICKLES

Enjoy these pickles with a plate of crispy fried chicken and potato salad.

7 **pounds 4-inch long pickling cucumbers**
1 **cup pickling lime**
6 **cups white vinegar (5% acidity)**
6 **cups sugar**
2 **tablespoons pickling spice**
1 **tablespoon salt**

- **Cut** cucumbers lengthwise into ¼-inch-thick slices.
- **Combine** cucumber slices, pickling lime, and water to cover in a nonaluminum stockpot; stir well. Cover and let stand at room temperature 12 hours.
- **Drain** cucumbers; rinse with cold water, and return to stockpot. Add fresh cold water to cover, and let stand 1 hour. Repeat procedure twice. Drain cucumbers, and return to stockpot.
- **Combine** vinegar and next 3 ingredients in a saucepan; bring to a boil over medium heat, stirring until sugar dissolves. Pour vinegar mixture over cucumbers in stockpot; cover and let stand 6 hours or overnight.
- **Bring** cucumbers and vinegar mixture to a boil over medium heat; cover, reduce heat, and simmer 35 minutes, stirring gently occasionally.
- **Pack** cucumbers into hot sterilized jars. Pour vinegar mixture over cucumbers, leaving ½ inch headspace. Remove air bubbles; wipe jar rims. Cover at once with metal lids, and screw on bands.
- **Process** in boiling water bath 5 minutes. Store in refrigerator after opening. Yield: 8 pints.

Soups and Stews

Soups and stews are soul
satisfying foods. Simple or
dramatic, warm or chilled, light
or robust, they can be enjoyed year
round with very little effort
and usually only one pot.

Tortilla Soup (page 342)

CUCUMBER-DILL SOUP

make ahead

Chilled cucumber soup is a refreshing summertime treat; it's great matched with finger sandwiches. Fresh dill really enhances the flavor of cucumber.

2 cups half-and-half
1 (8-ounce) carton sour cream
2 medium cucumbers, peeled, seeded, and diced
3 tablespoons minced fresh dill or 1 tablespoon dried dillweed
2 tablespoons fresh lemon juice
1 green onion, sliced
¾ teaspoon salt
¼ teaspoon white pepper
Garnishes: thinly sliced cucumber, fresh dill

• **Combine** first 8 ingredients; stir well. Cover and chill thoroughly. Stir well before serving. Garnish, if desired. Yield: 5 cups.

CHILLED AVOCADO SOUP

This soup might surprise you. It hints of guacamole's best ingredients; even tortilla chips are sprinkled on top.

5 ripe avocados, peeled and coarsely chopped
2 cups chicken broth
2 cups half-and-half
1 teaspoon salt
½ teaspoon onion salt
Pinch of freshly ground pepper
2 teaspoons lemon juice
½ teaspoon hot sauce
Garnishes: coarsely crushed tortilla chips, chopped tomato, fresh cilantro

• **Process** avocado and chicken broth in container of an electric blender until smooth. Remove from blender, and stir in half-and-half, salt, onion salt, pepper, lemon juice, and hot sauce. Cover soup with plastic wrap (applying directly to surface of soup to keep a skin from forming). Chill thoroughly. Remove plastic wrap before serving. Garnish, if desired. Yield: 7 cups.

CREAMED BUTTERNUT-AND-APPLE SOUP

Simmer the deep orange flesh of butternut squash with apples in a cinnamon broth until both are very soft. Then puree the mixture for a full-flavored and brilliantly colored soup to serve as part of a Thanksgiving menu.

1 (2½-pound) butternut squash, peeled and cubed
¾ pound Granny Smith apples, peeled, cored, and quartered
4 cups chicken broth
1 (3-inch) stick cinnamon
1 cup half-and-half
¼ cup butter or margarine
2 tablespoons maple syrup
¼ teaspoon salt
¼ teaspoon ground nutmeg
¼ teaspoon ground ginger
Garnishes: sour cream, ground nutmeg

• **Combine** first 4 ingredients in a Dutch oven. Bring to a boil; cover, reduce heat, and simmer 30 minutes or until squash is tender. Discard cinnamon stick.
• **Process** half of squash mixture in container of an electric blender until smooth. Repeat with remaining mixture; return to Dutch oven.
• **Stir** in half-and-half and next 5 ingredients. Cook over low heat, stirring constantly, until thoroughly heated. Serve hot. Garnish, if desired. Yield: 9 cups.

Velvety Roquefort Vichyssoise

◦ make ahead ◦

Vichyssoise is a luxuriously rich potato and leek soup that's served chilled. This version gets a big hit of Roquefort cheese that makes it marvelous.

2 cups finely chopped onion or leeks (white part only)
¼ cup butter or margarine
4 cups chicken broth
2 cups peeled, diced baking potato
¼ teaspoon salt
⅛ teaspoon ground white pepper
4 ounces Roquefort cheese, divided
½ cup dry white wine
1 cup whipping cream
2 tablespoons minced fresh chives or parsley

• **Sauté** onion in butter in a large Dutch oven until tender and barely golden. Stir in broth, potato, salt, and pepper; bring to a boil. Reduce heat, and simmer, uncovered, 15 minutes or until potato is tender.
• **Process** half of potato mixture in container of an electric blender until smooth. Repeat with remaining mixture; return to Dutch oven.
• **Crumble** 3 ounces cheese. Add cheese and wine to potato mixture; cook over low heat, stirring constantly, about 5 minutes or until cheese melts. Cool; cover and chill at least 4 hours. Stir in whipping cream before serving. Crumble remaining cheese and chives over each serving. Yield: 6 cups.

Easy Cream of Corn Soup

◦ quick ◦

Simple soups are the solution when you're in a hurry. Try this yummy corn soup which starts with cans of cream-style corn.

2 tablespoons minced onion
2 tablespoons butter or margarine
2 tablespoons all-purpose flour
1 teaspoon salt
¼ teaspoon pepper
1 (14.75-ounce) can cream-style corn
1 (8¾-ounce) can cream-style corn
3 cups milk or half-and-half
Salt and pepper to taste

• **Sauté** onion in butter in a saucepan over medium heat until tender. Stir in flour, salt, and pepper. Cook over low heat, stirring constantly, until smooth. Stir in corn; bring to a boil, and boil 1 minute.
• **Stir** in milk. Heat thoroughly (do not boil). Remove from heat; cool slightly. Process in container of an electric blender until smooth, if desired. Add additional salt and pepper to taste. Yield: 5 cups.

CURRIED CARROT SOUP

A delicious blend of flavors evolves when you simmer curry, fennel, and carrots for this soup.

1 small onion, chopped
2 tablespoons butter or margarine, melted
2 (14½-ounce) cans ready-to-serve vegetable or
    chicken broth
½ cup water
2 cups sliced carrot
1 tablespoon sugar
1 teaspoon salt
½ teaspoon curry powder
¼ to ½ teaspoon freshly ground pepper
¼ teaspoon fennel seeds
1 cup milk or half-and-half
Sour cream (optional)
Croutons (optional)

• **Sauté** onion in butter in a Dutch oven over medium-high heat until tender. Add broth and next 7 ingredients. Bring to a boil; cover, reduce heat, and simmer 20 minutes or until carrot slices are tender.

• **Process** mixture in container of an electric blender or food processor until smooth. Return mixture to Dutch oven; add milk, and simmer 10 to 12 minutes. If desired, serve with sour cream and croutons. Serve warm or chilled. Yield: 6 cups.

BEER-CHEESE SOUP

This is the perfect soup for a crowd. It pairs well with a French Dip or other roast beef sandwich or entrée.

6 cups milk
2 (12-ounce) cans beer, divided
1 (32-ounce) loaf process cheese spread, cubed
1 (8-ounce) loaf process cheese spread, cubed
1 (10½-ounce) can chicken broth
2 teaspoons hot sauce
2 teaspoons Worcestershire sauce
¼ cup plus 2 tablespoons cornstarch
Ground red pepper (optional)

• **Combine** milk and 2½ cups beer in a large Dutch oven. Cook over low heat 20 minutes or until thoroughly heated, stirring constantly. Add cheese, broth, hot sauce, and Worcestershire sauce. Cook over low heat, stirring constantly, until cheese melts and soup is thoroughly heated.

• **Combine** cornstarch and remaining beer, stirring well. Add to cheese mixture; simmer, stirring constantly, until thickened and thoroughly heated (do not boil). Sprinkle lightly with ground red pepper before serving, if desired. Yield: 1 gallon.

PEACH-PLUM SOUP

make ahead

Cinnamon and red wine enhance the flavors of fresh peaches and plums. This soup could be dessert.

½ pound fresh peaches, peeled and sliced
½ pound fresh plums, peeled and sliced
1 cup plus 2 tablespoons sugar
2 cups dry red wine
1¾ cups water
1 (3-inch) stick cinnamon
1 teaspoon cornstarch
¼ cup water
½ cup whipping cream, whipped
Additional whipped cream (optional)
Ground cinnamon (optional)

• **Combine** first 6 ingredients in a Dutch oven. Bring to a boil; reduce heat, and simmer, uncovered, 10 minutes or until fruit is tender. Discard cinnamon stick. Transfer fruit mixture to a bowl.
• **Process** 2 cups fruit mixture in container of an electric blender until smooth, stopping once to scrape down sides. Transfer pureed fruit mixture to Dutch oven. Repeat procedure, using remaining fruit mixture.
• **Combine** cornstarch and ¼ cup water, stirring until smooth. Bring pureed mixture to a boil. Stir cornstarch mixture into soup; boil 1 minute, stirring constantly. Remove from heat. Cover and chill at least 3 hours.
• **Stir** whipped cream into soup, and ladle soup into bowls. If desired, dollop additional whipped cream onto each serving, and sprinkle with ground cinnamon. Yield: 6 cups.

STRAWBERRY SOUP

make ahead

In celebration of strawberries whip up a simple strawberry soup. Serve it chilled as an appetizer or a dessert.

1 cup fresh strawberries, hulled
1 cup orange juice
¼ cup honey
¼ cup sour cream
½ cup sweet white wine (optional)

• **Process** all ingredients in container of an electric blender until smooth, stopping once to scrape down sides. Cover and chill thoroughly. Stir well before serving. Yield: 3 cups.

CANTALOUPE SOUP

quick

Choose a dessert wine such as a Muscat, Sauternes, or late harvest Riesling to sweeten this chilled fruit soup.

8 cups cubed cantaloupe (about 2 medium), chilled
¾ cup sweet white wine, chilled
¼ cup whipping cream
Garnish: fresh mint sprigs

• **Process** half each of cantaloupe, white wine, and whipping cream in container of an electric blender until smooth. Transfer pureed mixture to a large container. Repeat procedure, using remaining cantaloupe, white wine, and whipping cream. Ladle soup into bowls, and garnish, if desired. Yield: 7 cups.

Rich Onion Soup Gratinée

RICH ONION SOUP GRATINÉE

Gratinée is a French term that refers to a dish with a topping of cheese and/or buttery breadcrumbs that gets crispy and browned in the oven. Each serving of this soup is crowned with croutons covered in Gruyère cheese.

¼ cup plus 2 tablespoons butter or margarine, melted
2 tablespoons olive oil or vegetable oil
3 large onions (2 pounds), thinly sliced
½ teaspoon sugar
½ teaspoon salt
½ teaspoon dry mustard
4 (14½-ounce) cans ready-to-serve beef broth
1½ cups dry white wine (such as Chardonnay)
3 tablespoons all-purpose flour
3 tablespoons water
9 French bread slices, toasted
3 cups (12 ounces) shredded Gruyère cheese

• **Combine** butter and oil in a large Dutch oven. Separate onion into rings; add to Dutch oven. Cook over medium-low heat 30 minutes, stirring often. Stir in sugar, salt, and mustard; cook 30 minutes, stirring occasionally. Add broth and wine.
• **Combine** flour and water; add to onion mixture, stirring constantly. Bring to a boil; cover, reduce heat, and simmer 30 minutes.
• **Place** toast slices on a baking sheet; sprinkle with cheese. Bake at 450° until cheese melts. Cut into croutons, if desired. Sprinkle over soup just before serving. Yield: about 9 cups.

GARDEN VEGETABLE SOUP

family favorite

2 tablespoons butter or margarine
1 cup thinly sliced carrot
1 cup sliced celery with leaves
1 cup chopped onion
1 clove garlic, crushed
9 medium tomatoes, peeled and chopped
2 teaspoons salt
½ teaspoon pepper
1 (14½-ounce) can ready-to-serve beef or vegetable broth
½ pound fresh green beans, cut into 1-inch pieces
1 medium zucchini, halved lengthwise and sliced
¼ cup chopped fresh parsley
1 tablespoon chopped fresh oregano or 1 teaspoon dried oregano
1 tablespoon chopped fresh basil or 1 teaspoon dried basil
Freshly grated Parmesan cheese (optional)

• **Heat** butter in a large Dutch oven over medium-high heat. Add carrot and next 3 ingredients; sauté 5 minutes or until onion is tender. Add tomato, salt, and pepper; bring to a boil. Reduce heat, and simmer 15 minutes, stirring occasionally.
• **Add** broth and green beans; simmer 20 minutes. Add zucchini and next 3 ingredients; simmer 10 minutes. Spoon into soup bowls; sprinkle with cheese, if desired. Yield: about 11 cups.

VEGETABLE-CHEDDAR SOUP

2 stalks celery, chopped
2 carrots, scraped and diced
1 medium onion, chopped
1 cup chopped cauliflower
1 cup chopped broccoli
1 clove garlic, minced
1 tablespoon vegetable oil or olive oil
½ cup butter or margarine, melted
½ cup all-purpose flour
3 cups chicken broth
1 tablespoon Worcestershire sauce
¼ teaspoon salt
½ teaspoon pepper
2½ cups milk
2 cups (8 ounces) shredded sharp Cheddar cheese
¼ cup sliced almonds, toasted
Croutons

• **Sauté** first 6 ingredients in oil in a Dutch oven over medium heat until crisp-tender; remove vegetables. Add butter to Dutch oven; add flour, stirring until smooth. Cook 1 minute, stirring constantly. Gradually add chicken broth; cook over medium heat, stirring constantly, until mixture is thickened and bubbly.
• **Return** sautéed vegetables to Dutch oven. Cover, reduce heat, and simmer 20 minutes or until tender. Add Worcestershire sauce and next 4 ingredients. Cook over low heat 10 minutes or until cheese melts, stirring occasionally. Sprinkle each serving with sliced almonds and croutons. Serve immediately. Yield: 8 cups.

POTATO-BEET SOUP

This potato soup is good even without the beets. You can substitute one 15-ounce can of quartered beets, drained, for the fresh beets.

1½ pounds fresh beets
4 large leeks
3 tablespoons butter or margarine, melted
3 large baking potatoes, peeled and cut into chunks
6 cups chicken broth
¾ cup half-and-half
¾ cup milk
¼ teaspoon salt
¼ teaspoon ground white pepper
Garnish: fresh dill

• **Leave** root and 1 inch of stem on beets; scrub beets with a brush. Place beets in a saucepan; add water to cover. Bring to a boil; cover, reduce heat, and simmer 35 to 40 minutes or until beets are tender. Drain, reserving 2 tablespoons liquid. Pour cold water over beets, and drain. Cool. Trim off beet stems and roots, and rub off skins. Cut beets into chunks. Measure 2 cups beets; reserve remaining beets for another use.
• **Remove** roots, tough outer leaves, and tops from leeks, leaving 1 inch of dark leaves. Wash leeks thoroughly, and coarsely chop.
• **Sauté** leeks in butter in a large Dutch oven over medium-high heat 3 minutes or until wilted. Add potato and chicken broth; cover and cook 20 minutes or until potato is tender. Remove vegetable mixture from Dutch oven. Process half of potato mixture in container of an electric blender until smooth. Return to Dutch oven. Repeat with remaining potato mixture.
• **Stir** in half-and-half, milk, salt, and pepper. Cook over low heat, stirring constantly, until heated.
• **Process** 2 cups beets and reserved 2 tablespoons beet liquid in container of an electric blender until smooth. Drizzle beets into each serving of potato soup, and swirl gently with a knife to create a marbled effect. Garnish, if desired. Yield: 9 cups.

ACORN SQUASH SOUP

3 acorn squash
3 carrots, scraped and sliced
1 medium onion, sliced
3½ cups chicken broth, divided
⅓ cup water, divided
2 tablespoons butter or margarine
1 tablespoon all-purpose flour
½ cup sherry
1 teaspoon salt
½ to 1 teaspoon black pepper
½ teaspoon ground nutmeg
⅛ teaspoon paprika
Dash of ground allspice
Dash of ground red pepper
1 cup half-and-half
Garnish: fresh thyme sprigs

• **Cut** each squash in half lengthwise; remove seeds. Place halves, cut side down, in a shallow pan; add hot water to pan to depth of 1 inch. Bake, uncovered, at 350° for 55 minutes or until tender. Drain squash halves on paper towels, cut side down. Scoop out and reserve pulp; discard shells.
• **Cook** carrot and onion in boiling water to cover 12 to 15 minutes or until very tender; drain. Combine half of carrot mixture, half of reserved squash pulp, ½ cup chicken broth, and half of water in container of an electric blender; process until smooth. Repeat procedure with remaining carrot mixture, pulp, ½ cup chicken broth, and water; set aside.
• **Melt** butter in a Dutch oven over low heat; add flour, stirring until smooth. Cook 1 minute, stirring constantly. Gradually add pureed mixture, remaining 2½ cups chicken broth, sherry, and next 6 ingredients; bring to a boil over medium heat. Cover, reduce heat, and simmer 1 hour, stirring occasionally. Stir in half-and-half; cook just until thoroughly heated. (Do not boil.) Ladle soup into bowls; garnish, if desired. Yield: 11½ cups.

BROCCOLI CHEESE SOUP

family favorite, quick

Kids will enjoy this soup that's quick to fix. Just add sandwiches to make the meal complete.

1 (10-ounce) package frozen chopped broccoli
½ cup chopped onion
¼ cup chopped green pepper
1½ tablespoons butter or margarine, melted
1½ cups milk
1 cup water
1 (10¾-ounce) can cream of chicken soup, undiluted
12 ounces loaf process cheese spread, cubed

• **Cook** broccoli according to package directions, omitting salt; drain well.
• **Cook** onion and pepper in butter in a large saucepan over medium heat, stirring constantly, until tender. Add broccoli, milk, and remaining ingredients; cook until cheese melts and mixture is thoroughly heated, stirring often. Yield: 6 cups.

TORTILLA SOUP

This Southwestern-tasting soup begins with a long simmering tomato broth. Then crushed chips and several toppings are added just before serving.

1 onion, chopped
2 fresh jalapeño peppers, seeded and chopped
4 cloves garlic, minced
¼ cup vegetable oil
2 (14.5-ounce) cans stewed tomatoes
2 (10-ounce) cans diced tomatoes and green chiles
2 (10½-ounce) cans beef consommé, undiluted
2 (10½-ounce) cans chicken broth
2 (10½-ounce) cans tomato soup, undiluted
3 cups water
2 teaspoons ground cumin
½ teaspoon dried crushed red pepper
1 (9-ounce) bag tortilla chips, broken
3 tablespoons chopped fresh cilantro
1 cup (4 ounces) shredded Monterey Jack cheese
    with peppers
Garnish: fresh cilantro

• **Sauté** first 3 ingredients in oil in a large Dutch oven until tender; add stewed tomatoes and next 7 ingredients. Bring to a boil; cover, reduce heat, and simmer 1 hour. Stir in most of tortilla chips just before serving. Top each serving with additional tortilla chips, chopped cilantro, and cheese. Garnish, if desired. Serve immediately. Yield: 12 cups.

BLACK BEAN SOUP

Black bean soup is a meal in itself. This version is flecked with bits of ham and topped with some familiar favorites—sour cream, tomato, and green onions.

1 (16-ounce) package dried black beans
1 quart water
1 (10½-ounce) can beef consommé,
    undiluted
1 large meaty ham hock
6 black peppercorns
3 cloves garlic, halved
2 bay leaves
1 dried red chile pepper, cut in half
    crosswise
1 medium onion, chopped
1 medium carrot, scraped and chopped
1 small green pepper, seeded and chopped
1 stalk celery, chopped
1½ teaspoons ground cumin
1½ teaspoons ground coriander
¼ cup dry sherry
1 teaspoon salt
½ teaspoon freshly ground pepper
½ teaspoon hot sauce
Sour cream
Seeded, chopped tomato
Chopped green onions

• **Sort** and wash beans; place in a Dutch oven. Cover with water 2 inches above beans; let soak 8 hours. Drain beans, and return to Dutch oven. Add 1 quart water, consommé, and ham hock.
• **Place** peppercorns, garlic, bay leaves, and chile pepper on an 8-inch square of cheesecloth; tie with string. Add cheesecloth bag to bean mixture. Bring to a boil; cover, reduce heat, and simmer 1 hour.
• **Add** onion and next 5 ingredients to bean mixture; cover and cook over medium-low heat 45 to 50 minutes or until beans are tender.
• **Discard** cheesecloth bag. Remove ham hock; cool slightly. Remove meat from bone; discard fat and bone.

Chop meat. Add chopped meat, sherry, and next 3 ingredients to Dutch oven; cook until thoroughly heated, stirring gently. Serve soup with sour cream, chopped tomato, and chopped green onions. Yield: 8 cups.

HEARTY BEAN-AND-BARLEY SOUP

2 pounds dried Great Northern beans
1 pound ground chuck
2 quarts water
2 cups coarsely chopped cooked ham
1 cup fine barley
6 carrots, scraped and sliced
4 cloves garlic, minced
1 large onion, chopped
1 large meaty ham hock
4 (10½-ounce) cans beef consommé, undiluted
¼ cup Worcestershire sauce
1 teaspoon salt
1 teaspoon pepper
½ teaspoon hot sauce
2 fresh jalapeño peppers, seeded

• **Sort** and wash beans; place in a large Dutch oven. Cover with water 2 inches above beans; let soak 8 hours. Drain beans; return to Dutch oven.
• **Brown** ground chuck in a large skillet, stirring until it crumbles. Drain. Add meat, 2 quarts water, and next 7 ingredients to beans. Bring to a boil; cover, reduce heat, and simmer 2 hours, stirring occasionally.
• **Remove** ham hock; cool slightly. Remove meat from bone; discard fat and bone. Chop meat. Add chopped meat, Worcestershire sauce, and remaining ingredients to Dutch oven. Bring to a boil; cover, reduce heat, and simmer 30 minutes, stirring occasionally. Discard jalapeño peppers before serving. Yield: 20 cups.

FRENCH MARKET SOUP

This soup mix makes a great recipe gift.

1 (2-cup) package French Market Soup Mix
2 quarts water
1 large ham hock
1 (16-ounce) can whole tomatoes, undrained and coarsely chopped
1½ cups chopped onion
3 tablespoons lemon juice
1 chile pepper, coarsely chopped
1 clove garlic, minced
1¼ teaspoons salt
¼ teaspoon pepper

• **Sort** and wash soup mix; place in a Dutch oven. Cover with water 2 inches above soup mix; let soak 8 hours.
• **Drain** soup mix, and return to Dutch oven; add 2 quarts water and ham hock. Bring to a boil; cover, reduce heat, and simmer 1½ hours or until beans are tender. Stir in tomatoes and next 4 ingredients. Bring to a boil; reduce heat, and simmer, uncovered, 30 minutes. Remove ham hock; remove meat from bone. Chop meat, and return to soup. Stir in salt and pepper. Yield: 12 cups.

French Market Soup Mix
1 pound dried black beans
1 pound dried Great Northern beans
1 pound dried navy beans
1 pound dried pinto beans
1 pound dried red beans
1 pound dried black-eyed peas
1 pound dried green split peas
1 pound dried yellow split peas
1 pound dried lentils
1 pound dried baby limas
1 pound dried large limas
1 pound pearl barley

• **Combine** all ingredients in a very large bowl. Divide mixture into 13 (2-cup) packages to give with recipe for French Market Soup. Yield: 26 cups.

WILLIAMSBURG TURKEY SOUP

After you've roasted and feasted on your holiday bird, here's a great use for the carcass.

1 turkey carcass
4 quarts water
1 cup butter or margarine
1 cup all-purpose flour
3 medium onions, chopped (about 5 cups)
2 large carrots, scraped and diced (about 1 cup)
2 stalks celery, diced (about 1 cup)
1 cup uncooked long-grain rice
1 tablespoon salt
¾ teaspoon pepper
2 cups half-and-half

• **Place** turkey carcass and water in a large Dutch oven; bring to a boil. Cover, reduce heat, and simmer 1 hour. Remove carcass from broth, and remove meat from bones. Set broth and meat aside. Measure broth; add water, if necessary, to measure 3 quarts.
• **Heat** butter in a large Dutch oven; add flour, and cook over medium heat 5 minutes, stirring constantly. (Roux will be a blond color.)
• **Add** onion, carrot, and celery to roux; cook over medium heat 10 minutes, stirring often. Add 3 quarts broth, turkey meat, rice, salt, and pepper; bring to a boil. Cover, reduce heat, and simmer 20 minutes or until rice is tender. Add half-and-half; cook until thoroughly heated. Yield: 20 cups.

CRAB-AND-CORN BISQUE

Serve this thick seafood bisque with hot crusty bread.

½ cup chopped celery
½ cup chopped green onions
¼ cup chopped green pepper
½ cup butter or margarine, melted
2 (10¾-ounce) cans cream of potato soup, undiluted
1 (14.75-ounce) can cream-style corn
1½ cups half-and-half
1½ cups milk
2 bay leaves
1 tablespoon fresh thyme or ½ to 1 teaspoon dried thyme
¼ teaspoon ground white pepper
⅛ teaspoon hot sauce
1 pound fresh lump crabmeat
Garnish: chopped fresh parsley or chives

• **Sauté** celery, green onions, and green pepper in butter in a Dutch oven until tender. Add potato soup and next 7 ingredients; cook until thoroughly heated. Gently stir in crabmeat, and heat thoroughly. Discard bay leaves before serving. Garnish, if desired. Yield: 8 cups.

GUMBO YA YA

make ahead

Don't skip the step of chilling Gumbo Ya Ya for eight hours. The refrigerating procedure not only enables you to remove solidified fat from the surface of the soup, but also allows the rich flavors of the gumbo to blend and to intensify.

1 **(4- to 5-pound) dressed duckling**
1 **(3- to 3½-pound) broiler-fryer**
1 **gallon water**
1½ **teaspoons salt**
½ **teaspoon pepper**
1 **pound smoked sausage, cut into ½-inch slices**
6 **stalks celery, chopped**
3 **large onions, chopped**
2 **large green peppers, seeded and chopped**
2 **cloves garlic, minced**
1 **tablespoon vegetable oil**
1 **cup bacon drippings**
1 **cup all-purpose flour**
1 **(10-ounce) can diced tomatoes and green chiles, undrained**
2 **teaspoons salt**
1 **teaspoon seasoned pepper**
1 **teaspoon hot sauce**
1 **(16-ounce) package frozen sliced okra, thawed**
Hot cooked rice
Filé powder (optional)

• **Combine** first 5 ingredients in a large Dutch oven or stockpot. Bring to a boil; cover, reduce heat, and simmer 1 hour or until duck and chicken are tender. Remove duck and chicken from broth, reserving broth. Let duck and chicken cool. Transfer broth to another container; set aside. Skin, bone, and coarsely chop duck and chicken; set meat aside.

• **Cook** sausage and next 4 ingredients in hot oil in Dutch oven over medium-high heat, stirring constantly, until sausage is browned and vegetables are tender. Remove sausage and vegetables from Dutch oven; drain and set aside.

• **Combine** bacon drippings and flour in Dutch oven; cook over medium heat, stirring constantly, until roux is chocolate colored (about 20 minutes). Gradually add reserved broth, stirring constantly. Stir in chopped meat, sausage mixture, tomatoes and green chiles, 2 teaspoons salt, seasoned pepper, and hot sauce.

• **Bring** to a boil; cook over medium heat, uncovered, 3 hours, stirring occasionally. Add okra; cook, uncovered, 30 minutes, stirring occasionally. Remove from heat; cool to almost room temperature, stirring occasionally. Cover and chill gumbo at least 8 hours.

• **Remove** gumbo from refrigerator; skim as much solidified fat from top of gumbo as possible. Cook gumbo over medium heat until mixture is thoroughly heated, stirring often. Serve over rice; sprinkle with filé powder, if desired. Yield: 20 cups.

CHICKEN-SEAFOOD GUMBO

1 (2½- to 3-pound) broiler-fryer
6 cups water
⅓ cup vegetable oil
⅓ cup all-purpose flour
4 cloves garlic, minced
2 medium onions, chopped
1 (16-ounce) package frozen sliced okra
2½ cups chopped celery
½ cup chopped green pepper
6 live or frozen blue crabs, steamed and broken
   in half
1 (12-ounce) container oysters, undrained
1 (8-ounce) can tomato sauce
¼ pound chopped cooked ham
1 tablespoon chopped fresh parsley
1½ tablespoons Worcestershire sauce
1 tablespoon lemon juice
1 tablespoon browning-and-seasoning sauce
2 teaspoons Creole seasoning
1 teaspoon dried thyme
¼ teaspoon garlic powder
¼ teaspoon liquid smoke
2 bay leaves
Hot cooked rice
Filé powder (optional)

• **Combine** chicken and water in a Dutch oven. Bring to a boil; cover, reduce heat, and simmer 1 hour or until chicken is tender. Remove chicken from broth, reserving broth. Let chicken cool. Skin, bone, and coarsely chop chicken. Skim fat from broth; reserve 4 cups broth. Reserve any remaining broth for another use, if desired. Set chicken and 4 cups reserved broth aside.
• **Combine** oil and flour in Dutch oven; cook over medium heat, stirring constantly, until roux is caramel colored (about 15 minutes). Add garlic and next 4 ingredients; cook 20 to 30 minutes or until vegetables are tender, stirring occasionally.
• **Add** reserved 4 cups chicken broth, chicken, crabs, and next 12 ingredients. Bring to a boil; reduce heat,

and simmer, uncovered, 2½ hours, stirring occasionally. Discard bay leaves before serving. Serve gumbo over rice; sprinkle with filé powder, if desired. Yield: 14 cups.

DOVE AND SAUSAGE GUMBO

If there are hunters in your family, you'll want to tuck this robust recipe away and remember it often. The combination of dove breasts, smoky sausage, and earthy spices simmered in a rich broth is unbeatable. Serve this gutsy gumbo over rice or toasted cornbread.

15 dove breasts
1 (10½-ounce) can beef consommé,
   undiluted
1 beef bouillon cube
½ cup vegetable oil
½ cup all-purpose flour
1½ cups finely chopped onion
1 cup finely chopped celery
2 cloves garlic, minced
2 bay leaves
2 tablespoons Worcestershire sauce
½ teaspoon dried basil
¼ teaspoon poultry seasoning
¼ teaspoon freshly ground black pepper
⅛ teaspoon ground red pepper
⅛ teaspoon ground allspice
⅛ teaspoon ground cloves
¾ pound smoked sausage, thinly sliced
¼ cup dry red wine
⅛ teaspoon hot sauce
Hot cooked rice
Filé powder (optional)

• **Place** dove breasts in a Dutch oven; add water to cover. Bring to a boil; cover, reduce heat, and simmer 10 minutes. Remove dove from broth, reserving broth.

Let dove cool. Bone and coarsely chop dove; set aside. Add enough water to reserved broth to measure 3 cups.
• **Combine** broth, consommé, and bouillon cube in a saucepan; cook over medium heat until bouillon cube dissolves. Set aside.
• **Brown** dove meat in hot oil in Dutch oven over medium heat. Remove dove meat, reserving drippings in Dutch oven; add flour to drippings. Cook over medium heat, stirring constantly, until roux is caramel colored (about 15 minutes). Gradually add 1½ cups broth; cook over medium heat, stirring constantly, until mixture is thickened and bubbly. Add onion and celery; cook 5 minutes or until vegetables are tender, stirring occasionally. Add remaining broth, garlic, and next 8 ingredients to roux; stir well.
• **Brown** sausage in a large skillet over medium heat. Add sausage and dove meat to gumbo. Bring to a boil; cover, reduce heat, and simmer 1½ hours, stirring occasionally. Stir in wine and hot sauce. Discard bay leaves before serving. Serve gumbo over rice; sprinkle with filé powder, if desired. Yield: 7 cups.

NOTE: You can freeze this gumbo in an airtight container up to 3 months.

POTATO-CHEESE CHOWDER

½ cup chopped celery
½ cup chopped onion
½ cup chopped green pepper
¼ cup butter or margarine, melted
3 cups chicken broth
1 medium potato, unpeeled and cubed
1 large carrot, scraped and chopped
½ cup all-purpose flour
2 cups milk, divided
12 ounces sharp American cheese, cubed
2 tablespoons chopped fresh parsley

• **Cook** first 3 ingredients in butter in a Dutch oven over medium-high heat until tender, stirring constantly. Add chicken broth, potato, and carrot; bring to a boil. Cover, reduce heat, and simmer 20 minutes or until vegetables are tender.
• **Combine** flour and ¾ cup milk, stirring until smooth. Gradually stir flour mixture into vegetable mixture. Add remaining 1¼ cups milk, cheese, and parsley. Cook over medium-low heat, stirring constantly, 8 minutes or until thickened and bubbly. Yield: 8 cups.

MANHATTAN-STYLE SEAFOOD CHOWDER

4 medium onions, chopped
1 large green pepper, seeded and chopped
¼ cup vegetable oil
2 tablespoons all-purpose flour
3 (14½-ounce) cans stewed tomatoes, undrained
1 tablespoon celery salt
1 teaspoon garlic powder
1 teaspoon hot sauce
½ teaspoon pepper
2 pounds unpeeled medium-size fresh shrimp
½ pound fresh crabmeat, drained and flaked
½ pound firm white fish fillets, cut into bite-size pieces
1 (12-ounce) container oysters, drained
Garnish: celery leaves

• **Cook** onion and green pepper in oil in a Dutch oven over medium-high heat, stirring constantly, until tender.
• **Add** flour; cook, stirring constantly, 1 minute. Stir in tomatoes and next 4 ingredients. Bring to a boil; cover, reduce heat, and simmer 15 minutes.
• **Peel** shrimp. Add shrimp, crabmeat, fish, and oysters to Dutch oven; cover and simmer 15 minutes. Garnish, if desired. Yield: 12 cups.

CLAM CHOWDER

～ quick ～

Clam chowder is a thick, chunky seafood stew. This is the New England version made with milk and/or cream. And, of course, it includes crisp bits of bacon and crackers crushed on top.

4 slices bacon, chopped
2 (10-ounce) cans whole shelled baby clams
½ cup chopped celery
½ cup chopped onion
2 green onions, chopped
1 large baking potato, chopped (about 2 cups)
3 tablespoons butter or margarine
3 tablespoons all-purpose flour
2 cups milk
2 cups half-and-half
¼ teaspoon hot sauce
½ teaspoon salt
¼ teaspoon ground white pepper
Paprika
Garnish: fresh parsley sprigs
Oyster crackers

• **Cook** bacon in a Dutch oven over medium heat until crisp; pour off drippings.
• **Drain** clams, reserving 1 cup juice; set clams aside. Add clam juice, celery, and next 3 ingredients to bacon in Dutch oven. Bring to a boil; cover, reduce heat, and simmer 15 minutes or until potato is tender.
• **Melt** butter in a saucepan over low heat; add flour, stirring until smooth. Cook 1 minute, stirring constantly. Gradually add milk, stirring until smooth. Cook over medium heat until thickened; add to potato mixture in Dutch oven. Stir clams, half-and-half, and next 3 ingredients into chowder. Cook over medium heat until thoroughly heated, stirring constantly. Sprinkle each serving with paprika; garnish, if desired. Serve with oyster crackers. Yield: 8 cups.

HARVEST CHOWDER

～ quick ～

4 slices bacon
2 stalks celery, thinly sliced
2 carrots, scraped and thinly sliced
1 green onion, thinly sliced
1 (14.75-ounce) can cream-style corn
2 cups milk
2 cups cooked mashed potato
1 cup (4 ounces) shredded sharp Cheddar cheese
½ cup frozen English peas
¾ teaspoon salt
1 small tomato, cut into 8 slices
Freshly ground pepper

• **Cook** bacon in a Dutch oven until crisp; remove bacon, reserving 1 tablespoon drippings in Dutch oven. Crumble bacon, and set aside.
• **Sauté** celery, carrot, and green onion in drippings over medium heat 5 minutes or until tender. Stir in corn and next 5 ingredients; cook, stirring constantly, until cheese melts.
• **Ladle** chowder into bowls. Top each serving with a tomato slice. Sprinkle with crumbled bacon and pepper. Yield: 8 cups.

FRESH CORN CHOWDER

~ family favorite ~

There's nothing quite like fresh sweet corn for a thick homemade chowder.

6 ears fresh corn
1 large onion, chopped
¼ cup butter or margarine
1 bay leaf
2 whole cloves
1 sprig fresh rosemary or pinch of dried rosemary
1 sprig fresh thyme or pinch of dried thyme
3 (14½-ounce) cans ready-to-serve chicken broth
Dash of ground nutmeg
Dash of pepper
1 cup whipping cream
2 tablespoons cornstarch
Garnishes: fresh parsley, fresh rosemary, or fresh thyme sprigs

• **Cut** off tips of corn kernels into a large bowl, scraping cobs as well to remove all milk.
• **Sauté** onion in butter in a Dutch oven over medium heat 4 minutes or until onion is tender. Add 2 cups corn; cook 3 minutes.
• **Tie** bay leaf, cloves, rosemary, and thyme in a cheesecloth bag. Add cheesecloth bag, broth, nutmeg, and pepper to onion mixture, stirring well. Simmer, uncovered, 45 minutes.
• **Discard** cheesecloth bag. Strain soup mixture, reserving liquid. Process strained vegetables in a food processor 2 minutes or until smooth, stopping once to scrape down sides. Add pureed mixture to strained liquid; stir in remaining corn. Bring soup to a boil; reduce heat, and simmer, uncovered, 5 minutes.
• **Combine** whipping cream and cornstarch; stir into soup. Simmer 2 minutes or until chowder is thickened, stirring gently. Garnish, if desired. Yield: 6 cups.

BRUNSWICK STEW

~ family favorite ~

Freeze this hearty stew in several small containers. It will provide you with multiple meals up to three months.

1 (2½- to 3-pound) broiler-fryer
1½ pounds beef stew meat, cut into 1-inch pieces
1 pound pork tenderloin
3 (16-ounce) cans whole tomatoes, undrained and chopped
1 (16-ounce) package frozen white corn
1 (6-ounce) can tomato paste
6 round red potatoes, peeled and cubed
3 medium jalapeño peppers, seeded and chopped
4 cups frozen lima beans
4 cups chopped onion
2 cups sliced carrot
2 cups frozen sliced okra
1 cup frozen English peas
1 cup chopped cabbage
1 tablespoon sugar
3 tablespoons Worcestershire sauce
2 tablespoons lemon juice
2 teaspoons salt
½ to 1 teaspoon pepper

• **Combine** chicken, beef, and pork in a large Dutch oven; add water to cover. Bring to a boil; cover, reduce heat, and simmer 2 hours or until chicken and meats are tender. Strain stock, reserving chicken and meats. Let chicken and meats cool.
• **Skin,** bone, and coarsely chop chicken. Coarsely chop beef and pork. Skim fat from stock, reserving 7 cups stock. Reserve any remaining stock for another use, if desired.
• **Combine** reserved 7 cups stock, chopped chicken, chopped meats, tomatoes, and next 10 ingredients in Dutch oven. Bring to a boil; cover, reduce heat, and simmer 2 hours. Stir in sugar and remaining ingredients just before serving. Yield: 2 gallons.

IRISH STEW

Irish Stew has chunks of beef, potato, carrots, and onion that simmer to a perfect tenderness.

1 cup dry red wine
1 clove garlic, minced
1 teaspoon salt
½ teaspoon freshly ground pepper
¼ teaspoon dried thyme
3 pounds beef stew meat, cut into 1-inch cubes
¼ cup olive oil or vegetable oil
½ cup all-purpose flour
2½ cups water
2 (10½-ounce) cans condensed beef broth
6 carrots, cut into 2-inch slices
12 boiling onions
1½ pounds new potatoes, cut in half
2 bay leaves

• **Combine** first 5 ingredients; pour over beef in a shallow dish. Cover and marinate in refrigerator 8 hours. Drain beef, reserving marinade.
• **Heat** oil in a large Dutch oven over medium heat. Dredge beef in flour; brown beef in batches in hot oil.
• **Return** all browned beef to Dutch oven. Add water, broth, and reserved marinade; bring to a boil. Cover, reduce heat, and simmer 1½ hours. Add carrot, onion, potato, and bay leaves; cover and cook 30 minutes. Uncover and simmer 15 more minutes or until stew is thickened. Discard bay leaves before serving. Yield: 10 cups.

HUNTER'S STEW

This venison stew is packed with bold flavors. Serve it with crusty French bread and a simple slaw.

1½ pounds boneless venison, cut into ½-inch cubes
½ pound smoked sausage, cut into ½-inch slices
2 tablespoons vegetable oil
½ cup chopped onion
½ cup chopped celery
2 (28-ounce) cans whole tomatoes, undrained and chopped
1 (12-ounce) can beer
1 teaspoon salt
1 teaspoon sugar
1 teaspoon chopped fresh rosemary
¾ teaspoon freshly ground pepper
2 carrots, scraped and diced
2 medium-size baking potatoes, chopped

• **Brown** venison and sausage in hot oil in a large Dutch oven. Add onion and celery; cook 5 minutes or until tender, stirring often. Add tomatoes and next 5 ingredients; cover, reduce heat, and simmer 30 minutes. Add carrot; cook, uncovered, 30 minutes. Add potato, and cook, uncovered, 25 more minutes or until meat is very tender. Yield: 12 cups.

TEXAS STEW

2 pounds beef tips, cut into 1-inch pieces
1 (14½-ounce) can Mexican-style stewed tomatoes
1 (10½-ounce) can condensed beef broth, undiluted
1 (8-ounce) jar medium or mild picante sauce
1 (10-ounce) package frozen whole kernel corn
3 carrots, scraped and cut into ½-inch slices
1 medium onion, cut into thin wedges
2 cloves garlic, minced
1 teaspoon ground cumin
½ teaspoon salt
⅓ cup water
¼ cup all-purpose flour

- **Combine** first 10 ingredients in a 3- or 4-quart electric slow cooker. Cover and cook on HIGH 5 hours or on LOW 10 hours or until meat is tender.
- **Combine** water and flour, stirring until smooth; stir into meat mixture in slow cooker. Cook stew, uncovered, on HIGH 15 minutes or until thickened, stirring often. Yield: 10 cups.

MEXICAN CHILI
family favorite

2 pounds ground chuck
1 cup chopped onion
¾ cup chopped green pepper
1 clove garlic, minced
1 (16-ounce) can kidney beans, drained
1 (16-ounce) can whole tomatoes, undrained and
    chopped
2 (8-ounce) cans tomato sauce
1 tablespoon plus 1 teaspoon chili powder
2 teaspoons ground cumin
½ teaspoon salt
½ teaspoon dried basil
¼ teaspoon pepper
¼ teaspoon hot sauce
1 fresh or canned green chile, seeded and chopped
Shredded Cheddar cheese (optional)
Corn chips (optional)

- **Combine** first 4 ingredients in a Dutch oven; cook over medium heat until meat is browned, stirring until it crumbles. Drain. Add beans and next 9 ingredients; cover, reduce heat, and simmer 20 minutes, stirring occasionally. If desired, top with cheese, and serve with corn chips. Yield: 9 cups.

FRIDAY NIGHT CHILI
family favorite

*The name invites you to make
this a weekend meal.*

2 pounds ground chuck
2 large onions, chopped
3 large cloves garlic, minced
2 (16-ounce) cans kidney beans, undrained
1 (16-ounce) can whole tomatoes, undrained and
    chopped
1 (8-ounce) can tomato sauce
2 cups water
2 tablespoons chili powder
2 teaspoons garlic salt
1½ teaspoons ground cumin
1 teaspoon dried oregano
1 teaspoon black pepper
½ teaspoon ground red pepper
¼ teaspoon hot sauce
Corn chips (optional)
Shredded sharp Cheddar cheese (optional)
Sliced green onions (optional)

- **Cook** ground chuck, chopped onion, and garlic in a Dutch oven over medium-high heat until meat is browned and onion is tender, stirring until meat crumbles; drain. Stir in beans and next 10 ingredients. Bring to a boil; reduce heat, and simmer, uncovered, 1 hour, stirring occasionally. If desired, serve chili with corn chips, cheese, and green onions. Yield: 9 cups.

Vegetarian Chili

VEGETARIAN CHILI

2 cups dried pinto beans
3½ cups water
1 (15.25-ounce) can whole kernel corn, drained
1 (15-ounce) can tomato sauce
3 carrots, scraped and chopped
1 large onion, chopped
1 (4.5-ounce) can chopped green chiles
1 clove garlic, minced
1 teaspoon salt
3 tablespoons chili powder
1 teaspoon dried oregano
1 bay leaf
1 cup (4 ounces) shredded Monterey Jack cheese or 1 cup sour cream
Garnish: green onions

• **Sort** and wash beans; place in a Dutch oven. Cover with water 2 inches above beans. Bring beans to a boil; cover, remove from heat, and let stand 1 hour. Drain beans, and return to Dutch oven.
• **Add** 3½ cups water and next 10 ingredients to beans in Dutch oven. Bring to a boil; cover, reduce heat, and simmer 2 hours, stirring occasionally. Uncover and cook 30 more minutes or to desired consistency. Discard bay leaf before serving. Serve chili with cheese or sour cream. Garnish, if desired. Yield: 10 cups.

In the Red

Next to barbecue bragging rights, few things steam up a Southerner like chili preferences. *Southern Living* has contributed over 135 recipes to the discussion. We strongly believe in freedom of chili choice, no matter what the meat, what the heat, and whether or not there are beans. Our variations have spanned the chili universe: Chili Hominy Bake, Chuck Wagon Chili, Chili in a Biscuit Bowl, Beef and Sausage Chili con Carne, Chili-Tamale Pie, Tex-Mex Chili, Vegetarian Chili, and Old-Fashioned Spicy Chili. We may have every recipe, except yours.

Vegetable and Fruit Side Dishes

The abundance of vegetables
and fruits available in the marketplace
these days is mouthwatering and
beautiful. As a result, the Southern
vegetable plate is more enticing than
ever. Success with side dishes
begins with buying produce in season
and choosing recipes that let the
natural flavor of the food
shine through.

*Crusty Broiled Tomatoes (page 384), Italian Green Beans (page 359), and
Glazed Carrots and Onions (page 366)*

ARTICHOKE FLAN

*Artichoke hearts flavor this flan
as a vegetable side dish.*

½ (15-ounce) package refrigerated piecrusts
1 egg white
1 (9-ounce) package frozen artichoke hearts
3 large eggs, lightly beaten
1½ cups whipping cream
1½ cups (6 ounces) shredded Swiss cheese
½ teaspoon salt
¼ teaspoon dried thyme
Dash of ground red pepper

• **Fit** 1 piecrust into a 9-inch pieplate following package directions; fold edges of piecrust under, and crimp. Brush piecrust with egg white; set aside.
• **Cook** artichoke hearts according to package directions; drain well.
• **Combine** eggs and remaining 5 ingredients in a bowl; pour mixture into prepared piecrust. Arrange artichoke hearts over filling.
• **Bake** at 375° for 45 minutes or until a knife inserted in center comes out clean. Serve warm. Yield: 8 servings.

HAM-AND-MUSHROOM-STUFFED ARTICHOKES

*It's not hard to prepare and cook artichokes
once you get the hang of it. Here's a tasty
recipe for two to indulge.*

2 medium-size fresh artichokes
Lemon wedge
1½ tablespoons fresh lemon juice
1 cup sliced fresh mushrooms
1 teaspoon olive oil or vegetable oil
3 ounces smoked ham, cut into strips (about ½ cup strips)
2 tablespoons chicken broth
¼ cup whipping cream
½ cup (2 ounces) shredded Swiss cheese
2 tablespoons chopped fresh chives

• **Hold** artichokes by stems, and wash by plunging up and down in cold water. Cut off stem end, so artichokes will sit flat; trim about ½ inch from top of each artichoke. Remove any loose bottom leaves. With kitchen scissors, trim one-fourth off top of each outer leaf, and rub top and edges of leaves with lemon wedge to prevent discoloring.
• **Place** artichokes in a large nonaluminum Dutch oven; cover with water, and add lemon juice.
• **Bring** to a boil; cover, reduce heat, and simmer 35 minutes or until lower leaves pull out easily. Drain; place artichokes in a baking pan.
• **Cook** mushrooms in oil in a large skillet over medium-high heat 3 minutes, stirring often. Add ham, and cook 3 minutes, stirring often. Add chicken broth and whipping cream; cook 3 minutes. Remove from heat; stir in cheese and chives.
• **Spoon** mixture over artichokes and between the leaves. Broil 5½ inches from heat 3 minutes or until golden. Serve immediately. Yield: 2 servings.

ASPARAGUS WITH CASHEW BUTTER

⌁ quick ⌁

1½ pounds fresh asparagus
1 cup chicken broth
½ cup butter or margarine, softened
¼ cup chopped salted cashews

• **Snap** off tough ends of asparagus. Place asparagus in a large skillet; add chicken broth. Bring to a boil over medium heat; cover, reduce heat, and simmer 5 to 6 minutes. Drain.
• **Combine** butter and cashews; beat at high speed with an electric mixer until fluffy. Serve cashew butter with hot cooked asparagus. Yield: 6 servings.

ASPARAGUS WITH CURRY SAUCE

⌁ quick ⌁

½ cup mayonnaise
2½ teaspoons curry powder
1½ teaspoons lemon juice
1 pound fresh asparagus
2 tablespoons capers

• **Combine** first 3 ingredients; stir well. Chill.
• **Snap** off tough ends of asparagus. Place asparagus in a large saucepan of boiling water. Cover and cook 5 to 6 minutes or until asparagus is crisp-tender; drain. Arrange asparagus on a serving platter; top with curry mixture, and sprinkle with capers. Yield: 4 servings.

ASPARAGUS WITH ORANGE BUTTER SAUCE

⌁ quick ⌁

Use the juice and rind from a plump orange to dress this asparagus.

1½ pounds fresh asparagus
⅓ cup butter or margarine
2 tablespoons grated orange rind
¼ cup orange juice
Garnish: orange slices

• **Snap** off tough ends of asparagus. Arrange asparagus in a steamer basket over boiling water; cover and steam 6 to 8 minutes or until asparagus is crisp-tender.
• **While** asparagus steams, combine butter, orange rind, and juice in a saucepan. Bring to a boil over high heat; reduce heat to medium, and cook, uncovered, until mixture is reduced by half and slightly thickened, stirring occasionally.
• **Arrange** asparagus in a serving dish; pour sauce over asparagus. Garnish, if desired. Yield: 6 servings.

ASPARAGUS VINAIGRETTE

◦ make ahead ◦

*Pair red and green in this easy
do-ahead vegetable dish.*

3 pounds fresh asparagus
1 sweet red pepper, seeded and cut into strips
½ cup vegetable oil, divided
¼ cup white wine vinegar
2 tablespoons water
1 tablespoon grated onion
1 teaspoon dry mustard
½ teaspoon salt
Pinch of pepper

• **Snap** off tough ends of asparagus. Arrange asparagus in a steamer basket over boiling water. Cover and steam 8 minutes or until crisp-tender. Plunge asparagus into ice water; drain.
• **Sauté** red pepper strips in 1 tablespoon hot oil in a skillet over medium-high heat until crisp-tender. Plunge pepper strips into ice water to stop the cooking process; drain.
• **Place** asparagus spears and pepper strips in a large shallow dish. Combine remaining oil, wine vinegar, and remaining 5 ingredients; pour over vegetables. Cover and chill at least 8 hours. Serve with a slotted spoon. Yield: 12 servings.

SAVORY GREEN BEANS

◦ family favorite ◦

1½ pounds fresh green beans
1 clove garlic, minced
2 tablespoons chopped onion
3 tablespoons olive oil or vegetable oil
½ cup boiling water
1 tablespoon fresh basil or 1 teaspoon dried basil
¾ teaspoon salt
½ teaspoon sugar
¼ teaspoon pepper

• **Wash** beans; trim ends, and remove strings. Cut beans in half.
• **Sauté** garlic and onion in hot oil just until tender. Add beans, boiling water, basil, salt, sugar, and pepper. Cover and cook over medium heat 20 to 25 minutes or until beans are tender. Yield: 6 servings.

SNAP BEANS AND POTATOES

*These vegetables and seasonings remind us of
the Old South, but the crisp-tender preparation
of the beans is definitely this age.*

4 red potatoes, peeled and quartered (1½ pounds)
2¼ teaspoons salt, divided
1 pound fresh green beans, broken into 1½-inch
    pieces
3 slices bacon
1 large onion, sliced
¼ cup cider vinegar
2 teaspoons fresh or dried rosemary, crushed
¼ teaspoon sugar
¼ teaspoon freshly ground pepper

• **Cook** potato and 1 teaspoon salt in boiling water to cover in a saucepan 10 minutes or until tender. Drain.

• **Cook** beans and 1 teaspoon salt in boiling water to cover in saucepan 3 to 4 minutes or until crisp-tender. Remove from heat; plunge into ice water to stop the cooking process. Drain; set aside.

• **Cook** bacon in a large skillet until crisp; remove bacon, reserving drippings in skillet. Crumble bacon.

• **Sauté** onion in hot drippings until crisp-tender. Stir in remaining ¼ teaspoon salt, vinegar, and next 3 ingredients. Add potato and green beans; cook until heated, stirring occasionally. Sprinkle with bacon. Yield: 6 servings.

ITALIAN GREEN BEANS

~ *family favorite* ~

Mushrooms, water chestnuts, and Parmesan cheese adorn these flavorful beans.

2½ pounds fresh green beans
3 cups water
1 cup sliced fresh mushrooms
⅓ cup chopped onion
3 cloves garlic, minced
¾ teaspoon salt
½ teaspoon freshly ground pepper
½ teaspoon dried basil
1 teaspoon dried Italian seasoning
⅓ cup olive oil
1 (8-ounce) can sliced water chestnuts, drained
¼ cup freshly grated Parmesan cheese

• **Wash** green beans; trim ends, and remove strings. Combine beans and water in a Dutch oven. Bring to a boil; cover, reduce heat, and simmer 8 minutes or until beans are crisp-tender. Drain. Plunge beans into ice water. Drain and set aside.

• **Sauté** mushrooms and next 6 ingredients in hot oil in a Dutch oven. Stir in beans and water chestnuts, and cook until thoroughly heated. Sprinkle with Parmesan cheese before serving. Yield: 8 to 10 servings.

FRESH POLE BEANS

~ *family favorite* ~

These beans and some of their cooking liquid are delicious served with cornbread.

1 pound fresh pole beans
½ pound salt pork or ham hock
2 teaspoons vegetable oil
3 cups water
½ teaspoon salt
½ teaspoon freshly ground pepper

• **Wash** beans; trim ends. Cut beans into pieces, and set aside.

• **Brown** salt pork on all sides in oil in a large saucepan over medium heat. Add water, salt, and pepper; bring to a boil. Cover, reduce heat, and simmer broth mixture 15 minutes.

• **Add** beans. Cover and cook over medium heat 25 minutes or until beans are tender. Serve with a slotted spoon. Yield: 4 servings.

EASY BAKED BEANS

family favorite

Baked beans are always a welcome and favorite dish. Pair this recipe with pork chops, ham, or burgers from the grill.

2 slices bacon, halved
1 small onion, diced
1 small green pepper, finely chopped
1 (15-ounce) can pork and beans with tomato
     sauce
2 teaspoons prepared mustard
1 teaspoon chili powder
¼ to ⅓ cup molasses
3 tablespoons ketchup

• **Cook** bacon in a medium skillet until partially cooked; remove bacon, and set aside, reserving drippings in pan.
• **Sauté** onion and green pepper in bacon drippings until tender; drain.
• **Combine** sautéed onion mixture, beans, and remaining 4 ingredients, stirring well. Spoon mixture into a lightly greased 1½-quart baking dish. Top with bacon slices. Bake, uncovered, at 350° for 30 to 40 minutes or until beans are thickened and bacon is cooked. Yield: 4 servings.

CUBAN BLACK BEANS

Pile these seasoned beans high with cheese, tomato, and green onions. It's a meatless main dish.

1 pound dried black beans
1 large onion, chopped
1 medium-size green pepper, chopped
6 cloves garlic, minced
¼ cup olive oil
4 cups water
1 (6-ounce) can tomato paste
1 teaspoon sugar
1 teaspoon pepper
1½ teaspoons cumin seeds
1 tablespoon red wine vinegar
2½ teaspoons salt
Hot cooked rice
Shredded Cheddar cheese
Chopped tomato
Chopped green onions

• **Sort** and wash beans; place in a large Dutch oven. Cover with water 2 inches above beans; let soak 8 hours or quick soak according to package directions. Drain well.
• **Sauté** onion, green pepper, and garlic in oil until tender.
• **Combine** beans, sautéed vegetables, water, and next 4 ingredients in Dutch oven; bring to a boil. Cover, reduce heat, and simmer 1½ hours or until beans are tender, stirring occasionally. Stir in vinegar and salt. Serve bean mixture over rice.
• **Top** each serving with cheese, tomato, and green onions. Yield: 7 cups.

BEETS IN ORANGE SAUCE

This recipe is a wonderfully simple way to prepare fresh beets. Use rubber gloves while working with beets to avoid staining your hands.

2½ pounds small beets
1 tablespoon cornstarch
½ cup plus 2 tablespoons firmly packed brown sugar
½ (6-ounce) can orange juice concentrate, thawed
⅓ cup cider vinegar
1 tablespoon butter or margarine

• **Leave** root and 1 inch of stem on beets; scrub beets with a vegetable brush.
• **Cook** beets in boiling water to cover 30 minutes or until tender. Drain beets, reserving ⅓ cup liquid. Pour cold water over beets, and drain. Trim roots and stems; rub off skins. Cut beets into quarters; set aside.
• **Combine** reserved ⅓ cup beet liquid, cornstarch, and next 3 ingredients in a small saucepan. Bring to a boil over medium heat, stirring constantly; boil 1 minute. Stir in butter. Add beets, and heat thoroughly. Yield: 6 to 8 servings.

NOTE: To save time, substitute 2 (16-ounce) cans quartered beets for fresh, and omit precooking them.

BROCCOLI AND WALNUT SAUTÉ

~ quick ~

A splash of balsamic vinegar and some toasted walnuts dress up this easy broccoli dish.

1½ pounds fresh broccoli
½ cup water
2 tablespoons balsamic vinegar
2 teaspoons cornstarch
1 teaspoon chicken bouillon granules
1 clove garlic, minced
1 cup thin onion strips (cut vertically)
½ cup thin strips sweet red pepper
2 tablespoons vegetable oil
½ cup chopped walnuts, toasted

• **Remove** and discard broccoli leaves and tough ends of stalks; cut broccoli into flowerets. Peel broccoli stems, and thinly slice. Set broccoli aside.
• **Combine** water and next 3 ingredients; set cornstarch mixture aside.
• **Sauté** garlic, onion, red pepper, and broccoli in oil in a large skillet over medium heat 3 minutes or until broccoli is crisp-tender.
• **Add** cornstarch mixture to vegetable mixture, and bring to a boil, stirring constantly. Cook 1 minute, stirring constantly.
• **Spoon** vegetable mixture into a serving dish; sprinkle with walnuts. Yield: 6 servings.

BROCCOLI WITH STUFFING

Here's a new way to enjoy stuffing—in a broccoli casserole. Team it with turkey or roasted chicken.

2 (10-ounce) packages frozen broccoli spears
1 cup (4 ounces) shredded Cheddar cheese
2 large eggs, lightly beaten
1 (10¾-ounce) can cream of mushroom soup, undiluted
½ cup mayonnaise
½ cup finely chopped onion
¾ cup herb-seasoned stuffing mix
2 tablespoons butter or margarine, melted

• **Cook** broccoli according to package directions; drain. Arrange broccoli in a lightly greased 11- x 7-inch baking dish. Sprinkle with cheese.
• **Combine** eggs and next 3 ingredients; spread over cheese. Combine stuffing mix and butter; sprinkle over casserole.
• **Bake** casserole at 350° for 30 minutes or until thoroughly heated. Yield: 8 servings.

BROCCOLI PARMESAN

quick

1 (16-ounce) package fresh broccoli flowerets
2 tablespoons butter or margarine
3 tablespoons chopped onion
2 tablespoons all-purpose flour
1 teaspoon chicken bouillon granules
1¾ cups milk
½ cup freshly grated Parmesan cheese
½ teaspoon salt
½ teaspoon pepper
½ teaspoon dry mustard
Grated Parmesan cheese (optional)

• **Arrange** broccoli in a steamer basket over boiling water. Cover; steam 5 minutes or until broccoli is crisp-tender. Keep warm.
• **Melt** butter in a heavy saucepan; add onion, and sauté until tender.
• **Add** flour and bouillon granules, stirring until blended. Cook 1 minute, stirring constantly. Gradually add milk; cook over medium heat, stirring constantly, until thickened and bubbly.
• **Stir** in cheese and next 3 ingredients; pour over broccoli. Sprinkle with additional cheese, if desired. Yield: 6 servings.

Southern Living "Casser-Rolls" of Honor

70ˢ Butternut Squash Casserole, Cauliflower and Asparagus Supreme, Beefy Vegetable Casserole

80ˢ Spinach and Artichoke Casserole, Upside-Down Pizza Bake, Light Scalloped Potatoes

90ˢ Vegetable-Curry Casserole, Winter Root Vegetable Casserole, Mozzarella-Olive Orzo, Italian Sausage Lasagna

STIR-FRIED BOK CHOY

～ quick ～

Bok choy is a mild, versatile vegetable with crunchy white ribs and large dark green leaves.

½ cup soy sauce
⅓ cup rice wine vinegar
2 tablespoons sliced green onions
2 teaspoons peeled, chopped fresh ginger
1 teaspoon chopped garlic
1 teaspoon sugar
1 medium bunch bok choy
2 tablespoons sesame oil
3 cloves garlic, sliced

• **Stir** together first 6 ingredients; cover and let stand 2 hours.
• **Cut** stems from bok choy, and coarsely chop leaves.
• **Pour** oil around top of a nonstick wok or large skillet, coating sides; place over medium heat until hot.
• **Add** bok choy stems and sliced garlic to wok; stir-fry 3 to 4 minutes or until crisp-tender. Add bok choy leaves; stir-fry 2 minutes or until crisp-tender. Serve immediately with sauce. Yield: 4 servings.

BRUSSELS SPROUTS AND BABY CARROTS

～ quick ～

Serve this easy dish as part of a holiday feast.

1 (8-ounce) package frozen brussels sprouts
1 (9-ounce) package frozen baby carrots
2 tablespoons brown sugar
1 teaspoon grated orange rind
2 tablespoons fresh orange juice

• **Cook** brussels sprouts and carrots according to package directions; drain vegetables.
• **Bring** brown sugar, orange rind, and orange juice to a boil in a saucepan over medium heat, stirring until sugar dissolves. Toss with vegetables. Serve warm. Yield: 4 servings.

DIJON BRUSSELS SPROUTS

⅔ cup mayonnaise
⅔ cup sour cream
¼ cup Dijon mustard
½ teaspoon garlic salt
1 tablespoon Worcestershire sauce
Dash of hot sauce
4 (10-ounce) packages frozen brussels sprouts
3 tablespoons butter or margarine, melted
¼ cup finely chopped pecans, toasted

• **Combine** first 6 ingredients in a small saucepan; cook over low heat until heated, stirring often. Keep warm.
• **Cook** brussels sprouts according to package directions 5 minutes, and drain well.
• **Combine** brussels sprouts, butter, and pecans, tossing to coat. Serve with sauce. Yield: 12 servings.

LEMON-BUTTER CABBAGE

~ quick ~

1½ tablespoons butter or margarine
1½ tablespoons vegetable oil or olive oil
1 teaspoon caraway seeds
1 medium cabbage (about 1½ pounds), coarsely chopped
1 teaspoon grated lemon rind
2 tablespoons lemon juice
½ teaspoon salt
¼ teaspoon pepper

• **Heat** butter and oil in a large skillet over medium-high heat 2 minutes. Add caraway seeds; cook 1 minute, stirring often. Add cabbage; stir-fry 3 to 4 minutes. Cover, reduce heat, and steam 2 to 3 minutes or until cabbage is tender. Add lemon rind and remaining ingredients, tossing gently. Serve hot. Yield: 6 servings.

CABBAGE-ONION-SWEET PEPPER MEDLEY

½ small sweet red pepper
½ small sweet yellow pepper
½ small green pepper
2 slices bacon
1 onion, chopped
2 cups shredded cabbage
3 tablespoons white vinegar
1 tablespoon vegetable oil
1 tablespoon water
1½ teaspoons brown sugar
1½ teaspoons Dijon mustard
½ teaspoon salt
½ teaspoon pepper

• **Cut** peppers into 2-inch-long thin strips; cut bacon into 1-inch pieces.
• **Cook** bacon in a large skillet until crisp. Add pepper strips, onion, and cabbage, tossing gently.
• **Combine** vinegar and remaining 6 ingredients in a jar; cover tightly, and shake vigorously. Add to vegetable mixture in skillet, stirring gently.
• **Bring** to a boil; cover, reduce heat, and simmer 8 minutes or until cabbage is tender, stirring occasionally. Serve immediately. Yield: 3 servings.

GERMAN-STYLE RED CABBAGE

Cabbage and apples make a good mix. They're dressed with vinegar and brown sugar in this classic German dish.

3 tablespoons butter or margarine
3 Granny Smith apples, thinly sliced
1 small onion, chopped
1 small red cabbage, shredded
⅓ cup white vinegar
½ cup firmly packed brown sugar
2 teaspoons all-purpose flour
1 teaspoon salt
¼ teaspoon pepper
⅓ cup dry red wine

• **Melt** butter in a large skillet over medium-high heat. Add apple and onion; sauté 5 minutes. Add cabbage and vinegar. Sauté 1 minute.
• **Combine** sugar, flour, salt, and pepper; add to skillet. Add wine. Cover, reduce heat, and simmer 35 minutes. Yield: 6 servings.

GINGER-GLAZED CARROTS

∽ quick ∽

Fresh ginger and orange juice spruce up these sliced carrots.

3 pounds carrots, scraped and sliced
¾ cup minced onion
1 teaspoon grated fresh ginger or ground ginger
¼ cup butter or margarine, melted
¼ cup firmly packed brown sugar
¼ cup honey
¼ cup frozen orange juice concentrate, thawed and undiluted
¼ cup orange-flavored liqueur (such as Cointreau or Triple Sec)
2 teaspoons minced fresh thyme or ½ teaspoon dried thyme
Garnish: fresh thyme sprig

• **Place** sliced carrots in a steamer basket over boiling water. Cover and steam 8 to 10 minutes or until carrots are crisp-tender. Spoon carrots into a serving dish; cover and set aside.

• **Sauté** onion and ginger in butter until onion is tender. Add brown sugar and next 4 ingredients, and cook until mixture is thickened and bubbly. Pour ginger mixture over carrots, tossing gently to coat. Garnish, if desired. Yield: 12 servings.

BRANDIED CARROTS

These carrots are fit for a special occasion. Serve them with beef or pork tenderloin.

2 pounds fresh baby carrots with tops
¼ cup honey
¼ cup brandy
2 tablespoons Grand Marnier or other orange-flavored liqueur
2 tablespoons lemon juice
1½ teaspoons cornstarch
1 tablespoon water
Chopped fresh parsley

• **Scrape** and trim carrots, leaving ½ inch of green tops, if desired. Arrange carrots in a steamer basket over boiling water. Cover and steam 10 minutes or until carrots are crisp-tender. Set aside.

• **Combine** honey and next 3 ingredients in a large skillet; cook over medium heat 5 minutes, stirring occasionally.

• **Combine** cornstarch and water, stirring until smooth; add to honey mixture. Cook, stirring constantly, 1 minute or until slightly thickened. Add carrots; cook just until thoroughly heated, tossing gently. Transfer mixture to a serving bowl; sprinkle with chopped parsley. Yield: 8 servings.

GLAZED CARROTS AND ONIONS

~ quick ~

3 large carrots, scraped and diagonally sliced
1 teaspoon chicken bouillon granules
4 small boiling onions, halved
¼ cup butter or margarine
1 teaspoon sugar
1 tablespoon chopped fresh parsley, cilantro,
    or dill

• **Combine** carrot, bouillon granules, and water to cover in a small saucepan. Bring to a boil; cover, reduce heat, and simmer 8 minutes. Add onions, and cook 4 minutes or until vegetables are tender. Drain well. Spoon vegetables into a serving dish.
• **Melt** butter in a small saucepan; add sugar, and cook stirring constantly, until mixture turns golden. Pour over vegetables, and sprinkle with parsley, cilantro, or dill. Yield: 2 servings.

FREEZER-FRESH CREAMED CORN

~ family favorite ~

No need to wait for summer to make this foolproof creamed corn. The key is blending the corn with milk and butter for creamy results.

3 (16-ounce) packages frozen shoepeg corn,
    partially thawed and divided
½ cup butter or margarine
1¾ to 2 cups milk
1½ to 2 teaspoons salt
½ teaspoon pepper

• **Position** knife blade in food processor bowl; add 1 package corn. Process until smooth, stopping once to scrape down sides.
• **Melt** butter in a heavy skillet over medium heat; stir in pureed corn, remaining 2 packages corn, milk, salt, and pepper. Bring to a boil, stirring constantly; reduce heat, and simmer 20 minutes or until desired thickness, stirring often. Yield: 10 to 12 servings.

CORN FLAN

4 cups fresh corn kernels (about 8 ears)
1½ cups half-and-half
6 large eggs
1 teaspoon salt
½ teaspoon freshly ground pepper

• **Process** corn in a blender until smooth, stopping to scrape down sides. Add half-and-half and remaining 3 ingredients; process until smooth. Pour through a wire-mesh strainer into a bowl, discarding solids. Pour mixture into eight 6-ounce buttered custard cups or ramekins. Place cups in a 13- x 9-inch baking dish. Add hot water to dish to depth of 1 inch.
• **Bake** at 350° for 25 minutes or until set. Remove custards from water; cool 5 minutes on a wire rack. Invert onto plates. Yield: 8 servings.

Corn Pudding

~ *family favorite* ~

Creamy corn pudding continues to grace the dinner table as a preferred side dish.

2 large eggs
½ cup whipping cream
1 tablespoon butter or margarine, melted
1½ teaspoons sugar
¼ teaspoon salt
¼ teaspoon pepper
3 cups fresh corn kernels (about 12 ears)

• **Stir** together first 6 ingredients until well blended. Stir in corn kernels. Pour into a lightly greased 1½-quart baking dish.
• **Bake** at 350° for 30 minutes or until pudding is set. Let stand 5 minutes before serving. Yield: 4 servings.

Corn on the Grill

8 ears corn, unshucked
6 tablespoons unsalted butter, softened
2 tablespoons minced fresh thyme
1 teaspoon salt
1 teaspoon freshly ground pepper

• **Peel** husks from corn; do not remove. Remove silks.
• **Combine** butter and thyme; rub mixture over corn, and sprinkle with salt and pepper. Pull husks over corn, and tightly twist ends.
• **Grill,** covered with grill lid, over medium heat (300° to 350°) 20 to 25 minutes or until tender, turning often. (Husks will blacken in spots.) Remove husks, and serve corn immediately. Yield: 8 servings.

Buttermilk Fried Corn

You can serve these fried corn niblets as a side dish or sprinkle some on salads, soups, or casseroles.

2 cups fresh corn, cut from cob
1½ cups buttermilk
⅔ cup all-purpose flour
⅔ cup cornmeal
1 teaspoon salt
½ teaspoon pepper
Corn oil

• **Combine** corn and buttermilk in a large bowl; let stand 30 minutes. Drain; discard buttermilk.
• **Combine** flour and next 3 ingredients in a large heavy-duty, zip-top plastic bag. Add corn to flour mixture, a small amount at a time, and shake bag gently to coat corn.
• **Pour** oil to depth of 1 inch in a Dutch oven; heat to 375°. Fry corn, a small amount at a time, in hot oil 3 minutes or until corn is golden. Drain on paper towels. Yield: 2 cups.

BATTER-FRIED EGGPLANT

If you buy a small very fresh eggplant you won't need to peel it. Older eggplants should be peeled.

1 medium eggplant (about 1 pound)
2 teaspoons salt, divided
1 cup all-purpose flour
1 teaspoon baking powder
2 teaspoons Italian seasoning
1 teaspoon onion powder
⅛ teaspoon ground red pepper
⅛ teaspoon garlic powder
⅔ cup milk
1 tablespoon olive oil or vegetable oil
2 large eggs, lightly beaten
Vegetable oil

• **Peel** eggplant, if desired, and cut into finger-sized strips. To extract bitterness, sprinkle 1 teaspoon salt on eggplant strips; let stand 30 minutes. Rinse and pat dry with paper towels.
• **Combine** flour, remaining 1 teaspoon salt, baking powder, and next 7 ingredients in a bowl; stir until blended and smooth.
• **Pour** oil to depth of 2 to 3 inches into a Dutch oven; heat to 375°. Dip eggplant strips, one at a time, into batter, coating well. Fry eggplant strips, a few at a time, 3 to 5 minutes or until golden. Drain well on paper towels. Serve immediately. Serve with marinara sauce, if desired. Yield: 4 servings.

EGGPLANT PARMESAN

family favorite

4 cups diced fresh tomato (about 3 to 4 medium tomatoes)
2 tablespoons tomato paste
½ cup olive oil or vegetable oil, divided
1 teaspoon sugar
1¾ teaspoons salt
¼ teaspoon freshly ground pepper
1 clove garlic, minced
1 medium eggplant (about 1¼ pounds)
2 cups soft breadcrumbs (homemade)
2 tablespoons chopped fresh parsley or thyme
½ cup grated Parmesan cheese
1 (6-ounce) package sliced mozzarella cheese

• **Combine** tomato and tomato paste, 2 tablespoons oil, sugar and next 3 ingredients in a large saucepan. Bring to a boil; reduce heat, and simmer, uncovered, 15 minutes or until thickened. Set aside.
• **Peel** eggplant, if desired, and cut into ½-inch slices. Heat remaining ¼ cup plus 2 tablespoons oil in a large skillet. Add a few slices of eggplant at a time, and brown on both sides. Place fried eggplant in a lightly greased 11- x 7-inch baking dish.
• **Combine** breadcrumbs, parsley, and Parmesan cheese; sprinkle half of mixture over eggplant. Cover with tomato sauce. Top with remaining breadcrumb mixture; place mozzarella slices over top.
• **Bake,** uncovered, at 350° for 25 to 30 minutes or until cheese melts and edges are browned. Serve hot. Yield: 8 servings.

CREAMY CHARD AND POTATOES

Swiss chard is a member of the beet family. It has broad green leaves and red ribs. Cook the leaves as you would spinach. Here, potatoes are added for another texture and stirred into the cream sauce.

10 small new potatoes (about 2 pounds)
1 pound Swiss chard
1 teaspoon salt, divided
1 tablespoon dried onion flakes
¼ cup butter or margarine
3 tablespoons all-purpose flour
2 cups milk
¼ teaspoon pepper

• **Cook** potatoes in boiling water to cover in a Dutch oven 20 minutes or until tender; drain and cool slightly. Cut potatoes in half, and keep warm.
• **Remove** and discard ribs from Swiss chard. Rinse Swiss chard with cold water; drain and shred.
• **Cook** chard, ¼ teaspoon salt, and onion flakes in boiling water to cover in Dutch oven 10 minutes; drain and return to Dutch oven. Add potato; keep warm.
• **Melt** butter in a heavy saucepan over low heat; whisk in flour, and cook 1 minute, whisking constantly. Gradually whisk in milk; cook over medium heat, whisking constantly, until sauce is thickened and bubbly. Stir in remaining ¾ teaspoon salt and pepper. Pour sauce over vegetables; toss gently. Serve hot. Yield: 6 servings.

NOTE: To make ahead, spoon mixture into a lightly greased 11- x 7-inch baking dish. Chill until ready to serve. To reheat, bake at 350° for 10 to 15 minutes.

COLLARDS WITH APPLES

2 pounds fresh collard greens, cleaned and chopped
2 cloves garlic, minced
3 green onions, chopped
1 tablespoon olive oil
1 cooking apple, diced
½ cup dry white wine
1 teaspoon sugar
1 teaspoon Greek seasoning
½ teaspoon salt
¼ teaspoon pepper

• **Cook** greens in boiling water to cover in a Dutch oven 30 minutes; drain.
• **Sauté** garlic and green onions in hot oil in Dutch oven over medium-high heat until tender; add collards, apple, and remaining ingredients. Bring to a boil; cover, reduce heat, and simmer 15 minutes or until apple is tender, stirring occasionally. Yield: 6 servings.

MESS O' GREENS WITH WARM PECAN DRESSING

~ quick ~

As far as greens go, this recipe is tops. A small amount of delicious dressing wilts and coats the greens perfectly. And the pecans are a nice nutty surprise.

6 cups fresh mustard greens, shredded, or fresh turnip greens, shredded
2 tablespoons balsamic vinegar
2 teaspoons honey
1 tablespoon Dijon mustard
⅓ cup coarsely chopped pecans
1 tablespoon vegetable oil or olive oil

• **Place** greens in a large bowl.
• **Stir** together vinegar, honey, and mustard. Simmer vinegar mixture and pecans in hot oil in a small skillet over medium heat 2 minutes, stirring often. Remove from heat. Pour warm dressing over greens; toss. Serve immediately. Yield: 2 servings.

FRIED OKRA

~ family favorite ~

Work quickly and with a light hand when tossing okra in this breadcrumb batter. The secret to enjoying fried okra at its best is to be ready to eat it right away.

1 pound okra
3 tablespoons all-purpose flour
Vegetable oil
2 egg whites
1½ cups soft breadcrumbs (homemade)
¾ teaspoon salt

• **Wash** okra, and drain well. Trim ends; cut okra into ½-inch slices. Toss okra with flour.
• **Pour** oil to depth of 2 inches into a Dutch oven; heat to 350°.
• **Beat** egg whites at high speed with an electric mixer until stiff peaks form; gently fold in okra. Gradually stir in breadcrumbs, coating okra well. (Mixture will be sticky.)
• **Fry** okra in batches 4 minutes or until golden, separating pieces with a metal spoon. Drain well on paper towels. Sprinkle with salt. Serve hot. Yield: 4 servings.

LIMPING SUSAN

Hopping John has a delicious cousin here. It's okra that typifies this dish. You can simplify it by serving it without the rice or toppings.

2 ears fresh corn
4 slices thick bacon
⅔ cup finely chopped onion
½ cup finely chopped celery
⅓ cup diced carrot
2½ cups thickly sliced okra
½ cup water
6 fresh thyme sprigs
1 clove garlic, crushed
1 bay leaf
¼ teaspoon ground red pepper
3 cups hot cooked rice
1 medium tomato, chopped
2 green onions, chopped
1 cup (4 ounces) shredded sharp Cheddar cheese

• **Slice** whole kernels from cob; set aside.
• **Cook** bacon in a large skillet over medium heat until crisp. Remove bacon, reserving drippings in skillet. Crumble bacon, and set aside.
• **Sauté** onion, celery, and carrot in bacon drippings over medium heat 5 minutes or until tender. Add reserved corn, okra, and next 5 ingredients; cover and cook over medium heat 12 minutes or until tender. Remove from heat; stir in bacon. Discard bay leaf. Serve corn mixture over rice. Sprinkle each serving with tomato, green onions, and cheese. Yield: 6 servings.

FRENCH-FRIED ONION RINGS

～family favorite～

Everyone's favorite burger companion makes a crispy debut in this recipe.

3 large Spanish or Bermuda onions
3 cups buttermilk or ice water
2 cups all-purpose flour
2 teaspoons salt
1 tablespoon baking powder
1⅓ cups water
2 tablespoons vegetable oil
2 teaspoons lemon juice
½ teaspoon ground red pepper
2 large eggs, beaten
Peanut oil or vegetable oil

• **Peel** onions; cut into ½-inch-thick slices, and separate into rings. Place onion rings in a large bowl, and cover with buttermilk; let stand 30 minutes. Drain well, and spread onion rings on paper towels.
• **Combine** flour and next 7 ingredients; stir until blended and smooth. Dip onion rings into batter, coating well.
• **Pour** oil to depth of 2 to 3 inches into a Dutch oven; heat to 375°. Fry onion rings, a few at a time, 3 to 5 minutes or until golden on both sides. Drain well on paper towels. Serve immediately. Yield: 10 servings.

SMOKY SWEET ONIONS

4 large sweet onions, unpeeled
¼ cup butter or margarine, melted
2 beef bouillon cubes, halved
4 teaspoons dry sherry
½ teaspoon freshly ground pepper

• **Cut** tops off onions, and discard. Cook onions in boiling water to cover 10 minutes; drain and cool. Make a shallow well in center of each onion, and place each onion in center of a 12-inch square of heavy-duty aluminum foil.
• **Add** butter and remaining 3 ingredients evenly into well of each onion. Bring opposite corners of foil together; twist to seal each onion.
• **Grill,** covered with grill lid, over medium-high heat (350° to 400°) 50 minutes or until onions are tender. Yield: 4 servings.

ENGLISH PEAS WITH MUSHROOMS

quick

2 tablespoons butter or margarine
2 tablespoons grated onion
2 cloves garlic, crushed
1 (8-ounce) package sliced fresh mushrooms
1 (10-ounce) package frozen English peas
½ teaspoon chopped fresh rosemary
¼ teaspoon ground nutmeg
¼ teaspoon salt
¼ teaspoon pepper

• **Melt** butter in a large skillet over medium heat; add onion, garlic, and mushrooms, and sauté 3 to 4 minutes or until liquid evaporates.
• **Stir** in peas and remaining ingredients; cover and cook 4 minutes. Uncover and cook, stirring constantly, 4 minutes or until thoroughly heated. Yield: 4 servings.

SOUTHERN BLACK-EYED PEAS

family favorite

1 pound dried black-eyed peas
3 ham hocks
1 medium onion, chopped
2 tablespoons bacon drippings
1 bay leaf
¼ teaspoon freshly ground pepper
5 cups water
1 teaspoon salt
2 teaspoons hot sauce

• **Sort** and wash peas; place in a large Dutch oven. Add water 2 inches above peas, and bring to a boil. Boil 2 minutes; cover, remove from heat, and let stand 1 hour. Drain peas.
• **Brown** ham hocks and onion in bacon drippings in Dutch oven 2 minutes. Add peas, bay leaf, and pepper. Add 5 cups water. Bring to a boil; reduce heat, and simmer, partially covered, 1 to 1½ hours or until peas are tender. Discard bay leaf.
• **Remove** ham hocks from saucepan. Remove meat from bones, and add meat to peas. Add salt and hot sauce to peas. Serve with a slotted spoon. Yield: 8 cups.

CHILLED BLACK-EYED PEAS

~ make ahead, quick ~

Serve these peas as a chilled side dish or an appetizer.

2 (15-ounce) cans black-eyed peas, drained
⅓ cup vegetable oil
⅓ cup red or white wine vinegar
¼ cup finely chopped onion
½ teaspoon salt
¼ teaspoon cracked pepper
1 clove garlic, minced

• **Combine** all ingredients in a bowl; cover and chill 24 hours to blend flavors. Serve with a slotted spoon. Yield: 6 servings.

SPICY CREOLE PEAS

Creole seasoning and chili powder spice up these peas, Southern style.

1 pound dried black-eyed peas
5 cups water
2 tablespoons minced green onions
1 tablespoon Creole seasoning
1 teaspoon dried parsley flakes
1 teaspoon garlic powder
1 teaspoon chili powder
¾ teaspoon pepper
3 chicken bouillon cubes

• **Sort** and wash peas; place in a Dutch oven. Cover with water 2 inches above peas. Let soak 8 hours. Drain peas; return to Dutch oven. Add 5 cups water and remaining ingredients. Bring to a boil; cover, reduce heat, and simmer 45 minutes or until tender. Serve with a slotted spoon. Yield: 8 to 10 servings.

THREE-PEPPER SAUTÉ

~ quick ~

Use just one color of pepper in this sauté, if desired.

1 large sweet red pepper, seeded and cut into thin strips
1 large sweet yellow pepper, seeded and cut into thin strips
1 large green pepper, seeded and cut into thin strips
1 small onion, chopped
1 clove garlic, minced
3 tablespoons olive oil
1 teaspoon dried basil
½ teaspoon salt
¼ teaspoon ground pepper

• **Sauté** first 5 ingredients in hot oil in a large skillet over medium-high heat 5 minutes or just until tender. Stir in basil, salt, and ground pepper. Serve hot. Yield: 4 servings.

Roast 'em, toast 'em, grill 'em

90s Many twentieth century Southerners identify with boiled vegetables of all kinds. Late '90s style took veggies out of the saucepan and put them into the oven to roast and on the grill to sizzle. High heat, short cooking time, and low-fat preparation make onions, potatoes, sweet peppers, eggplant, tomatoes, and mushrooms even more attractive for side dishes, sandwich fixings, and pizza and pasta toppings. And don't forget them in soups and sauces.

Lemon-Buttered New Potatoes

LEMON-BUTTERED NEW POTATOES

family favorite

Peel a strip of skin from the potatoes for a striking presentation.

2 pounds new potatoes
¼ cup butter or margarine
2 tablespoons chopped fresh parsley
1 teaspoon grated lemon rind
2 tablespoons fresh lemon juice
½ teaspoon salt
¼ teaspoon pepper
⅛ teaspoon ground nutmeg
Garnish: fresh parsley

• **Peel** a thick strip around middle of each potato, using a vegetable peeler. Cover and cook potatoes in boiling water to cover 10 minutes or just until tender; drain.
• **Combine** butter and next 6 ingredients in a small saucepan; cook over medium heat, stirring until butter melts. Pour butter mixture over potatoes; toss gently to coat. Garnish, if desired. Yield: 6 servings.

SOUTHERN-FRIED POTATOES

quick

Fried potatoes from a cast-iron skillet are a favorite Southern side dish for breakfast or dinner.

3 large red potatoes, peeled and cut into 1½-inch chunks
½ cup vegetable oil
1 small onion, chopped
Salt and pepper to taste

• **Fry** potato chunks in hot oil in a 9- or 10-inch cast-iron skillet over medium-high heat 12 minutes, stirring often. Add onion, and cook 5 more minutes. Remove mixture to a serving bowl, using a slotted spoon. Sprinkle with salt and pepper to taste. Yield: 4 servings.

SCALLOPED POTATOES

family favorite

A golden cheese top develops as these potatoes bake in a rich cream sauce.

2½ pounds round red potatoes, unpeeled and thinly sliced
¼ cup all-purpose flour
1 large clove garlic, minced
1 shallot, chopped
½ teaspoon dried crushed red pepper
3 tablespoons butter or margarine, melted
1¼ cups milk
1½ cups whipping cream
½ teaspoon salt
¼ teaspoon freshly ground pepper
1½ cups (6 ounces) grated Gruyère cheese
½ cup (2 ounces) freshly grated Parmesan cheese

• **Toss** sliced potatoes with flour in a large bowl until potatoes are coated.
• **Sauté** garlic and shallot with crushed red pepper in butter in a Dutch oven 2 minutes. Add coated potatoes, milk, and next 3 ingredients, stirring well. Bring to a boil; reduce heat, and simmer until thickened.
• **Spoon** half of potato mixture into a lightly greased 3-quart au gratin dish. Sprinkle mixture with half of Gruyère cheese. Repeat procedure with remaining potatoes and Gruyère cheese. Top with Parmesan cheese. Cover and bake at 350° for 30 minutes. Uncover and bake 35 to 40 more minutes or until potatoes are tender and cheese is browned. Yield: 8 servings.

HOLIDAY POTATO CASSEROLE

family favorite

3 pounds round red potatoes, peeled and
    quartered
½ cup butter or margarine
2 (3-ounce) packages cream cheese, softened
1 cup (4 ounces) shredded Cheddar cheese,
    divided
¾ cup finely chopped green pepper
¾ cup finely chopped green onions
1 (2-ounce) jar diced pimiento, drained
½ cup grated Parmesan cheese
½ cup milk
1 teaspoon salt

• **Cook** potato in boiling salted water to cover 15 minutes or until tender; drain and mash. Add butter and cream cheese; beat at medium speed with an electric mixer until smooth. Stir in ½ cup Cheddar cheese, green pepper, and remaining 5 ingredients.
• **Spoon** mixture into a lightly greased 11- x 7-inch baking dish. Cover and refrigerate up to 24 hours, if desired. Remove from refrigerator; let stand, covered, 30 minutes. Uncover and bake at 350° for 25 to 30 minutes or until thoroughly heated. Sprinkle with remaining ½ cup Cheddar cheese; bake 5 more minutes or until cheese melts. Yield: 8 servings.

GARLIC-GRUYÈRE MASHED POTATOES

quick

3 pounds Yukon Gold potatoes
¾ cup hot milk
½ cup sour cream
¼ cup butter or margarine, softened
1 teaspoon salt
⅛ teaspoon ground red pepper
1 clove garlic, minced
½ cup (2 ounces) shredded Gruyère cheese
2 green onions, thinly sliced
⅓ cup chopped baked ham (optional)
Garnish: sliced green onions

• **Peel** potatoes, if desired; cut into 1-inch cubes. Cook in boiling water to cover 15 minutes or until tender. Drain and mash. Add milk and next 5 ingredients. Mash until fluffy.
• **Stir** in cheese, thinly sliced green onions, and, if desired, ham. Garnish, if desired. Yield: 8 servings.

CREAM CHEESE POTATOES

make ahead

3 pounds round red potatoes, peeled and quartered
2 (3-ounce) packages cream cheese, softened
⅔ cup sour cream
¼ cup milk
2 tablespoons butter or margarine
¾ teaspoon salt
1 tablespoon butter or margarine, melted
½ teaspoon paprika

• **Cook** potato in boiling salted water to cover 15 minutes or until tender; drain and mash.

• **Combine** potato, cream cheese, and next 4 ingredients in a large mixing bowl; beat at medium speed with an electric mixer until smooth. Spoon mixture into a greased 11- x 7-inch baking dish. Brush with melted butter, and sprinkle with paprika. Cover and refrigerate up to 24 hours, if desired.

• **Remove** from refrigerator; let stand, covered, 30 minutes. Uncover and bake at 350° for 30 minutes or until heated. Yield: 8 servings.

MISSY POTATOES

This big dish of cheesy, crusty hash browns is potluck food at its best.

1 (2-pound) package frozen hash brown potatoes, thawed
1 (16-ounce) carton sour cream
1 (10¾-ounce) can cream of celery soup, undiluted
1 cup (4 ounces) shredded sharp Cheddar cheese
½ cup butter or margarine, softened
1 teaspoon salt
1 teaspoon coarsely ground pepper
½ cup round buttery cracker crumbs

• **Combine** first 7 ingredients in a large bowl; stir well. Spoon mixture into a greased 13- x 9-inch baking dish; sprinkle with cracker crumbs. Bake at 350° for 55 minutes or until bubbly. Yield: 12 servings.

Smash Hits

90s In 1993, mashed potatoes starred as the single most-often published recipe in U.S. food and women's magazines. *Southern Living* has done the smashed potato as roasted garlic, dill-sour cream, buttermilk-basil, horseradish, feta, Mexican, and pesto. Mashed potatoes with skins—purple, yellow, creamy white—or without skins are anything you want them to be.

ULTIMATE STUFFED POTATOES

family favorite

Stuffed potatoes can easily become a filling meal. Just add a green salad.

6 slices bacon
4 large baking potatoes
¼ cup butter or margarine
¼ cup whipping cream
1 (8-ounce) carton sour cream
¾ cup (3 ounces) shredded sharp Cheddar cheese
½ cup chopped green onions
3 tablespoons grated Parmesan cheese
½ teaspoon garlic salt
¼ teaspoon pepper
Chopped fresh or frozen chives, thawed

• **Place** bacon on a microwave-safe rack in an 11- x 7-inch baking dish; cover with paper towels. Microwave at HIGH 5 to 7 minutes or until bacon is crisp. Drain bacon; crumble and set aside.

• **Scrub** potatoes; prick several times with a fork. Place potatoes 1 inch apart on microwave-safe rack or on paper towels. Microwave at HIGH 14 minutes or until done, turning and rearranging after 5 minutes. Let stand 2 minutes.

• **Cut** potatoes in half lengthwise; carefully scoop out pulp, leaving ¼-inch-thick shells. Combine pulp, butter, and whipping cream in a large bowl; mash until fluffy. Stir in sour cream and next 5 ingredients.

• **Spoon** mixture evenly into potato shells, and place on a baking sheet. Bake at 400° for 10 minutes or until thoroughly heated. Sprinkle with bacon and chives. Yield: 8 servings.

BOURBON SWEET POTATOES

A toasty ring of pecans crowns these mashed sweet potatoes.

6 medium-size sweet potatoes, unpeeled (4 pounds)
½ cup butter or margarine, melted
½ cup firmly packed brown sugar
⅓ cup orange juice
¼ cup bourbon
½ teaspoon salt
½ teaspoon pumpkin pie spice
½ cup chopped pecans

• **Cook** sweet potatoes in boiling water to cover 30 to 35 minutes or until tender. Let cool to touch; peel and mash potatoes.
• **Combine** sweet potato, butter, and next 5 ingredients; mash until blended. Spoon mixture into a lightly greased 1½-quart baking dish. Sprinkle chopped pecans around edge of dish. Bake at 375° for 45 minutes. Yield: 8 servings.

MISS SALLIE'S CANDIED YAMS

family favorite

In the South sweet potatoes are often called yams, though the two are from different plant species. Cook these slices long and slow in brown sugar and butter for delicious candied results.

4 large sweet potatoes (about 4½ pounds)
¾ cup water
1 cup firmly packed brown sugar
½ teaspoon salt
½ teaspoon ground nutmeg
⅓ cup butter or margarine

• **Peel** sweet potatoes; cut lengthwise into ¼-inch-thick slices. Place sweet potatoes in a roasting pan; add water. Cover pan tightly with aluminum foil. Bring to a boil over medium heat; cook 8 minutes or until most of water evaporates. Remove from heat.
• **Combine** brown sugar, salt, and nutmeg; sprinkle mixture over sweet potatoes. Dot with butter. Bake, uncovered, at 350° for 30 to 45 minutes or until sweet potatoes are tender and candied, basting occasionally. Yield: 8 servings.

RUTABAGA-SPINACH TART

Sliced rutabaga forms the crust and top for this spinach tart.

1 rutabaga
1 cup fine, dry breadcrumbs (store-bought)
¼ cup all-purpose flour
¾ cup grated Parmesan cheese, divided
½ cup milk
1 (10-ounce) package frozen spinach, thawed
6 slices bacon, cooked and crumbled
¼ cup butter or margarine, melted

• **Place** a baking sheet on bottom rack of oven. Heat oven to 400°.
• **Peel** rutabaga. Cut a thin slice from 1 side, allowing it to stand upright. Cut rutabaga into ¼-inch-thick slices.
• **Stir** together breadcrumbs, flour, and ¼ cup cheese in a shallow dish. Pour milk into a shallow bowl.
• **Dip** 1 rutabaga slice in milk; dredge in breadcrumb mixture. Place slice in center of a greased 8-inch round cakepan.
• **Cut** remaining rutabaga slices in half. Dip half of slices in milk, and dredge in breadcrumb mixture. Arrange in pan, allowing outer edges of rutabaga to fit around edge of pan.
• **Drain** spinach well, pressing between layers of paper towels. Arrange over rutabaga. Sprinkle with bacon and

remaining ½ cup cheese, and drizzle with 2 table-spoons butter.

• **Dip** remaining rutabaga slices in milk; dredge in breadcrumb mixture. Arrange over cheese. Drizzle with remaining 2 tablespoons butter. Top with a sheet of aluminum foil; press an 8-inch round cakepan onto tart. Place tart in oven on a preheated baking sheet, and top with a large heavy ovenproof skillet. Bake tart at 400° for 40 to 45 minutes. Yield: 1 (8-inch) tart.

SPINACH WITH LEMON AND PEPPER

~ quick ~

1 teaspoon olive oil
1 teaspoon dark sesame oil
¼ teaspoon salt
⅛ teaspoon dried crushed red pepper
1 (10-ounce) package fresh spinach
½ lemon

• **Heat** first 4 ingredients in a large skillet over high heat just until hot; add spinach, and cook 3 to 4 minutes or until wilted, stirring often. Squeeze lemon over spinach; discard lemon. Remove spinach from heat, and serve immediately. Yield: 4 servings.

SPINACH SOUFFLÉ

1 (10-ounce) package frozen chopped spinach, thawed
Butter
¼ cup all-purpose flour
¼ cup butter or margarine, softened
1 teaspoon salt
⅛ teaspoon ground red pepper
¾ cup milk, heated
5 large eggs, separated

• **Place** spinach between paper towels, and squeeze until barely moist.
• **Lightly** butter bottom of a 1½-quart soufflé dish.
• **Process** spinach, flour, ¼ cup butter, salt, red pepper, and milk in a food processor 30 seconds or until mixture is blended, stopping once to scrape down sides. Pour mixture into a saucepan. Cook over medium heat until thickened, stirring constantly.
• **Beat** egg yolks until thick and pale. Gradually stir about one-fourth spinach mixture into yolks; add to remaining spinach mixture, stirring constantly.
• **Beat** egg whites at high speed with an electric mixer until stiff but not dry; fold into spinach mixture. Pour into soufflé dish. Bake at 375° for 30 minutes or until puffed and golden. Serve immediately. Yield: 4 servings.

SPINACH-ARTICHOKE CASSEROLE

2 (14-ounce) cans artichoke hearts, drained and halved
2 (10-ounce) packages frozen chopped spinach
½ cup chopped onion
⅓ cup butter or margarine, melted
½ cup sour cream
¼ cup grated Parmesan cheese
¾ teaspoon salt
¾ teaspoon ground white pepper
Dash of ground red pepper
2 tablespoons grated Parmesan cheese

• **Arrange** artichoke hearts in a lightly greased 8-inch square baking dish. Set aside.
• **Cook** spinach according to package directions; drain well. Sauté onion in butter in a large skillet over medium heat until tender. Stir in spinach, sour cream, and next 4 ingredients. Spoon spinach mixture over artichokes; sprinkle with 2 tablespoons Parmesan cheese.
• **Bake,** uncovered, at 350° for 25 to 30 minutes or until thoroughly heated. Yield: 8 servings.

Yellow Squash Casserole

family favorite

Made with Cheddar cheese, bacon, and buttery cracker crumbs, squash casserole beckons you to a (second) helping.

2 **pounds yellow squash, sliced**
1 **cup water**
2 **small onions, minced**
2 **tablespoons butter or margarine, melted**
1½ **cups (6 ounces) shredded Cheddar cheese**
1¼ **cups round buttery cracker crumbs, divided**
¼ **teaspoon salt**
¼ **teaspoon pepper**
4 **slices bacon, cooked and crumbled**
2 **large eggs, lightly beaten**

• **Combine** squash and water in a large saucepan; bring to a boil. Cover, reduce heat, and simmer 15 minutes or until squash is tender. Drain well, and mash. Drain again, and set aside.
• **Sauté** onion in butter in a large skillet over medium-high heat until tender. Combine squash, onion, cheese, ¾ cup cracker crumbs, salt, and remaining 3 ingredients; stir well.
• **Spoon** mixture into a lightly greased 2-quart casserole; sprinkle with remaining ½ cup cracker crumbs. Bake, uncovered, at 350° for 40 to 45 minutes or until thoroughly heated. Yield: 6 servings.

Garden-Stuffed Yellow Squash

The curvy shape of crookneck squash makes an interesting presentation for stuffed shells.

6 **medium-size yellow squash**
1 **cup chopped onion**
1 **cup chopped tomato**
½ **cup finely chopped green pepper**
1 **tablespoon chopped fresh basil**
¼ **teaspoon salt**
Dash of freshly ground pepper
1 **cup (4 ounces) shredded Cheddar cheese**
2 **tablespoons butter or margarine**
3 **slices bacon, cooked and crumbled**

• **Wash** squash thoroughly; cover with water, and bring to a boil. Cover, reduce heat, and simmer 8 to 9 minutes or until squash is tender but still firm. Drain and cool slightly. Cut squash in half lengthwise; remove and discard seeds, leaving a firm shell.
• **Combine** onion, tomato, green pepper, basil, salt, and pepper in a bowl. Stir in cheese. Place squash shells in a 13- x 9-inch baking dish. Spoon vegetable mixture into shells; dot with butter. Sprinkle with bacon. Bake, uncovered, at 400° for 20 minutes. Yield: 6 servings.

*Garden-Stuffed
Yellow Squash*

APPLE AND PECAN ACORN SQUASH

The best flavors of fall are wrapped up in this simple stuffed acorn squash.

2 medium acorn squash (about 1¼ pounds each)
1 cup peeled, chopped cooking apple
¼ cup firmly packed brown sugar
¼ cup butter or margarine, melted
¼ teaspoon apple pie spice
¼ cup chopped pecans, toasted

• **Cut** squash in half crosswise, and remove seeds. Cut a thin slice from bottom of each squash half to sit flat, if necessary. Place squash halves, cut side up, in a 13- x 9-inch baking dish. Add hot water to dish to depth of 1 inch.
• **Combine** apple and next 3 ingredients; spoon evenly into squash halves. Cover and bake at 350° for 1 hour or until squash is tender. Sprinkle with pecans. Yield: 4 servings.

BUTTERNUT SQUASH SOUFFLÉ

½ cup butter or margarine
½ cup all-purpose flour
1½ cups half-and-half
6 large eggs, separated
2 cups cooked, mashed butternut or acorn squash
½ teaspoon salt
½ teaspoon ground nutmeg

• **Melt** butter in a heavy saucepan over low heat; add flour, whisking until smooth. Cook 1 minute, whisking constantly. Gradually add half-and-half; cook over medium heat, whisking constantly, until thickened and bubbly.
• **Whisk** egg yolks until thick and pale. Gradually stir about one-fourth of hot mixture into yolks; stir into remaining hot mixture. Stir in mashed squash, salt, and nutmeg.
• **Beat** egg whites at high speed with an electric mixer until stiff peaks form; fold one-fourth of egg whites into squash mixture. Fold in remaining egg whites, and pour into a lightly buttered 2-quart soufflé dish.
• **Bake** at 350° for 1 hour or until puffed and brown. Serve immediately. Yield: 6 servings.

MARINATED ZUCCHINI

make ahead

3 medium zucchini, thinly sliced (about 1¼ pounds)
¼ cup chopped onion
¼ cup chopped green pepper
¼ cup chopped celery
1 tablespoon chopped pimiento
⅓ cup cider vinegar
¼ cup sugar
¼ cup vegetable oil
1 tablespoon white wine vinegar
½ teaspoon salt
¼ teaspoon pepper
⅛ teaspoon hot sauce

• **Combine** first 5 ingredients in a large bowl; toss lightly.
• **Combine** cider vinegar and remaining 6 ingredients; pour over zucchini mixture. Cover and marinate in refrigerator at least 8 hours, stirring occasionally. Serve with a slotted spoon. Yield: 4 servings.

ZUCCHINI TOSS

⸺ quick ⸺

Here's a simple side dish that will go with just about any entrée.

1 pound medium zucchini, cut into ¼-inch-thick slices
1½ teaspoons olive oil
1 tablespoon freshly grated Parmesan cheese
¼ teaspoon grated lemon rind
¼ teaspoon salt
¼ teaspoon pepper

• **Sauté** zucchini in hot oil in a large skillet over medium-high heat 5 minutes or until crisp-tender. Remove from heat; cover and let stand 5 minutes.
• **Combine** cheese and remaining 3 ingredients. Spoon zucchini into a serving dish, and sprinkle with cheese mixture; toss gently. Serve immediately. Yield: 3 servings.

ZUCCHINI PIE

2 cups shredded zucchini
¾ cup biscuit mix
¾ cup (3 ounces) shredded Cheddar cheese
1 small onion, chopped
½ teaspoon salt
¼ teaspoon pepper
¼ teaspoon rubbed sage
2 large eggs, lightly beaten
¼ cup vegetable oil

• **Stir** together all ingredients. Pour into a greased 9-inch pieplate. Bake at 350° for 45 minutes. Cool 10 minutes before serving. Yield: 1 (9-inch) pie.

GRILLED VEGETABLE KABOBS

Red pepper and zucchini get a brief grilling on short skewers. Pair them with chicken, pork, or beef for dinner.

4 medium-size sweet red peppers, seeded and cut into ½-inch strips
4 small zucchini, cut into ½-inch-thick slices
½ cup vegetable oil
¼ cup lemon juice
¼ cup white wine vinegar
1 tablespoon plus 1 teaspoon Worcestershire sauce
2 teaspoons dried Italian seasoning
1 teaspoon salt

• **Thread** pepper strips and zucchini slices onto eight 6-inch bamboo skewers. Place kabobs in a large shallow dish.
• **Combine** oil and remaining 5 ingredients; pour over kabobs. Cover and marinate in refrigerator 8 hours, turning once.
• **Remove** kabobs from marinade, reserving marinade. Grill kabobs, covered with grill lid, over medium-hot coals (350° to 400°) 10 to 12 minutes or until vegetables are crisp-tender, turning and brushing with marinade occasionally. Yield: 4 servings.

BASIL-MARINATED TOMATOES

⌐ make ahead ⌐

Enjoy the sweet tang of vine-ripened tomatoes, fresh basil, and garlic in this summertime specialty.

3 large tomatoes
⅓ cup olive oil
¼ cup red wine vinegar
2 to 3 tablespoons chopped fresh basil
2 tablespoons chopped onion
1 teaspoon salt
¼ teaspoon pepper
1 clove garlic, crushed

• **Cut** tomatoes into ½-inch-thick slices; arrange in a thin layer in a large shallow dish.
• **Combine** oil and remaining 6 ingredients in a jar; cover tightly, and shake vigorously. Pour mixture over tomato slices. Cover and marinate in refrigerator at least 8 hours before serving. Yield: 6 servings.

CRUSTY BROILED TOMATOES

⌐ family favorite, quick ⌐

Fresh thyme, crusty crumbs, and shreds of Parmesan cap these juicy red jewels of summer. See them on page 354.

4 large tomatoes
2 tablespoons Dijon mustard
½ cup Italian-seasoned breadcrumbs or French breadcrumbs
½ cup freshly shredded Parmesan cheese
½ teaspoon fresh thyme leaves
⅛ teaspoon salt
⅛ teaspoon freshly ground black pepper
⅛ teaspoon ground red pepper
¼ cup plus 2 tablespoons butter or margarine, melted

• **Cut** tomatoes in half crosswise. Pat cut surfaces of tomato halves with paper towels to remove excess moisture. Spread mustard evenly over cut sides of tomato halves.
• **Combine** breadcrumbs, cheese, thyme, salt, black pepper, red pepper, and butter; stir well. Spoon breadcrumb mixture evenly over tomato halves.
• **Place** tomato halves on a rack of a broiler pan. Broil 5½ inches from heat 2 to 4 minutes or until lightly browned. Serve hot. Yield: 8 servings.

SWEET-AND-TANGY TOMATOES

make ahead

10 small firm, ripe tomatoes
½ cup sugar
½ cup white vinegar
2 tablespoons vegetable oil
1 tablespoon minced onion
1 tablespoon minced celery
1 tablespoon minced green pepper
1 teaspoon salt
½ teaspoon pepper
½ teaspoon Worcestershire sauce
Lettuce leaves

• **Blanch** each tomato in boiling water 30 seconds. Drain and immediately place in ice water. Remove tomato from ice water, and peel tomato, using a sharp paring knife. Core each tomato.
• **Combine** sugar and next 8 ingredients in a large heavy-duty, zip-top plastic bag. Place tomatoes in bag, and seal. Shake gently to coat, and marinate in refrigerator 8 hours, turning occasionally.
• **Remove** tomatoes from marinade, reserving some marinade as dressing. Quarter tomatoes, and arrange 4 wedges on lettuce leaves for each serving. Drizzle lightly with dressing. Yield: 10 servings.

TURNIPS AU GRATIN

The mild flavor of turnips may surprise you in this well-seasoned casserole.

9 medium turnips, peeled and diced (about 3 pounds)
1 teaspoon salt
1 teaspoon sugar
2 tablespoons butter or margarine
2 tablespoons all-purpose flour
1½ cups milk
¾ cup (3 ounces) shredded Cheddar cheese
1 teaspoon seasoned salt
⅛ teaspoon pepper
¼ cup fine, dry breadcrumbs (store-bought)

• **Combine** first 3 ingredients in a Dutch oven; add water to cover. Bring to a boil; cover, reduce heat, and simmer 10 to 12 minutes or until diced turnips are tender. Drain well, and set aside.
• **Melt** butter in a large heavy saucepan over low heat; add flour, stirring constantly. Gradually add milk; cook over medium heat, stirring constantly, until slightly thickened. Add cheese, seasoned salt, and pepper, stirring until cheese melts. Remove from heat; stir in diced turnips.
• **Spoon** turnip mixture into a lightly greased 1½-quart casserole; sprinkle with breadcrumbs. Bake at 350° for 20 to 25 minutes or until thoroughly heated. Yield: 6 servings.

CHEESE APPLES

~ family favorite ~

Use Granny Smith apples or your favorite baking apples in this comfort food that can be a side dish or dessert.

¾ cup sugar
½ cup all-purpose flour
¼ teaspoon salt
¼ cup butter or margarine, cut up
1 cup (4 ounces) shredded sharp Cheddar cheese
6 peeled, sliced Granny Smith apples
⅓ cup water
1 tablespoon lemon juice

• **Combine** sugar, flour, and salt; cut in butter with a pastry blender until mixture is crumbly. Stir in cheese, and set aside.
• **Combine** sliced apples, water, and lemon juice; toss lightly. Spoon into a greased 8-inch square baking dish. Sprinkle cheese mixture over sliced apples. Bake, uncovered, at 350° for 40 minutes. Yield: 6 servings.

BAKED CINNAMON APPLES

Red hot cinnamon candies flavor and color these apples as they bake. They're best enjoyed alongside baked ham or grilled pork.

1 cup water
1 cup sugar
1 cup red cinnamon candies
6 Rome apples, peeled, cored, and quartered

• **Combine** water and sugar in a medium saucepan; bring to a boil. Add candies, and cook, stirring constantly, until melted.
• **Place** apple quarters in a 13- x 9-inch baking dish; pour candy syrup over apples. Bake, uncovered, at 400° for 20 minutes. Turn apples over; bake 15 more minutes, basting often with syrup. Yield: 6 servings.

HOT CURRIED FRUIT

1 (29-ounce) can pear halves, undrained
1 (29-ounce) can peach halves, undrained
1 (20-ounce) can pineapple chunks, undrained
1 (17-ounce) can apricot halves, undrained
1 (16½-ounce) can pitted Royal Anne cherries, undrained
¼ cup sugar
3 tablespoons all-purpose flour
3 tablespoons butter or margarine
¼ cup dry white wine or fruit juice
1 teaspoon curry powder

• **Drain** first 5 ingredients, reserving juices in a bowl. Combine fruit in a large bowl; set aside. Stir juice mixture; reserve ¾ cup. Reserve remaining juice mixture for another use.
• **Combine** sugar and flour in a heavy saucepan; gradually stir in reserved ¾ cup juice mixture. Add butter, and cook over medium heat, stirring constantly, until

mixture is thickened and bubbly. Remove from heat; stir in wine and curry powder.

• **Add** sauce mixture to fruit mixture, stirring gently. Spoon mixture into a lightly greased 13- x 9-inch baking dish. Cover and bake at 350° for 30 minutes or until thoroughly heated. Yield: 10 to 12 servings.

SPICED PEACHES

make ahead

2 (29-ounce) cans peach halves in heavy syrup, undrained
1 teaspoon cornstarch
½ teaspoon ground cinnamon
½ teaspoon ground cloves
¼ teaspoon grated orange rind
⅛ teaspoon ground nutmeg
⅛ teaspoon ground allspice

• **Drain** peach halves, reserving syrup; set peach halves aside. Combine syrup, cornstarch, and remaining 5 ingredients in a small Dutch oven. Bring to a boil, stirring constantly. Reduce heat; add peach halves, and simmer 1 minute. Remove from heat, and let cool. Cover and chill peaches up to 24 hours. Yield: 6 servings.

SCALLOPED PINEAPPLE

This pineapple casserole gains a crusty sugared top as it bakes. Serve it with pork or ham.

3 cups (1-inch cubes) French bread
1¼ cups sugar
⅓ cup butter or margarine, melted
3 large eggs, lightly beaten
1 (20-ounce) can crushed pineapple, undrained

• **Combine** all ingredients in a large bowl; stir well. Spoon mixture into a lightly greased 2-quart casserole.
• **Bake,** uncovered, at 350° for 45 to 50 minutes or until golden and bubbly. Yield: 8 to 10 servings.

RECIPE INDEX

CREDITS

OXMOOR HOUSE WISHES TO THANK
THE FOLLOWING MERCHANTS:

Barney's, New York, NY
Birmingham Antiques Mall, Birmingham, AL
Bromberg and Co. Inc., Mountain Brook, AL
Christine's, Birmingham, AL
Eigen Arts, Inc., Jersey City, NJ
Henhouse Antiques, Birmingham, AL
Lamb's Ears, Ltd., Birmingham, AL
Mariposa, Manchester, MA
McKenzie Childs, Aurora, NY
Pier I Imports, Fort Worth, TX
Ronnie Ceramics, San Francisco
Sabré, Dallas, TX
Stonefish Pottery, Hartford, CT
Table Matters, Birmingham, AL
Tricia's Treasures, Birmingham, AL
Vaban Gille, Inc., San Francisco, CA
Vietri, Hillsborough, NC

CONTRIBUTING PHOTOGRAPHERS:
(PAGES 6-11)

Tina Cornett
Jerome Drown
J. Savage Gibson
Mary-Gray Hunter
Taylor Lewis
Charles Walton IV

METRIC EQUIVALENTS

The recipes that appear in this cookbook use the standard United States method for measuring liquid and dry or solid ingredients (teaspoons, tablespoons, and cups). The information on this chart is provided to help cooks outside the U.S. successfully use these recipes. All equivalents are approximate.

METRIC EQUIVALENTS FOR DIFFERENT TYPES OF INGREDIENTS

A standard cup measure of a dry or solid ingredient will vary in weight depending on the type of ingredient.
A standard cup of liquid is the same volume for any type of liquid. Use the following chart when converting standard cup measures to grams (weight) or milliliters (volume).

Standard Cup	Fine Powder (ex. flour)	Grain (ex. rice)	Granular (ex. sugar)	Liquid Solids (ex. butter)	Liquid (ex. milk)
1	140 g	150 g	190 g	200 g	240 ml
¾	105 g	113 g	143 g	150 g	180 ml
⅔	93 g	100 g	125 g	133 g	160 ml
½	70 g	75 g	95 g	100 g	120 ml
⅓	47 g	50 g	63 g	67 g	80 ml
¼	35 g	38 g	48 g	50 g	60 ml
⅛	18 g	19 g	24 g	25 g	30 ml

USEFUL EQUIVALENTS FOR LIQUID INGREDIENTS BY VOLUME

¼ tsp					=	1 ml
½ tsp					=	2 ml
1 tsp					=	5 ml
3 tsp	=	1 tbls		= ½ fl oz	=	15 ml
		2 tbls	= ⅛ cup	= 1 fl oz	=	30 ml
		4 tbls	= ¼ cup	= 2 fl oz	=	60 ml
		5⅓ tbls	= ⅓ cup	= 3 fl oz	=	80 ml
		8 tbls	= ½ cup	= 4 fl oz	=	120 ml
		10⅔ tbls	= ⅔ cup	= 5 fl oz	=	160 ml
		12 tbls	= ¾ cup	= 6 fl oz	=	180 ml
		16 tbls	= 1 cup	= 8 fl oz	=	240 ml
		1 pt	= 2 cups	= 16 fl oz	=	480 ml
		1 qt	= 4 cups	= 32 fl oz	=	960 ml
				= 33 fl oz	= 1000 ml	= 1 l

USEFUL EQUIVALENTS FOR DRY INGREDIENTS BY WEIGHT

(To convert ounces to grams, multiply the number of ounces by 30.)

1 oz	=	¹⁄₁₆ lb	=	30 g
4 oz	=	¼ lb	=	120 g
8 oz	=	½ lb	=	240 g
12 oz	=	¾ lb	=	360 g
16 oz	=	1 lb	=	480 g

USEFUL EQUIVALENTS FOR LENGTH

(To convert inches to centimeters, multiply the number of inches by 2.5.)

1 in				=	2.5 cm	
6 in	= ½ ft			=	15 cm	
12 in	= 1 ft			=	30 cm	
36 in	= 3 ft	= 1 yd		=	90 cm	
40 in				=	100 cm	= 1 m

USEFUL EQUIVALENTS FOR COOKING/OVEN TEMPERATURES

	Fahrenheit	Celsius	Gas Mark
Freeze Water	32° F	0° C	
Room Temperature	68° F	20° C	
Boil Water	212° F	100° C	
Bake	325° F	160° C	3
	350° F	180° C	4
	375° F	190° C	5
	400° F	200° C	6
	425° F	220° C	7
	450° F	230° C	8
Broil			Grill